The Story of Jesus

The Story of Jesus

The Reader's Digest Association, Inc.
Pleasantville, New York   Montreal

Framed within the letter Q are two joyful moments: the angel's announcement to Zechariah that Elizabeth will bear a son and (at lower right) the birth of Jesus. This ornate manuscript illumination is dated about the year 1000.

Frontispiece: *Jesus blesses and distributes bread to the disciples in this detail from a painting of the Last Supper by Paolo Veronese (1528–1588).*

DESIGNED AND EDITED BY
GARDNER ASSOCIATES
Editorial Director: Joseph L. Gardner
Art Editor: Barbara Marks
Picture Editor: Laurie Platt Winfrey
Associate Picture Editor: Robin J. Sand
Senior Contributing Editor: Thomas L. Robinson
Contributing Writer: Charles Flowers
Research Editors: Guadalupe Morgan, Josephine Reidy,
    Robert Melzak (Art)
Copy Editor: Felice Levy
Indexer: Cynthia Crippen
Calligrapher: Carole Lowenstein

PROJECT STAFF FOR READER'S DIGEST
Senior Editor: James Cassidy
Art Editor: Robert M. Grant

READER'S DIGEST GENERAL BOOKS
Editor in Chief: John A. Pope, Jr.
Managing Editor: Jane Polley
Executive Editor: Susan J. Wernert
Art Director: David Trooper
Group Editors: Will Bradbury, Sally French, Norman B. Mack,
    Kaari Ward
Group Art Editors: Evelyn Bauer, Robert M. Grant, Joel Musler
Chief of Research: Laurel A. Gilbride
Copy Chief: Edward W. Atkinson
Picture Editor: Richard Pasqual
Rights and Permissions: Pat Colomban
Head Librarian: Jo Manning

The Scripture quotations contained herein (with the exceptions noted on pages 52 and 212 and with the exception of some quotations within excerpts) are from the Revised Standard Version of the Bible, copyright 1946, 1952, 1971 by the Division of Christian Education of the National Council of the Churches of Christ in the U.S.A.
Used by permission.

The acknowledgments that begin on page 371 are hereby made a part of this copyright page.

Library of Congress Cataloging in Publication Data
The Story of Jesus
        p.   cm.
    Includes index.
    ISBN 0-89577-472-0
    1. Jesus Christ—Popular works.   2. Jesus Christ—Art.
I. Reader's Digest Association.
BT199.S84   1993
232.9'01—dc20   92-42206

About This Book

THE LIFE OF JESUS was comparatively brief—played out in a remote corner of the all-powerful Roman empire nearly 2,000 years ago. It is known to us almost exclusively from the four Gospels: Matthew, Mark, Luke, and John—with a few scattered references to be gleaned from the Acts of the Apostles (a continuation of Luke's narrative) and the various Epistles. Yet, more has been written about Jesus than about any other man in history, and the events of his life are better known to more people than those of any other individual who ever lived.

There is no physical description of Jesus in the New Testament, nor did his contemporaries leave any record of his appearance. Yet, again, no other individual inspired so many artists to recreate the events of his life. Christianity, it can be said without fear of challenge, claims the world's richest artistic legacy.

The Story of Jesus brings together hundreds of selections from this unparalleled literary and artistic heritage in a keepsake collection of stories, poems, hymns, and prayers illustrated with the best Christian art of two millennia. There are many voices in these pages: reformer Martin Luther, Roman Catholic prelate Fulton J. Sheen, Presbyterian preacher Peter Marshall, Jewish scholar Joseph Jacobs, novelists Pearl S. Buck and Lloyd C. Douglas, poets Joyce Kilmer, Carl Sandburg, and Henry Wadsworth Longfellow, humanitarians Albert Schweitzer, Mahatma Gandhi, Martin Luther King, Jr., and Mother Teresa of Calcutta, to name a few. They all have one thing in common—the enormous impact of Jesus on their lives.

In addition, the work of many artists is reproduced here: anonymous craftsmen who fashioned stained glass windows for Europe's great cathedrals; monks who preserved the Bible in lavishly illuminated medieval manuscripts; Renaissance painters who placed biblical stories in the Italy of their time; Old Masters who brought their profound personal values to depictions of Jesus and his disciples; and modern masters who have reinterpreted the story of Jesus for our own century. The variety and vitality of these works are testimony to the universal, enduring appeal of Jesus.

Biblical quotations introduce the selections and serve to weave the views and visions of many people through the ages and around the world into a coherent and revealing narrative. Carefully selected illustrations complement the text. But *The Story of Jesus* is more than a highly illustrated biography—though it is arranged, as far as possible, chronologically. It is, rather, a celebration of the greatest life ever lived, reverently offered by writers and artists whose own lives were indelibly shaped and given direction by the wise, compassionate man from Nazareth.

THE EDITORS

The wise men's gifts, a 16th-century enamel

The Annunciation in gold and precious stones

Jesus among the teachers in the temple

His Ministry on Earth

119

The baptism of Jesus by Veronese

The calling of Peter and Andrew by Duccio

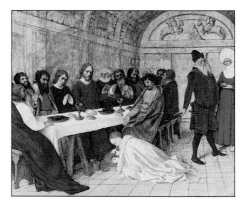

*Ministering to Jesus by
Jean Fouquet (c. 1416–1480)*

*The woman at the well
by Lorenzo Lippi (1606–1664)*

The prodigal son among the swine

The Final Days

227

*Washing the disciples' feet by Ford
Madox Brown (1821–1893)*

*Jesus scourged and mocked,
a 16th-century enamel*

Jesus carrying his cross
by El Greco (c. 1548–1614)

The crucified Jesus in his mother's arms
by Il Bronzino (1502–1572)

Savior and Redeemer

295

The Resurrection by Taddeo
Gaddi (1300–1366)

*Jesus bestowing a blessing,
a 13th-century enamel*

*The supper at Emmaus by Mathieu
Le Nain (1607–1677)*

*Pentecost, a 14th-century
manuscript illumination*

Jesus Among Us

347

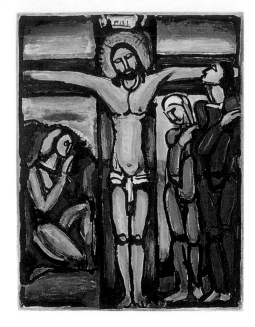

Crucifixion by Georges Rouault
(1871–1958)

Opposite: *Mary and*
her child, flanked by
Nativity scenes; a
14th-century reliquary
shrine believed to
have been made for
the queen of Hungary

The Story of Jesus

The Messiah

The name Jesus, meaning "he will save," was given to Mary's son to signify that he would save his people from their sins. Linked to it throughout the New Testament is the title Christ, or in Hebrew, Messiah, "the Anointed One." At the time of Jesus' birth there was an intense hope among Jews that the Anointed One was about to come and that he would be an ideal king, standing alongside an ideal high priest or embodying both figures in one person. When Jesus asked his disciples, "Who do you say that I am?" Peter responded with a simple phrase but one bearing centuries of yearning, "You are the Christ" (Mark 8:29).

The Evangelists were well versed in the Hebrew Bible. Thus, the Gospels are replete with references to Old Testament prophecies being fulfilled in the New Testament. The links made between the two on the following pages set the stage for the subsequent presentation of the life of Jesus, starting with "The Nativity" on page 33.

Jesus' ancestry is traced back to King David's father in this tree of Jesse, a 15th-century stained glass window from the church of St. Lazare in Autun, France.

Jesus and his apostles are seated beneath the cupola of this late-12th-century German reliquary; the Old Testament prophets who predicted the Messiah's coming stand in the church arches below.

TO US A CHILD OF HOPE IS BORN

To us a Child of hope is born,
To us a Son is given
Him shall the tribes of earth obey,
Him, all the hosts of heav'n.

His name shall be the Prince of Peace,
For evermore adored,
The Wonderful, the Counselor,
The great and mighty Lord!

His pow'r, increasing, still shall spread,
His reign no end shall know;
Justice shall guard His throne above,
And peace abound below.

JOHN MORRISON, 1749–1798

"*Do not be afraid, Mary, for you have found favor with God. And behold, you will conceive in your womb and bear a son, and you shall call his name Jesus. He will be called great, and will be called the Son of the Most High; and the Lord God will give to him the throne of his father David, and he will reign over the house of Jacob for ever; and of his kingdom there will be no end.*"

LUKE 1:30-33

A LIGHT SHINING IN THE DARKNESS

In his momentous announcement to Mary, the angel Gabriel was alluding to verses in Isaiah that describe a savior-king. Writing in about 732 B.C., the prophet observed with dismay the disaster of King Ahaz's alliance with Assyria. Nonetheless, he spoke of a hopeful future with such certainty that he used the past tense as though the anticipated events had already taken place.

BUT THERE WILL BE no gloom for her that was in anguish. In the former time he brought into contempt the land of Zebulun and the land of Naphtali, but in the latter time he will make glorious the way of the sea, the land beyond the Jordan, Galilee of the nations.

The people who walked in darknesss
   have seen a great light;
those who dwelt in a land of deep darkness,
   on them has light shined.
Thou hast multiplied the nation,
   thou hast increased its joy;
they rejoice before thee
   as with joy at the harvest,
   as men rejoice when they divide the spoil.
For the yoke of his burden,
   and the staff for his shoulder,
   the rod of his oppressor,
   thou hast broken as on the day of Midian.
For every boot of the tramping
   warrior in battle tumult

and every garment rolled in blood
    will be burned as fuel for the fire.
For to us a child is born,
    to us a son is given;
and the government will be upon his shoulder,
    and his name will be called
"Wonderful Counselor, Mighty God,
    Everlasting Father, Prince of Peace."
Of the increase of his government and of peace
    there will be no end,
upon the throne of David, and over his kingdom,
    to establish it, and to uphold it
with justice and with righteousness
    from this time forth and for evermore.
The zeal of the Lord of hosts will do this.

                                    ISAIAH 9:1–7

THE LIGHT OF THE WORLD

*Isaiah's image of a light shining in the darkness was
adopted by Jesus himself (John 8:12), appropriately during
his visit to Jerusalem at the Feast of Tabernacles,
a festival marked by the lighting of lamps in the temple
court. The great prophet spoke on several occasions of
Israel as a light to the world.*

"I am the Lord, I have called you in righteousness,
    I have taken you by the hand and kept you;
I have given you as a covenant to the people,
    a light to the nations,
    to open the eyes that are blind,
to bring out the prisoners from the dungeon,
    from the prison those who sit in darkness. . . ."

                                    ISAIAH 42:6–7

Arise, shine; for your light has come,
    and the glory of the Lord has risen upon you.
For behold, darkness shall cover the earth,
    and thick darkness the peoples;
but the Lord will arise upon you,
    and his glory will be seen upon you.
And nations shall come to your light,
    and kings to the brightness of your rising.

                                    ISAIAH 60:1–3

*The words of Isaiah are frequently cited in the New Testament to show
how Jesus' life fulfilled Old Testament prophecies; Isaiah's mosaic portrait is from the
sixth-century church of San Vitale in Ravenna, Italy.*

Now the birth of Jesus Christ took place in this way. When his mother Mary had been betrothed to Joseph, before they came together she was found to be with child of the Holy Spirit; and her husband Joseph . . . resolved to divorce her quietly. But as he considered this, behold an angel of the Lord appeared to him in a dream, saying, "Joseph, son of David, do not fear to take Mary your wife, for that which is conceived in her is of the Holy Spirit."

MATTHEW 1:18–20

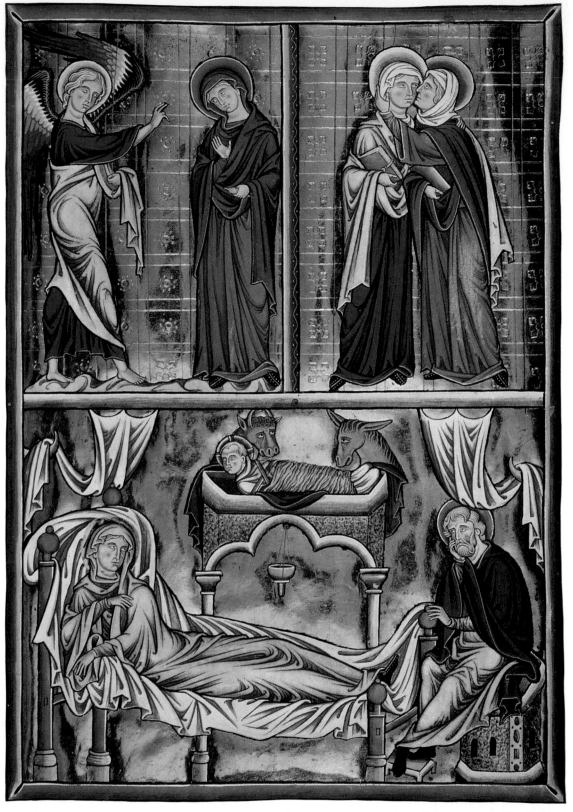

Three events echoing the Old Testament—the angel's Annunciation to Mary, her response to Elizabeth's greeting, and Jesus' birth in Bethlehem—appear in this 13th-century manuscript illumination.

UNDERSTANDING PROPHECIES IN LIGHT OF THEIR FULFILLMENT

The angel's startling revelation to Joseph ends with a reference to a prophecy fulfilled that makes it even more astonishing. In this excerpt from THE GOSPEL ACCORDING TO ST. MATTHEW, *the German scholar Wolfgang Trilling tells why.*

WHAT THE ANGEL HAS DECLARED is important and breathtaking. Part of what he says tells clearly what will happen, the rest hints at far-reaching consequences which the well-informed like Joseph know or at least suspect. St. Matthew ends the passage with a reference to the fulfillment of a prophecy. Now it is perfectly clear that this is no everyday event. The event is full of meaning for the present in which the miracle of the Holy Spirit takes place, for the future in which this child will accomplish the salvation of his people, and for the past which appears in a new light.

In a situation full of menace the prophet Isaiah had announced to King Ahaz a divine sign which was to portend disaster for him. Now this word becomes a message of joy: "Behold, a virgin shall conceive." The mysterious circumstances that had filled Joseph with dismay are not so disturbingly new. The virgin birth wrought by the Spirit was already intimated in the Old Testament. The eyes of faith recognize the action of God across the centuries and know how to understand the promises of the prophet in light of their fulfillment.

There is something else in the prophecy: a name which is just as profound and rich as the name "Jesus": "Emmanuel," or "God with us." The knowledge that Yahweh was always with his people was something deeply ingrained in the faith of Israel. It was Israel's distinction and its glory. As it was in the past, so will it also be in the future which the prophets proclaim: "Fear not, for I redeem you; I call you by thy name, you are mine! When you go through the waters, I am with you; and when you go through rivers they shall not submerge you. When you pass through fire, you shall not be burned and the flames shall not scorch you" (Isaiah 43:1–2).

God was always with his people—in the wars of the patriarchs, in the assemblies at the cultic shrines in the time of the judges, and then especially on the sacred hill of Zion and in the temple, at the anointing of its kings and at the mission of its prophets, in his faithfulness and the bestowal of his salvation, and also as they were scattered among the nations in captivity.

During the years of captivity there remained the lively hope that God would be with his people in the future. It was a fact, and yet it was still but a promise. They could experience the presence of God—and still they had to wait for it. The manner of God's future presence to his people, which remained to be realized, was clearly to be something quite new.

And now it seems to have become reality. The child who is to be born bears the name which is the full description of this hope: "God with us." The nearness of God given here is, therefore, not to be made manifest in any thing or place, but in a man whose nature it is to be God with us. In him and through him God is near and present, more closely and more really than ever before.

O COME, O COME, EMMANUEL

O come, O come, Emmanuel,
And ransom captive Israel,
That mourns in lonely exile here,
Until the Son of God appear.

Rejoice! Rejoice! Emmanuel
Shall come to thee, O Israel!

O come, thou Day-spring, come and cheer
Our spirits by thine advent here;
Disperse the gloomy clouds of night,
And death's dark shadows put to flight.

O come, thou Wisdom from on high,
And order all things, far and nigh;
To us the path of knowledge show,
And cause us in her ways to go.

O come, Desire of nations, bind
All peoples in one heart and mind;
Bid envy, strife and quarrels cease;
Fill the whole world with heaven's peace.

JOHN M. NEALE
1851 translation of a Latin hymn

A spectral Isaiah hovers above this Annunciation scene, a panel of the famed Isenheim altarpiece painted by Matthias Grünewald about 1515.

The long-barren Hannah (here shown in a 12th-century manuscript) rejoiced at the birth of Samuel, as Mary would later exult at her conception of Jesus.

In those days Mary arose and went with haste into the hill country, to a city of Judah, and she entered the house of Zechariah and greeted Elizabeth. And when Elizabeth heard the greeting of Mary, the babe leaped in her womb; and Elizabeth was filled with the Holy Spirit and she exclaimed with a loud cry, "Blessed are you among women, and blessed is the fruit of your womb!"

LUKE 1:39–42

A JOY THAT FILLED HER SOUL AND SPIRIT

Mary's response to Elizabeth—called the Magnificat from the first word of the Latin translation—is among the most beautiful passages in the Bible (see page 52). In the following excerpt from THE GOSPEL ACCORDING TO ST. LUKE, the German scholar Alois Stöger analyzes her hymn of praise.

THE DEPTHS OF MARY'S HEART were penetrated with God's praise, and a messianic joy filled her soul and her spirit. She counts herself among the lowly, the poor, and the insignificant to whom the prophets and the psalms repeatedly promise salvation. Jesus is to adopt this promise as one of his Beatitudes: "Blessed are the meek, for they shall inherit the earth."

Mary's praises which Elizabeth inaugurated will never end. All ages will raise their voices to bless her. The kingdom of the king who is her child will never end, and the king's mother will be praised eternally.

Might, holiness, and mercy are the most brilliant traits of the Old Testament God. The force of his vital power is directed outwards in an effort aimed at making everything in the world belong to God, and it is in this power that God shows he is holy. A holy God, he is also merciful. He is a savior and a redeemer for the faithful remnant of Israel because he is God, and not a human being. The great things God accomplishes in his might are proof of his merciful love.

Mary expresses the experience of her own race, re-corded in Deuteronomy 26:6–9: "The Egyptians mistreated us; they tormented us and imposed a harsh slavery on us. We cried out to the Lord, the God who is our Father. The Lord listened to our cry and saw our torment, our labor, and our distress. He brought us out of Eygpt with a strong hand and an outstretched arm, showing signs and wonders with awe-inspiring power. He brought us to this place and gave us this land, a land flowing with milk and honey."

Mary's great hour is also the great hour of her people. The promise of salvation made to Abraham and his posterity Mary sees fulfilled in herself. And the people of God will receive its benefits.

Mary's words of praise take up the hymn sung by a barren woman to whom God had granted a child: Samuel's mother, Hannah (1 Samuel 2:1–2):

My heart exults in the Lord;
  my strength is exalted in the Lord.
My mouth derides my enemies,
  because I rejoice in thy salvation.
There is none holy like the Lord,
  there is none besides thee;
  there is no rock like our God.

Mary and Joseph kneel in adoration of the infant Jesus; the tender scene is the work of Fra Bartolommeo (1475–1517).

And he [Joseph] rose and took the child and his mother by night, and departed to Egypt, and remained there until the death of Herod. This was to fulfil what the Lord had spoken by the prophet, "Out of Egypt have I called my son."

MATTHEW 2:14–15

Angels guide the Holy Family's flight into Egypt in this painting by Giotto di Bondone (c. 1276–1337).

DELIVERED FROM BONDAGE IN EGYPT

After citing Micah's prophecy of a ruler to come from Bethlehem, Matthew draws yet another parallel between the New Testament and the Old: Joseph's flight to and return from Egypt with Mary and her child and the deliverance of the Israelites from Egyptian bondage. In Hosea 11:1–7, the Lord addresses Israel as a loving father would in reproving an erring son.

When Israel was a child, I loved him,
   and out of Egypt I called my son.
The more I called them,
   the more they went from me;
they kept sacrificing to the Baals,
   and burning incense to idols.

Yet it was I who taught Ephraim to walk,
   I took them up in my arms;
   but they did not know that I healed them.
I led them with cords of compassion,
   with the bands of love,
and I became to them as one
   who eases the yoke on their jaws,
   and I bent down to them and fed them.

They shall return to the land of Egypt,
   and Assyria shall be their king,
   because they have refused to return to me.
The sword shall rage against their cities,
   consume the bars of their gates,
   and devour them in their fortresses.
My people are bent on turning away from me;
   so they are appointed to the yoke,
   and none shall remove it.

> **The word of God came to John the son of Zechariah . . . and he went into all the region about the Jordan, preaching a baptism of repentance for the forgiveness of sins.**
>
> LUKE 3:2–3

A VOICE IN THE WILDERNESS

All four Evangelists, in introducing John the Baptist, quote the prophet Isaiah. The original verses (Isaiah 40:1–11) are a message of consolation to the Jews during their Babylonian exile in the sixth century B.C. Proclaiming that the time of suffering has passed, the prophet conjures up the image of preparations for a royal procession back to Jerusalem.

Comfort, comfort my people, says your God.
Speak tenderly to Jerusalem, and cry to her
   that her warfare is ended,
   that her iniquity is pardoned,
   that she has received from the Lord's hand
     double for all her sins.

A voice cries:
"In the wilderness prepare the way of the Lord,
   make straight in the desert a highway for our God
   Every valley shall be lifted up,
   and every mountain and hill be made low;
the uneven ground shall become level,
   and the rough places a plain.
   And the glory of the Lord shall be revealed,
   and all flesh shall see it together,
   for the mouth of the Lord has spoken."

A voice says, "Cry!"
   And I said, "What shall I cry?"
All flesh is grass,
   And all its beauty is like the flower of the field.

John the Baptist fulfilled a prophecy of Isaiah. In this painting by Tommaso Guidi (1401–1428), known as Masaccio, Peter perpetuates the rite of baptism for neophyte Christians.

Gathering manna is paired with the Last Supper in a 15th-century manuscript.

The grass withers, the flower fades;
  when the breath of the Lord blows upon it;
  surely the people is grass.
The grass withers, the flower fades;
  but the word of our God will stand for ever.

Get you up to a high mountain,
  O Zion, herald of good tidings;
lift up your voice with strength,
  O Jerusalem, herald of good tidings,
  lift it up, fear not;
say to the cities of Judah,
  "Behold your God!"
Behold, the Lord God comes with might,
  and his arm rules for him;
behold, his reward is with him,
  and his recompense before him.
He will feed his flock like a shepherd,
  he will gather the lambs in his arms,
he will carry them in his bosom,
  and gently lead those that are with young.

JESUS: HE WAS INDEED THE COMING ONE

The Gospels do not always cite specific Old Testament passages in describing Jesus as the fulfillment of ancient prophecies. Some of these indirect references are explained in the following excerpt from F. F. Bruce's THE TIME IS FULFILLED, *a lecture series published in 1978.*

THERE ARE UNMISTAKABLE ECHOES of the book of Daniel in the form and content of Jesus' proclamation, and many of his hearers must have been aware of the words of Daniel 7:22, "the time came for the saints to receive the kingdom." But whether it reminded them of that precise text or not, the general implication of the announcement was plain: the time had come when God was to inaugurate the indestructible kingdom which would supersede all other forms of world dominion.

When the imprisoned John the Baptist sent his messengers to ask Jesus if he was the Coming One after all, or if they had to look for someone else, he was perhaps disturbed by the discrepancy between the purifying judgment by wind and fire which he had said the Coming One would execute and the ministry in which Jesus was actually engaged.

When Jesus told John's messengers to go back and tell their teacher what they had seen him do and heard him say—"the blind receive their sight, the lame walk, lepers are cleansed, and the deaf hear, the dead are raised up, the poor have good news preached to them" (Luke 7:22)—he knew that John would recognize the fulfillment of those prophetic words of Isaiah 35:5–6:

  Then the eyes of the blind shall be opened,
    and the ears of the deaf unstopped;
  then shall the lame man leap like a hart,
    and the tongue of the dumb sing for joy.
Above all, the proclamation of the good news to the poor or afflicted was a sign that the year of Yahweh's favor had come, according to the announcement of the Spirit-anointed speaker of Isaiah 61:1–2:
  The Spirit of the Lord God is upon me,
    because the Lord has anointed me
  to bring good tidings to the afflicted;
    he has sent me to bind up the brokenhearted,

Now after John was arrested, Jesus came into Galilee, preaching the gospel of God, and saying, "The time is fulfilled, and the kingdom of God is at hand; repent, and believe in the gospel."

MARK 1:14–15

Ezekiel (lower left) envisions New Testament figures as inner spokes of a wheel and Old Testament personalities as outer spokes. The painting is by Fra Angelico (1387–1455).

DESCRIBING HIS MISSION IN WORDS TAKEN FROM ISAIAH

Following his baptism by John and the temptation in the wilderness, Jesus returned to Galilee to begin teaching. But the proclamation of his messianic mission in the synagogue at Nazareth scandalized his countrymen (Luke 4:16–30). Alois Stöger explains why in this selection from THE GOSPEL ACCORDING TO ST. LUKE.

T HE PASSAGE OF SCRIPTURE which Jesus chose to read was from the book of Isaiah, the favorite prophet of those who waited for God's kingdom in Jesus' time. Mary sensed his relevance at the Annunciation, Simeon was enlightened and inspired by him, and it was through him that the Baptist realized what his mission was.

Jesus now described his mission in words taken from Isaiah 61:1–2. Only one line is changed: "to let the oppressed go free" (Isaiah 58:6) replaces the words: "to bind up the brokenhearted." This change gives the whole passage its articulation.

The reading from scripture was followed by an instruction. This is summed up in one lapidary sentence with words which are as impressive as they are forceful: "Today this scripture has been fulfilled in your hearing." Jesus proclaimed the time of salvation and ushered it in. This is what is new and extraordinary about this moment. The hallowed customs of the Jews and the words of scripture which contained a promise were now fulfilled.

Jesus stood before his hearers as one who had come to the end of his period of training and had been anointed with the Spirit. Now he had begun to fulfill his mission. God's favor was displayed to the full.

However, Jesus' hearers took offense the very next moment: "Is not this Joseph's son?" His humanity was a stumbling block; his words represented a challenge and they were scandalized. They welcomed his message, but they rejected the savior who brought the message because he was one of themselves and he offered no proof in support of his claim to be the savior.

The people of Nazareth wanted a sign that Jesus was the savior who had been promised. Jesus offered no such proof, and so the people felt obliged to condemn him as a blasphemer and stone him to death. The incident made it clear that Jesus' message to his own people would be frustrated.

    to proclaim liberty to the captives,
        and the opening of the prison to those who are
        bound;
    to proclaim the year of the Lord's favor,
        and the day of vengeance of our God . . .

No wonder, then, that John was encouraged with the blessing invoked by Jesus on the one who refused to think that Jesus had let him down: Jesus was indeed the Coming One.

The enemy which Jesus confronted and challenged in his ministry was not the Roman oppressor but the spiritual power of darkness, the dominion of Satan. "But if it is by the finger of God that I cast out demons," he said, "then the kingdom of God has come upon you" (Luke 11:20). The proclamation of the advent of the divine kingdom stirred up specially hostile activity in the realm of evil, which felt its dominion threatened. The superior power of the kingdom of God was seen in the release of those whose minds and bodies were held in spiritual bondage: Jesus not only proclaimed but effected "liberty to the captives, and the opening of the prison to those who are bound" (Isaiah 61:1). In doing so he knew himself to be the agent of the Father who desired the well-being, not the suffering, of his children.

Witnesses to the life of Jesus as a fulfillment of Old Testament prophecies, the four Evangelists—Luke and Mark (top), Matthew and John (below)—appear in a 12th-century manuscript.

The 30 pieces of silver Judas received for betraying Jesus was the Old Testament price of a slave. An unknown artist painted this early Renaissance fresco for a church in Assisi, Italy.

Christ also suffered for you, leaving you an example, that you should follow in his steps. . . . When he was reviled, he did not revile in return; when he suffered, he did not threaten; but he trusted to him who judges justly. He himself bore our sins in his body on the tree, that we might die to sin and live to righteousness. By his wounds you have been healed. For you were straying like sheep, but have now returned to the Shepherd and Guardian of your souls.

1 PETER 2:21–25

A NEW AND FAITHFUL SON

Although he does not explicitly quote Isaiah 53:5–12 in his brief description of Jesus' suffering on the cross, Peter revealed how the words of the prophet could be used to shape the way the story of his master's death was to be remembered—just as the words of Psalm 22 were used by Matthew. In this excerpt from THE OLD TESTAMENT ROOTS OF OUR FAITH, Paul and Elizabeth Achtemeier tell how Jesus fulfills the words of the prophets.

THROUGH EVERY BOOK of the New Testament this fulfillment in Christ can be traced. He is the new Israel and the new Messiah, upon whom the spirit of God is poured out. He is the descendant of David, ruling over a universal kingdom. He is the Messiah of peace, bringing justice, righteousness and faithfulness to his people in the strength of the Lord. In infinite detail, the New Testament proclaims that he is the One expected; on page after page, it testifies that God has kept his solemn promise.

Perhaps first and foremost, however, we should understand Jesus Christ as the fulfillment of Israel's obedience. The people of the old covenant were called to serve the Lord as his son. God brought them out of Egypt into a good land, flowing with milk and honey. He gave them a law to govern their life and fought before them in their battles. He set a king to reign over them, and raised up prophets to guide them. He asked only in return that they love him and trust him and let him rule their hearts and wills. He asked of this son surrender, in order that the son might be the instrument of God's redemption of the world. But Israel could not trust the Lord or walk in his commandments. Israel was a rebellious son.

God therefore replaced Israel with a new and faithful Son, a Son who in every respect was tempted like Israel, and like we are, yet without sinning. Through the course of the Gospel stories we can trace his obedience: his refusal in his desert temptations to serve any other ruler but God, his rejection of even the closest human ties as more important than his relationship with his heavenly Father, his total subjection of man's life with man to God's will and purpose for the community, his constant refusal in his dealings with the scribes and Pharisees to conform to merely human standards of morality and religion. In every deed and word, Jesus acknowledged the sole lordship of God, until his obedience brought him finally to a dark garden called Gethsemane, where in sorrow and agony, he sweated out his final surrender, "Father, if thou art willing, remove this cup from me; nevertheless not my will, but thine, be done."

Here was the true Son of God. Here was the descendant of Abraham and of David who perfectly followed his heavenly Father. Here was the new Israel, the one of unshakeable faith. Here was the obedient Israel whom God could use for his purpose.

Psalm 22 illustrated with a Crucifixion

FROM THE CROSS, AN ECHO

My God, my God, why hast thou forsaken me?
　Why art thou so far from helping me, from the
　words of my groaning?
O my God, I cry by day, but thou dost not answer;
　and by night, but find no rest.

Yet thou art holy,
　enthroned on the praises of Israel.
In thee our fathers trusted;
　they trusted, and thou didst deliver them.
To thee they cried, and were saved;
　in thee they trusted, and were not disappointed.

But I am a worm, and no man;
　scorned by men, and despised by the people.
All who see me mock at me,
　they make mouths at me, they wag their heads;
"He committed his cause to the Lord;
　　let him deliver him,
　let him rescue him, for he delights in him!" . . .

I am poured out like water,
　and all my bones are out of joint;
my heart is like wax,
　it is melted within my breast;
my strength is dried up like a potsherd,
　and my tongue cleaves to my jaws;
　thou dost lay me in the dust of death.

Yea, dogs are round about me;
　a company of evildoers encircle me;
　they have pierced my hands and feet—
I can count all my bones—
　they stare and gloat over me;
they divide my garments among them,
　and for my raiment they cast lots.

But thou, O Lord, be not far off!
　O thou my help, hasten to my aid!
Deliver my soul from the sword,
　my life from the power of the dog!
Save me from the mouth of the lion,
　my afflicted soul from the horns of the wild oxen!

PSALMS 22:1–8, 14–21

Giotto's depiction of the Crucifixion hangs in the church of Santa Maria Novella in Florence, Italy.

"This Jesus God raised up, and of that we all are witnesses. Being therefore exalted at the right hand of God, and having received from the Father the promise of the Holy Spirit, he has poured out this which you see and hear. For David did not ascend into the heavens; but he himself says, 'The Lord said to my Lord, Sit at my right hand, till I make thy enemies a stool for thy feet.'"

ACTS OF THE APOSTLES 2:32–35

Jesus' Resurrection is paired with Jonah's emergence from the big fish.

THE EXALTED MESSIAH

Peter's Pentecost sermon concluded with the lines of Psalm 110:1—the Old Testament passage most frequently quoted in the New Testament. Used by Jesus himself in his discourse with the Pharisees (Matthew 22:44), the words fortified the Christian belief that Jesus was the son of God.

The Lord says to my lord: "Sit at my right hand,
  till I make your enemies your footstool."
The Lord sends forth from Zion
  your mighty scepter.
  Rule in the midst of your foes!
Your people will offer themselves freely
  on the day you lead your host
  upon the holy mountains.
From the womb of the morning
  like dew your youth will come to you.
The Lord has sworn
  and will not change his mind,
"You are a priest for ever
  after the order of Melchizedek."
The Lord is at your right hand;
  he will shatter kings on the day of his wrath.
He will execute judgment among the nations,
  filling them with corpses;
he will shatter chiefs over the wide earth.
He will drink from the brook by the way;
  therefore he will lift up his head.

PSALMS 110:1-7

HIS ONLY BEGOTTEN SON

Why do the nations conspire,
  and the peoples plot in vain?
The kings of the earth set themselves,
  and the rulers take counsel together,
  against the Lord and his anointed, saying,
"Let us burst their bonds asunder,
  and cast their cords from us."

He who sits in the heavens laughs;
  the Lord has them in derision.
Then he will speak to them in his wrath,
  and terrify them in his fury, saying,
"I have set my king
  on Zion, my holy hill."

I will tell of the decree of the Lord:
He said to me, "You are my son,
  today I have begotten you.
Ask of me, and I will make the
    nations your heritage,
  and the ends of the earth your possession.
You shall break them with a rod of iron,
  and dash them in pieces like a potter's vessel."

PSALMS 2:1–9

A MESSIAH FOR ALL NATIONS

There shall come forth a shoot from the stump of Jesse,
    and a branch shall grow out of his roots.
And the Spirit of the Lord shall rest upon him,
    the spirit of wisdom and understanding,
    the spirit of counsel and might,
    the spirit of knowledge and the fear of the Lord.
And his delight shall be in the fear of the Lord.

He shall not judge by what his eyes see,
    or decide by what his ears hear;
but with righteousness he shall judge the poor,
    and decide with equity for the meek of the earth;
and he shall smite the earth with the rod of his mouth,
    and with the breath of his lips he
        shall slay the wicked.
Righteousness shall be the girdle of his waist,
    and faithfulness the girdle of his loins.

The wolf shall dwell with the lamb,
    and the leopard shall lie down with the kid,
and the calf and the lion and the fatling together,
    and a little child shall lead them.
The cow and the bear shall feed;
    their young shall lie down together;
    and the lion shall eat straw like the ox.
The sucking child shall play over the hole of the asp,
    and the weaned child shall put his hand
        on the adder's den.
They shall not hurt or destroy
    in all my holy mountain;
    for the earth shall be full of the
        knowledge of the Lord
    as the waters cover the sea.

In that day the root of Jesse shall stand as an ensign to
the peoples; him shall the nations seek, and his dwellings
shall be glorious.

ISAIAH 11:1–10

*Jesus surmounts this tree
of Jesse, an illumination
for a 13th-century Psalter
now in the Musée Condé
in Chantilly, France.*

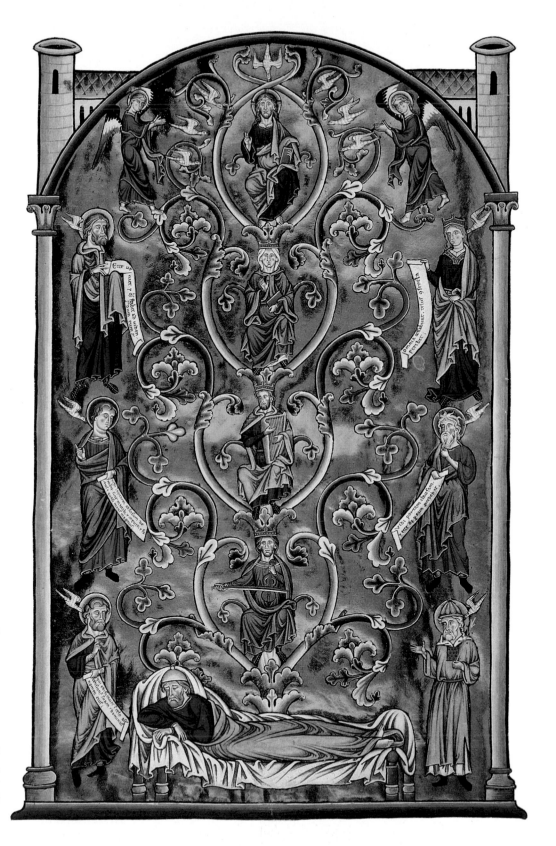

The Nativity

The events surrounding the birth of Jesus form perhaps the world's
most famous and beloved story. The Gospels of Matthew and
Luke agree on the major elements: the birth of the child Jesus in
Bethlehem during the reign of Herod the Great, a child
conceived of the Holy Spirit and destined to be the Savior.
Each Evangelist, however, offers separate, richly
detailed incidents that make the narrative even more
compelling and memorable.

Matthew's account is written more from the perspective of
Joseph, whose actions to protect his wife and the child are guided
by angels appearing to him in dreams. In Luke's
version Mary is the more central figure, suggesting to some
that the Evangelist heard the story directly from her.

On the following pages the two interwoven
Gospel narratives are interpreted by a variety of
writers and artists, inspired over the centuries by the
simple beauty of this cherished tale.

*Choirs of angels
summon shepherds
to worship the
newborn Jesus in
this Nativity scene
painted in 1500
by the Italian master
Sandro Botticelli.*

Gabriel appears to Zechariah in one of 20 scenes from the life of John the Baptist that decorate the bronze doors of the baptistery of the cathedral of Florence in Italy; the carvings, by the sculptor Andrea Pisano, were created between 1329 and 1336.

In the days of Herod, king of Judea, there was a priest named Zechariah, of the division of Abijah; and he had a wife of the daughters of Aaron, and her name was Elizabeth. And they were both righteous before God.

LUKE 1:5–6

THE ANSWERED PRAYER

One day it fell by lot for Zechariah, of the Abijah division of the priesthood, to burn incense at the temple in Jerusalem. What happened after the aged priest entered the inner sanctuary is told by Pearl Buck, winner of the Nobel Prize for literature in 1938. The selection is from THE STORY BIBLE, a retelling of the biblical narrative published in 1971, two years before her death at the age of 81.

THOSE JEWS WHO WERE deeply dedicated to the God of Israel made frequent pilgrimages to the city of Jerusalem to celebrate the feasts and holy days with the priests and wise men of the temple. Those who lived in Jerusalem worshiped in the temple whenever the spirit came upon them. Thus, great crowds of people were praying outside in the temple court as Zechariah went into the inner sanctuary of the house of the Lord to burn incense upon the altar.

Now Zechariah and his wife Elizabeth loved the Lord and served him with all their hearts, but they had one great cause for sorrow. They were old, and yet they had no child. If there was any one thing that they prayed for more than anything else, it was for a son of their own.

Zechariah lit the tiny flame upon the altar. The sweet smell of incense rose in a cloud of smoke. And suddenly an angel of the Lord appeared on the right side of the altar of incense. When Zechariah saw this sudden apparition he was greatly startled and troubled in his heart. He felt afraid, and he bowed his head.

"Fear not," said the angel gently. "Your prayer is answered. Your wife will have a son, and you will name him John. He shall bring you joy and gladness; and many will rejoice at his birth, for he shall be great in the sight of the Lord. He will drink neither wine nor strong drink and, filled with the Holy Spirit, he will turn many of the children of Israel to the Lord their God. His spirit and power shall be that of Elijah, so that he will go before the Lord and turn the hearts of the fathers to the children, and the disobedient to the wisdom of the just. Thus he will make ready a people prepared to meet the Lord."

Zechariah was full of wonderment. "How can this be?" he asked. "How shall I know that this is true? For my wife and I are old, too old to have a child."

And the angel answered: "I am Gabriel, who stands in the presence of God. The Lord has sent me to you to tell you these glad tidings. But because you do not believe my words, which nevertheless will be fulfilled when the right time comes, you shall be dumb and not able to speak until the day that these things shall be performed. Let that be your sign that what I say is true." Zechariah looked again, but the angel was no longer there.

The crowds of people praying in the temple court outside began wondering why the priest stayed so long within the inner sanctuary. When at last the old man came out his lips were moving silently and his hands made gestures in the air as if he had been taken with a sudden illness. As they stared at him, astonished, they became aware that some strange and wonderful thing had happened to him. All he could do was beckon to them dumbly and make signs that he had lost his speech; yet on his face there was a radiance that they had never seen before.

It came to them, then, that he must have seen a vision in the temple, and they were filled with awe. They waited for some time to see what else might happen or what he might say when he regained his voice, but there was no sign. The old man remained speechless for all the time they waited, until at last they went away and forgot what they had seen.

When Zechariah was finished with his days of duty in the temple he departed to his own house in the rolling hills of Judea. He still could not speak, nor did he speak for several months thereafter. But soon after he came home his wife Elizabeth told him that they were, at last, to have a child.

"Thus has the Lord dealt with me after these many years!" she said joyfully. And the old man gave thanks in the silence of his heart.

The people gathered for prayer at the temple seem unaware of Zechariah's astonishing encounter with the angel Gabriel, who tells him that Elizabeth will bear him a son. The fresco for the church of Santa Maria Novella in Florence was painted by Domenico Ghirlandaio; the 15th-century artist often included portraits of his wealthy patrons in such biblical scenes.

STRUCK DUMB FOR HIS DISBELIEF

*The faith of Zechariah and Elizabeth is stressed
in this excerpt from* THE MYSTERY OF BETHLEHEM
*by Herman Hoeksema, a Protestant theologian.
His series of meditations on the events
surrounding the birth of Jesus
was published in 1944.*

 ECHARIAH AND ELIZABETH! Did not these very names testify that both were of the generations that feared the Lord and hoped for his salvation? Or does it not speak of that faith, which is an evidence of things unseen and clings to the Invisible, when one names his son Zechariah, Jehovah remembereth, in times when it appears that God has forgotten to be kind; when one calls his daughter Elizabeth, my God is my oath, in a period when the promises of the Almighty seem to fail?

In the hill country of Judah they lived and waited. Waited and prayed! Prayed for a son, for they were childless, though in late years this prayer had died in their hearts. They were now both well stricken in years, and according to all human experience and expectations it must have become evident that the Lord was not pleased to grant them this petition.

And also prayed for the realization of Israel's hope, for they were both righteous and walked in all the commandments and ordinances of the Lord.

United they were by a common faith. Waiting, praying, believing, hoping, looking for the break of day in the enveloping darkness!

And yet not waiting in vain, for presently their prayers would be answered.

It was the division of Abijah's turn to minister in the sanctuary, and to that course belonged the gray-haired Zechariah. Many times he had obeyed the summons and hastened in company with a multitude of priests to the Holy City, there to minister unto the Lord. For, although no less than twenty-four divisions of the priesthood had been instituted by Israel's great king of old, and these different courses had been restored and maintained after the return from Babylon,

Jerusalem's Three Temples

Herod the Great's magnificent temple, which Zechariah enters in the first chapter of Luke's Gospel, was begun in 20 B.C., but the outlying structures were still incomplete 46 years later. The despised tyrant hoped that erecting the greatest of all temples on Jerusalem's Mount Zion would consolidate his disputed kingship over the Jews, but it was not grandiose architecture that made the site sacred.

An angel is said to have shown King David the spot, and fire descended from Heaven to ignite his first offering there. In about 960 B.C. his son Solomon built the first temple. As predicted by Old Testament prophets who foresaw punishment for the people's sins, the building was razed and its furnishings carted away to Babylon in 587 B.C. Jews returning from the Babylonian Captivity began building a second temple in 520; it was completed five years later. Herod leveled it to erect his own monument. Ironically, his temple had the shortest life of all, for the Romans destroyed it in A.D. 70.

*A stone inscription from Herod's temple (fragment at left)
once warned gentiles not to enter the sacred precincts on penalty
of death; right, a model in present-day Jerusalem.*

yet each course was summoned to work in the sanctuary at least twice a year. And a well-known figure this pious son of Aaron of more than three-score years had become to the worshipers in Jehovah's house.

Yet, even so, a unique honor was bestowed upon him as again he had obeyed the summons and in the dusk of early dawn presented himself for the ministration. For, as the different functions had been apportioned by lot among the many priests of his course, the third lot had pointed to him as the one who was to enter into the holy place and burn incense before Jehovah on the golden altar, a distinction so rare and unique, that only once in a lifetime it was bestowed on one, and ever after he was accounted "rich."

Thankful and rejoicing the aged priest enters into the holy place, where already the lamps on the seven-armed candlestick had been trimmed, and the coals upon the altar had been laid, ready to consume the incense and make it rise as a sweet-smelling savor to the throne of grace. He stands before the altar, to the left of which is placed the table of shewbread, while on the right the seven-armed lamp spreads a shimmering light in the darkness. He prays: for the people; for Israel's hope and salvation; for the coming of the promised day; meanwhile mingling the smoke of the incense with his priestly intercessions. Now he will return to the prostrate worshipers in the court, to spread his hands in priestly benediction upon them and bless them in the name of Jehovah!

Then, he stops, amazed, spell-bound, troubled and fearful. Who is that shining figure that suddenly appears between the altar and the candlestick?

A messenger of joy; Gabriel, that standeth before God, whose special function is to bring good tidings of great joy, of the salvation of Jehovah to His praying saints. And he speaks:

"Fear not, Zechariah! Jehovah remembereth! Thy prayer is heard! Thy prayer of long ago and the prayer of the present. Thy wife shall bear a son! And thou shalt call his name John! Thou shalt have joy and gladness, and many shall rejoice at his birth!"

Zechariah asks: "Whereby shall I know this?"

"O, thou of little faith! Why askest thou a sign, now the night is passing and day breaking? I am Gabriel, that standeth before God! Dumb shalt thou be!

"Thou shalt not speak these glad tidings, till the day that all these things shall be accomplished. For, in the dispensation of faith, only he that believeth shall confess with the mouth. And shall be saved!"

Two panels from an 11th-century German Gospel book: Offering incense in the temple sanctuary, Zechariah is greeted by the angel Gabriel (top); emerging, he motions to the people that he is unable to speak (bottom).

Carved from wood, painted, and decorated with fabric, this angel was once part of a 17th-century Neapolitan Nativity scene.

THE ANNUNCIATION

The angel and the girl are met.
Earth was the only meeting place.
For the embodied never yet
Travelled beyond the shore of space.
The eternal spirits in freedom go.

See, they have come together, see,
While the destroying minutes flow,
Each reflects the other's face
Till heaven in hers and earth in his
Shine steady there. He's come to her
From far beyond the farthest star,
Feathered through time. Immediacy
Of strangest strangeness is the bliss
That from their limbs all movement takes.
Yet the increasing rapture brings
So great a wonder that it makes
Each feather tremble on his wings.

Outside the window footsteps fall
Into the ordinary day
And with the sun along the wall
Pursue their unreturning way.
Sound's perpetual roundabout
Rolls its numbered octaves out
And hoarsely grinds its battered tune.

But through the endless afternoon
These neither speak nor movement make,
But stare into their deepening trance
As if their gaze would never break.

EDWIN MUIR, 1887–1959

The angel Gabriel was sent from God to a city of Galilee named Nazareth, to a virgin betrothed to a man whose name was Joseph, of the house of David; and the virgin's name was Mary. . . . And the angel said to her, "Do not be afraid, Mary, for you have found favor with God. And behold, you will conceive in your womb and bear a son, and you shall call his name Jesus."

LUKE 1:26–27, 30–31

BLESSED AMONG WOMEN

So vivid is Luke's account of the angel Gabriel's appearance to Mary that some scholars suggest he heard it directly from her. Among the many writers who have expanded the biblical story is Fulton Oursler, from whose THE GREATEST STORY EVER TOLD *the following version of the Annunciation is taken.*

IT WAS AN EXPERIENCE shattering to the very roots of her being. For hours after it happened she was unable to speak; she could scarcely even breathe. It was so inexplicable, so dazing and frightening that for the time she could not force herself to tell her mother or father or even Joseph. How could she ask them to believe that she had actually known such a wonder? Yet she *had* known it.

Joachim and Anna had been chatting up on the roof, the hens and rooster were perched and fast asleep, the dog was out barking behind the garden, and the sheep and goats were dozing. Feeling a little chill, for the night was damp, Mary had crossed the lower floor inside the house and mounted to the inner terrace. As she went up the steps to the platform she realized that she was not alone. A tall figure was standing near the farther wall!

A stranger. An odd and altogether different stranger! Because he seemed to stand in light where there was no lamp, and a kind of silvery mist enveloped him as if the light were his cap and gown. Mary opened her mouth to speak, to demand who he was and what he wanted there, but he anticipated her with an unexpected greeting.

"Hail, Mary!"

The voice was kind and fathomlessly deep; such a voice as Mary had never heard before—bass and yet tender. "Full of grace!" the voice continued.

Hail, Mary, full of grace! She felt embarrassed and even more frightened.

"The Lord is with you. Blessed are you among women."

She folded her hands and she knew then how she was trembling in every muscle. The stranger saw.

"Fear not, Mary."

She bowed her head. She must not be afraid. She knew she could trust this deep and tender voice. But she could not still her quaking. She closed her eyes and listened to the astounding words this stranger was speaking to her. She had found grace with God. She would conceive in her womb and bring forth a son.

"And you shall call his name Jesus!"

"Jesus! He will be my son. Jesus! Jesus, son of Mary! I shall bring him forth and hold him in my arms. . . ." Her mind was a place of wild, birdlike thoughts; yet she must listen to all that the stranger continued to tell her: her son Jesus was to have the throne of David, his father—

"And of all his kingdom there shall be no end."

Then came her instant need for reality. Who this stranger was she did not know; yet the maiden who heard his words felt bound to question him. "How shall this be done?" she asked in a whisper. "Seeing I know not a man?"

But there came no frown on the austere and shadowy face of the stranger. Instead, in the starry blaze of his eyes she read only compassion. He took a step nearer and she saw the folded wings and knew him for what he was.

His voice lower and deeper still: "The Holy Ghost shall come upon you. The power of the Most High shall overshadow you and the child which shall be born of you shall be called the Son of God."

The announcement to Mary is the principal panel of this French manuscript page dated about 1505. The other scenes (clockwise from top right) depict her visit to Elizabeth, the birth of Jesus, the angel appearing to the shepherds, the wise men, and the presentation of the baby in the temple.

The Messengers of God

Angels play important roles in the Nativity narratives of both Matthew and Luke: bringing news that the aged Elizabeth and the virgin Mary will each conceive a son and conveying messages to Joseph and the wise men from the East. Indeed, the word "angel" comes from a Greek word for messenger, and these heavenly beings become visible in order to take communications directly from God's throne to his subjects on Earth both before and after Jesus' mission here. (During the ministry, however, no angels are needed as messengers, for Jesus himself is bringing God's word to those who will hear it.)

According to tradition, angels were created by God as moral beings, capable of choosing between good and evil. When wicked angels rebelled under the leadership of the angel Satan, they were defeated and cast out of Heaven by the archangel Michael and other loyal angels. Unlike humans who err, these evil rebels are considered irredeemable.

Only three angels are named in the Bible and Apocrypha — Gabriel, Michael, and Raphael. Nonscriptural Jewish writings also mention Uriel frequently. Several references in the New Testament suggest that there was a distinct hierarchy of angels, with archangels at the top. The exact number of archangels varied in both Jewish and Christian writing but eventually became fixed, under the influence of the Book of Revelation, at seven. Early church teaching held that these celestial beings were grouped in nine choirs: angels, archangels, cherubim, seraphim, and the five groups mentioned in Paul

(virtues, powers, principalities, dominions, and thrones).

Gabriel, whose name means "hero of God" in Hebrew, appears four times in the Scriptures. Twice in the Book of Daniel he helps the prophet understand the true significance of mystic visions. Perhaps drawing upon that tradition, Luke names Gabriel as the divine messenger who tells a skeptical Zechariah the amazing news that he is going to have a son, John the Baptist, and visits Mary to announce the birth of Jesus. Although Daniel describes him as coming "in swift flight," the wings usually depicted in religious art are never specifically mentioned in the Bible. In Daniel, Gabriel is simply described as "having the appearance of a man." Outside the Bible, in folklore and nonscriptural writing, Gabriel has been named as God's agent in the destruction of Sodom as well as an intercessor for mankind during the Flood.

The unnamed angels who appear throughout the New Testament help the world prepare for the coming of Jesus, as when an angel tells the shepherds about his birth, or interpret his mission, as when the angels at the tomb explain that he is risen from the dead.

For believers, angels have always been a source of comfort and renewed faith. Throughout the Christian era, many people have claimed that everyone has been assigned a "guardian angel" and that angels come at the hour of death to lead the soul into Paradise.

Angels with traditional wings are depicted in the detail above from an Italian missal and in the French plaque at left.

Mary felt stifled, suffocated, as she heard these incredible words. She was to be the mother of a son who would be called the Son of God?

How could one little Nazareth girl take all that in? She looked up at him plaintively, her eyes half closed, her words coming so softly that she could barely hear herself speak. "Behold the handmaid of the Lord. Be it done unto me according to your word."

As if by incantation the angel vanished; one instant he was there, gone the next. And Mary, swaying and murmuring, sank to her knees, closed her eyes, and wept and prayed.

THE THREE MIRACLES

The great Protestant reformer Martin Luther left behind enough sermons to fill five volumes totaling nearly 3,000 pages. From this massive body of work, Roland H. Bainton, a professor at Yale University, assembled and translated a number of the writings and published them in 1962 as LUTHER'S MEDITATIONS ON THE GOSPELS. In this passage Luther comments on the Annunciation to Mary.

MARY WAS A POOR MAID. To be sure, she was of the house of David, but the priests had arrogated power to themselves until the house of David had fallen into such disrepute that to expect a king from the tree of Jesse was like looking for a flower from a shriveled, rotten, old root. Mary was a waif, perhaps an impoverished orphan and despised, because she said of herself that God "regarded the low estate of his handmaiden."

The angel Gabriel might have gone to the daughter of Caiaphas, rich, fair, and clad in gold-embroidered raiment. Instead he went to Mary, whose name means bitterness in view of the bitter plight of her people.

To this poor maid the marvelous announcement was given that she should be the mother of the Most High, who would be called a Son of God. He would be a king and of his Kingdom there would be no end. She might well have said, "Who am I, little worm, that I should give birth to a king?" She might have doubted, but she shut her eyes and trusted in God that He is powerful and can bring all things to pass, though reason and all creatures be against it. Because she be-

lieved, the word of the angel was fulfilled in her. At first she held back, and said, "How shall this be, seeing I know not a man?"

Early Christian scholars saw here three miracles: the first, that God became man; the second, that a virgin was a mother; and the third, that the heart of man should believe this.

Really the virgin birth is not such a great miracle, because Jesus was made out of flesh and blood. This was not so extraordinary as making Adam out of mud and Eve out of a rib, but we do not regard any of these as miraculous because we have heard about them so often. I do not suppose Adam and Eve believed their creation to have been miraculous. We do not believe that our own births are miraculous. Where in the seed is the material for eyes and teeth and nails? So all God's works are incredible. Mary believed, and yet she overlooked the greater miracle that her child would be the Son of God. She did not ask how that could be and how his Kingdom could be without end. She forgot all this. Her thought centered on herself, and she asked only how *she* could conceive, though the other was more marvelous. It is only a little miracle for God to make a virgin conceive, but to create a man who is also eternal, that is a great miracle.

The Holy Spirit in the form of a dove hovers over this Annunciation scene; surrounded by angels, God watches from top right. Such glazed terra-cotta reliefs were the supreme achievement of 15th-century Florentine artist Luca della Robbia; this is the work of his nephew and successor Andrea della Robbia.

HIS UNWORTHY SERVANT

*The surprise and fear Mary must have experienced when
the angel made its appearance was imagined by the
inspirational writer Marjorie Holmes in her
novel TWO FROM GALILEE, subtitled "A Love Story."*

ONE DAY TOWARD SUNDOWN Mary had gone down the path a little way, into the stable cave to water the ass. She had emptied the skins into the trough and the stubby creature had bent its head to drink, when its pointed ears laid back. It shied and made an odd whimpering sound. "Hush now, what's wrong?" Mary stroked its quivering nose to gentle it, following its blank stare toward the doorway where a shaft of sunlight poured through.

Mary. "Yes, Father?" she answered dutifully, though it seemed strange that he should be home from the fields so early. *Mary!*

Suddenly she realized that it was not her father's voice that called. She could not place it, nor the source of it, though she went to the low leaning doorway and peered out. The yard and the grove and the adjoining fields lay quivering with the falling light, peaceful and undisturbed. There was no one by the old stone cistern, no one by the vine-covered fence.

Puzzled, she turned back to the donkey. It had bent its prickly nose again to the water, but only hovered there, not drinking. She could hear its uneasy breath. And now her own heart began to pound.

Then she saw that the shaft of light pouring dustily through the doorway had intensified. It had become a bolt, a shimmering column, and in it she dimly perceived a presence. Neither man nor beast, rather a form, a shape, a quality of such beauty that she was shaken and backed instinctively away.

Mary. Little Mary. The voice came again, gently, musically. *Have I frightened you? I'm sorry. Be still now, be at ease, there is nothing to fear. I am sent from God, who has always loved you. He has a message of great importance. So listen carefully, my child, and heed.*

---

*As God and the Holy Spirit (represented by a dove)
give their blessing, the angel offers Mary the lily of purity;
this fresco, by the 15th-century artist Melozzo da Forli,
decorates the Pantheon in Rome.*

"I am his unworthy servant," Mary whispered, though she scarcely believed her own voice. Why was she speaking thus, alone with only the beast in the sun-white stall? "What . . ." it was difficult to form the words, "what is it that the Lord would have of me?"

There was a second of silence. Then, in clear ringing tones the answer came: *Behold, you will conceive in your womb and bear a son and you shall call his name Jesus. He will be great and will be called the Son of the Most High.*

"The *Messiah!*" Mary gasped. "But I am unworthy! How can I be the mother of this long awaited child?"

God knows the secrets of his handmaiden's heart. He does not expect perfection. This child that he will send you will be human as well as holy. God wills it so, in order that man, who is human, can find his way back to God.

"But I am not yet married," Mary protested. "How can this thing be?"

With God all things are possible, the voice said. *Now the Holy Spirit will come upon you, and the power of the Most High will overshadow you; and the child that is born unto you will be the Son of God.*

"I will strive to be worthy," Mary whispered. She closed her eyes. When she opened them again, the shaft of light still slanted through the doorway, although its intensity was diminished. And the voice of her destiny was gone.

THE ANNUNCIATION

God whispered, and a silence fell; the world
  Poised one expectant moment, like a soul
Who sees at heaven's threshold the unfurled
White wings of cherubim, the sea impearled,
  And pauses, dazed, to comprehend the whole;
Only across all space God's whisper came
And burned about her heart like some white flame.

Then suddenly a bird's note thrilled the peace,
  And earth again jarred noisily to life
With a great murmur as of many seas.
But Mary sat with hands clasped on her knees,
  And lifted eyes with all amazement rife,
And in her heart the rapture of the spring
Upon its first sweet day of blossoming.

THEODOSIA GARRISON, 1874–1944

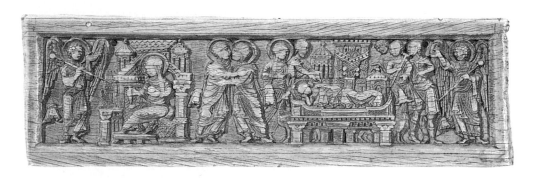

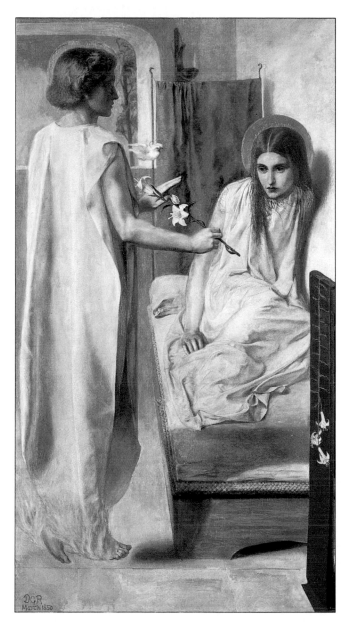

Some 800 years separate these two versions of the Annunciation: a detail (above, far left) from an 11th-century casket plaque in ivory, which also shows Mary's visit to Elizabeth, the birth of Jesus, and the shepherds summoned by an angel; and, at left, Dante Gabriel Rossetti's hauntingly evocative painting of 1850.

He did as the angel of the Lord commanded him; he took his wife, but knew her not until she had borne a son.

MATTHEW 1:24–25

The betrothal of Mary to Joseph—the formality of the ceremony reflecting the importance attached to engagement—is among the many masterpieces of Raffaello Sanzio, known as Raphael (1483–1520). The artist stamped the temple dominating the scene with his name, origin (Urbinas, Latin for "of Urbino"), and date he created the work (MDIIII, Roman numerals for 1504).

An 18th-century Jewish marriage contract

Betrothal Customs

Joseph's remarkably calm reaction to the discovery of Mary's pregnancy is even more unusual in light of ancient Jewish marriage customs. Betrothal, or engagement, often lasted up to a year, and it carried most of the rights and obligations of marriage. Had Joseph died during betrothal, for example, Mary would have been legally considered his widow. A child born to the couple during this period would be deemed legitimate. By the same token, the apparently unfaithful Mary could have been stoned to death for adultery, just as if the marriage had taken place. Nonetheless, Joseph was willing to end the betrothal quietly without exposing Mary to public ridicule or legal punishment.

Perhaps because of his calm kindness, legend has portrayed Joseph as much older than his betrothed, although the Bible does not say so. Usually, Jewish girls were betrothed at age 12 or soon thereafter, boys at 18. Typically, the boy's father arranged a marriage with the prospective bride's father, who would be given a bride price for her; romantic love was rarely considered. Although a man could divorce his wife for almost any cause, Jewish tradition frowned on the practice.

Now the birth of Jesus Christ took place in this way. When his mother Mary had been betrothed to Joseph, before they came together she was found to be with child . . . and her husband Joseph, being a just man and unwilling to put her to shame, resolved to divorce her quietly. But as he considered this, behold, an angel of the Lord appeared to him in a dream, saying, "Joseph, son of David, do not fear to take Mary your wife, for that which is conceived in her is of the Holy Spirit."

MATTHEW 1:18–20

TOO MUCH TO EXPECT OF ANY MAN?

Matthew's Nativity narrative begins with the discovery by Joseph that his intended bride is pregnant. In THE GREATEST STORY EVER TOLD, *Fulton Oursler focuses on the torment this caused him.*

O N THE WOODEN TABLE the rush lights were lit and fluttering, and the shadows were like jumpy phantoms on the white plaster of the wall. Mary was standing before the door, and the lambent yellow flames of the candles inside were playing over her face in shivering light. But the sportive light only showed clearer to Joseph how much Mary had changed; she looked like a phantom of the girl he remembered.

She was so pale now that she might have been a specter, not of the dead but of the living. She whose cheeks had been ripe orchard red with the warmth of health; whose strong arms could swing the household baskets, heavily burdened, and take pleasure in her own strength; whose stride was young and free and full of the energy of earth, was now a wraith of her former self, yet she had grown taller. There was a primrose pallor in her skin. Especially the enlarged glow of her eyes startled Joseph—it summed up the mystical, frightening change in her.

The dream in which the angel appeared to reassure Joseph is the subject of this 12th-century manuscript page. It is from the Bavarian State Library in Munich, Germany.

"Peace be with you, Mary!"

"And the Lord be with you, Joseph."

"Beloved, are you ill?"

"Don't come nearer to me. Not—just yet. There is something I have to tell you."

He stood, straight and tall, twisting his cap nervously in knotty fingers, his brow heavily creased.

"Say it, Mary, whatever it is. I am listening."

"Joseph, I am with child."

If the world had broken in two and dropped away into bottomless space, her words could not have sounded more unlikely. Mary with child! Joseph stood, unmoving; his fingers stopped playing with the cap; it was as if he had fallen into a trance. "But you have not known me," he spoke in a far-off whisper.

"I have not known man."

"But you say you are with child!" he cried, and in his wounded tone was the pain of a man who cannot believe his own anguish. "Whose child?" he groaned.

"Not the child of any man," she answered. "It is from God. The angel Gabriel came to me. And now I am the handmaid of the Lord and shall be the mother of the Promised One!"

"Mary! Do you know what you are saying? If the elders hear you, they will have you put to death."

"Still it is true, Joseph."

He threw his cap to the ground and flung himself after it on a pile of chips and sawdust.

"Tell me this strange thing," he invited glumly. "I shall listen and no more interruptions."

Step by step Mary rehearsed for him the incredible proceedings. The meeting with the stranger on the inner terrace of her home, the annunciation, the folded wings, the vanishing of the angel whom she knew to be Gabriel. She was a virgin and she was going to bring a child into the world.

And then there was a long silence. At last Mary said: "You are thinking deep thoughts, Joseph."

"I am thinking," muttered Joseph, slowly scrambling to his feet, "it is a curious thing that no angel came to me. Surely I have a right to be shown the truth of this matter!" he cried. "Am I expected to take this shocking story casually? I have no wish to quarrel. The Lord knows that I have loved you, Mary, with all my mind and all my heart and all my soul. But if this thing has happened, why is it that no angel reassured me? Don't I count at all?"

She wept. Joseph had only her word for what had happened. That was a great deal to ask of any man.

DOUBT, SADNESS,
THEN JOY FLOODING HIS HEART

In 1927 Alice M. Darton published HIS MOTHER, *subtitled
"The Life History of Mary, The Mother of Christ,"
an imaginative reconstruction based on her reading of
the Bible. Her Mary, betrothed to Joseph at perhaps no
more than 12 years of age, is shattered by the angel's
announcement and flees in confusion to the home of
Elizabeth and Zechariah. Only when she returns,
according to this version, does Joseph discover that his
intended bride is to have a child.*

*An elderly Joseph is
wedded to the youthful
Mary in this pious
work by Giovanni da
Fiesole (1387–1455), an
Italian monk known
as Fra Angelico. The
lying-in scene at left
may represent the birth
of John the Baptist,
which would have
occurred at about the
same time.*

WHEN FIRST THEY MET again after Mary's return to Nazareth, Joseph noticed the intangible change that had come over her character, the radiance that shone from her shyly raised eyes, the inward joy she seemed trying to conceal. Joseph noticed something else too. The maiden whose childlike modesty, whose angelic virtues had won his tenderest affections, was to become a mother.

How could he reconcile this with all that he had believed of Mary, with what he knew of her life, of her upbringing, her character? His being was shaken to its foundations, for if Mary was capable of what the malicious would be quick to suspect, how could he ever have faith in human nature again?

He had loved her dearly; he had desired to cherish her, and even now he could not bear to think of his delicate lovely lady as a target for the world's revilement and criticism. His sense of justice demanded that he shut her out from the shrine which he had given her in his heart but he could not endure to divorce her publicly, as was his right.

He considered these matters long and sadly, wavering in favor of the maiden whom by human standards he was justified in casting aside, inclining to sacrifice himself rather than let her be exposed to contempt.

Not until he had made up his mind to the kind and generous course did God interfere. Then after he had fallen asleep, tired with the emotional ordeal, the angel of the Lord appeared to him in his sleep, saying "Joseph, son of David, fear not to take unto thee Mary thy wife, for that which is conceived in her, is of the Holy Ghost. And she shall bring forth a son; and thou shalt call his name Jesus. For he shall save his people from their sins."

How gently, almost reverently, the angel addressed this noble man. Joseph awoke with a paean of joy in his soul. His world had righted itself. Mary was restored to her throne in his heart, and seated there more securely than before. She had been chosen by the Holy Ghost. That unprecedented tribute to her virtue, her saintliness, signified to Joseph that Mary was all and more than in his fondest imaginings he had dreamed. And her child, Jesus—and his heart leaped out to the babe. The Promised One was coming, God was showing Israel mercy once again, the great day was dawning for which His people and His house had been longing through centuries of sorrow and dismay.

Joseph sought Mary at once. Well did he now understand that irradiation of her being with joy; he felt it flooding his own heart. Mary recognized it on him before a single word was spoken. Their eyes, meeting, flashed the message of a happy comprehension. God had again provided a confidant for Mary and another home in which she should be safe.

They were married soon. Everything was done in the marriage celebration with due regard for form. Mary was to be shielded from unwelcome publicity; therefore the ceremonies must be strictly orthodox so as to avoid comment. The day selected was a Wednes-

Jewish elements such as a Hebrew scroll on an altarpiece, topped with the figure of Moses bearing the Ten Commandments, are incorporated into this depiction of the marriage of Mary and Joseph; the work is that of a 15th-century German artist known only as the Master of the Life of Mary.

day, which was the rule when the bride was a maiden.

The bridal couple were escorted to the bridegroom's home accompanied by musicians playing. Invited guests, known in Galilee as "children of the bride-chamber," encircled them bearing branches of palm and myrtle out of which they made a canopy for the bridal pair. All who met them joined in procession as a religious duty. The bride could be recognized by her flowing hair, or by a bridal veil or bridal crown. At their new home friends were waiting to receive them, bearing aloft long-handled lamps consisting of wicks burning in cups of oil. A feast was then served. But poverty may have forced them to curtail these customary marriage festivities.

Joseph and Mary then withdrew gradually from the world. She occupied herself with the responsibilities of her new home, with the care and comfort of Joseph, but most ardently of all, with the preparation of the swaddling cloths for the child that was to be born of her. These articles were fashioned by her with infinite tenderness. They were not made of rich fabrics bought in the bazaars, but Mary spun and wove the cloth herself and all she made was precious because so much of love entered into its creation.

JOSEPH'S SUSPICION

And the angel spoke and made an effort
with the man, who clenched his fists:
But dost thou not see by every fold
that she is cool as God's early day.

Yet the other looked somberly at him,
murmuring only: What has changed her so?
But at that the angel cried: Carpenter,
dost thou not yet see that the Lord God is acting?

Because thou makest boards, in thy pride,
wouldst thou really call him to account
who modestly out of the same wood
makes leaves burgeon and buds swell?

He understood. And as he now raised his eyes
very frightened, to the angel,
he was gone. He pushed his heavy
cap slowly off. Then he sang praise.

RAINER MARIA RILKE, 1875–1926

SEEKING ONE WHO COULD UNDERSTAND

In Luke's Gospel, Mary departs for the hill country of Judea immediately after the Annunciation. In his book A QUIET TALK ABOUT THE BABE OF BETHLEHEM, *published in 1915, Samuel D. Gordon imagines Mary's thoughts following the angel Gabriel's visit.*

AND MARY IS LEFT ALONE. She glances up perhaps. Yes, quite alone. Is it a dream? Will she be awaking? Ah! no, it is too real a thing ever to be questioned. No one who ever had a message direct from God doubts it.

She rises to go about her usual common tasks, but there's a touch of sacredness in the day. It has been made holy to her by God's choice of her for the simple bit of service she *could* give. It has been made holy by this visit of the messenger of God. It was made yet more holy by her own action, her simple full consent to God's plan for her life.

That evening in the twilight she sat on the hill looking out over plain and mountain and sea in holy wordless communion. Perhaps, if she had access to an old Scripture roll in the home, she turned to that Psalm of Asaph's, the Seventy-seventh. And her slender finger traced anew the line: *"I will remember thy wonders of old."* And she paused and mused. Then, with a holy hush coming anew over her spirit, her finger dropped down and traced the yet more wondrous line: "Thou art the God that *doest* wonders."

And now Mary's thought turns naturally to her kinswoman in the southland, Elizabeth, who was much Mary's senior. It is not improbable that there was also a kinship of spirit between them. On some previous visit they may have had simple fellowship and understanding in the deep things of the spirit.

Elizabeth may have been to her as a wise mother in spiritual things. And now Elizabeth was also having unusual experience these days of the wonder-working power of God. There would be no one with whom she could better commune of what had been told her. No one else could understand. As she thinks it over it comes strongly to her that this is the Spirit's suggestion and plan for her.

And so speedily the visit is arranged. And the journey south to the hill country of Judea is made. And no one suspects how much this quiet young traveller knows in her own spirit of God's plan.

The young virgin Mary and her elderly kinswoman Elizabeth— strangely of equal youthfulness—greet each other in these two-foot-high gilded and painted wood statuettes, produced in Germany in about 1310. Inset stones covered cavities in which relics were placed.

In those days Mary arose and went with haste into the hill country, to a city of Judah, and she entered the house of Zechariah and greeted Elizabeth. And when Elizabeth heard the greeting of Mary, the babe leaped in her womb; and Elizabeth was filled with the Holy Spirit and she exclaimed with a loud cry, "Blessed are you among women, and blessed is the fruit of your womb!"

LUKE 1:39–42

RAISING HER VOICE IN A SONG OF PRAISE

Mary's journey to Elizabeth's home would have taken her through some of the Holy Land's wildest and most beautiful territory. The Polish writer Sholem Asch describes her traveling with her new husband Joseph. Though his novel is titled MARY in the English translation, Asch refers to the mother of Jesus as Miriam, the Hebrew version of her name.

IT WAS A LONG JOURNEY that took almost a full week. But it was late spring, the kindest season to travelers. The fields were blanketed with an abundance of varied greens, and men and women were tending the vegetable gardens with which the Plain of Jordan was so thickly planted. On all sides, wherever fell the random glance of the travelers, they saw the sparkling multicolored pattern of beets, radishes, artichokes, fat Egyptian gourds and melons, herbs, spices, and flowering shrubs.

Yet the Jordan is not everywhere so lenient to men. The river meanders through the valley, winds in and out with a serpentine motion, sealing off sometimes whole tracts of land. Only a little way upstream it seemed to flow blithely through gardens and meadows, cajoling fishermen and farmers to its shores— then suddenly it turns abruptly off and, before veering back farther downstream, bequeaths to the fisherman a half-circle of inaccessible marshland, overgrown with writhing waterplants in fulsome profusion. Stumps of dead trees and fallen trunks and branches

Angels bless the reverent greeting Elizabeth extends to Mary as an aged Zechariah sits at rest in the background of this richly detailed tapestry, the work of 16th-century Flemish craftsmen.

The Annunciation to Mary (left) and her subsequent visit to Elizabeth are both depicted in this fragment of a sixth-century Coptic, or Egyptian Christian, tapestry.

THE MAGNIFICAT

My soul doth magnify the Lord,
and my spirit hath rejoiced in God my Saviour.
For he hath regarded the low estate of his handmaiden:
for, behold, from henceforth all generations shall call me blessed.
For he that is mighty hath done to me great things;
and holy is his name.
And his mercy is on them that fear him
from generation to generation.
He hath shewed strength with his arm;
he hath scattered the proud in the imagination of their hearts.
He hath put down the mighty from their seats,
and exalted them of low degree.
He hath filled the hungry with good things;
and the rich he hath sent empty away.
He hath holpen his servant Israel,
in remembrance of his mercy;
as he spake to our fathers,
to Abraham, and to his seed for ever.

LUKE 1:46–55 (King James Version)

bar every access to the river bank. These are areas of real danger, and the most practiced travelers—not to mention the pilgrims journeying to Jerusalem—avoid their treacherous undergrowth and choose detours that take them through the settlements at the foot of the hills. For there are savage animals that lurk in the thickets; wildcats leap from the branches, boars show their hard, bristling snouts, and with the fall of night comes the cry of the jackal.

Joseph was unfamiliar with this region, and at one point, leading the donkey along the river bank which he had taken for his guide, he lost the hackneyed path which had abandoned the Jordan for the security of the hills. But eventually he brought Miriam safely into the date groves of Jericho.

Southward from Jericho the little ass was forced to climb and clamber over rolling masses of stone, the sunken ghosts of ancient cities that once barred Joshua's way into the Promised Land. With wary steps, as though it knew the nature of its burden, the donkey picked a path between sharp razing crags and headlong chasms, digging its hooves into the rocky groove it had chosen to follow and conscious of the yawning gorge that opened a few feet away. Joseph did not for a moment leave its side, feeling Miriam's hand on his shoulder and ready any moment to help if the donkey should misjudge its step.

A stillness as of extinction reigned among these stones. No man or animal or habitation, as far as the eye could reach—nothing but the colossal bulk of stone and precipice falling off steeply into wadis of pulverized rock whose mounting dust seemed like the steam of cauldrons stirred by a witch's brood. Never the sound of running water; never a glimpse of a tree; only the grueling cry of the hyena pursued by a bird of prey that circled overhead biding its victim's exhaustion. The vulture's flitting shadow was the only sign of life in this wilderness, and sometimes, very rarely, a fugitive gazelle perched for a moment on a mountain peak to disappear as quickly as it had come.

There were several scattered oases in the Wilderness of Judah, and in one of these forsaken settlements the aged priest and his wife awaited the future.

Twilight was falling when at last they reached the mountain town—a small square with a well to hold the spring water and a few scattered palms. The dwellings, some twenty in all, were concealed within the face of the rock at various levels. Joseph asked the whereabouts of the priest Zechariah and was directed to a rock-hewn stairway that ran up the mountain wall.

"Zechariah, Zechariah, come forth to welcome your guests!" His call faded away without answer, but within a few seconds the tall frame of the priest appeared. With joy written over his old face, the priest stretched out his arms toward Joseph and embraced him and all the while motioned upward with his hands toward the cave.

Down the stone steps now came another figure—as thin and almost as tall as the priest's. It was the aged Elizabeth, her dress of dark sackcloth taut over a bulging belly, a lighted earthenware lamp in her hand.

Miriam slipped down from her saddle and at once buried her face in the old woman's breast. "I have made this long journey, cousin Elizabeth, to rejoice with you in the gift God has bestowed on you."

As Elizabeth heard these words the blood rushed to her head and her face colored crimson like a skin of wine. Her sunken eyes suddenly kindled like bright fires. She rose briskly to her full length, so that the high dome of her head almost touched the ceiling. Strands of her hair trembled under her black kerchief and, for a moment, she stared at Miriam with mixed terror and exultation before dropping heavily to her knees and crying loudly: "Blessed are you among women, and blessed is the fruit of your womb. For no sooner had your greeting reached my ears but the babe in my womb leapt for joy!"

Joseph did not stir; he kept his eyes cast down as was his wont. But the old priest suddenly raised himself up and stood motionless against the rocky wall so that even the fine hairs of his beard seemed frozen into immobility. For a moment his eyes gaped wildly at the two women and an inarticulate moan wrung itself from his chest. Then he, too, lowered his eyes as though to see were to trespass, and both men held their breath, for it seemed to them that the air of the cave was charged with the substance of another world, all mankind, disembodied, gathered under the palm roof and paying homage to the virgin seated by the wall, an infinity of unfleshed souls—the generations of the living, the dead, and the unborn.

Then Miriam rose, her face so radiant one would have said the sun had set behind the whiteness of her skin, and she opened her lips in a song of praise, singing for sky and earth, for man and angel, for the quick and the dead, singing to all the ends of the earth from the day of creation to the end of time. "My soul doth magnify the Lord," she began.

WILLING TO BE A MAID

Martin Luther drew a lesson of humility from Mary's visit to her kinswoman Elizabeth. His sermon on the subject was translated and edited by Roland H. Bainton for his 1962 publication LUTHER'S MEDITATIONS ON THE GOSPELS.

WHEN MARY HEARD that her cousin Elizabeth was with child, she set out to help her. Mary was of royal lineage and was to be the true, natural mother of God. Yet she set out on foot on a journey of two or three days to do maid service for Elizabeth. Shame on all of us for our pride! No peasant and no townsman of good family among us would stoop so far. If one of us is descended from a noble or a prince, there is no end of bragging. Yet no queen of the Romans or empress could be compared with Mary. What honor is there in the world to be compared with her honor, and she was of royal seed! She might well have said: "Why should I go to help that priest's old lady? It is beneath me, for I am of David's house, and I am carrying the Son of God.

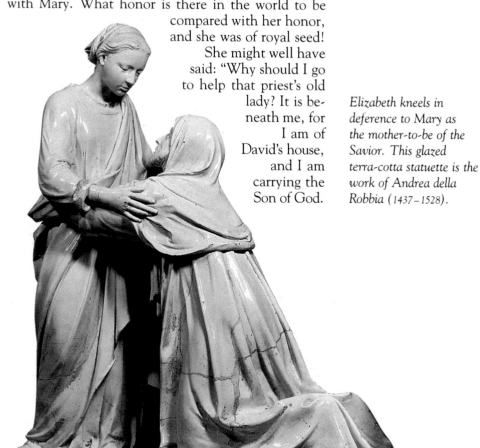

Elizabeth kneels in deference to Mary as the mother-to-be of the Savior. This glazed terra-cotta statuette is the work of Andrea della Robbia (1437–1528).

The angels should take me in a chariot of gold with wheels studded with jewels." Nevertheless she went on foot to visit her cousin. Though she was carrying the Son of God, she was willing to be a maid.

John knew before his mother that Mary was carrying the Savior. When he leaped in the womb, then his mother perceived what she had not discerned by the sight of the eyes, for Mary's condition was not yet evident. Elizabeth was then so overcome that she did not thank Mary, nor did she greet her with the familiarity of a kinswoman but said instead: "Blessed art thou among women, and blessed is the fruit of thy womb. And whence is this to me, that the mother of my Lord should come to me?" One humility confronted another. Mary humbled herself, and Elizabeth considered herself unworthy to have her come.

In Mary and Elizabeth we see how mighty a thing is genuine faith, for it changes a person in soul and body. Elizabeth had become another woman full of inexpressible joy. Her body and tongue were so joyous that she became a prophetess. She was also filled with such assurance that were the world with devils filled she would have trembled not for them. So also Mary. Such a change happens when faith is in the heart.

Elizabeth had said to Mary, "Blessed art thou among women."

And Mary accepted this statement and responded: "Behold, from henceforth all generations shall call me blessed."

Was that not pride for a young girl? No, there is no humility in denying the gifts which God has given. If you have gifts, you should say, "These gifts are from God; I did not confer them upon myself." One should not be puffed up on their account. If someone else does not have the gifts I have, then he has others. If I exalt my gifts and despise another's, that is pride. The sun does not vaunt himself, though more fair than the earth and the trees but says, "Although, tree, you do not shine, I will not despise you, for you are green and I will help you to be green." That is what Mary did here.

Graceful arches frame these sequential scenes from the life of John the Baptist by Francesco Granacci (1469–1544): at left, Elizabeth kneels to greet Mary; center, the aged mother tenderly regards her newborn son; far right, the news of John's birth is conveyed to Zechariah.

*Now the time came for Elizabeth to be
delivered, and she gave birth to a son. And
her neighbors and kinsfolk heard that
the Lord had shown great mercy to her, and
they rejoiced with her. And on the eighth
day they came to circumcise the child;
and they would have named him
Zechariah after his father, but his mother
said, "Not so; he shall be called John."*

LUKE 1:57–60

A NAME FROM HEAVEN

*In his work of devout meditations on events related
to the Nativity,* THE MYSTERY OF BETHLEHEM,
*Herman Hoeksema pictures the scene in which the future
John the Baptist receives his name.*

*Still unable to speak,
Zechariah writes out the
name he has chosen for
his newborn son: John.
Fra Angelico, like many
artists of the Renaissance,
took liberties such as placing
the scene in the courtyard
of an Italian villa and
dressing his figures in
15th-century costumes.*

ZECHARIAH'S MOUTH had been silent the past nine months, so that he had not been able to speak of the marvellous works of God, of the Word of God through the angel, that was being fulfilled before his eyes.

Now the Word was realized. He who was to go before the face of the Lord to prepare the way before him was born. Already he had received the sign of the old covenant. Already the question of his name had been settled, though this had been an occasion of dispute.

Neighbors and relatives had considered it a matter of course that he should be named after his father. In fact, they called him Zechariah. What was more natural? Was he not the only child of his aged parents? Besides, what could be a more suitable name with a view to the wonder of God embodied in this child? Did not the name Zechariah signify that Jehovah remembers and was not this child a tangible and marvellous proof of this truth? What wonder, then, that they called him by the name of his father? And why should it be considered impertinent that, over the protest of Elizabeth and against her strange assertion that the child should be called John, they appealed to the authority of his father?

But now all this is settled.

When they had made signs to the aged, deaf-mute Zechariah, and at his request had supplied him with the necessary implements, he had written a statement that left no room for dispute.

His name *is* John! He had been so named from heaven!

And when the tongue of the thankful father, that had been silent so long, was loosed, he broke forth in praise to Jehovah before a marvelling audience.

The sure and glorious promise has now entered upon its fulfillment! That, in brief, is the theme of this beautiful, inspired song of the aged father of John the Baptist.

Zechariah, filled with the Spirit of prophecy and considering the wonder-child of his old age, sings that God hath visited and redeemed His people.

And thou, child!

A prophet of the Most High he would be called. Greater indeed he would be than all the prophets that were before him. For, though his position would still be on the threshold of the kingdom of heaven, yet he would point with his finger to the Lamb of God that taketh away the sins of the world. And while all the prophets of the old dispensation could only see the Promise afar off, his would be the mission to announce that the Kingdom of heaven had come near, very near indeed! Before his face he would go to prepare his ways!

Repentance he would preach!

Interpreting the Gospel of Luke's cryptic reference to John's upbringing, Fra Filippo Lippi (c. 1406–1469) imagined the saddened parents bidding farewell to their son (detail at right); above, John sits serenely amid a bizarre menagerie in the wilderness.

And the child grew and became strong in spirit, and he was in the wilderness till the day of his manifestation to Israel.

LUKE 1:80

> *In those days a decree went out from Caesar Augustus that all the world should be enrolled. . . . And all went to be enrolled, each to his own city.*
>
> LUKE 2:1, 3

IN OBEDIENCE TO THE IMPERIAL EDICT

How was the decree of Caesar Augustus made known in Palestine? Denis O'Shea, canon of the Church of the Holy Sepulchre in Jerusalem, attempted to answer such questions in THE FIRST CHRISTMAS, *a description of events surrounding the birth of Jesus based on his scholarly studies and observations in the Holy Land. The edict, he suggests, was read to the people of Nazareth by a messenger sent from Herod.*

PEACE BE TO YE! An edict has gone forth from Caesar Augustus that the whole world shall be enrolled. As I, the King, am the friend of Caesar, I have decreed that this enrolling shall be made throughout my kingdom. Wherefore, let every man repair to the place of origin of his house and family and have his name inscribed in the public registers. I, the King, have spoken."

"Long live the King!" shouted the Roman soldiers accompanying the messenger.

But there was no demonstration of loyalty from the townspeople assembled in the marketplace. Instead, the Nazarenes looked gloomily at one another, angry at this disturbance of their daily lives. This was the first census ordered by Rome in the Holy Land, and they resented it. Moreover, once their names were inscribed in the lists they might not so easily evade the payment of the poll tax of a denarius. Their land, too, would be more accurately assessed for taxation. A muttering of discontent broke out, and imprecations were uttered by the hardier patriots.

It was clear that the Nazarenes regarded the edict as an offense to their religion, their patriotism, and their purses. But no man dared come forward and protest openly, for fear of the king lay like a shadow across the whole land.

The Wilderness Years of John the Baptist

John the Baptist's mission takes on new meaning when viewed in light of ancient Hebrew attitudes toward the wilderness. Linked in tradition with the punishing Sinai wasteland of the Exodus, the barren desert was also associated with wild animals, enemy marauders, hunger and thirst — even with monsters and demons from the nether world. On the other hand, God had made his covenant with the Israelites during their 40 years of wandering there, and the desert could be seen as a place of purity and cleansing.

John, six months older than his kinsman Jesus, went to the desert in his youth. By the time he was attracting followers with his fiery preaching, he had assumed the camel's hair garb and inflammatory language of the Old Testament prophets, emphasizing the need for repentance and submission to God's will through the act of baptism. His austerity, his warnings against sin, and his years in the desert have suggested to some scholars that John had once been an Essene. This Jewish sect lived periodically in a closed community on desolate cliffs near the Dead Sea. Idealists who shared property and practiced sexual continence in preparation for a coming war between the forces of good and evil, the Essenes engaged in ritual bathing, believed themselves to be the true Israel, and prayed for the day when they would gain control of the temple from a worldly and wicked priesthood.

John's message, however, was addressed to all men, not just one sect, and specifically dealt with the coming of one greater than himself. His rite of baptism, unlike the Essenes' ritual bathing, was a onetime act symbolizing that a sinful life was being washed away to make the new believer ready for the establishment of God's kingdom.

The remarkable Dead Sea Scrolls, including the fragment pictured above, were discovered in a cave near the desert cliff community of Qumran (left), not far from Jericho. They offer many insights into the beliefs and practices of the Essene sect.

Majestically enthroned, Caesar Augustus (top center) orders his minions to take a census; obedient to the imperial will, Joseph (bottom) takes his pregnant wife Mary to Bethlehem for the enrollment.

Slowly, gloomily, in the fading light of the short winter day, the good folk of Nazareth dispersed and returned to their homes to resume their interrupted occupations. Among them was Joseph the carpenter, who was deeply troubled. He had to bring home to Mary the news of the census and discuss with her, in the privacy of their home, the details of his departure. Her days were nearly accomplished that she should be delivered, and yet he saw himself compelled to leave her and journey across the mountains to Bethlehem.

Night was falling when Joseph returned home from the meeting in the marketplace. It was too dark to work any longer and just time enough to close up the shop for the day. At night Joseph's workshop became the stable of his donkey, the sturdy beast used in transporting logs of wood too heavy for his own back. In the fading light Joseph made up his donkey's bed from bales of straw and filled the crib with meal. He tidied up his workshop, put away his tools in their racks, and barred up the entrance to make all secure for the night. Then he entered the inner room to discuss with Mary the edict of Caesar and its bearing on their lives.

She was seated on a cushion near the oven engaged in making swaddling clothes by the light of the lamp. The carpenter bowed and sat down beside her. He began to talk, while the winter rain drummed on the flat roof overhead, and the north wind, cold and raw from the snows of Mount Hermon, blew piercingly through the narrow streets. Much as he disliked leaving her alone under the circumstances, he was compelled to go to Bethlehem, for he dared not disobey the King's command. There was no need for her to leave home, for he could have his wife's name enrolled with his own. Ten days or more might elapse before he would be back in Nazareth.

There was a pause while Mary pondered over Joseph's words. She would not be parted from him in her hour of need. Since he had to go to Bethlehem, she would go with him. She would endure the discomforts of the journey rather than be separated from the just man into whose care she had been committed by God. Now she tells him so, and he bows his head, overwhelmed by this proof of her trust and love.

To the difficulties of his long winter journey he would add the burden of a woman in a delicate condition. A burden? It was rather a privilege and a joy to have her accompany him. Together they knelt down for their night prayers. Soon they would leave Nazareth—for a much longer time than they anticipated.

*The census at Bethlehem was given a 16th-century setting in Flanders by Pieter Brueghel the Elder (c. 1525–1569);
at center foreground, Joseph leads an ox and the ass on which Mary is seated.*

The apparent contradictions between the genealogy, or family tree, given for Jesus in Matthew and that given in Luke have puzzled Christian scholars for centuries. Indeed, certain questions remain unanswerable, but much of the mystery disappears if the intent of the Evangelists and the customs of the age are taken into account. In the first place, many of the expressions used in ancient genealogies could have more than one meaning. For example, the Hebrew word for "son" could also indicate "grandson" or even the vague "descendant." Similarly, "beget" could also mean something like "become the ancestor of." Second, a genealogy was set down in order to make a connection with a historical figure or establish a relationship with a specific community, tribe, or race; therefore, the intervening names were not all of equal importance and might be skipped. Finally, a genealogy could descend from an ancestor as in Matthew or rise from a descendant as in Luke.

Matthew places his genealogy at the beginning of his story, clearly intending to give Jesus an ancestry befitting the Messiah. The list links him to the royal house of David as well as to the patriarch Abraham, from whose progeny "shall all the nations of the earth bless themselves" (Genesis 22:18). In other words, Jesus is both heir to God's promises made to the Jewish hero-king and the fulfillment of the divine plan for all humankind. The first part of Matthew's genealogy resembles a list found twice in the Old Testament (Ruth 4:18-22, 1 Chronicles 2:1–15), and

highlights the names of four women: Tamar, Rahab, Ruth, and Bathsheba. Matthew's motive for the choice of these four has long been debated. St. Jerome proposed that the women were all sinners, thus showing that Jesus meant to save the sinful. Martin Luther suggested that all would have been considered foreigners by the ancient Hebrews and Matthew was showing that Jesus, though certainly the Jewish Messiah promised in prophecy, was also related to gentiles. Neither of these theories is completely consistent with the scriptural histories of the four women. Today, experts are inclined to believe that Matthew named the four because each, like Jesus' mother, had an irregular union with a man and each performed some action that made her an instrument of God's plan. The second part of Matthew's genealogy more or less matches a list popularly used for the expected Messiah, with the names of Joseph and Jesus added. The Evangelist claims that the complete genealogy reveals a pattern of three groups with 14 generations each. In fact, it does not, since many names have been omitted from the historical record; also, there are only 13 generations in the third group.

Luke, too, wanted to prove to the people of his day that the Messiah had already appeared in history, but his genealogy also reveals his emphasis on Jesus' role as spiritual leader. He inserts his genealogy right after Jesus' baptism, when a heavenly voice affirms that he is God's Son; therefore, Luke's list, which goes back to Adam, is effectively the only scriptural genealogy to connect a bloodline to God.

Illustrations of Jesus' genealogy are called trees of Jesse, for the father of David. In the one above, the lineage rises through David and Mary to a Jesus blessed by the Holy Spirit. The inclusion of Adam and Eve in the manuscript illumination at right indicates the artist was following the genealogy in Luke's gospel.

BOUND FOR BETHLEHEM

Since so little is known of Mary and Joseph, writers across the ages have attempted to fill in the details of their lives. Henri Jules Charles Petiot, using the pen name Daniel-Rops, combined his skills as a novelist and a scholar to produce JESUS AND HIS TIMES, from which the following selection is taken.

WHAT DO WE KNOW of this couple who set out on the road to obey the order of Caesar? That they were united by the sacred tie of marriage and, moreover, by affection, for it was not essential that the young wife in her condition should have accompanied her husband since only males were required to present themselves for registration. They were poor people of the working class, richer in courage than in money and docile and resigned as the humble generally are.

He was an artisan, presumably a carpenter, one of those craftsmen and husbandmen who formed the bulk of the population of Palestine, and whose piety, industry and discipline had permitted the Jewish community on its return from exile to establish themselves once more in the land of their forefathers. The Gospels leave him in silence and obscurity; we guess him, rather than see him, as a man of mature age whom the experience of life has taught wisdom and tolerance. She, his wife, would certainly be much younger than he, for it was customary to marry girls very early.

Though they were both so humble, it need not surprise us that they belonged to Israel's royal family. Not all of the innumerable descendants of the populous harems of David and Solomon were rich or in high places. It would seem that both Joseph and Mary were of the line of David. In the case of Joseph it is expressly stated in the Gospels: by Matthew at the beginning of his book; and by Luke, when he comes to the account of the public ministry of Jesus where it was important, because it was known that the Messiah would be born of the race of the great king. The relation of Mary to the royal house of David is traditional, confirmed by Paul in his letter to the Romans and having the authority of Jewish custom behind it, for marriages within the same family group, often for legal reasons, were common.

And so the two, Joseph and Mary, set out for Bethlehem, the town which the sacred writings had designated as the birthplace of the Messiah. For it was of Bethlehem that the prophet Micah had said, "But thou, Beth-lehem Ephratah, though thou be little among the thousands of Judah, yet out of thee shall he come forth unto me that is to be ruler in Israel. . . ."

Joseph and Mary, descended from David, would remember this prophecy for they knew that the child which Mary bore was the pledge of a miracle. So great would be the hope in their hearts that it might well seem that it was for this that Caesar all unknowing had signed his decree, and mobilized his army of functionaries, for the ways of God are obscure to men and the mightiest are but instruments in his hands.

In response to Caesar's call, Mary and Joseph appear before the seated monarch to pay their enrollment taxes. The 14th-century Italian manuscript is in the library of Oxford University's Corpus Christi College.

And Joseph also went up from Galilee, from the city of Nazareth, to Judea, to the city of David, which is called Bethlehem, because he was of the house and lineage of David, to be enrolled with Mary, his betrothed, who was with child. And while they were there, the time came for her to be delivered.

LUKE 2:4–6

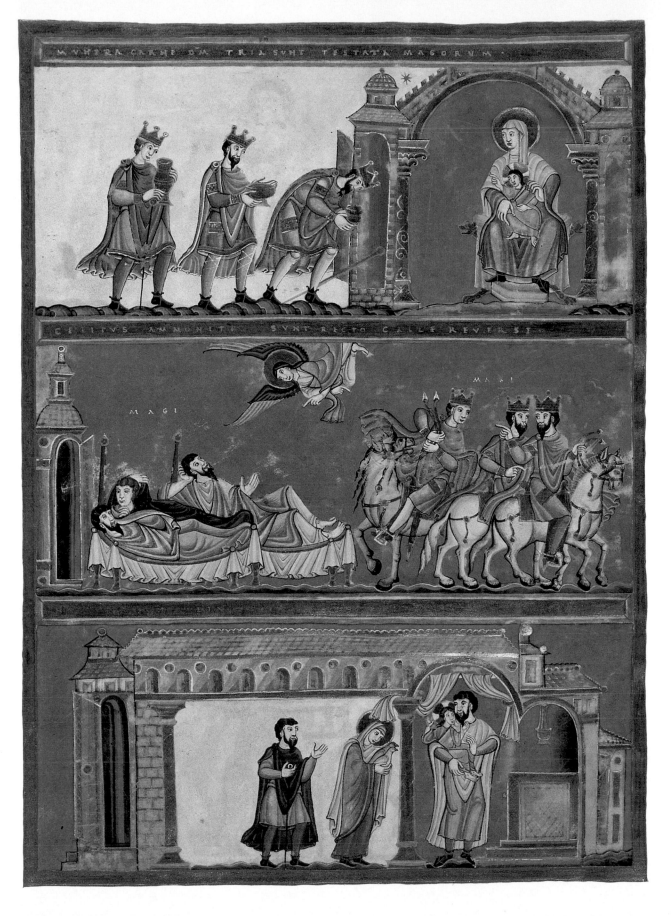

Key events pertaining to the birth of Jesus are illustrated in these pages reproduced from the 11th-century Codex Aureus of Echternach, one of the treasures of the German National Museum in Nürnberg. Opposite, from left to right, top to bottom: the angel Gabriel appearing to Mary and Mary's visit to Elizabeth, the birth of Jesus and the angel bearing tidings to the shepherds, the wise men before Herod; this page: the wise men offering gifts to Jesus, the dream of the wise men and their clandestine departure, the presentation of the infant in the temple at Jerusalem.

And she gave birth to her first-born son
and wrapped him in swaddling cloths, and
laid him in a manger, because there was
no place for them in the inn.

THE SADDEST WORDS OF ALL

*An auxiliary bishop of New York, Fulton J. Sheen
was one of the American Catholic Church's
most prominent spokesmen for three decades—as host
of radio and television programs from 1930 to 1957
and author of a number of books. In his
LIFE OF CHRIST, Bishop Sheen blends narrative
history and biblical commentary.*

JOSEPH WAS FULL OF EXPECTANCY as he entered the city of his family, and was quite convinced that he would have no difficulty in finding lodgings for Mary, particularly on account of her condition. Joseph went from house to house only to find each one crowded. He searched in vain for a place where he, to whom heaven and earth belonged, might be born. Could it be that the Creator would not find a home in creation?

Up a steep hill Joseph climbed to a faint light which swung on a rope across a doorway. This would be the village inn. There, above all other places, he would surely find shelter. There was room in the inn for the soldiers of Rome who had brutally subjugated the Jewish people; there was room for the daughters of the rich merchants of the East; there was room for those clothed in soft garments, who lived in the houses of the king; in fact, there was room for anyone who had a coin to give the innkeeper; but there was no room for him who came to be the Inn of every homeless heart in the world. When finally the scrolls of history are completed down to the last words in

*Mary and the child Jesus fondly gaze at one another
in this detail from a stained glass window at the cathedral
of Freiburg im Breisgau, Germany.*

time, the saddest line of all will be: "There was no room in the inn."

There was no room in the inn, but there was room in the stable. The inn is the gathering place of public opinion, the focal point of the world's moods, the rendezvous of the worldly, the rallying place of the popular and the successful. But the stable is a place for the outcasts, the ignored, the forgotten.

No worldly mind would ever have suspected that he who could make the sun warm the earth would one day have need of an ox and an ass to warm him with their breath; that he, who clothed the fields with grass, would himself be naked; that he, from whose hands came planets and worlds, would one day have tiny arms that were not long enough to touch the huge heads of the cattle; that the feet which trod the everlasting hills would one day be too weak to walk; that the Eternal Word would be dumb; that Omnipotence would be wrapped in swaddling cloths; that Salvation would lie in a manger; that God coming to this earth would ever be so helpless.

AT THE MANGER MARY SINGS

O shut your bright eyes that mine must endanger
With their watchfulness; protected by its shade
Escape from my care: what can you discover
From my tender look but how to be afraid?
Love can but confirm the more it would deny.
    Close your bright eye.

Sleep. What have you learned from the womb that
    bore you
But an anxiety your Father cannot feel?
Sleep. What will the flesh that I gave do for you,
Or my mother love, but tempt you from His will?
Why was I chosen to teach His Son to weep?
    Little One, sleep.

Dream. In human dreams earth ascends to Heaven
Where no one need pray nor ever feel alone.
In your first few hours of life here, O have you
Chosen already what death must be your own?
How soon will you start on the Sorrowful Way?
    Dream while you may.

W. H. AUDEN, 1907–1973

The beloved folk tale that animals worshiped the infant Jesus is reverently shown in a gold and enamel cross made between the sixth and eighth centuries.

The Ox and the Ass

"The ox knows its owner, and the ass its master's crib, but Israel does not know . . ." This famous prophecy in Isaiah 1:3 inspired the enduring folk belief, frequently illustrated in religious art, that an ox and an ass were present at the Nativity and recognized Jesus as God's son. For believers, the charming story implies that the humblest of domestic animals, in their simplicity, understood the spiritual truths that King Herod and established leaders of the Jews did not.

The patient, gentle ass is depicted carrying Mary and Jesus on the Holy Family's flight into Egypt and as Jesus' mount on the triumphal entry into Jerusalem. It also plays a part in the popular legends about early Christian saints, as when St. Jerome's donkey carries wood for his monastery.

Because the ox was sometimes offered as sacrifice by the Jews of biblical times, Renaissance painters adopted the beast as a symbol of the Jewish nation. To early Christians, however, the ox represented Jesus, who had become a sacrifice for the sins of mankind. Since the animal uses its great strength for others, it was also considered symbolic of people who endure life's burdens while patiently doing good for their fellow men.

This Byzantine ivory statuette of Mary and Jesus was originally part of a plaque carved in the 11th century.

*The image of Mary and the
infant Jesus has attracted
the talents of artists through the
centuries and around the world.
The faces on the Russian icon
at right are nearly lost amid the
gold and precious-stone setting.
The Korean painting opposite and
the Chinese ivory statuette below
right give the figures Oriental
features. In carving the statuette
below, an African artist made Mary
and Jesus people of his own race.*

DOING THE RIGHT THING

*Overwhelmed by secular pre-Christmas pressures
one year, the writer Jean Jones Andersen
found herself wondering about the bystanders
at the birth of Jesus so many centuries ago.
From her musings came a series of dialogues and
meditations published in 1985 under the title
ENCOUNTERS AT BETHLEHEM. Following are the
thoughts she attributed to the innkeeper.*

WHAT'S A POOR INNKEEPER to do? We've barely
enough money to pay the bills, and not
enough feed for the animals for the winter:
I can't be expected to turn aside those who
can pay for food and lodging. Not that they're any too
generous, mind you—but at least they don't expect
credit. It's hard to say "no," but I have to be reasonable. I'm in business, after all.

It was a pity about that young couple: I felt bad
about that. Couldn't let them know it, of course, or
they'd have badgered me to death, without a doubt. I
could see the woman was far along . . . wouldn't surprise me if she gave birth this very night. But I just
can't afford sympathy: once you start that, there's no
end to it—and every beggar in the area would be
beating a track to my door. No, no—I did the only
thing I could: the only reasonable, rational thing. I
really had no choice in the matter.

So if what I did was right, how come I can't let go
of it? How come I'm feeling so tormented by it? I keep
seeing their faces . . . going over the whole scene
again and again in my mind. It's like there's something there that's so plain, but I'm just missing it. I
must be too tired: going soft in the head, no doubt.
Can't begin thinking that way. I'd better go look at
the account books, get things straight in my head.

"Hey, who are you, wandering around out here in
the dark? Oh—it's you again. I thought I said . . .

"Oh, it really is late for her, isn't it? Well, I'm kind
of embarrassed to suggest it, but there is a stable out
beyond here, in the side of the hill. It'd be better than
outdoors, with the warmth of the animals at least.
And I'll see if I can find a couple of things to make
you a little more comfortable. Follow me.

"Here, I've found a blanket, and a bucket of water;
and—well, I'm afraid it's just kitchen scraps, but it's
nourishing, if not fancy. No, no, there's no charge—

Journalist Jim Bishop gained fame with a literary form in which his hour-by-hour recreation of an historical event makes the reader feel like a spectator. In 1960 he used that method to describe THE DAY CHRIST WAS BORN, *from which this selection is taken.*

M Y WIFE, SAID JOSEPH, in a tone this side of begging, is outside. She will have her first-born in an hour or two. Can you not please find room? A little room? The owner became irritable. Every house, every field in Bethlehem was filled with people from all over Judea. Where then could a woman have a baby? Nowhere. Some people were even sleeping below in the valley, surrounded by bleating sheep looking for grass.

The owner's wife heard part of the plea. She called her husband aside and asked questions. The night was chill, she said. Why could not the young man take his wife to the cave below, the cave where the animals were kept?

The owner shrugged. The young man was welcome to it, if one wanted to bring a baby into the world in a place like that. Joseph inclined his head. "I am grateful," he said. "I thank you."

Returning to Mary, he dragged his feet and told her the news. She seemed relieved. "Take me," she said. "The time grows short."

Joseph apologized, ashamed that he had failed her in this hour. For a moment, Mary studied her husband. She brought a tender smile to her face. She told her husband that he had not failed her; he had been good and tender and lawful. Mary looked around at the haltered cattle, the few lambs, some asses and a camel. If it is the will of God, she said, that his son should be born in a place like this, she would not question the wisdom of it.

She asked Joseph to build a small fire on the path outside, and to fetch some water from the goatskin. Joseph did as she directed. He found an extra lamp and lit it. As the stable brightened, the animals watched in glistening-eyed silence, their breaths making small gray plumes in the gloom.

Joseph collected clean straw from the feed boxes, cleaned out a stall, and arranged the straw as a bed and placed his cloak over it. Then he looked for wood

don't thank me: it's such a poor thing to offer you . . . I'm really mortified. Please . . . if there's anything you think I can do for you, just come and find me. I'll do what I can, even though it's not much."

Whatever has gotten into me? I don't understand at all! What I just did made no sense—but I feel somehow good about it. It goes against all my training, all my experience and common sense—but somehow it's *right.* I don't feel so much that I did a "right thing" as that it just somehow happened through me—in spite of me . . . almost as though I'm the one who got a gift, and I should be giving thanks.

And I don't feel so drained and tied in knots any more. Tired, yes—in fact, very tired. But it feels good, and I think I could sleep now, even right here, near the entrance to the stable . . . so if they want anything, they can find me easily.

outside, and found none. He went back up to the inn and bought some charcoal from the owner. When the water was hot, he filled a jar, and brought it to Mary with some cloths. She was standing, hanging onto the wall of the stall with both hands. Her head was down, and he could not see her face. In fear, he asked her to name what he could do. She said to go outside and tend the fire and heat more water and to remain there until she called him. The animals watched impassively as Mary sank to the straw.

The fire outside burned brightly in the southerly breeze and little trains of ruddy sparks flew off into the dark night. Joseph sat beside it, heating the water and praying. Time was slow; there was an infinity of silence; a timeless time when the future of mankind hung in empty space.

Joseph looked up toward the east, and his dark eyes mirrored a strange thing: three stars, coming over the Mountains of Moab, were fused into one tremendously bright one. His eyes caught the glint of bright blue light, almost like a tiny moon, and he wondered about it and was still vaguely troubled by it when he heard a soft call, "Joseph." At once, he picked up the second jar of water and hurried inside. The lamp still shed a soft glow over the stable, even though it seemed years since it had been lighted.

The first thing he noticed was his wife. Mary was sitting tailor-fashion with her back against a manger

Simplicity of style does not conceal the obvious piety with which an unknown Catalan artist of the 12th century painted this version of the Nativity. Although Joseph's halo is traditional, those of Mary and the infant are strangely oval in shape.

wall. Her face was clean; her hair had been brushed. There were blue hollows under her eyes. She smiled at her husband and beckoned him to come closer. Joseph, mouth agape, peered into a little manger. It had been cleaned but, where the animals had nipped the edges of the wood, the boards were worn and splintered. In the manger were the broad bolts of white swaddling she had brought on the trip. They were doubled underneath and over the top of the baby.

Mary smiled at her husband as he bent far over to look. There, among the cloths, he saw the tiny red face of an infant. This, said Joseph to himself, is the one of whom the angel spoke. He dropped to his knees beside the manger. This was the Messiah.

A HYMN FOR THE NATIVITY
OF MY SAVIOUR

I sing the birth was born tonight,
The Author both of life and light;
  The angels so did sound it.
And like the ravished shepherds said,
Who saw the light and were afraid,
  Yet searched, and true they found it.

The Son of God, the eternal King,
That did us all salvation bring,
  And free the soul from danger;
He whom the whole world could not take,
The Word which heaven and earth did make,
  Was now laid in a manger.

The Father's wisdom willed it so,
The Son's obedience knew no No,
  Both wills were in one stature:
And as that wisdom had decreed,
The Word was now made flesh indeed,
  And took on Him our nature.

What comfort by Him do we win,
Who made Himself the price for sin,
  To make us heirs of Glory!
To see this Babe all innocence,
A martyr born in our defence;
  Can man forget this story?

BEN JONSON, 1572–1637

Surrounding Jesus in the Limoges enamel plaque at left, as well as in the four details from Aachen's 11th-century gold altar, are the symbols of the Evangelists (clockwise from upper left): a man, an eagle, an ox, and a lion.

The Four Evangelists

A rich symbolic tradition for the four Evangelists — Matthew, Mark, Luke, and John — developed early in the Christian era. Borrowing from Greek and Roman styles of depicting writers or philosophers, Christian artists showed the authors of the Gospels either seated at their writing desks or standing, sometimes holding a copy of the Gospel each had contributed to the Scriptures.

From a scene described in Revelation 4:6-8 came an association with four winged creatures — a man, a lion, an ox, and an eagle. Matthew was linked with the man because his Gospel starts with the earthly genealogy and human birth of Jesus. Since Mark begins his account with John the Baptist as "the voice of one crying in the wilderness," he is assigned the lion as his symbol. The ox or calf became Luke's symbol because he tells of Zechariah's sacrifice in the Temple. The Evangelist John begins his Gospel with the image of "the Word" in Heaven with God, so tradition has linked him with the soaring eagle. In addition, each of these symbols of the tetrad, or group of four, has meaning in the life of Jesus. The man representing Matthew recalls the human form taken by Jesus. Because people in the Middle Ages believed that a lion could bring its stillborn cubs to life by roaring, Mark's lion was thought to symbolize the Resurrection, just as Luke's sacrificial ox stands for the Crucifixion. The Ascension of Jesus into Heaven is recalled by John's eagle. Clerics of the Middle Ages associated the four Evangelists with the four greatest prophets of the Old Testament — Isaiah, Jeremiah, Ezekiel, and Daniel. Toward the end of the medieval period, the Evangelists were linked with the Roman Catholic saints revered then as the foremost doctors of the church — Jerome, Augustine, Ambrose, and Gregory. Although biblical scholars have raised many questions about authorship, most agree that Mark's Gospel is the oldest.

After an angel appeared to them (upper right), the shepherds hastened to worship the infant Jesus—a scene reverently recreated by 15th-century French court painter Jean Fouquet for a book of devotions.

And in that region there were shepherds out in the field, keeping watch over their flock by night. And an angel of the Lord appeared to them, and the glory of the Lord shone around them, and they were filled with fear. And the angel said to them, "Be not afraid; for behold, I bring you good news of a great joy which will come to all the people; for to you is born this day in the city of David a Savior, who is Christ the Lord."

LUKE 2:8–11

WINTER TURNED TO SPRING

Not to the high and mighty but rather to lowly shepherds was the birth of Jesus first proclaimed. Seldom has a writer better captured the awe these humble herdsmen must have felt than did Sholem Asch in his novel MARY.

OUTSIDE, THE NIGHT was growing brighter—not with the light of day, nor yet with the star-light of the night; it was a brightness as though beams of pearl were being woven through the ether. The stars grew larger, multiplied, and seemed to wend toward the earth. They rained down rays of light which lent a virgin whiteness to the land they touched upon, rendering all things bright and transparent, so that one could not say whether the landscape was of solid substance or not rather a pattern of veiled, dancing chimeras. Hills, houses, valleys, and flocks of sheep revealed themselves in an instant and retired from sight.

A thin white flurry of snow swept down from the heights, as the poor, shivering shepherds, who could not provide roofed cover for their flocks and who were pasturing them far from their homes, tried bravely to keep the sheep warm in their own body heat, crowding them against each other as closely as possible. The shepherds were wrapped in sack-like coats, but most of them were soaked to the skin by windswept snow. Some had thatched themselves over with burlap rags, cloths of goat's hair, or crudely woven wool. And here and there they could be seen to crouch about a small brushwood fire.

For several hours past they had observed an unfamiliar radiance pouring down from the sky. It was not the unusual size and brightness of the stars, nor even their exceptional profusion on this night, that made the herdsmen raise their heads again and again as though the sky owed them an answer; it was their terrified realization that all the floating glimmer of the Milky Way was hanging over Bethlehem, that the white buoyant skyways, blown like drifting veils from the horizon, were straining to a stop over their slumbering town. Never had they seen the blended galaxy emitting a more radiant light, nor seen it strike such pearly iridescence from the snow on the hills. Never before had they seen stars so closely thronged that their flash and scintillation seemed like the sparking of metallic bodies in collision.

And suddenly they saw their flocks disband, abandoning the woolen wombs of warmth which their commingling bodies had posed against the cold. With flaring nostrils they sniffed fresh vapor rising up from shrubs and pasture grasses and began scattering through the vales and even climbing the hills. The very landscape changed its aspect. A current of warmth swept through the atmosphere as earth shook off the winter, breathing forth a waft of spring. Each bush and shrub exhaled a balm as of flowering blossoms, filling the world with a smell of youth and revival. And suddenly the shepherds saw their winter transfigured into spring. Every valley shone with the green of young grass, and on the hills fresh pastures showed through the retreating white, and a pearly light fell on the sheep grazing in the meadows. A stillness settled over all creation.

Squatting on their haunches around their small fire, the shepherds remained motionless with terror and dared not speak a word. And in another moment they looked up fearfully, for they heard, above their heads, a suppressed whirr as of fanned air. The sound could not be placed; they saw only the veiled white trails of the eastern sky, stretched low like tenuous clouds and streaking toward Bethlehem.

Then suddenly the sky-veils parted and revealed a fiery flame, fluttering down toward the kneeling shepherds. And within the flame stood the form of an angel, and a voice said: "Fear not: for, behold, I bring you good tidings of great joy. . . ."

The shepherd story in miniature (left) adorns a page of the devotional book illuminated for the duc de Berry by Pol de Limbourg and his two brothers early in the 15th century. An unknown artist lavished gold paint on the shepherd scene created for a 13th-century French Psalter (below)—and included black goats nibbling at imagined palm trees.

And when the shepherds lifted up their eyes to see who it was that spoke, they saw the angel surrounded by a multitude of the heavenly host, and they were praising the Lord: "Glory to God in the highest, and on earth peace, good will toward men."

The song faded out, and with the song, the vision of the host. Then, when the shepherds regained their speech, they turned to one another, saying: "Why do we linger here? Let us hasten to Bethlehem and see with our own eyes what God has given us to know."

The shepherd in this scene from an English devotional book carries a bagpipe—an instrument associated with shepherds across Europe, though not particularly appropriate for a field near Bethlehem.

CHRISTMAS CAROL

From the starry heav'ns descending
   Herald angels in their flight,
     Nearer winging,
     Clearer singing,
   Thrilled with harmony the night:
"Glory, glory in the highest!"
   Sounded yet and yet again,
     Sweeter, clearer,
     Fuller, nearer—
"Peace on earth, good will to men!"

Shepherds in the field abiding,
   Roused from sleep, that gladsome morn,
     Saw the glory
     Heard the story
   That the Prince of Peace was born:
"Glory, glory in the highest!"
   Sang the angel choir again,
     Nearer winging,
     Clearer singing:
"Peace on earth, good will to men!"

Swept the angel singers onward,
   Died the song upon the air;
     But the glory
     Of that story
   Grows and triumphs everywhere;
And when glow the Yuletide heavens,
   Seems that glorious song again
     Floating nearer,
     Sweeter, clearer—
"Peace on earth, good will to men!"

J. R. NEWELL

TOO GLORIOUS FOR MORTAL EYES TO LOOK UPON

Was the memory of that night preserved by the shepherds who were there and carefully handed down from generation to generation? In "The Shepherd's Story," Washington Gladden imagined one of the shepherds recounting the miraculous appearance of the angel 50 years later to his grandson.

BRING THAT SHEEPSKIN, Joseph, and lay it down on this bank of dry earth, under this shelving rock. The wind blows chilly from the west, but the rock will shelter us. The sky is fair and the moon is rising, and we can sit here and watch the flock on the hillside below. Your young blood and your father's coat of skins will keep you warm for one watch, I am sure. At midnight, my son, your father and his brother will take our places; for the first watch you and I will tend the sheep."

"Yes, grandfather; you shall sit in that snug corner of the rock, where you can lean back and take your comfort. I will lie at your feet. Now and then I will run and see whether the sheep are wandering, and that will warm me, if I grow cold."

"Do you know, my boy, that this is the night of the year on which the Lord Christ was born?"

"Oh yes," answered the lad. "My father told me you were with the sheep that night. How long ago was that, grandfather?"

"Just fifty years ago this night."

"And how old were you then?"

"Fourteen, and a stout boy for my age. I had been for two years in the fields with my father and had tasted to the full the hardships and dangers of the shepherd's life. My father and his brother James, and Hosea, a neighbor and kinsman of ours, were with me. On that year, as on this year and often, there came in the mid-winter a dry, warm season between the early and latter rain. We had driven forth our flock from Bethlehem and were dwelling by night in the shelter of the tower on the hillside yonder, watching and sleeping, two and two. My father and I were wont to keep the earlier watches. At midnight we would call James and Hosea to relieve us, and they would watch till morning.

"But that night, when the sun went down and the stars came out, we were all sitting here, upon this hill-

The candle Joseph holds casts a radiant glow on the swaddled infant and his mother Mary (left) in this intimate scene of worshiping shepherds. Such illumination from within was a favorite device of French painter Georges de La Tour (1593–1652).

As the heavenly host gives benediction, awed shepherds approach Mary to pay obeisance to the infant Jesus.
The work of French court painter Charles Lebrun (1619–1690), this canvas now hangs in the Louvre museum in Paris.

side, talking of the troubles of Israel and the promises of deliverance spoken of by the prophets; and James and Hosea were asking my father questions, and he was answering them, for he was older than they, and all the people of Bethlehem reverenced him as a wise and devout man.

"Suddenly I saw my father rise to his feet. Then the other men sprang up, with astonishment and wonder upon their faces. It had grown light all at once, lighter than the brightest moon; and as I turned my face in the direction in which the others were looking I saw, standing there upon that level place, a figure majestic and beautiful beyond the power of words to describe. My heart stopped beating. The others were standing, but I had no power to rise. I lay there motionless upon the earth. My eyes were fixed upon that wonderful face, upon those clear, shining eyes, upon that brow that seemed to beam with the purity of the soul within. It was not a smile with which that face was lighted. It was something too noble and exalted to call by that name. It was a look that told of power and peace, of joy and triumph."

"Did you know that it was an angel?"

"I knew not anything. I only knew what I saw was glorious, too glorious for mortal eyes to look upon. Yet while I gazed, the terribleness of the look began to disappear, the sweetness and grace of the soul shone forth, and I had almost ceased to tremble before the angel opened his mouth. And when he spoke, his voice, clearer than any trumpet and sweeter than any lute, charmed away all my fears.

" 'Be not afraid,' he said, 'for behold I bring you good tidings of great joy. For there is born to you this day, in the city of David, a Saviour.'

"Oh, that voice, my boy! It makes my heart beat now to remember its sweetness. It seemed to carry these words into our innermost hearts; to print them on our memories, so that we never could forget one syllable of what he said. And then, before we had time to make reply, he turned aside a little and lifted his face toward heaven, and in a tone far louder than that in which he had spoken to us, but yet so sweet that it did not startle us at all, came forth from his lips the first strain of that great song:

" 'Glory to God in the highest!'

"When he had uttered that he paused a moment, and the echoes, one after another, from the hills that were near and the hills that were far away, came flying home to us; so that I knew for once what the prophet

Holding an olive branch to symbolize Jesus' mission of peace, the angel announces his birth to the shepherds in this work by the Italian miniaturist Sano di Pietro.

Shepherds Keeping Watch

Descended from generations of seminomadic herders who lived by keeping flocks of sheep and goats, ancient Hebrews held shepherds in high esteem. Patriarchs, kings, and prophets, including Jacob, David, and Amos, had tended sheep. Job, a rich man in his day, owned 14,000 sheep, and 100 sheep a day were consumed by Solomon's court. Yet, as the Israelites settled in Canaan and turned to farming, social attitudes toward shepherds began to change.

The shepherds mentioned in Luke were probably men of modest means, either owning a small flock or working for someone else. Theirs was a harsh, lonely life on the fringes of cultivated land. Dressed in a rude cloak of homespun wool or sheepskins, the typical shepherd carried simple weapons to protect his charges — a goat's hair sling for hurling stones, a 30-inch-long wooden club embedded with iron nails. Thieves — not to mention such predators as wolves, hyenas, jackals, lions, and bears — were a constant danger. During the day, the flocks wandered over unfenced, rocky ground, nibbling at scarce forage. Following on the alert, shepherds carried a water bag and such basic fare as dates, olives, cheese, and bread. Crude huts made of poles and a thatched roof might be set up at lookout points to protect the men from the glaring desert sun. At night, if the weather turned inclement or cold, sheep and shepherd would return to camp — perhaps a cave or a stone-walled sheepfold. The shepherds sometimes set up tents for themselves, but in warmer months, they often slept beside their flocks in the wilds.

The angel's announcement to the shepherds underscored Jesus' role as the Good Shepherd who would sacrifice his life for humankind — just as the shepherds of his time were literally expected to give their lives to protect their flocks.

Shepherds gathered in worship are depicted by the 17th-century Dutch master Rembrandt van Rijn (near right), one of the many biblical scenes he engraved. Two centuries earlier, Germany's greatest engraver of the period, Martin Schongauer, devoted his talents to the same scene (opposite).

meant when he said that all the mountains and the hills should break forth into singing. But before the echoes had all faded we began to hear other voices above our heads, a great chorus, taking up the strain that the first angel had sung. At first it seemed dim and far away; but gradually it came nearer and filled the air, filled all the earth, filled all our souls with the most entrancing sweetness. 'Glory to God in the highest!'—that was the grandest part. It seemed as though there could be no place so high that the strain would not mount up to it, and no place so happy that that voice would not make it thrill with new gladness. But then came the softer tones, less grand, but even sweeter—'Peace on earth, good-will toward men.' "

"Did you see the choir of angels overhead?"

"I saw nothing. The brightness was too dazzling for mortal eyes. We all stood there, with downcast eyes, listening spellbound to the wonderful melody, until the chorus ceased, and the echoes, one after another, died away, and the glory faded out of the sky, and the stars came back again, and no sound was heard but the faint voice of a young lamb calling for its mother.

"The first to break the silence was my father. 'Come,' he said in a solemn voice. 'Let us go at once to Bethlehem, and see this thing which is come to pass, which the Lord hath made known unto us.' "

WHILE SHEPHERDS WATCHED THEIR FLOCK BY NIGHT

Like small curled feathers, white and soft,
    The little clouds went by,
Across the moon, and past the stars,
    And down the western sky:
In upland pastures, where the grass
    With frosted dew was white,
Like snowy clouds the young sheep lay,
    That first, best Christmas night.

The shepherds slept; and glimmering faint,
    With twist of thin, blue smoke,
Only their fire's crackling flames
    The tender silence broke—
Save when a young lamb raised his head,
    Or, when the night wind blew,
A nesting bird would softly stir,
    Where dusky olives grew—

With finger on her solemn lip,
    Night hushed the shadowy earth,
And only stars and angels saw
    The little Saviour's birth;
Then came such flash of silver light
    Across the bending skies,
The wondering shepherds woke, and hid
    Their frightened, dazzled eyes!

And all their gentle sleepy flock
    Looked up, then slept again,
Nor knew the light that dimmed the stars
    Brought endless peace to men—
Nor even heard the gracious words
    That down the ages ring—
"The Christ is born! the Lord has come,
    Good-will on earth to bring!"

Then o'er the moonlit, misty fields
    Dumb with the world's great joy,
The shepherds sought the white-walled town,
    Where lay the baby boy—
And oh, the gladness of the world,
    The glory of the skies,
Because the longed-for Christ looked up
    In Mary's happy eyes!

MARGARET DELAND, 1857–1945

A Nativity scene, complete with the traditional ass and ox, is framed within the letter P in this late-14th-century Italian choral manuscript from the workshop of Silvestro dei Gherarducci.

HARK!
THE HERALD ANGELS SING

Hark! the herald angels sing,
"Glory to the new-born King;
Peace on earth, and mercy mild,
God and sinners reconciled."
Joyful all ye nations, rise,
Join the triumph of the skies;
With th' angelic host proclaim,
"Christ is born in Bethlehem!"
Hark! the herald angels sing,
"Glory to the new-born King!"

Christ, by highest heaven adored,
Christ, the everlasting Lord!
Come, Desire of Nations, come,
Fix in us thy humble home.
Veiled in flesh the Godhead see;
Hail th' Incarnate Deity,
Pleased as man with man to dwell;
Jesus, our Emmanuel;
Hark! the herald angels sing,
"Glory to the new-born King!"

Hail, the heaven-born Prince of Peace!
Hail, the Sun of Righteousness!
Light and life to all he brings,
Risen with healing in his wings;
Mild he lays his glory by,
Born that man no more may die,
Born to raise the sons of earth,
Born to give them second birth;
Hark! the herald angels sing,
"Glory to the new-born King!"

CHARLES WESLEY, 1707–1788

Trumpeting the joyous news, one of three details from a Neopolitan manuscript (others at right)

O LITTLE TOWN OF BETHLEHEM

O little town of Bethlehem,
  How still we see thee lie!
Above thy deep and dreamless sleep
  The silent stars go by;
Yet in thy dark streets shineth
  The everlasting Light;
The hopes and fears of all the years
  Are met in thee tonight.

For Christ is born of Mary,
  And, gathered all above,
While mortals sleep, the angels keep
  Their watch of wond'ring love.
O morning stars, together
  Proclaim the holy birth!
And praises sing to God the King,
  And peace to men on earth.

How silently, how silently
  The wondrous gift is given!
So God imparts to human hearts
  The blessings of his heaven.
No ear may hear his coming;
  But in this world of sin,
Where meek souls will receive Him still,
  The dear Christ enters in.

O holy child of Bethlehem,
  Descend on us, we pray;
Cast out our sin, and enter in,—
  Be born in us today.
We hear the Christmas angels
  The great, glad tidings tell;
O come to us, abide with us
  Our Lord Emmanuel!

PHILLIPS BROOKS, 1835–1893

A lady strumming a medieval musical instrument

SILENT NIGHT, HOLY NIGHT

Silent night, holy night!
All is calm, all is bright,
'Round yon Virgin Mother and Child!
Holy Infant, so tender and mild,
Sleep in heavenly peace,
Sleep in heavenly peace.

Silent night, holy night!
Shepherds quake at the sight!
Glories stream from heaven afar,
Heav'nly hosts sing Alleluia;
Christ the Saviour is born,
Christ the Saviour is born.

Silent Night, Holy Night!
Son of God, love's pure light,
Radiant beams from Thy holy face,
With the dawn of redeeming grace
Jesus, Lord, at Thy birth,
Jesus, Lord, at Thy birth.

Silent Night, Holy Night!
Guiding star, lend thy light,
See the eastern wise men bring,
Gifts and homage to our King,
Jesus, the Saviour is born,
Jesus, the Saviour is born.

JOSEPH MOHR, 1792–1848

IT CAME UPON A MIDNIGHT CLEAR

It came upon a midnight clear,
That glorious song of old,
From angels bending near the earth,
To touch their harps of gold;
"Peace on the earth, good-will to men,
From Heaven's all-gracious King";
The world in solemn stillness lay,
To hear the angels sing.

Still through the cloven skies they come,
With peaceful wings unfurled;
And still their heavenly music floats
O'er all the weary world;
Above its sad and lowly plains
They bend on heavenly wing,
And ever o'er its Babel sounds
The blessed angels sing!

And ye, beneath life's crushing load,
Whose forms are bending low,
Who toil along the climbing way
With painful steps and slow,
Look now! for glad and golden hours
Come swiftly on the wing;
O rest beside the weary road,
And hear the angels sing.

For lo! the days are hastening on,
By prophet-bards foretold,
When, with the ever-circling years
Comes round the age of gold;
When peace shall over all the earth
Its ancient splendors fling,
And the whole world give back the song
Which now the angels sing.

EDMUND HAMILTON SEARS, 1810–1876

A royal figure, possibly King David, with a lyre

And at the end
of eight days,
when he was
circumcised, he
was called
Jesus, the name
given by the
angel before he
was conceived
in the womb.

LUKE 2:21

A youthful Mary
and an aged Joseph
(right) attend the
ceremonial
circumcision of
the infant Jesus in
Federico Barocci's
painting dated
1590. The artist
included a bound
sacrificial lamb in
the left foreground.

And when the time came for their purification according to the law of Moses, they brought him up to Jerusalem to present him to the Lord.

THE FIRST SHADOW FALLS

After Mary and Joseph sacrificed the pair of turtledoves or young pigeons as prescribed for a firstborn son, an aged man approached them in the temple. His greeting, as Alice M. Darton suggests in this excerpt from HIS MOTHER, a fictional biography of Mary, held not only confirmation of their belief in the child as Messiah but also a chilling warning for the future.

SIMEON WAS AN OLD MAN going down to his grave at the end of a life of righteousness. Ardently had he prayed for the consolation of Israel, so sorely beset and so sadly in need of redemption. And his faith had been rewarded: the Holy Spirit had revealed that he should not see death before he had seen the Christ.

How this was to be fulfilled, Simeon did not know. Probably like most Jews, he expected to see an angelic sort of being with unlimited earthly power at his command—a kind of superman. Simeon, however, had no arrogance of spirit. When he entered the temple, led by the Spirit, and perceived that the child of this poor, inconspicuous mother was the expected Messiah, he accepted this fact with perfect submission of his will and blessed God.

Again Mary and Joseph found that God had disclosed his mercy, and in the same unexpected way as to the shepherds. Had the priest who had redeemed their child uttered the words of Simeon, they would not have been surprised; he stood to them as the churchly authority, as the chosen of God. But he had held this Holy Child in his arms, entirely unconscious of his identity; he had received the redemption sum and recited the benedictions in a purely perfunctory manner. They had turned from him, believing that God intended to conceal the identity of Jesus even in his temple. But Simeon—not a priest, not a Levite, but simply a just and devout man—accosted them.

Simeon's heart yearned over this little family and as he restored the child again to his mother's arms he blessed Mary and Joseph, upon whom rested the responsibility of this glorious child. And God permitted him to see some of the future, and he spoke to Mary the first words of warning: "Behold this child is set for the fall, and for the resurrection of many in Israel, and for a sign which shall be contradicted: And thy own soul a sword shall pierce, that, out of many hearts, thoughts may be revealed."

This was the first shadow that fell upon Mary and the babe. Their future together, even though unknown, had seemed to stretch radiantly before her. This radiance was now dimmed. What sword could pierce her soul but sorrow for him? This child, for whom she would lay down her life, whom as "handmaiden" she would serve forever, was to meet opposition and suffering. That message of Simeon was the shock which took away the last traces of girlishness from the young mother, implanting in her in its stead that serious and understanding conformity to the will of God which was to increase with the years and hold her steadfast at the foot of the cross.

Faithful to Luke's account of the presentation ceremony, Fra Angelico included Joseph bearing birds for sacrifice, Mary and the infant Jesus, the devout Simeon, and the aged prophetess Anna—and then curiously added two children at play in what is obviously an Italian Renaissance chapel.

**Now when Jesus was born in Bethlehem of
Judea in the days of Herod the king,
behold, wise men from the East came to
Jerusalem, saying, "Where is he who has
been born king of the Jews? For we
have seen his star in the East, and have
come to worship him."**

MATTHEW 2:1–2

FINDING THEIR WAY

*On the way to Bethlehem, according to legend, the three
wise men lost sight of the star that was guiding them.
In THE WELL OF THE STAR, published in 1941,
English novelist Elizabeth Goudge tells how they found it
with the help of a poor carpenter's son named David.*

AVID SAT CROSS-LEGGED by himself in a corner of the room. If only he were a rich man, then it would not matter that storms had destroyed the barley, that their vines had failed, or that their father was ill and could no longer ply his trade.

Suddenly there came to David's mind the thought of the wishing well far down below on the road to Bethlehem. It was a well of clear sparkling water, and it was said that those who stood by it at midnight, and prayed to the Lord God from a pure heart, were given their heart's desire. He crept noiselessly through the shadows to the door, pulled it open, and slipped out into the great cold silent night.

The sky was streaming with light, so jeweled with myriads of blazing stars that it seemed the weight of them would make the sky fall down and crush the waiting earth to atoms. With his knees shaking, David raced down the road until he saw the water of the well gleaming only a few feet away.

He leaned against the stone parapet and looked gravely into the water. Covering his face with his fingers he prayed that he might have gold to buy food and wine and oil for that stricken house up above him on the hill. And so hard did he pray that he forgot everything but his own longing, forgot his fears and the cold wind that nipped him through his rags, saw nothing but the darkness of his closed eyes and heard nothing but his own desperate whispering.

Then, sighing a little like a child awaking from sleep, he opened his eyes and peeped anxiously through his fingers at the water in the well. Was that something glittering in the well? He dropped his hands from his face and leaned closer, the blood pounding so in his ears that it sounded like drums beating. Yes, it was gold! Circles of gold lying upon the surface of the water, as though the stars had dropped down from heaven. But his cry of joy changed to a cry of terror, for framed in those twinkling golden points of light he saw the reflection of a

Following the star in the East, the three wise men seek the newborn king of the Jews; the stained glass panel, created in about 1200, graces Canterbury cathedral in England.

LORD, WHEN THE WISE MEN CAME FROM FAR

Lord, when the wise men came from far,
Led to thy cradle by a star,
Then did the shepherds too rejoice,
Instructed by thy angel's voice;
Blest were the wise men in their skill,
And shepherds in their harmless will.

Wise men in tracing nature's laws
Ascend unto the highest cause;
Shepherds with humble fearfulness
Walk safely, though their light be less;
Though wise men better know the way,
It seems no honest heart can stray.

There is no merit in the wise
But love (the shepherds' sacrifice).
Wise men, all ways of knowledge past,
To th' shepherds' wonder come at last;
To know, can only wonder breed,
And not to know, is wonder's seed.

A wise man at the altar bows
And offers up his studied vows
And is received; may not the tears
Which spring too from a shepherd's fears,
And sighs upon his frailty spent,
Though not distinct, be eloquent?

'Tis true, the object sanctifies
All passions which within us rise;
But since no creature comprehends
The cause of causes, end of ends,
He who himself vouchsafes to know
Best pleases his creator so.

When then our sorrows we apply
To our own wants and poverty,
When we look up in all distress
And our own misery confess,
Sending both thanks and prayers above,
Then though we do not know, we love.

SIDNEY GODOLPHIN, 1610–1643

*Albrecht Altdorfer (c. 1480–1538) depicted
one of the wise men as black in a scene set
in the ruins of a Gothic church.*

man's face, a bearded swarthy face with gleaming teeth and eyes.

"Do not cry out, little son. I will not hurt you." The man stretched out a hand and gave David's shoulder a reassuring little shake. "I but looked over your shoulder to see what you stared at so intently."

The stranger was tall, and wore a purple robe girdled at the waist with gold and a green turban to which were stitched gold ornaments that shook and trembled round his proud, hawk-nosed face. David had one pang of agonized disappointment as he realized that it was only the reflection of these gold ornaments he had seen in the water, and not God's answer to his prayer, and then amazement swept all other thoughts from his mind.

For the star-lit road to the well that a short while ago had been empty was now full. While David prayed, his ears closed to all sounds, a glittering cavalcade had come up out of the night. There were richly caparisoned camels and two more splendid grave-faced men even more richly dressed than the man who had startled him. Surely these men were kings!

"And for what were you looking so intently, little son?" the first king asked.

"They say," said David, "that if you pray to God for your heart's desire from a pure heart, you will see a vision of it in the water."

"And you saw yours?"

David shook his head. "You came, great lord," he explained. "I saw you."

One of the other kings, an old white-bearded man in a sea-green robe, was listening with a smile to their talk. "We three have lost a star, little son," he said to David. "Should we find it again in your well?"

David thought it might be a joke, for what could three great lords want with a star? But when he looked up into the fine old eyes gazing down into his he saw trouble and bewilderment in them.

"If your heart is pure, great lord."

A shadow passed over the old man's face and he turned back to the third king, a young man with a boy's smooth skin and eyes that were bright and gay.

"Gaspar," he said. "You are young and pure of heart, you look."

Obediently Gaspar stepped up to the well, his scarlet robe swirling about him and the curved sword that he wore slapping against his side. After bowing his head in prayer, he bent over the well.

"I can see only a part of the sky," he murmured,

"and each star is like another in glory—no—yes." He paused and suddenly gave a shout of triumph. "I have found it, Melchior! It shines in the center of the well, like the hub of a wheel or the boss of a shield."

He straightened himself and flung back his head, his arms stretched up toward the sky. "There! There!" he cried, and David and the elder kings, gazing, saw a great star blazing over their heads, a star that was mightier and more glorious than the sister stars that shone around it like cavaliers round the throne. And as they gazed it suddenly moved away, streaking through the sky like a comet.

"Look!" cried David. "A shooting star! It is shining over Bethlehem!"

The three kings stood behind him, gazing where he pointed, and saw at the end of the road, faintly visible in the starlight, slender cypress trees rising above the huddled roofs of a little white town upon a hill, and above them the blazing star.

"Bethlehem," said the first king. "At long last, the end of our journey."

Above, a black servant removes the crown of the youngest wise man (left foreground), who joins his two older, and already bareheaded, comrades in worshiping Jesus. Domenico Ghirlandaio's crowded canvas is dated 1487. The stylized bas-relief of the three wise men offering gifts at left is from the cathedral of Cividale del Friuli, some 70 miles northeast of Venice.

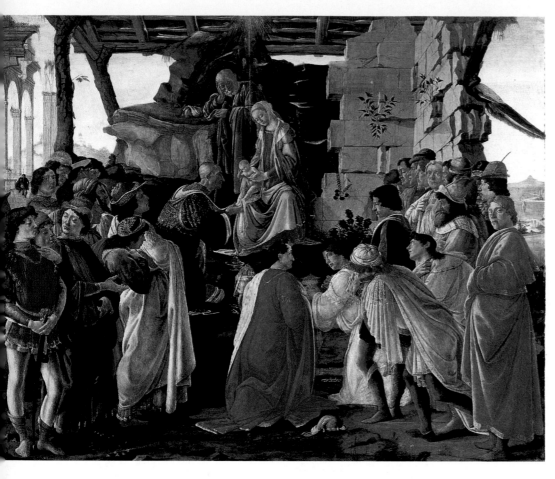

Although the grotto in which Joseph and Mary receive the wise men who have come to worship Jesus is realistically humble, the artist, Sandro Botticelli (c. 1445–1510), peopled his scene with richly attired courtiers typical of his native Florence at the height of the Italian Renaissance.

THE HEAVENLY STRANGER

No warm, downy pillow His sweet head pressed;
No soft silken garments His fair form dressed;
    He lay in a manger,
    This heavenly Stranger,
The precious Lord Jesus, the wonderful child.

No jubilant clang of rejoicing bell
The glorious news the world did tell;
    But angels from glory
    Sang sweetly the story
Of Bethlehem's Stranger, the Saviour of men.

Thou heavenly Stranger, so gentle and mild,
Though born in a manger, the Father's own Child,
    We'll worship before Thee
    And praise and adore Thee,
And sing the glad story again and again.

ADA BLENKHORN

*Then Herod summoned the wise men . . .
and he sent them to Bethlehem, saying,
"Go and search diligently for the
child, and when you have found him bring
me word, that I too may come and
worship him." When they had heard
the king they went their way;
and lo, the star which they had seen
in the East . . . came to rest over
the place where the child was.*

MATTHEW 2:7–9

GIFTS FOR THE KING

*The arrival of the exotic caravan before the simple abode
where Jesus had been born no doubt surprised and startled
Joseph. In* TWO FROM GALILEE, *her 1972 inspirational
novel, Marjorie Holmes depicted the event.*

JOSEPH STOOD ONE NIGHT at the stable door. He had been to the well for water, but he could not go in just yet. The night was cold and clear; it was exhilarating and yet peaceful to stand for a moment before joining his loved ones inside. From this little distance he stood savoring the sweet communion of the stable.

They had made the place more comfortable. The innkeeper's wife had come down, incredulous before the star. She was a fat, bustling, loquacious woman, childless, poor thing, and she had fallen in love with the baby. She had urged them to stay. "You will be hard put to find better quarters in Bethlehem," she told them, accurately reading their poorness. "Remain here at least until the time of your purification." She had brought down a table and bench from the inn, and a brazier to augment the fire in the pit. Now it too glowed through the long cold nights.

And now the forty days had passed. Tomorrow they must take the little Jesus and travel to the temple, there to redeem him with an offering. After that, Joseph reasoned, it would be well to come back to Bethlehem and find work until the baby was old enough to attempt the treacherous journey back to Nazareth.

Would the star follow them? he wondered. Would it continue to blaze above their heads like a torch to light the way?

Where now, star? he thought. Guide me, lead me.

A quiet joy filled him. Wherever they went they would be together, he and Mary and the child that had leapt into their lives. The miracle of that smote him with new significance. For the miracles we beg of God are seldom those we receive. The miracle that had come to them that night was the miracle of birth itself. The living child, fashioned out of nothing, a mystery of love, yet swelling and growing and coming forth as blood and bone and hungry mouth!

Taking up the cool bulging skins of water, he was about to go in when he heard the pluck of approaching hooves and the jingle of harness, and saw, flowing slowly down the pathway from the inn, three camels. He paused. Rich merchants, evidently, dark princes from some far country. And it flashed through his consciousness that it was strange they had not summoned a servant to stable their mounts instead of themselves riding down from the inn.

Joseph turned hastily, not wishing to be seen, and was about to duck into the cave when one of them called out to him. "Wait! You there in the doorway." The camel drew nearer. "Tell me, is this the place where the new child lies?"

Joseph stood rigid, silent in the grip of a terrible apprehension.

"Of course it is, it has to be." The second rider was making a gesture of triumph toward the star. "See, it no longer moves."

"But—a stable!" The third rider drew abreast. "Surely this is no fit birthplace for a king."

Joseph's heart had begun to beat in heavy strokes. Obviously these were men of travel and learning, men on a vital mission, and he was afraid. A great foreboding rose up in him, and a fierce rebellion. What did such men want with his child? Were the dread momentous things hinted at so darkly in the prophets already about to begin? He would not have it. Not yet, not yet! The child was not ready; his little life had only just begun.

He stood blocking the doorway as the strangers prepared to dismount, rapping the growling beasts on the neck so that they folded their thin legs to crouch.

"Why do you ask?" Joseph demanded. "What do you want?"

"To see him. Is there not a newborn child within?"

The central scene in this page from a music score—the adoration of the Magi—is nearly lost in the tangle of vegetation and mythical sea creatures that form the letter Q about it. The exquisite manuscript is among the treasures of the cathedral library in Siena, Italy.

Joseph hesitated. "Only my wife and son."

They regarded him. One was tall and handsome, with a curling black beard and teeth that flashed white in his swarthy face. The other two were fairer. All had the look of wisdom and splendor about them, humbling Joseph, a sense of purpose and wills that were not easily to be denied.

"You are the father of this holy child?"

"My wife has borne a son," he said. "Is not every child sacred in the sight of God?"

"Yes. Yes, truly," said the tall one after a second. "But the stars have foretold this event for years. We have studied the stars. We are Magi from Persia and Chaldea, philosophers and physicians, and we have traveled for weeks following the star that stands over this doorway. It has become the sole purpose of our existence, my friend—to see him, if only for a few minutes, this child of yours who is to change the course of all history. This one who is to become King of the Jews." The voice was grave, at once stern and imploring. "Surely you would not turn us away?"

Joseph gazed into the stranger's impassioned eyes. And he knew that it was ended, the peaceful dream of the stable with the child as only a child at its center and heart. For cradled there in the manger lay all the portent and the promise, the man of destiny.

"Wait," he said brusquely, "I must go and consult my wife."

A sweet desperate pain drove through Joseph's breast when he entered the cave. "I'm sorry I was gone so long," he said. "But there are strangers at the door insisting they must see him. They are wise men, Mary, come all the way from Persia and Chaldea."

Mary gasped. And she too was bewildered and suddenly stricken. "Wise men? You must not keep them waiting."

She closed her eyes, forced now to remember all the suffering and hope that had led to this moment. And all the threat and promise that lay ahead of him—this innocent little being, kicking and chewing his fist, unaware of his fate. She took him up and

kissed him; blindly then she put him down and began preparing the child so that he should not be found wanting in the strangers' eyes.

"Bid them come in."

In a few moments she could hear the slapping of sandals and the swish of robes as they approached; it was like the ominous rush and pound of some majestic but overpowering sea. They filled the room with their turbaned strangeness, their exotic smell of spices and perfume. But one by one they knelt at her feet, there in the straw, and kissed the hem of her gown. And they gazed long upon the baby, who smiled at them with his great liquid eyes and strove within his bindings, as if to reach out to them. And they laughed gently, and opening their embroidered shawls, presented their gifts—jars of precious myrrh and frankincense, a bolt of silk shot through with gold, a ruby in a velvet case.

"For the king," they said, rising unsteadily and brushing their eyes. "For the hope of the ages."

The papier-mâché wise men below, the work of a Mexican folk artist, are designed to be viewed in the round— here, with the central figure facing the rear.

THE GIFT

Caspar, Melchior, Balthazar,
These are they who followed the star.

Myrrh, and incense, gems and gold,
These are the gifts they brought of old;—

These are the precious wonderful things
They brought as befitting three wise Kings.

The humble Shepherds were quite too poor
To lay such gifts on the stable floor;

But one left his cloak, and mittens; another
His shepherd's crook and cap; and his brother,

Who had carried a lamb across the wild,
Left that as gift for the Holy Child.

Oh, Mary might better have liked a gem—
(For the best of women are fond of them)—

And Joseph no doubt the gold approved;—
'Tis a thing men's hearts have always loved;

These things I suspect;—but sure I am
The Little Lord Christ preferred the lamb.

LAURA SPENCER PORTOR

An astrological map of the heavens

Who Were the Wise Men?

Mentioned only in Matthew, the Magi who sought the child Jesus were probably members of a priestly class in Persia. Skilled in astrology, the belief that stars and other celestial bodies directly affect human events, these "wise men from the East" undoubtedly thought that any unusual phenomenon signaled the birth or death of an important person. In 7 B.C., quite near the birth of Jesus, the planets Jupiter and Saturn came close together in the constellation Pisces, a rare and unusually brilliant occurrence. Jupiter symbolized kingship of the world, Saturn was associated with Palestine, and Pisces was a sign of Earth's last days. Documents from the period prove that Mesopotamian astrologers could have predicted this planetary conjunction.

Astrology is disdained throughout the Bible as idolatry, but Matthew portrays the Magi with great sympathy, perhaps to show that people from all nations, not just Jews, are included in Jesus' mission on Earth. Some scholars speculate that the Magi could have known about Old Testament prophecies of the coming of a Messiah through the Jews who had remained behind when others returned to Jerusalem from the Babylonian Captivity.

The unique, highly stylized version of the wise men appearing before Mary and the infant Jesus at left— a silk-screen print on rice paper—is the work of contemporary Japanese artist Sadao Watanabe. The unknown 14th-century artist who depicted the dream of the wise men below allowed them to wear their crowns to bed.

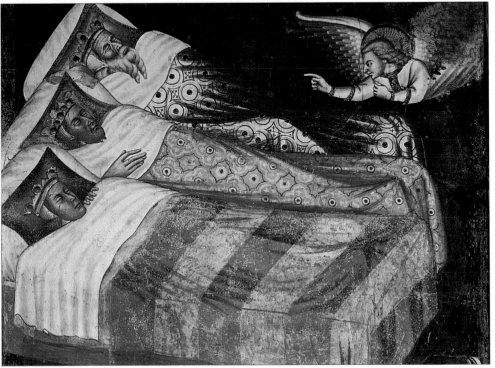

The angel's warning to Joseph is the subject of the ninth-century ivory plaque above; the subsequent flight into Eygpt at right is from a 14th-century devotional book in London's Victoria and Albert Museum.

An angel of the Lord appeared to Joseph in a dream and said, "Rise, take the child and his mother, and flee to Egypt, and remain there till I tell you; for Herod is about to search for the child, to destroy him."

MATTHEW 2:13

> **Then Herod, when he saw that he had been tricked by the wise men, was in a furious rage, and he sent and killed all the male children in Bethlehem and in all that region who were two years old or under.**
>
> MATTHEW 2:16

THE WRATH OF HEROD

Old, wasted by disease, yet loath to relinquish power, Herod had been startled and angered by the news the wise men brought of a new king of the Jews. When he learned that they had returned to the East without telling him where the child could be found, he took the drastic measures described by Jim Bishop in THE DAY CHRIST WAS BORN.

As Joseph leads Mary and the infant to safety in Egypt (background), an implacable Herod ignores the plea of a mother to stop the carnage he has ordered; the German engraving is dated 1491.

THE KING'S PALACE was a place of splendid courtyards and many oil lamps on the west side of Jerusalem, about three hundred yards from a place called Golgotha. Men of importance were rushing, on this night, in and out of the palace. Herod the Great was in a towering rage. He arose from his couch, a man with deepset eyes like caves in a forest, and his gray beard parted and his tongue spat words. Many, he said, would pay for the trick which had been played upon him. Many would die. His courtiers trembled because, if lives could be sacrificed at a whim, their lives were less than worthless.

Spies had come to him from several quarters. The first ones said that the Magi had remained in Bethlehem two days and had left for Persia, skirting Jerusalem to the south. This showed that they had no intention of keeping their promise to return to the king with news of the newborn Messiah. Other spies had been sent at once to Bethlehem to find the baby and his parents and bring them to the august presence of Herod. But these had returned with bad news indeed: the little family, it seemed, had lived in a stable beneath the inn, and the stable was now empty.

Herod's soldiers had arrested the innkeeper and his wife, but torture could bring no further information than that they had no room at the inn for the expectant mother, and had permitted her to live in the stable with her husband and newborn. The king was seventy years of age, and very ill, but his rage enslaved him and he tore fabrics and drapes from the walls and screamed until the saliva hung on his beard.

The census, he roared. That would provide a solution to the problem of the make-believe Messiah who had come to exact tribute from the gullible Jews. The census. He called an aide and ordered him to go to the Roman tribune now in quarters at Fortress Antonia and to ask in the name of the king for the names of all families who had infants. The aide was about to run outdoors when Herod stopped him. Wait, the king screamed. We must first find out how old this particular baby is. Call my councilors!

The learned ones came in, their striped cloaks betraying the trembling underneath. How long, said Herod, had that accursed star been in the sky? No one

ACTO FALCONIS hABENTE hOC OPUS IN CURA NEC NON OPERE QUO QUE TUR hEST PISIS PA

This gruesome version of the slaughter of the innocents (above) appeared in a 13th-century French Psalter. The same scene was rendered in high relief (above right) by the late medieval Italian sculptor Giovanni Pisano for the cathedral at Pisa, of which he was the chief architect in the years following 1278.

knew. They had not looked for a star. Herod moaned and sobbed and pounded the wall with his withered fists. If the Magi could see such a star, why cannot my councilors see it? Can it be that my learned assistants are in league with the little one who aspires to usurp my throne?

The soothsayers said that the strange bright star could not have been in the heavens long, or else astrologers among the Jews would have broadcast the news. They would also have made their own dire predictions about it. This, they reasoned, made it likely that the star was on a path across Persia toward Bethlehem and that it had begun its flight recently.

A year ago? shouted Herod. A week ago? I must find out the age of his little majesty. The councilors looked at each other and said surely no more than a year. Probably far less. Herod the Great leaned his hands on his couch and gasped for air. Then, he said, I know what to do. I know what to do. He punched the couch arm with his hand.

He sent the courier to the Roman tribune to ask, in the name of the king, for a list of all Jewish families

who had male sons two years of age or less. The census would reveal the status of every family—how many members, what age. When the list was copied, he wanted it given to his chief of guards and he wanted squads of soldiers sent to Bethlehem, Jerusalem and every town and village in the area. The soldiers were under orders from the king to tear the babies from their parents and to either kill them on the spot with the short sword, or take them out in batches and cast them from the cliffs.

One councilor coughed politely and asked if it wouldn't be more prudent to kill only those babies up to the age of one, and only those who were born of the family of David in the town of Bethlehem.

Herod shrieked. He held his fists against the sides of his head and rocked with pain. When he again caught his breath, he said the order was to kill all babies from the age of one hour to the age of two years, and this would include all babies in the vicinity of Bethlehem. There would be no exemptions, even among the babies of the soldiers themselves. This must be done at once, so that no spurious pretender to the throne could grow up and lift the scepter from Herod's cold hands.

Within a few days, the slaughter of the innocents began. Soldiers in squads hurried from house to house, tearing babies from the arms of screaming mothers, throwing them on earthen floors and running short swords through the little bodies. In every village, anguish and wailing followed the running visit of death. In Jerusalem, some bereft mothers tried to carry their dead infants into the temple, as sacrifices.

No newborn babies were killed in Bethlehem, because the only one born there in the past year had been taken away. Older ones were killed, and some were cast from the cliffs down into the valley of the shepherds. In Jerusalem, some of Herod's soldiers wept because they had to kill the babies of fellow soldiers. All up to the age of two were slain because to fail by one baby would have brought death to many soldiers.

Some of the elders shook their heads sadly and wiped their eyes as they remembered the old words of the prophet Jeremiah:

> A cry was heard at Rama,
> there was weeping and sore lament.
> Rachel wept for her children;
> She would not be consoled,
> because they were no more.

Herod asked many questions about the killings and was pleased that his officers had done an efficient job. Surely the so-called baby king was among the many who died in the swift raids. There was no chance that any infant had escaped the holocaust. There were weeping and mourning all over the land and only Herod was happy.

The king began to eat again and managed to feel a little surge of joy at sight of the rising sun. Then he was seized with a fit, and fell to the floor of his palace. His councilors and officers were summoned and they stood around in a little group and watched the king strangle slowly. There was nothing they could do to help him, and, apparently, there was no wish to ameliorate his last hour.

They stood polite and mute in the presence of majesty, and watched him grovel and tear at his throat, the dark eyes bulging from his head, a plea for assistance in the dying eyes. When Herod's final gasp subsided in a sigh of resignation, the councilors moved to inform the nation, and Caesar Augustus in Rome, that the king was dead. He had followed the infants, but he did not join them.

HEROD'S SUSPICION

Why art thou troubled, Herod? what vain fear
    Thy blood-revolving breast to rage doth move?
Heaven's King, who doffs himself weak flesh to wear,
    Comes not to rule in wrath, but serve in love;
Nor would he this thy feared crown from thee tear,
    But give thee a better with himself above.
    Poor jealousy! why should he wish to prey
    Upon thy crown, who gives his own away?

Make to thy reason, man, and mock thy doubts;
    Look how below thy fears their causes are;
Thou are a soldier, Herod; send thy scouts,
    See how he's furnished for so feared a war.
What armour does he wear? A few thin clouts.
    His trumpets? tender cries. His men, to dare
    So much? rude shepherds. What his steeds? alas,
    Poor beasts! a slow ox and a simple ass.

RICHARD CRASHAW, c. 1612–1649

As its unlikely decoration, this 1566 ceramic plate features the massacre of Bethlehem's male infants decreed by Herod. The architectural details in the background are clearly drawn from 16th-century Italy.

The Hidden Years

All we know of Jesus from the time of the
Holy Family's return to Nazareth, perhaps when the child was two,
to his baptism by John, which marked the beginning
of his public ministry at about the age of 30, is contained in
Luke 2:41–52. Accompanying his parents as
Passover pilgrims to Jerusalem at the age of 12, Jesus
astonished the teachers in the temple by his
precocious understanding. Thereafter, according
to Luke, the youth "increased in wisdom and in stature,
and in favor with God and man."

Jesus' family upbringing and education, his likely
apprenticeship to Joseph, his growth to physical maturity—these
important details of his early years are unrecorded in the Gospels.
Not surprisingly, poets, writers, and artists—as the
following pages attest— have not hesitated to speculate about
events that occurred out of the sight of history.

*In this painting
of Jesus discovered
in the temple,
the 14th-century Italian
artist Simone Martini
captured the moods
of his three subjects:
Mary, gently reproving;
Joseph, puzzled; and
Jesus, obedient
but annoyed to be
summoned from
his "Father's house."*

Depicting the flight into Egypt, the Spanish painter Bartolomé Estéban Murillo (1618–1682) emphasized the tender concern Mary feels for her baby as Joseph guides the donkey on the road to safety.

An angel of the Lord appeared to Joseph in a dream and said, "Rise, take the child and his mother, and flee to Egypt, and remain there till I tell you; for Herod is about to search for the child, to destroy him." And he rose and took the child and his mother by night, and departed to Egypt, and remained there until the death of Herod.

MATTHEW 2:13–15

TAMING BEASTS, FINDING SUCCOR ON THE ROAD TO EGYPT

Matthew offers no further details of the flight into Egypt or the sojourn there of Mary, Joseph, and the child Jesus. However, THE GOSPEL OF PSEUDO-MATTHEW, a sixth-century compilation of unknown authorship, describes a number of miraculous incidents that supposedly occurred during the Holy Family's journey. Never accepted as Scripture by religious scholars, this "gospel" can be considered a work of pious and vividly imaginative fiction.

HAVING COME TO A CERTAIN CAVE, and wishing to rest in it, the blessed Mary dismounted from her beast, and sat down with the child Jesus. And lo, suddenly there came forth from the cave many dragons, and she cried out in great terror. Then Jesus stood on his feet before the dragons; and they adored Jesus, and thereafter retired. Then was fulfilled that which was said by David the prophet, saying: Praise the Lord from the earth, ye dragons; ye dragons, and all ye deeps. And the young child Jesus, walking before them, commanded them to hurt no man. But Mary and Joseph were very much afraid lest the child should be hurt by the dragons. And Jesus said to them: Do not be afraid, and do not consider me to be a little child; for I am and always have been perfect; and all the beasts of the forest must needs be tame before me.

Lions and panthers adored him likewise, and accompanied them in the desert. Wherever Joseph and

Left, Vittore Carpaccio (c. 1450–1525) depicted Joseph as the traditionally older man but put the fleeing Holy Family in a landscape typical of his native Italy. The 13th-century ivory panel above was crafted in south-central Germany.

the blessed Mary went, they went before them showing them the way and bowing their heads; and demonstrating their submission by wagging their tails, they adored him with great reverence.

Now at first, when Mary saw the lions and the panthers, and various kinds of wild beasts, coming about them, she was very much afraid. But the infant Jesus looked into her face with a joyful countenance, and said: Be not afraid, mother; for they come not to do thee harm, but they make haste to serve both thee and me. With these words he drove all fear from her heart. They walked among wolves, and feared nothing; and no one of them was hurt by another.

And it came to pass on the third day of their journey, while they were walking, that the blessed Mary was fatigued by the excessive heat of the sun in the desert; and seeing a palm tree, she said to Joseph: Let me rest a little under the shade of this tree. Joseph therefore made haste, and led her to the palm, and made her come down from her beast. And as the blessed Mary was sitting there, she looked up to the foliage of the palm, and saw it full of fruit, and said to Joseph: I wish it were possible to get some of the fruit

of this palm. And Joseph said to her: I wonder that thou sayest this, when thou seest how high the palm tree is; and that thou thinkest of eating of its fruit. I am thinking more of the want of water, because the skins are now empty, and we have none wherewith to refresh ourselves.

Then the child Jesus, with a joyful countenance, said to the palm: O tree, bend thy branches, and refresh my mother with thy fruit. And immediately at these words the palm bent its top down to the very feet of the blessed Mary; and they gathered from it fruit, with which they were all refreshed. And after they had gathered all its fruit, it remained bent down, waiting the order to rise from him who had commanded it to stoop.

Then Jesus said to it: Raise thyself, O palm tree, and be strong, and be the companion of my trees, which are in the paradise of my Father; and open from thy roots a vein of water which has been hid in the earth, and let the waters flow, so that we may be satisfied from thee. And it rose up immediately, and at its root there began to come forth a spring of water exceedingly clear and cool and sparkling.

A Spanish colonial folk artist provided the Holy Family with a guide (above), while a German artist showed Joseph cooking (right), and Rembrandt depicted them fording a brook (below).

WHEN A KING GREATER THAN SOLOMON PASSED BY

The legend of a palm tree miraculously succoring Mary, Joseph, and Jesus during their flight to Egypt can be traced back to the early Christian era. Selma Lagerlöf, Swedish winner of the Nobel Prize for literature in 1909, wrote the following version of the tale.

FAR AWAY IN AN EASTERN DESERT many, many years ago grew a palm tree, which was both exceedingly old and exceedingly tall. All who passed through the desert had to stop and gaze at it, for it was much larger than other palms; and they used to say of it, that some day it would certainly be taller than the obelisks and pyramids.

Where the huge palm tree stood in its solitude and looked out over the desert, it saw something one day which made its mighty leaf-crown sway back and forth on its slender trunk with astonishment. Over by the desert borders walked two human beings. They were still at the distance at which camels appear to be as tiny as moths; but they were certainly a man and a woman who had neither guide nor pack-camels; neither tent nor watersack.

"Verily," said the palm to itself. "A seven-fold death awaits these travelers. The lions will devour them, thirst will parch them, the sandstorm will bury them, robbers will trap them, sunstroke will blight them, fear will destroy them." Sad at heart, it tried to think of a seventh.

"By the drought and the storm!" said the palm, calling upon Life's most dangerous enemies. "What is it that the woman carries on her arm? I believe these fools also bring a little child with them!

"The child hasn't even sufficient clothing on. I see that the mother has tucked up her skirt and thrown it over the child. She must have snatched him from his bed in great haste and rushed off with him. I understand now: these people are runaways.

"I can imagine how the whole thing came about. The man stood at his work; the child slept in his crib; the woman had gone out to fetch water. When she was a few steps from the door, she saw enemies coming. She rushed back to the house, snatched up her child and fled. Unless an angel protects them, they would have done better to have let their enemies do their worst, than to venture into this wilderness.

"They are so frightened that, as yet, they feel neither fatigue nor suffering. But I see their thirst by the strange gleam in their eyes." And as the palm began thinking of thirst, a shudder passed through its trunk.

"I hear my leaves rustle louder and louder," said the palm, "and it sounds as melancholy as a dirge."

The palm assumed that the death-rustle in its leaves must apply to the two lone wanderers. It is certain that they too believed that their last hour was nearing. One saw it from their expression as they walked past the skeleton of a camel which lay in their path. One saw it from the glances they cast back at a pair of passing vultures. It couldn't be otherwise; they must perish!

They had caught sight of the palm and oasis and hastened thither to find water. But when they arrived at last, they collapsed from despair, for the well was dry. The woman, worn out, laid the child down and seated herself beside the well-curb, and wept. The man flung himself down beside her and beat upon the dry earth with his fists.

"God will help us," said the woman.

"We are alone among beasts of prey and serpents," said the man. "We have no food and no water. How should God be able to help us?"

The woman sat erect, with her hands clasped over her knees. But the looks she cast toward the desert spoke of a hopelessness beyond bounds.

The palm heard the melancholy rustle in its leaves growing louder and louder. The woman must have heard it also, for she turned her gaze upward toward the palm-crown.

"Oh, dates, dates!" she cried. There was such intense agony in her voice that the old palm wished itself no taller than a broom and that the dates were as easy to reach as the buds on a brier bush. It probably knew that its crown was full of date clusters, but how could a human being reach such a height?

The man had already seen how beyond all reach the date clusters hung. He did not even raise his head. He begged his wife not to long for the impossible.

But the child, who had toddled about by himself and was playing with sticks and straws, had heard the mother's outcry.

ALL THE ROAD TO EGYPT

All the road to Egypt
    Sang to see them pass,
The Child asleep on Mary's arm,
Old Joseph, shielding them from harm,
The Angel, beautiful as hope,
Leading by a twist of rope
    The little, gray-coat ass.

All the road to Egypt
    Knelt to see them pass,
The Child's dear head haloed gold,
Madonna's robe in many a fold
Of changing blue like shimmering wave,
Whose falling grace a glory gave
    Even to the dusty ass.

All the road to Egypt
    Danced to see them pass,
Old Joseph's cloak of cinnamon,
The Angel's restless wings that shone
Green as the trees of Paradise,
And like some curious, chased device
    A little silver ass.

All the road to Egypt
    Bloomed to feel them pass,
So raced the sap in stem and root
The withered fig tree sprang to fruit;
The palm and olive bowed their load
To Mary's lips; that purple road
    Bore thistles for the ass. . . .

KATHARINE LEE BATES, 1859–1929

Carved of walnut and painted by a Spanish artist in the early 16th century, the depiction at right, above, of the legend of the palm tree is from New York's Metropolitan Museum of Art.

Nicolas Poussin (1594–1665) showed the refugees at rest, with the monuments of Egypt clearly in sight.

Of course, the little one could not imagine that his mother should not get everything she wished for. The instant she said dates, he began to stare at the tree. He pondered and pondered how he should bring down the dates. His forehead was almost drawn into wrinkles under the golden curls. At last a smile stole over his face. He had found the way. He went up to the palm, stroked it with his little hand, and said in a sweet, childish voice: "Palm, bend thee!"

The palm leaves rustled as if a hurricane had passed through them, and up and down the long trunk traveled shudder upon shudder. And the tree felt that the little one was its superior. It could not resist him.

And it bowed its long trunk before the child, as people bow before princes. In a great bow it bent itself towards the ground, and finally it came down so far that the big crown with the trembling leaves swept the desert sand.

The child appeared to be neither frightened nor surprised; with a joyous cry he loosened cluster after cluster from the old palm's crown. When he had plucked enough dates, and the tree still lay on the ground, the child came back and caressed it and said, in the gentlest voice: "Palm, raise thee!"

Slowly and reverently the big tree raised itself on its slender trunk, while the leaves played like harps.

"Now I know for whom they are playing the death melody," said the palm to itself when it stood erect once more. "It is not for any of these people."

The next time a caravan passed through the desert, the travelers saw that the great palm's leaf-crown had withered. "How can this be?" said one of the travelers. "This palm was not to die before it had seen a King greater than Solomon."

"Mayhap it hath seen him," answered another of the desert travelers.

THE WINDFLOWERS
AND THE SAGE

While Mary and the Christ-Child
    Fled from King Herod and death,
The patient ass that carried them
    Stumbled and failed for breath.

Where curved the steep hill downward,
    Mary's heart stood still to see
That Herod's soldiers, sword in hand,
    Came riding bloodily.

"Oh, holy little Son!" she cried,
    "How hide thy tenderness?"
Then saw she, growing by the road,
    Windflowers in lovely dress.

"Oh, windflowers, lovely windflowers!
    Be good and open wide
Your tender leaves and blossoms that
    My Lord therein may hide!"

But lest they spoil their loveliness
    The windflowers answered "Nay!"
Then Mary turned with pleading
    Where by the dusty way

A humble sage-bush blossomed,
    Who, when the same request
Was made of her, bent humbly down
    And opened her sweet breast;

And spread her leaves so widely kind,
    So reverently deep,
The little Lord might shelter find,
    And hide Him there, and sleep.

Then the most blest of women
    Bowed low, and blessed it there;
Since when the humble sage-brush breathes
    Sweet fragrance on the air.

LAURA SPENCER PORTOR

*A cherub guides the Holy Family's flight in a
painting by Guido Reni (1575–1642).*

Egypt as a Place of Refuge

When Joseph and Mary took the infant Jesus to Egypt to escape the wrath of Herod, they were following a well-worn path. In the ancient world the land of the Nile epitomized stability and security. Insulated by forbidding deserts, Egypt lived off the bounty of its river, which annually replenished and irrigated the soil and allowed the people to maintain a reasonable prosperity.

Palestine, on the other hand, appeared less hospitable and more vulnerable, suffering both drought-induced famines and the instability of political turbulence. Thus, the Bible repeatedly tells how people fled from the problems of Palestine to the apparent safety of Eygpt. Almost as soon as Abraham entered the land of Canaan, severe famine forced him to seek food in Egypt. Two generations later, in Jacob's time, the entire clan migrated to the Nile Delta in search of provender; their descendants remained there for centuries, until Moses led them back to the Promised Land.

In later generations, Eygpt served as a political haven. Among those who fled there were Hadad the Edomite, escaping King David; Jeroboam, seeking asylum after Solomon tried to kill him but returning later to lead the rebellious tribes of northern Israel; and the prophet Uriah, trying unsuccessfully to elude King Jehoiakim.

This medieval map of the Mediterranean world shows Egypt separated from Palestine by a Red Sea that is really red.

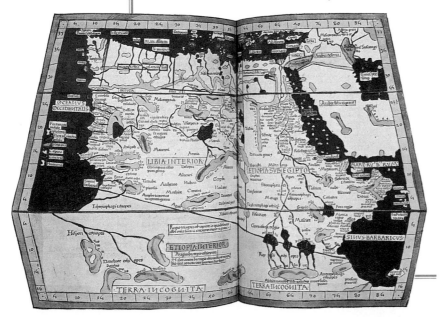

And when they had performed everything according to the law of the Lord, they returned into Galilee, to their own city, Nazareth. And the child grew and became strong, filled with wisdom; and the favor of God was upon him.

LUKE 2:39–40

WAITING FOR MORE MIRACLES

In Luke's Gospel, Joseph and Mary return to Nazareth immediately following the presentation of Jesus in the temple at Jerusalem. In his short story "The Second Christmas," John Haynes Holmes imagines the letdown Mary must have felt after the wondrous events at Bethlehem.

IT HAD BEEN A DREARY YEAR FOR MARY. Such a disappointment after that thrilling experience in Bethlehem! Was there ever such a birth-day? Had ever a mother been so blessed? There had been miracles that night! Surely, more miracles would come.

So all the long year she had waited. Every night she had watched for visitors from afar, or listened for music from the skies. But nothing had happened. The rains had come—the earlier rains, and then the latter rains. The lilies of the field had blossomed, and the hot summer had ripened the grapes and olives. Now the winter had come again. And she was still waiting—in vain! It was all so disappointing—as if heaven had been opened to her, and then been closed.

Sometimes in the evening, when the day's work was done, and Jesus was safely cradled, and the supper was cleared away, and Joseph, poor man, was tired and had gone to bed, she would climb to the roof of the house—the flat roof that looked up to the stars. And she would sit, and gaze far off to the south, to that place among the hills which was Bethlehem.

It was there that the heavens had opened to the shepherds abiding in the fields. And an angel of the Lord brought them good tidings of a child born in the city of David, which was Christ the Lord. And they had come to Bethlehem, and found Jesus in the manger, and worshipped him.

And she would recall the Magi, as they came to her that morning out of the East, following the star which had led them to Bethlehem. It had all seemed unreal—like some kind of strange and wonderful dream.

What did all this mean? Patiently she had waited for an answer but none had come. There were shepherds on the hills of Nazareth—but none to seek her out. And there were men who came from afar to Nazareth, rich merchants, traveling sages, perhaps kings and princes. But there were no Magi among them.

As for the heavens, they were silent—no angel-songs any more! And the star, after those nights in Bethlehem a year ago, had dimmed and gone. Mary did not dare to tell how many nights, when all Nazareth was still, she had listened for the song and watched for the star. She began to fear that perhaps it had only been a dream—that night in Bethlehem.

And now was the birth-night! She must make everything ready for the morrow, for it was to be a day of feasting and revelry.

It was late when Mary's work was done. The threshold had been swept and the floor cleaned. The chairs and stools were in order about the table, and the cups in their places. Joseph himself was sleeping, for the first peep of dawn must see him up.

Mary never knew just what happened next. But before she went to sleep—yes, before she closed her eyes!—there came a kind of glow across the door. At first soft and dim, it brightened and spread, like the sun in the east at dawn. Slowly, silently, the light gathered into the bright form of an angel.

"Mary, blessed of women," said the angel, "thou hast been sad all this year. Thou hast not found joy in thy child, nor content within thine heart. For always thou hast looked for miracle and sign."

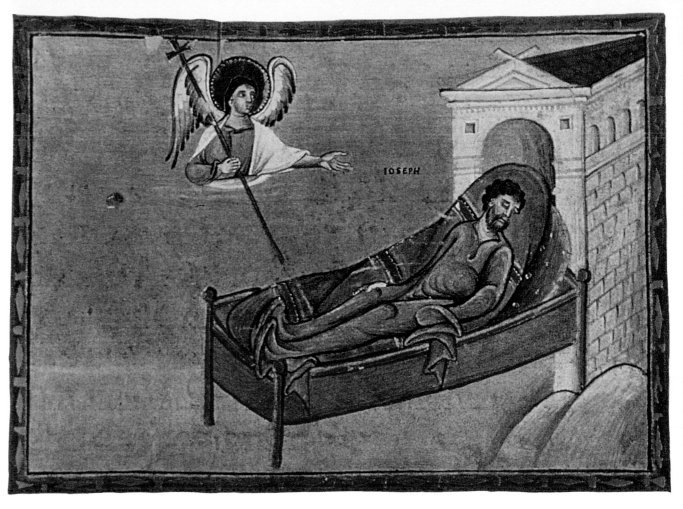

"But, my Lord," interrupted Mary, "there *was* miracle and sign, when Jesus was born in Bethlehem of Judaea this night a year ago."

"Yea, miracle and sign," said the angel, gently; "such miracle and sign as accompany the wonder of every birth. To those who have eyes to see, a star shines when any child is born. To those who have ears to hear, the morning stars sing together and all the sons of God shout for joy when a new soul comes into the world. But, Mary, look not for wonders in the heavens or on the earth—for cloven skies and marching stars, for earthquakes and famines, for wars and victories of arms. These show not God! Look rather for wonders within.

"Delve deep into thy son's life, as a miner delves deep into the earth for precious treasure. What thou findest guard, though thou art dazzled and afraid. For Jesus, thy son, is given thee of God to rear and fashion for His service.

"Be patient, Mary. Be brave. Though there be no sign nor wonder more, thy work is sure."

In Matthew's Gospel, an angel appears to Joseph in a dream on four occasions: to tell him that the child Mary has conceived is of the Holy Spirit; to order the flight to Egypt; to advise him that Herod's death makes it safe to return to the land of Israel; and, finally, to warn him that Judea is to be avoided in favor of Galilee. The 10th-century manuscript painting above is from the Codex Egberti in the City Library of Trier, Germany.

By placing Jesus in the workaday surroundings of a modest carpenter's shop, the English artist Sir John Everett Millais (1829–1896) stressed the child's secular upbringing rather than depicting a spiritual environment. His 1850 painting was widely criticized by contemporaries unprepared for such an unconventional point of view.

A Very Special Son

Although the Gospels are silent on the subject, it is reasonable to assume that Jesus, growing up in Nazareth, would have been educated as were other Jewish boys of his time. In her novel THREE FROM GALILEE, Marjorie Holmes imagines a precocious student questioning the ancient traditions.

OR JESUS, SCHOOL WAS AT FIRST A SHOCK. The synagogue, always noisy and crowded on the Sabbath, seemed strangely empty, echoing to the boys' voices and that of the schoolmaster rabbi sitting on the platform before them, austere and at first frightening, his dark bearded face peering at them from under his draped prayer shawl.

The boys sat in a semicircle on the hard bare floor. At one end of the room stood the curtained chest containing the sacred scrolls. Small ruby lamps burned before it like alert red eyes, giving off an acrid smell of oil and incense and slightly filming the air. There was the fragrance of the cedar benches along the walls, the smell of well-scrubbed boys; beyond the open slits of windows birds sang, carts rattled by. The boys sat trapped and anxious yet excited, as the master slowly unrolled the scroll.

"We always start with Leviticus," he said. "The third book of the Torah. A very important book, for it teaches us the essence of our religion. Can anyone tell us what that is?"

"You shall be holy, for I, the Lord your God am holy!" several voices responded eagerly. "You shall love your neighbor as yourself!"

"Yes, yes, good—and what else?"

Jesus was leaning forward, shy, hopeful, anxious to do well, yet trembling, filled with a nameless fear and dread. He strove to answer—about the rules for being healthy and clean—but his voice could not be heard above the babble. "Sacrifice!" the others were saying. "It teaches us about sacrifice."

"Yes. The first half of Leviticus deals with sacrifice, which has always been an important part of worship among all races of men." The teacher paused, searching them with his stern but kindly eyes. "But for Jews what kind of sacrifice? Human sacrifice like those pagans who worship Molech and other false gods?"

"No, never!" the boys murmured in horror.

"That's right, *never*. And what do we offer up to die in our place? That's right—animals, the finest of our flocks, beasts and birds. They are our substitute.

"Follow me as I recite for you the first passages wherein the Lord gives to Moses the manner of the sacrifice. *And he shall put his hand upon the head of the burnt offering. . . . And he shall kill. . . and flay . . . and cut it into its pieces . . . and shall put fire upon the altar.*"

Jesus hunched into himself, swallowed, covered his mouth. He was burning, drowning in a sea of blood and flame, fighting like some poor doomed thing to survive. Yet a wild and desperate protest filled him at the same time: Why should these innocent creatures die? No, no, he couldn't bear it.

To his horror Jesus realized the room had fallen silent. The rabbi, seeing the boy's white face, had halted. "Jesus," he asked, concerned. "Don't you feel well? Would you like to be excused?"

Shamed and stricken, he went home and told his parents, "They laughed at me! I have disgraced you."

"It's the animal sacrifice," Joseph told Mary later. "We talked about it at length. You know how much he loves every living thing. I hope I made it clear that God's laws are always for our own good. He will participate tomorrow, he promised. And it will be easier later when they deal with holiness. He will have no trouble with that part of the book."

His father was right. Jesus soon redeemed himself. He could even keep pace with the older students, although he strove to hold back, dreading the scorn that comes with envy. His head swam with the mystery of his own knowledge; it was as if everything he studied he already knew and yet must experience in ways he did not understand.

One afternoon the rabbi stopped in Joseph's shop. "I have come to discuss your son," the rabbi said uncomfortably. His tone was half complimentary, half concerned. "A very bright boy, yes, very bright, but your son's imagination goes well beyond his years."

"God gives different children different gifts."

"I meant no offense," said the rabbi. "You must realize you have a very special son."

Thoughtfully, Joseph stroked the board he was planing. Finally he lifted his eyes, his composure belying the tangled pain and pride in his breast. "His mother and I realize," Joseph told him.

The candle Jesus holds to shed light on Joseph's work in the carpentry shop also serves to reveal the child's radiant innocence. Georges de La Tour's 17th-century painting is in the Louvre museum in Paris.

Egyptian idols topple before Jesus, a legend preserved in the apocryphal Gospel of Pseudo-Matthew.

The Other "Gospels"

Luke begins his Gospel by acknowledging others who had already told the story of Jesus, as it had been handed down from "eyewitnesses and ministers of the word." Unfortunately, some of the sources available to Luke are now lost; but even after Luke's Gospel as well as those of Matthew, Mark, and John were written, other early Christians continued to compile lives of Jesus.

Most of these nonbiblical works have survived the centuries only in brief excerpts or in fragmentary manuscripts. Some were simple collections of Jesus' sayings; others were narratives much like the four Gospels of the New Testament; still others claimed to be the secret teachings of Jesus after the Resurrection. Many of these apocryphal gospels were sectarian works intended to make Jesus the spokesman for one heretical viewpoint or another. In 1946, for example, a remarkable discovery of ancient manuscripts in a clay jar buried at Nag Hammadi in Egypt brought to light the literature of the deviant Christians known as Gnostics, members of a variety of sects who believed that salvation lay in their knowledge (in Greek, *gnosis*) of their divine origin. Included in the cache were such clearly unorthodox works as the Gospel of Truth and a previously unknown collection of Jesus' sayings called the Gospel of Thomas.

A number of these apocryphal gospels perpetuate pious legends. The so-called Protevangelium (first gospel) of James, a second-century work, contains vivid stories about the miraculous birth and holy childhood of Mary and about the birth of Jesus himself. The Infancy Gospel of Thomas (different from the Nag Hammadi Gospel of Thomas), another compilation dating from the second century, attributes childhood miracles to Jesus. A much later work, dubbed the Gospel of Pseudo-Matthew by scholars, combines these two and adds a collection of colorful tales about the Holy Family in Egypt. To early Christians these other writings provided both entertainment and material for pious reflection as well as support for such popular religious movements as the veneration of Mary.

A Gift for Melchior

The silence of the Gospels on the years of Jesus' boyhood in Nazareth has prompted writers to fill in the gap with imagined events. In his short story "The Seventh Christmas," Coningsby Dawson describes Mary showing Jesus the gifts of the wise men as a special treat on his birthday—when an unexpected visitor arrives.

IN THE BARRENNESS OF THE PRESENT her heart cried out for a confirmation of the glories that were past. Rising, she entered the shop on tiptoe for fear of waking Joseph. From the place where she had hidden them in readiness for the arrival of charioteers and horsemen who should summon her son to his crowning, she brought them forth; with them she brought the royal robe that she had woven. In the shuttered street, with nothing stirring save the distant flocks and none to watch her save the stars, she put the robe upon him.

How often she had longed to array him in these splendors! Surely tonight, late though it was, some sign would come to tell her that God's angels still kept guard. Opening the first casket, she drew forth the crown and set it shining on his forehead. "It is for Power," she said. From the second she drew forth the frankincense and scattered it upon his raiment. "It is for Worship." But the third casket, containing the gift which signifieth Death, she did not open.

Suddenly, Jesus held up his hand, listening and saying nothing. Then she, too, heard it—the thud-thud-thudding of a swiftly approaching camel and a voice panting in the night, "Where is he? Where is he?"

Through olive groves, bare of leaves, a dromedary came racing, swaying and staggering from weariness. It was caparisoned in purple and gold; but the purple had faded and the gold was tarnished. Upon it sat a man, gaunt and haggard, whose raiment was gray with the dust of travel.

"Where is he who is born King of the Jews?" he questioned hoarsely. "Once, when I was young, on such a night as this I found him. Tonight there are many stars, but no star to guide me."

Mary came out from the shadow and stared up into the face of the stranger. "Whence art thou?"

Bending down from his dromedary, he gazed at her puzzled, as though she brought memories. "From the East," he whispered. "We had waited so long, I who was young, and Melchior who was old, and Balthazar who was midway between us. At last we found him, and all the gods of Persia fell upon their faces and called him blessed. Again we have waited. We have lost him, and the East grows doubting; for the world hath not changed from what it was. Melchior is dying; he longs for certainty. So with no star to guide me, because my faith is greatest, I, who am the youngest of we three kings, have journeyed forth. Where is he who is born King of the Jews? If thou canst tell me, I will give thee— But I can give thee nothing, for I have spent my all in the searching."

Mary turned her head, glancing back across her shoulder. The gaze of the young lord followed. Gropingly he descended. His eyes met the eyes of the child. In the moonlight he saw the crown which shone upon his forehead, the white robe which garbed him, and the three golden caskets, two of them open, which lay at his feet before him.

"I came to thee before with a lordly train and trumpets blowing," the visitor whispered; "now I come to thee stained with the dust of travel and empty-handed. What is there I can give thee?"

"My mother is hungry," said Jesus.

From about his waist the lord unloosed a pouch in which were bread and dates. "Were I in my own country," he said, "I would give thee a palace of white marble, with fountains playing and hanging gardens. Here I am poor; but such as I have I give thee."

When they had eaten, Mary reminded him: "Melchior is old and dying. It is a long journey. What can we send to him to make him certain?"

Then they thought of the crown; but he himself had given it and might be offended. And they thought of the frankincense; but that was all gone.

The child spoke: "Let us send him the third casket, for it hath not been opened."

"Nay," said Mary, for she knew what it contained: myrrh, which signifieth Death.

But Jesus said, "I will open it and look just once."

When he raised the lid, a dazzling light burst forth, so that all save Jesus were blinded. But Jesus clapped his hands and laughed, for instead of the gift which signifieth Death out from the casket drifted the star.

"The star we had lost!" the young lord cried.

Holding the hand of Jesus, Mary watched him depart. Directly he was mounted, the star moved eastward toward the dawn, going to bring faith to the dying eyes of Melchior.

IN THE CARPENTER'S SHOP

Mary sat in the corner dreaming,
Dim was the room and low,
While in the dusk the saw went screaming
To and fro.

Jesus and Joseph toiled together,
Mary was watching them,
Thinking of Kings in the wintry weather
At Bethlehem.

Mary sat in the corner thinking,
Jesus had grown a man;
One by one her hopes were sinking
As the years ran.

Jesus and Joseph toiled together,
Mary's thoughts were far—
Angels sang in the wintry weather
Under a star.

Mary sat in the corner weeping,
Bitter and hot her tears—
Little faith were the angels keeping
All the years.

SARA TEASDALE, 1884–1933

As Joseph works in the background, Mary looks up from her spinning to study young Jesus going about a household task. English historical painter John Rogers Herbert (1810–1890) set his intimate domestic scene in a landscape accurately representing the eastern Mediterranean world.

Most of the original paint and gilt has faded from this early 16th-century German sculpture-relief in oak, and Jesus (at top) has lost a hand; but the drama of the discourse in the temple remains.

CHILD

The young child, Christ, is straight and wise
And asks questions of the old men, questions
Found under running water for all children,
And found under shadows thrown on still waters
By tall trees looking downwards, old and gnarled,
Found to the eyes of children alone, untold,
Singing a low song in the loneliness.
And the young child, Christ, goes asking
And the old men answer nothing and only know love
For the young child, Christ, straight and wise.

CARL SANDBURG, 1878–1967

*Now his parents went to Jerusalem
every year at the feast of the Passover.
And when he was twelve years
old, they went up according to custom;
and when the feast was ended,
as they were returning, the boy Jesus
stayed behind in Jerusalem.*

LUKE 2:41–43

AN EAGER YOUNG MIND THIRSTING FOR KNOWLEDGE

The single incident known of Jesus' life between his infancy and the beginning of his public ministry at about the age of 30 is this journey to Jerusalem with his parents recorded by Luke. Elizabeth Goudge's version of what happened in the Holy City is from her 1951 work GOD SO LOVED THE WORLD.

FROM ALL THE SMALL TOWNS and villages perched upon the hilltops all over the country came companies of men and women and children, some of them riding upon donkeys, others walking, and all wearing their gayest clothes.

They laughed and talked as they journeyed and looked about them at the springtime beauty of their land; the high and distant hills splashed with heavenly color, the nearer ones striped silver and green with the vines and olives, the waving green corn in the valleys, and the fields full of flowers. At night they camped out near some village or inn, setting up their tents under the olive trees, lighting campfires, and sitting about them before they went to sleep, listening to the little tunes that the shepherd boys played on their pipes, and singing the songs of Israel. In the midday heat they stopped to rest by some wayside well and watched lizards darting over the stones and heard crickets chirping. They got footsore and tired sometimes, but every day Jerusalem came a little nearer.

Jesus had been a much-traveled baby, but he could not remember that, and so this to him was the first journey of his life. With eager delight he looked at the villages and fields and hills, at the men and women going about their business and the patient beasts at their toil, and stored all these things in his memory and pondered them in his heart.

His strong young body would have exulted in the walking that tired his father and mother. While their elders sat resting in the shade, the boys would have run races and climbed trees and played games, and Jesus would have run the fastest and tackled trees that baffled the others, and had brilliant ideas for new and wonderful games. But if he did things always a bit better than they did, the other boys would not have disliked him for it because he never boasted about his exploits. He did not seem to think about them at all.

His first sight of the Holy City must have held Jesus silent and still with awe. It was a city larger than anything he had ever imagined, built high upon its hill, with palaces and houses, towers and domes all enclosed within the old, powerful, tawny-colored walls that rose up so fiercely from the bare rock. But for Jesus the crowning glory of it all was the temple. This was the house of God, his Father, and in coming to it he had come home.

He went to the temple services with Joseph and Mary and stood with them to pray, but sometimes he went off by himself to pray alone, and they let him go, glad that he should learn to find his way about the holy place that meant so much to every Israelite. If they allowed him more freedom than parents usually gave to children of twelve, that was natural, for if he was fearless he was trustworthy and sensible too.

And so it was on the last day of the feast he discovered the quiet court where the rabbis, the teachers of the Jewish religion, were instructing the young boys who came to them as pupils. Jesus had been instructed too, at home in Nazareth, but not by such wise and learned men as were teaching here. In Nazareth they had not been able to tell him the half of all that he longed to know. His brilliant eager mind thirsted for knowledge. He wanted to know all about the history of his people and his religion, and to understand the law. Above all he wanted to read all the Scriptures, and have them explained to him, so that through them he might reach out to a deeper knowledge of his Father's purpose for him.

He took his place quietly among the other boys and sat down to listen, his chin propped on his hands, his eyes fixed on the old rabbi who sat with a roll of the Scriptures on his knees, talking to them of the Hope of Israel. As he listened, Jesus' heart beat hard, as it always did when men talked of the Christ. In five minutes he had forgotten all about the little party of travelers who today were to start the homeward journey to Nazareth. It was his Father's will that he should be here, listening and learning, and he had known long before he had been old enough to put what he knew into words, that to do the will of his Father was the reason why he had come into the world.

Mary and Joseph had been traveling for a whole day before they found that Jesus was missing. In great anxiety they looked for him among all their friends, and when they could not find him they went back to Jerusalem and spent three days searching for him.

They found him at last in the quiet court of the temple, and now he was not only listening to the rabbis but asking them questions. The boy was wise beyond his years and athirst for knowledge, and the rabbis were astonished at his understanding.

Jesus sitting among the teachers in the temple at Jerusalem is one of several scenes in his early life that 16th-century Swiss weavers chose for a tapestry that now hangs in the Historical Museum in Basel.

Mary interrupted with a cry of anguished reproach. "Son, why hast thou thus dealt with us? Your father and I have sought thee sorrowing."

He went at once to comfort them but could not understand Mary's reproach. "How is it that you sought me?" he asked her. "Know you not that I must be about my Father's business?"

But Mary and Joseph had had a bad fright and just at this moment they were incapable of understanding anything except that he must come home with them at once, and they would not take their eyes off him again until they had got him safely back to Nazareth.

"And he went down with them, and came to Nazareth, and was subject unto them."

There is sadness in that sentence, the sadness of a boy who had to say good-by to the Holy City, to the temple, and the learned men who could have taught him so much if he had stayed with them. But quietly and obediently he turned his back on it all and went home to Nazareth.

JESUS IN THE TEMPLE

With His kind mother, who partakes thy woe,
Joseph, turn back; see where your Child doth sit,
Blowing, yea blowing out those sparks of wit
Which Himself on the doctors did bestow.
The Word but lately could not speak, and lo!
It suddenly speaks wonders; whence comes it
That all which was, and all which should be writ,
A shallow-seeming child should deeply know?
His Godhead was not soul to His manhood,
Nor had time mellow'd Him to this ripeness;
But as for one which hath a long task, 'tis good,
With the sun to begin His business,
He in His age's morning thus began,
By miracles exceeding power of man.

JOHN DONNE, 1573–1631

Commemorating Passover

Passover linked the heart and soul of every Jew — those who lived in Jerusalem as well as those like Mary and Joseph who took the 12-year-old Jesus there to celebrate the feast — with the traumatic yet wonderful experiences that had created the Israelite nation. All in the pilgrim party from Nazareth that year would have joined in sacrificing a lamb and partaking of a solemn meal in reenactment of that awful night more than a thousand years earlier when Moses had commanded the Israelite slaves in Egypt to kill and roast a lamb but use some of its blood to mark their doorposts and lintels. God was about to compel the recalcitrant Pharaoh to release His people from slavery through one final, horrible plague: the death of all Egyptian firstborn. The blood above their doors would save the Israelites, for God had promised, "when I see the blood, I will pass over you, and no plague shall fall upon you to destroy you, when I smite the

land of Egypt." God's terrible vengeance prompted Pharaoh to let the Israelites depart — the dramatic night of terror and salvation burned forever into the hearts of the children of Israel.

The Israelites were never to allow the Passover events to recede into ancient history, but rather they were to preserve them as a living experience. Jewish tradition required that people of every successive generation think of themselves as personally having come forth out of Egypt. "Therefore are we bound to give thanks," it was written, "and to bless Him who wrought all these wonders for our fathers and for us. He brought us out of bondage to freedom, from sorrow to gladness . . . from darkness to a great light, and from servitude to redemption."

Regretting his decision to let the Israelites go after the death of the Egyptian firstborn, Pharaoh sent troops in pursuit. God parted the Red Sea to allow His chosen people to escape.

Coming Home to His Father's House

The excitement and wonder a boy of 12 must have felt at his first sight of the temple is imagined by Edna Madison Bonser in this extract from THE LITTLE BOY OF NAZARETH, published in 1930.

T WAS VERY EARLY when the little boy awoke. Only a faint glow in the eastern sky showed that it was morning. A sweet coolness and quiet lay over the crowded city that, with the full coming of the day, would hum with the voices of the joyous pilgrims to the feast of the Passover.

It had been dark when the group from Nazareth had reached Jerusalem. Father Joseph, mother and the little boy had gone at once to the home of a kinsman, where, after bathing and eating, they had slept, tired from their long, hard journey.

For days and days the little boy had been thinking of the temple. But when at last they had climbed the hills beyond Bethany, where in daylight hours the first glimpse of its snowy marble walls and golden turrets might be caught, it had been quite dark, a deep, soft engulfing blackness through which they walked slowly, for the road was crowded with travelers. Too weary for dreams, the little boy slept through long hours, but awoke with the thought, "Today I shall see the temple, the house of God, the wondrous holy Place of Peace." There was no more sleep for him.

He had lain close to father Joseph through the night, and now, as he stirred and sat up, father Joseph awoke also and said, softly, "What is it, Son?"

"The sky is growing bright," answered the little boy. "It will soon be full day. Couldn't we creep softly down and be the first to enter the temple?"

"A priest is standing on the highest pinnacle of the temple, watching for the first rays of the sun that he may give the signal to the trumpeters. When we hear the silver trumpet's call we shall know that the great gates of the temple will swing open and we may go in. Let us wait here for the call. From this roof we can see the sunlight as it strikes the pinnacle of the temple and the white-robed priests as they go about their duties. The sound of the chanting will come to us here also. Then, when it is full day, we may go in together to worship."

So while the dawn strengthened and the shadows of

darkness disappeared, the little boy and father Joseph watched and waited.

"Long, long ago," father Joseph almost whispered so that he might not disturb others who were sleeping, "our people worshiped at a tabernacle they carried with them in the wilderness. They had but lately escaped from Egypt and were poor and without suitable building-material, but God directed them."

While they talked the light had grown stronger. The sky was full of a soft, clear radiance. A breeze stirred the trees from which came the twitter of sleepy birds.

"What became of that tabernacle they carried in the wilderness?" asked the little boy.

"In a few years our people reached the Promised Land, and built their homes and worshiped at many altars, under oak trees and beside streams. I do not know what became of the tabernacle. It had been built so that it could be taken down and carried to a new location. So I have no doubt it was used for many years. But after many years our greatest king, Solomon the wise, built in Jerusalem a temple far larger and more costly than the tabernacle.

"For more than five hundred years our people worshiped there in peace, but it was destroyed at last; its

The precocious wisdom of the child Jesus amazed the learned men in the temple. English painter William Holman Hunt (1827–1910) captured the moment when Jesus' mother and Joseph came to claim the lost boy.

From a lofty perch the young Jesus interrupts his dialogue with the teachers in the temple to greet the arrival of Mary and Joseph. The carved and painted wood panel is in the cathedral at Naumburg, Germany.

walls were burned; its golden vessels and sacred symbols, the ark and the tables of the law, destroyed or left a smoking desolation, while they who had kept it with such loving devotion were driven away to exile and slavery, to years of suffering in foreign lands.

"For long years it lay so. Then the good King Cyrus allowed a few of the most loyal Hebrew people to return to Jerusalem and set, as best as they could, its ruined walls in place and establish once more a temple worship. This was called Zerubbabel's temple."

"Is it the same as this temple we now have?" asked the little boy.

"The temple of Zerubbabel was almost destroyed in battle when Pompey laid seige to Jerusalem and captured it for the Romans. But upon its ruins Herod the Great built this for us. He has spared no expense. Its walls are of marble and its steps and pinnacles of gold. But none who see it may fail to note the golden eagles of Rome emblazoned in the banner that floats over it, and few there are who trust or honor Herod, he who hated the Jews yet sought to win their tolerance by such costly gifts. Even the house of God must exist with Rome's permission. But hark! The trumpets! The watchman has seen the sun before its first rays have reached us. Now we may go in."

As the little boy and mother and father Joseph made their way through the narrow streets of Jerusalem to the first service, they were overtaken and carried along by a joyous crowd of people all in their holiday best, all eager and glad to see friends from the country, all full of happy plans for feasting and games and gossip once the sacrifices should be made and the prayers said. But to the little boy, the prayers and the sacrifices were of the greatest importance.

Leaving the dark streets, they entered the temple through the Gate Beautiful and immediately the noise and clamor died away. A sweet peace and quiet lay over all, broken only by the chanting of the priests and the music of harps and cymbals. Looking upward from the gate was like looking up the golden ladder into heaven, the little boy thought as he stood for a moment and gazed about him. Before them lay the fifteen golden steps on which the singers stood, while back of these, leading up and up, were more golden steps before the most holy place. On a golden altar the smoke of a sacrifice ascended into the blue of the sky, while priests repeated the sacred prayers, and the people, kneeling with their faces toward the altar, joined their voices in the deep responses.

The little boy dropped to his knees beside father Joseph and at once forgot everything except that he was here at last where he had longed to be, in the house of his heavenly Father, the place where one might speak with God. He was only a little country lad, up for the first time from the village of Nazareth. He had never seen a sacrifice or heard any service other than the simple prayers and readings of the synagogue, but he felt as one who had been on a long journey and had at last come home.

THE LITTLE CHILD

A simple-hearted Child was He,
    And He was nothing more;
In summer days, like you and me,
    He played about the door,
Or gathered, when the father toiled,
    The shavings from the floor.

Sometimes he lay upon the grass,
    The same as you and I,
And saw the hawks above Him pass,
    Like specks against the sky;
Or, clinging to the gate, He watched
    The stranger passing by.

A simple Child, and yet, I think,
    The bird-folk must have known,
The sparrow and the bobolink,
    And claimed Him for their own,
And gathered round Him fearlessly
    When He was all alone.

The lark, the linnet, and the dove,
    The chaffinch and the wren,
They must have known His watchful love,
    And given their worship then;
They must have known and glorified
    The Child who died for men.

And when the sun at break of day
    Crept in upon His hair,
I think it must have left a ray
    Of unseen glory there—
A kiss of love on that little brow
    For the thorns that it must wear.

ALBERT BIGELOW PAINE, 1861–1937

Three centuries separate these two images of the child Jesus in the temple: the 12th-century mosaic at left is from the cathedral of San Marco in Venice; Giovanni di Paolo's painting below dates to the 15th century.

*And he went down with them and
came to Nazareth, and was obedient
to them; and his mother kept all these
things in her heart. And Jesus
increased in wisdom and in stature,
and in favor with God and man.*

LUKE 2:51–52

PASSING FROM BOYHOOD INTO HIS
SUBLIME MANHOOD

*The youth and growth to maturity of Jesus remain a
blank in the biblical narratives. Among the authors who
have attempted to reconstruct these years is Winifred Kirkland,
from whose* DISCOVERING THE BOY OF NAZARETH
the following selection is taken.

JESUS OF NAZARETH AT EIGHTEEN, is it possible to picture him? Day in, day out, the Nazareth people went past the door of the carpenter shop, paying little attention to Jesus. If anybody in Nazareth had really noticed their carpenter, surely some item from these unknown years would somehow have floated down to us. Yet perhaps there were a few who did look at the young man with curiosity, trying to guess what was going on back of those clear eyes. If you and I had stopped opposite a door always open to anyone, what might we have seen?

There is a shaft of light from the doorway and in it we may pick out tools, homemade saw and auger and plane, so rude that we wonder at the skill that can produce with them yokes and boards and plows so smooth and so well-shaped. The young carpenter is perhaps singing at his work, for he loves work. And he is alone, master of the shop now. They have begun to call him "our carpenter," even though he is still only eighteen. All his movements are vigorous and flowing and sure. He has girded up his tunic. His arms and feet and close-curled head are bare. His dark cheeks have a touch of red as if he had brought the hilltop with him into the closeness of the shop.

While his hands never cease from their quick, capable activity, his face is strangely intent as you watch

*The tender scene above is the work of William C. T. Dobson
(1817–1898) and hangs in London's Tate Gallery. A still
youthful Mary and an aged, weary Joseph bear Jesus home
to Nazareth following the remarkable encounter with the
teachers in the temple at Jerusalem.*

him when he is alone. Sometimes thoughts go kindling across it, sometimes it is as still and grave as if carved out of marble. His eyes, ordinarily clear as brook water, at times turn as black and impenetrable as midnight. Sometimes Jesus' eyes seem to gaze farther off than anyone could measure.

Without his family or friends ever dreaming of what was going on in his mind, Jesus, right there at home, came to know people and came to understand God in all that amazing intimacy he later showed. Quietly and all alone, he set to work to discover his neighbors, his God, and himself.

We can imagine that in these years when Jesus was growing up he was learning how to live at peace with himself, for as a child he had often been shaken by changing moods. The day-by-day routine of carpentry has steadied him. The words of the prophets learned by heart in school still sing in his soul, but they have now fallen into tune with the swishing of his plane and the beating of his hammer.

Jesus at eighteen is a practical young workman, supporting a widowed mother. He still at times thinks about that glorious figure of his childhood's fancy, the Messiah, but the young man Jesus, being no daydreamer, often forgets that great Helper-to-come because he is so busy helping people himself, his neighbors right there in Nazareth. He has his hands and his heart full trying to get food for starving people, and clothes for the destitute, welcoming the stranger in the town, going to see the sick, and making visits to the jail. Those were harsh days of history, even in Nazareth, and Jesus, poor and hardworking as he was himself, poured himself out in pity for those poorer.

Sometimes those he tried to help hated him for it, resented his efforts and refused his advice. It hurt, of course, to have them feel like that toward him, but, while still young, Jesus must have learned his own cure for his own sensitiveness. "Father," he would say, for he had become quite accustomed to talking to God in silence, "forgive them. They don't really know what they're saying or doing."

In those unnoticed years in the Nazareth workshop Jesus passed from boyhood into his sublime manhood. How did he accomplish his magnificent growth? It could only have been by taking risks, for that is the only way anyone ever does grow. Now, far adventures were impossible for Jesus, though the distant glinting sea and the white highroads nearer by must have beckoned to his spirit. He was needed at home, he must remain year by year in a little town. The only adventure open to him was in Nazareth. He chose the adventure of loving everybody, whatever the cost.

In those silent years of his development in Nazareth, Jesus was not only growing into the greatest lover of humankind that ever lived, but he was also growing to be the greatest lover of God that humankind itself had ever brought forth. Just as Jesus, watching his neighbors in Nazareth, came to believe that the only way really to understand people is first to love them, so also did he come to believe that the only way really to know God is first to love Him, however shadowy and strange and distant He may seem. Clearly Jesus in little Nazareth was learning how to live and grow by taking risks, for surely there is no greater risk than loving people—they may hurt you. And it is as great a risk to love God, for He may sometimes seem to fail you. Jesus, boy and man, grew by choosing always these two roads of risk, and yet he never seems sorry for the choice he made while still a boy in Nazareth.

A FAREWELL TO CARPENTRY

Eventually, as we know, the time came for Jesus to take up his mission on earth. The poignant departure from Nazareth is recreated by Edwin McNeill Poteat in this extract from THESE SHARED HIS CROSS.

In another of his strikingly natural etchings depicting biblical events, Rembrandt van Rijn (1606–1669) shows Mary and Joseph hand in hand with Jesus en route home from Jerusalem.

NAZARETH HAD NO DISTINCTION to boast except that within a radius of forty furlongs most of the joinery throughout the countryside was done in its shops. Carpenter booths flanked both sides of the principal street, and all day long the industrious whisper of plane and saw issued from their dim interiors.

Up from the main street, toward the western limit of the low-roofed dwellings, was the house of Joseph. Mary, widowed for fourteen years, lived with her family of five, four sons and one daughter. Their house was near the open fields, and easy of access to herdsmen and tillers of the soil. Often, during the day, oxen were to be seen outside the mud wall, waiting for the fitting of a new yoke; and an occasional shepherd might stand testing the heft of a new crook, while a farmer brought a blunted plowshare for repair.

Since the death of Joseph, Jesus had managed the affairs of the shop, and taught the trade to the three younger sons, James, Simon and Judah. Throughout the countryside the reputation of the sons of Joseph had spread, and their fame rested on two specialities: they made the strongest and lightest yoke that was to be found anywhere, said to have been the invention of the eldest son; and he, furthermore, enjoyed a re-pute unique among the carpenters of the town as be-ing more expert in repair work than them all. No bro-ken tool, no article of furniture, no shattered staff or yoke but could be restored by him to a condition said to be better even than before the damage occurred.

One evening, long after the set of sun, a shepherd knocked on the gate and when admitted, exhibited his crook, broken sadly in half. Could the carpenter fix it before the morrow? Jesus picked up a wick that burned indifferently inside the house, and protecting it with a cupped hand, crossed the yard to the shop. The shepherd followed him, and watched silently while with practiced skill Jesus sawed the broken ends, smoothed them with a crude file, and joined them expertly with a dowel pin.

"You work swiftly and easily," the shepherd said. "Why do you make so much of repair work and so little of articles made new for common use?"

The carpenter vigorously rubbed dark wax over the fresh crack until it was all but invisible in the dim light. "It is easier to make than to repair," he an-swered pleasantly as he handed the stick to the shep-herd, who tested the repaired break under his knee.

"It is stronger than before," he ventured. "What can I do to repay your trouble?"

"Your thanks and your recollection," Jesus an-swered. He followed the shepherd to the gate and opened it. The man tried to thank him as the gate closed between them. Jesus stood for a moment and looked up at a cluster of bright stars, and then walked slowly across the yard, and sat down on the doorsill by Judah. There was a long interval of silence.

"How long," Judah asked finally, "do you think the thanks of shepherds for repairs to their broken crooks will keep this family in bread?" There was annoyance

This ninth-century ivory plaque, designed as a book cover, summarizes Jesus' early life, from the angel advising the flight into Egypt (top left) to the wedding at Cana (bottom). Jesus in the temple at age 12 is at right in the third panel.

in his tone and it was clear that his question was the resumption of a dispute begun earlier in the evening. He waited for a reply, but there was none.

Jesus stood up. His full height looked immensely tall in the darkness. He looked up at the cluster of burning stars again, stepped out into the yard, and moved toward the gate. Drawing the bar so gently it made no sound, he stepped through and breathed deeply of the darkness. Above the village, a short mile from the house, the summit of the ridge smouldered black against the sky. He was careful to make no sound as he closed the gate behind him, and his footsteps, as he turned into a familiar path that led to the crest where he would spend the night in prayer, were only heard by his bewildered brother.

The soft, bright edge of day had hardly pushed over the eastern ridge when the gate to the house of Joseph opened quietly and a tall figure bent slightly to enter. His step was elastic and his countenance was as bright as if he had captured all the radiance of the dawn in his face. Nothing about Jesus' manner bespoke an all-night vigil on the mountaintop.

He crossed the yard and listened at the door. No one seemed yet to be astir. He went into the shop. On a shelf was a toy he had whittled on in odd hours, a tiny yoke of oxen, hitched to a plow. He blew the dust off it, and put it on the bench as he brushed aside the debris of the previous day's work with his foot. He looked lovingly about the shop, then recrossed the yard to his mother's door. She called his name softly, and he entered her room and seated himself beside her on the bed. She stroked his face fondly, and noted the tiny wooden oxen in his hand.

"My time is come," he said suddenly. She clutched tightly at her heart and then breathed deeply as if in resignation to a destiny she had long known she could not escape.

"My time is come," he said again, his eyes lighted with an unearthly fire. "My Father is moving the hearts of the sons of men. Down in the valley John gathers to him those who need repair, whose hearts are broken with folly, whose bodies are broken with sin. They come from Jerusalem, and from Judea to be baptized, confessing their sins."

He paused and Mary leaned toward him. A look of desperate inquiry burned in her eyes. He stood up and gripped her shoulders at arms' length with his powerful hands, and then held her fiercely against him long and breathlessly. It was the moment of farewell she had so dreaded, but no word was given her to speak.

He smiled reflectively, and for a moment the austere mood seemed to drop from him. And then with a tenderness his mother was never to forget, he put his arm about her and led her to the door. He raised his hand and pointed down the valley. It was gold and blue in the early light. They walked slowly through the gate and stopped. Once again he pointed down the valley, but neither spoke. Her eyes were bright with tears as he kissed her forehead. Then down the alleyway he strode with strong, confident steps, and as he turned the corner that would lose him from her sight, she raised her hand weakly. He returned her salute boldly and then was gone, never again to be known as the son of Mary, but henceforth to be called the Son of Man.

THE HIDDEN YEARS AT NAZARETH

The hidden years at Nazareth,
How beautiful they seem,
Like fountains flowing in the dark
Or waters in a dream!
Like waters under Syrian stars
Reflecting lights above,
Repeating in their silent depths
The wonder of God's love!

The hidden years at Nazareth!
How marvelous they lie,
As open to the smile of God
As to the Syrian sky!
As open to the heart of man
As to the genial sun,
With dreams of high adventuring,
And deeds of kindness done!

The hidden years at Nazareth!
How radiant they rise,
With life and death in balance laid
Before a lad's clear eyes!
O soul of youth, forever choose
Forgetting fate or fear,
To live the truth, or die with God,
Who stands beside thee here!

ALLEN EASTMAN CROSS, 1864–1943

His Ministry on Earth

The wise and revolutionary teaching, the miracles,
the amazing proclamation of a kingdom to come—the public
years of Jesus lasted, by tradition at least, only
three short years. Yet the events of that brief time span
altered the course of history.

The Gospels actually account for no more than a few months,
perhaps, of Jesus' ministry, and it is impossible
to reconstruct those momentous three years with certainty.
The first three Evangelists—Matthew, Mark, and
Luke—follow a similar chronology, often using
identical language; their Gospels are called *synoptic*, from
a Greek word that means viewing together. John's narrative
often differs from theirs, not only in sequence but
in the events recorded. On the following pages, Jesus' ministry is
presented according to a chronology that combines the
synoptic Gospels with John (see time line, pages 154–157).

*"Let the children
come to me,
and do not hinder
them." Jesus'
love for children
is depicted in this
painting by Carl
Vogel von Vogelstein
(1788–1868).*

Casting off his finer attire, John the Baptist dons the camel's hair garment that Mark says he wore when John first appeared in the wilderness to preach his baptism of repentance. Domenico Veneziano's painting is dated about 1445.

*John the baptizer appeared in
the wilderness, preaching a baptism of
repentance for the forgiveness of sins.
And there went out to him all the
country of Judea, and all the people of
Jerusalem; and they were baptized
by him in the river Jordan.*

MARK 1:4–5

"BEHOLD THE LAMB OF GOD"

*Mark's vivid description of John as one clothed in camel's
hair, girded in leather, and sustained by a diet of
locusts and wild honey suggested to 19th-century novelist
Lew Wallace that John lived according to a Nazirite vow.
In the following scene from* BEN-HUR, *Wallace's hero is
accompanied by the wise man Balthasar, who has
returned to Judea 30 years after his first visit.*

ABOUT THE THIRD HOUR the party came upon the
barren steppe east of the river Jordan. Soon
they caught sight of booths, tents and teth-
ered animals; and then of the river, and a
multitude collected down close by the bank, and yet
another multitude on the western shore. Knowing
that John was preaching, they made greater haste;
yet, as they were drawing near, suddenly the mass began to break up and disperse. They were too late!

"Let us stay here, good Balthasar," Ben-Hur suggested. "The Nazirite may come this way."

The people were too intent upon what they had
heard, and too busy in discussion, to notice the new-
comers. When some hundreds were gone by, and it
seemed the opportunity to so much as see the Nazirite
was lost, up the river not far away they beheld a person coming towards them of such singular appearance
they forgot all else.

Outwardly the man was rude and uncouth, even
savage. Over a thin, gaunt visage of the hue of brown
parchment, over his shoulders and down his back below the middle, in witch-like locks, fell a covering of
sun-scorched hair. His eyes were burning-bright. A
shirt of the coarsest camel's-hair clothed his person to

the knees, being gathered at the waist by a broad girdle of untanned leather. His feet were bare. Every little while he tossed the unruly hair from his eyes, and
peered round as if searching for somebody.

"Is that the herald of thy King?" asked Balthasar.

"It is the Nazirite," Ben-Hur replied.

In truth, he was himself more than disappointed.
Ben-Hur's dream of the king who was to be so great
and do so much had colored all his thought of him, so
that he never doubted to find in the forerunner some
sign or token of the goodliness and royalty he was announcing. Gazing at the savage figure before him, he
could only repeat, "It is the Nazirite."

Another man had been sitting by himself on a
stone at the edge of the river, thinking yet, probably,
of the sermon he had heard. Now he arose and walked
slowly up from the shore, in a course to take him
across the line the Nazirite was pursuing.

And the two—the preacher and the stranger—
kept on until they came, the former within twenty
yards of Ben-Hur, the latter within ten feet. Then the
preacher stopped, flung the hair from his eyes, looked
at the stranger, and threw his hands up as a signal to
all the people in sight. And they also stopped, each in
the pose of a listener; and when the hush was perfect,
slowly the staff in the Nazirite's right hand came down
pointed at the stranger.

Balthasar and Ben-Hur fixed their gaze upon the
man pointed out. He was moving slowly towards them
in a clear space a little to their front, a form slightly
above the average in stature, and slender, even delicate. His action was calm and deliberate, like that ha-
bitual to men much given to serious thought upon
grave subjects; and it well became his costume, which
was an under-garment full-sleeved and reaching to the
ankles, and an outer robe called the talith; on his left
arm he carried the usual handkerchief for the head,
the red fillet swinging loose down his side. Except for
the fillet and a narrow border of blue at the lower edge
of the talith, his attire was of linen yellowed with dust
and road-stains. Possibly the exception should be extended to the tassels, which were blue and white, as
prescribed by law for rabbis. His sandals were of the
simplest kind.

The head was open to the cloudless light, except as
it was draped with hair long and slightly waved, and
parted in the middle, and auburn in tint, with a ten-
dency to reddish golden where most strongly touched
by the sun. Under a broad, low forehead, under black

*A wrathful John the
Baptist, gaunt from his
ascetic life in the
wilderness, was depicted
by Donatello (c.1386–1466),
a leading sculptor of the
early Italian Renaissance.
The statue is in the church
of I Frari in Venice.*

Poised on a natural pedestal in a landscape reminiscent of a rock quarry, John is the central figure in this detail from a painting by the 15th-century Italian artist Fra Filippo Lippi. Another detail appears on page 56.

well-arched brows, beamed eyes dark-blue and large, and softened to exceeding tenderness by lashes of great length. Never was a child that would not, with quick instinct, have given him its hand and whole artless trust; nor might any one have said he was not beautiful.

As he drew near, the hush was profound.

Presently the Nazirite, still pointing with his staff, cried, in a loud voice, "Behold the Lamb of God, which taketh away the sin of the world!"

The many standing still, arrested by the action of the speaker, and listening for what might follow, were struck with awe by words so strange and past their understanding; upon Balthasar they were overpowering. He was there to see once more the Redeemer of men.

"It is he, it is he!" Balthasar cried, with upraised tearful eyes. Next moment he sank down insensible.

All this time, Ben-Hur was studying the face of the stranger. Who is this man? And what? Messiah or king? Never was apparition more unroyal. Nay, looking at that calm, benignant countenance, the very idea of war and conquest, and lust of dominion, smote him like a profanation. Turning to a man at his side, he asked, "Who is the stranger?"

The man laughed mockingly and replied, "He is the son of a carpenter over in Nazareth."

A VOICE FROM THE DESERT

A voice from the desert comes awful and shrill:
   "The Lord is advancing—prepare ye the way!"
The word of Jehovah he comes to fulfill,
   And o'er the dark world pours the splendor of day.

Bring down the proud mountain,
     though towering to heaven;
   And be the low valley exalted on high;
The rough path and crooked
     be made smooth and even;
   For, Sion! your King, your Redeemer is nigh!

The beams of salvation his progress illume,
   The lone dreary wilderness sings of her God;
The rose and the myrtle shall suddenly bloom,
   And the olive of peace spread its branches abroad.

WILLIAM DRUMMOND, 1585–1649

In Token of Repentance: Baptism

John's call for repentance had a profound and disturbing effect on most of his listeners. The American scholar Edgar J. Goodspeed explained why in his book A LIFE OF JESUS, published in 1950.

THE SENSATION OF THE DAY, John revived Amos' message of a dreadful day of wrath and punishment for an unrepentant world. He lived the life of a hermit, eating raw food, wearing rough clothes, keeping away from towns and settlements. His manner of life stamped him as a prophet and irresistibly reminded people of Elijah, the fiery old desert prophet of nine centuries before.

John's vehement demand for repentance and obedience to the will of God soon created an immense impression. People streamed out to his camp meetings and listened spellbound to his message. They soon identified him as a returned Elijah, come back to earth as Malachi had foretold, to be God's messenger, sent to warn mankind and prepare them for the coming of the terrible day of the Lord.

In the boldest terms he warned the Jews who came in crowds to hear him that their descent from Abraham meant nothing compared with a life of helpfulness to others, with whom they must share their food and clothing. He told them bluntly that they must reform and warned them that someone greater than he was soon to come to institute a Messianic judgment and punish those who failed to repent.

But his sternest rebuke was called forth by the appearance in his wilderness audiences of people he recognized as members of the dominant religious sects: the Sadducees from in and about Jerusalem and the Pharisees, more generally scattered throughout the land. Who had told this brood of snakes, he bitingly inquired, that they would escape the wrath that was coming? If they were going to confess their sins and profess repentance, they had better show their sincerity in a complete change of conduct.

But the time was short; the ax was already lying at the roots of the trees, and any tree that failed to produce good fruit was going to be cut down and burned. In token of repentance John demanded that his followers accept baptism at his hands.

An ancient rite of Judaism, baptism was part of the Levitical purification prescribed in ridding oneself of certain types of impurity. It had also been adopted in the Jewish mission as one of the three demands made upon Jewish proselytes, or converts, from other peoples and religions, when they entered the Jewish fold—circumcision, baptism, and a sacrifice. To John it was the symbol of repentance and spiritual purification. He baptized his penitents in token of their repentance and sent his followers forth not just momentarily swayed toward a better life but, in their own minds at least, publicly committed, by accepting it, to a higher course of conduct. It was the symbol of a decision reached and acted upon, a public commitment to the abandonment of old sins and the entrance upon a new life. But what gave John's baptism everlasting significance was its effect upon Jesus.

The two men were cousins, born within a few months of each other, and probably had known each other at least slightly from boyhood. Very soon after news of John's work reached Nazareth, Jesus—a carpenter about thirty years of age—set forth with a little caravan of people attracted by what they had heard of John's personality and message. He found John on the banks of the lower Jordan, was soon satisfied that John's message expressed the will of God and pressed forward for baptism in the turbid waters.

It was a sublime moment in his life. For as he came up out of the water, serene in the consciousness that he was doing his utmost to carry out the will of God, a tremendous sense of vocation, selection and mission came over him. He heard a voice saying to him, "You are my Son, my Beloved! You are my Chosen!"

He felt filled with the Spirit of God, as never before. For an instant, the heavens had opened, and the Spirit had taken possession of him. A curtain had rolled up in his mind and he saw with a new and surpassing clearness the role God intended him to play in the drama of redemption. It was doubtless the climax of much religious reflection and experience, but it was nonetheless the great moment, the decisive hour, not only in Jesus' life but in human experience.

John is depicted here as a solitary wanderer in a forbidding wilderness, one of 20 scenes from the Baptist's life that appear on the bronze baptistery doors of the cathedral in Florence, Italy. They are the work of Andrea Pisano (c. 1270–1348).

Above is a 17th-century wood panel painting of John from the Kremlin in Moscow. The baptism of Jesus is the subject of the four-inch-square enamel on copper gilt plaque below; it dates to the 12th century.

Jesus came from Nazareth of Galilee and was baptized by John in the Jordan. And when he came up out of the water, immediately he saw the heavens opened and the Spirit descending upon him like a dove; and a voice came from heaven, "Thou art my beloved Son; with thee I am well pleased."

MARK 1:9–11

WAITING FOR HIS HOUR TO COME

The news of John's mission in Judea must have had a profound effect on his kinsman Jesus, working as a humble carpenter in an obscure Galilean village. French Nobel Prize-winner François Mauriac wrote of that turning point in his LIFE OF JESUS.

THE EXCITEMENT RAISED by the preaching of John the Baptist reached Nazareth. We can imagine, in his workshop there, the man waiting for his hour that was soon to come. Perhaps Mary spoke to him of John, of the son of her cousin Elizabeth and of his mysterious birth. Zechariah, the priest, and his wife Elizabeth, who was barren, had already reached old age. It was revealed to Zechariah while he was alone within the sanctuary offering incense and while the people waited without, that a male child would be born to them and this child would be filled with the Holy Spirit. Mary remembered the visit to her cousin she made six months later. But now, after so many years, the canticle she had sung upon the threshold did not rise again from her heart. "My *soul doth magnify the Lord, and my spirit hath exulted in God my Saviour*—" No, the silence of the last hours of the hidden life could not be troubled by the hymn of joy. Mary understood that the time had come; the sword was already moving a little.

For the Baptist who, they said, was clothed in camel's hair and wore a leathern girdle about his loins, and who fed on locusts and wild honey, was not content with preaching penance with threats, nor with baptizing by water, but he announced the early arrival of a stranger, the strap of whose sandal he was not worthy to stoop and untie. "He who cometh after me is mightier than I. . . . His winnowing-fan is in his hand, and he will clean out his threshing floor; he will gather his wheat into the barn, but will burn up the chaff with unquenchable fire."

The last days of the hidden life: the workman is no longer a workman; he refuses all orders and the workshop takes on an abandoned air. He had always prayed, but now day and night Mary would come upon him, his face against the earth. Perhaps he was already seized with impatience that all be accomplished, an impatience which he showed so often during the three years of his ascent to Calvary. How he longed to hear the first crackling of that fire he had come to light!

Until that hour, God had so far sunk Himself in man that even his mother, although the mystery had been made known to her, had forgotten it, and allowed herself to rest beneath the weight of her crushing knowledge; he was her child, like other children, whose brow she kissed, over whose sleep she watched; a young man whose tunic she mended. He earned his bread, seated himself at table to eat his meals, talked with the neighbors—and there was no lack of other artisans pious like himself and versed in the Scriptures. No doubt he was the same man who, during those last days, went to the door, listened with an absent expression and without comment to what the people said, but attentive to the rumours concerning John, now coming from every quarter. Already a power was manifesting itself in him which his mother alone was to see. Already he was far away, his thought entirely on what he loved, on humanity which he must win—from what an enemy! For Jesus was the light come into a world delivered over to the powers of darkness.

At this moment of his life, the Son of Man was the gladiator still hidden in obscurity but about to enter the blinding arena—the fighter awaited and feared by the beast. "I beheld," Christ was to cry one day in exaltation, "I beheld Satan fall like a lightning-flash from heaven." It was perhaps during those last hours of the hidden life that he had the vision of that fall. Did he also see that the vanquished archangel carried in his wake millions of souls, more numerous and thickly falling than the flakes of a snowstorm?

He took a cloak, he tied on his sandals. To his mother he said words of farewell we shall never know.

Surrounded by the 12 apostles, Jesus is baptized by John. This spectacular mosaic cupola caps the presbytery of the sixth-century church of San Vitale in Ravenna, Italy.

THE HEAVENS OPENED, THE LIGHT SHONE DOWN

The dramatic revelation at the time of Jesus'
baptism by John—also recorded in the Gospels of
Matthew, Mark, and Luke—has captured the imagination
of innumerable writers over the centuries. English
novelist Elizabeth Goudge re-created the moment in
GOD SO LOVED THE WORLD.

THE RIVER JORDAN flows swiftly and the water is fresh and clear. The climate in its sheltered valley is almost tropical. Flowering trees grow upon the riverbanks, among them the tamarisk with its feathery pink flowers and willows with their silvery leaves. The birds love these trees, and morning and evening their song mingles with the music of the flowing water.

One day John was baptizing in the Jordan. He stood knee-deep in the river and one by one his penitents came to him and he dipped up the water and poured it over them, and spoke to them just the few words that would help and comfort them. It was a day of light, one of those brilliant days that sometimes end in thunder. The streaming silvery sunshine danced on the water, on the leaves that rippled as the wind passed over them, and lit with beauty the wet faces of the penitent men. There was a pause in the stream of penitents, and he shut his eyes for a moment. Then he heard a light, quick, firm footfall. It had a dear familiarity about it and his heart leaped.

"John!"

He swung round and opened his eyes. Yes, it was he, coming down the path through the trees, taking off his coat as he came. His eyes met John's, and his smile flashed out like light over his face. Making himself one with the company of the penitents, he had come to John to be baptized too. Before John could stop him he had stepped down into the water and was humbly waiting.

John in his humility was in even deeper distress than he had been when they asked him if he was the

---

From heaven, God blesses "my beloved Son, with whom I am well pleased." The work of Italy's finest pre-Renaissance painter, Giotto di Bondone (c. 1276–1337), this fresco is one of a series created for the Scrovegni chapel in Padua, Italy.

A 12th-century bronze baptismal font from the cathedral in Hildesheim, Germany.

The Origins of Baptism

From the earliest days of Christianity, baptism has served as an initiation rite for converts — 3,000 were baptized on Pentecost alone. Scholars suggest at least four possible origins for the practice. To the ancient Jews, ritual ablutions, or washings, symbolized moral cleansing. The Jews also demanded baptism of their converts, along with a sacrificial offering and circumcision for males. The purification rites of the Essenes at Qumran included a baptism in flowing water, frequent ablutions, and a cold-water ritual bath each day at the fifth hour (about eleven o'clock). The most direct source of the Christian sacrament, however, was the ritual practiced by John the Baptist, who may have been influenced by the Essenes. His baptism in the river Jordan symbolized the need for reform and conversion even among the pious — a rite of repentance that prepared the believer for the imminent coming of God's judgment. Jesus was baptized by John, perhaps to symbolize a commitment to his own ministry on earth, and he remained in Judea baptizing others. After Pentecost, his disciples baptized all new converts "in the name of Jesus," and it has since remained one of Christianity's most important rituals.

The top of this ornate ivory pastoral staff encircles a miniature baptism scene in which an angel holds a towel for Jesus emerging from the Jordan; only a fragment of the figure of John remains at right.

Christ. "I have need to be baptized of thee," he said, "and comest thou to me?"

Jesus answered gently, "Suffer it to be so now: for thus it becometh us to fulfill all righteousness."

Then John understood. The first law of the heavenly kingdom that Jesus had come to establish was that a man should humble himself and be sorry for his sins before he could enter into it.

So Jesus bent his head, and John baptized him. Then he stood erect again, the silvery water shot through with sunshine streaming off him, and went up "straightway" out of the water. John watched with humble love, and it seemed to him that all the light of the bright day gathered itself about that quickly moving figure. It was as though the very heavens opened and the light shone down.

MEETING THE MASTER HE SOUGHT

Since the Gospels reveal so little about Jesus at the time of his baptism, scholars have probed deeply in their efforts to fill in the gaps. The following account is from a 1959 life of Jesus by the French cleric Jean Steinmann.

JESUS WAS ABOUT THIRTY when he joined John's desert entourage. Of his physical appearance—height, expression, mannerisms—we know nothing, much less any details concerning such things as his way of writing or how he looked when he smiled. From his capacity for lengthy fasts and journeys on foot, however, it has been deduced that he was probably tall, well-built, and muscular.

Like many of his compatriots, he was of royal descent—that is, a little of David's blood ran in his veins. But his circumstances were comparatively humble. He was from the village of Nazareth, a carpenter and cartwright who spoke Aramaic with a northern accent, and whose early education must have been restricted to the village school and the local synagogue. He knew Hebrew, and probably understood Greek too: people of many races passed through the villages of Galilee, and children brought up there tended to be fluently multilingual.

Life as a rural artisan was in no way incompatible with high spiritual development: many rabbis also

The 15th-century Italian master Piero della Francesca depicted the central figures in his painting of the baptism (right) with pious formality, but gave the attendant angels more casual poses and included a second figure in the background, preparing to be baptized. Angels hover with towels and curious fish swim up to Jesus in the scene below, the work of an early Egyptian Christian.

practiced manual crafts to earn their bread. In point of fact Jesus knew the Scriptures extremely well, and was passionately concerned about the religious future of his people. His Galilean origin also equipped him with traits characteristic of the better sort of northern provincial: hardheaded realism, broad-mindedness, the common touch, a certain prickly defiance when dealing with scornfully superior Judeans.

The religion which both he and his family followed was Orthodox Temple Judaism, modified in one or two respects by old-fashioned habits such as adherence to the old traditional calendar and a marked weakness for certain practices of the Essenes—ascetic self-denial, baptism, sharing property in common, communal meals of bread and wine, a contempt for money. On the other hand, he displayed little or no regard for the monastic ideal, with its strict discipline, blind obedience, and quasi-military organization.

Jesus had been brought up in a tradition of ideas very much akin to those held by good Pharisees. He believed firmly in the resurrection of the dead and intercession by angels in human affairs; yet there was much that he found to dislike about these strict sectarians: their ostentatious habits, their self-righteousness, their holier-than-thou attitude.

From his very first encounter with Jesus, the desert prophet got the impression that he had met the Master he sought. Jesus' insight into future events was so striking, his strength of character so self-evident, and his moral purity so absolute that when he asked John to baptize him the latter at first refused, though finally he capitulated and did as Jesus requested.

It seems possible that when the time came for Jesus to confess his sins, he instead—being without stain—declared his intention of taking upon himself the sins of all mankind. Not long afterward, John described him as "the Lamb of God, which taketh away the sin of the world"—that is to say, the suffering servant we read of in Isaiah, the immolated Paschal Lamb whose blood is to be shed, the victim who will one day rise in triumph.

When Jesus emerged from the green-slimed, sluggish water of the river Jordan, the bright heavens were opened to the Infinite, the breath of God blew upon his face, and he heard a voice that said: "Thou art my beloved Son, in whom I am well pleased."

Like the very first man, whom God fashioned from clay in Paradise, he received the lifegiving spirit direct. He heard himself addressed as the Son of God, a

title which in bygone days the kings of Israel had assumed. By means of this mystical vision, experienced in a state of ecstasy, Jesus was celebrating his own kingly consecration. The ancient kings, however, did not connect their divine adoption with the moment of consecration; they knew it applied from the very moment any one of them was conceived. So it was with Jesus. His baptism only confirmed that natural bond, existing between him and God, which lent such infinite richness to his inner life. In addition, this ritual act of initiation into the New Kingdom—preached so fervently by John—made Jesus feel more closely bound to humankind than ever before.

Carved in wood, then painted and gilded, this baptismal scene is the work of a pupil of Veit Stoss (c. 1450–1533), considered to be the master of German wood carving.

THE BAPTISM OF CHRIST

It was a green spot in the wilderness,
Touch'd by the river Jordan. The dark pine
Never had dropp'd its tassels on the moss
Tufting the leaning bank, nor on the grass
Of the broad circle, stretching evenly
To the straight larches, had a heavier foot
Than the wild heron's trodden. Softly in
Through a long aisle of willows, dim and cool,
Stole the clear waters with their muffled feet,
And hushing as they spread into the light,
Circled the edges of the pebbled tank
Slowly, then rippled through the woods away.

Hither had come th' Apostle of the wild,
Winding the river's course. 'Twas near the flush
Of eve, and, with a multitude around,
Who from the cities had come out to hear,
He stood breast-high amid the running stream,
Baptizing as the Spirit gave him power.
His simple raiment was of camel's hair,
A leathern girdle close about his loins,
His beard unshorn, and for his daily meat
The locust and wild honey of the wood—
But like the face of Moses on the mount
Shone his rapt countenance, and in his eye
Burn'd the mild fire of love—and as he spoke
The ear lean'd to him, and persuasion swift
To the chain'd spirit of the listener stole.

Silent upon the green and sloping bank
The people sat, and while the leaves were shook
With the birds dropping early to their nests,
And the gray eve came on, within their hearts
They mused if he were Christ. The rippling stream
Still turned its silver courses from his breast,
As he divined their thought. "I but baptize,"
He said, "with water; but there cometh One,
The latchet of whose shoes I may not dare
E'en to unloose. He will baptize with fire
And with the Holy Ghost." And lo! while yet
The words were on his lips, he raised his eyes

*Jesus' humility is stressed in the elegant painting at left,
the work of Ottavio Vannini (1585–1643).*

And on the bank stood Jesus. He had laid
His raiment off, and with his loins alone
Girt with a mantle, and his perfect limbs,
In their angelic slightness, meek and bare,
He waited to go in. But John forbade,
And hurried to his feet and stay'd him there,
And said, "Nay, Master, I have need of *thine*,
Not thou of *mine!*" And Jesus, with a smile
Of heavenly sadness, met his earnest looks,
And answer'd, "Suffer it to be so now;
For thus it doth become me to fulfill
All righteousness." And, leaning to the stream,
He took around him the Apostle's arm,
And drew him gently to the midst. The wood

Was thick with the dim twilight as they came
Up from the water. With his clasped hands
Laid on his breast, th' Apostle silently
Follow'd his Master's steps—when lo! a light,
Bright as the tenfold glory of the sun,
Yet lambent as the softly burning stars,
Enveloped them, and from the heavens away
Parted the dim blue ether like a veil;
And as a voice, fearful exceedingly,
Broke from the midst, "This is my much-loved Son,
In whom I am well pleased," a snow-white dove,
Floating upon its wings, descended through;
And shedding a swift music from its plumes,
Circled, and flutter'd to the Saviour's breast.

NATHANIEL PARKER WILLIS, 1806–1867

*American primitive artist
Ann Johnson called this
pious scene "Baptisam of
Our Savour." It is from
the folk art collection
at Colonial Williamsburg.*

And Jesus, full of the Holy Spirit,
returned from the Jordan, and was led
by the Spirit for forty days in
the wilderness, tempted by the devil.

LUKE 4:1–2

STANDING ON THE HEIGHTS WITH EVIL ITSELF

The acclamation of Jesus' divinity at his baptism in the
river Jordan was followed by a lonely, harrowing
experience for the man about to embark on his mission of
redemption. Fulton Oursler expanded on the Gospel
narrative in THE GREATEST STORY EVER TOLD.

Christian scholars long
sought to link incidents in
the life of Jesus with
Old Testament stories.
In the paired manuscript
illuminations below,
Jesus' temptation by the
devil (left) is compared
with the apocryphal tales
of Daniel unmasking
the god Bel and
poisoning the dragon.

TELLING NO ONE what he intended to do, Jesus made his way alone into the wilderness. He was both led by the Spirit of God and driven by it, impelled and compelled to a great and lonely test. This parched and arid place was to be his place of testing; here, with red-tailed buzzards wheeling overhead, he was to endure a hideous experience none the less frightful because he deliberately invited the trial upon himself.

On a hillside he found a cavern and there he made his solitary camp. His sole reason for retreating to this grotto was that he must become acquainted with human suffering and temptation. He had to know them at first-hand and altogether before he could begin his work. He must overcome temptation himself—as a man, not as God—before he advised other men what they must do.

That was why Jesus made his way into this gigantesque waterless region—an inchoate place like a piece of creation begun but not finished; a mountainous expanse of stone ravines, blistering hills, and beds of crumbling shale, where no birds ever roosted except the birds of prey; a lonely, scorched, and gloomy place fit only for panthers and wild boar.

Here Jesus forced upon himself a grueling discipline of fasting and solitude. For forty days he remained there eating nothing. And during those forty days the little home in Nazareth and the blessed face of Mary his mother seemed very far away.

It was only after those forty weakening days and nights that Jesus was subject to the ordeal of temptation. Not until he was faint and exhausted did the temptations come—at a time when he felt weakest, most lonely, and friendless.

He stood on the heights with evil itself. Around him lay a scene like the panorama of the world: near at hand the dead yellow rock baked in the merciless heat of the forsaken valley, down which, in clear view, a lion stalked a stag. Off in the southern distance lay the plain of Zoar, Sodom, and Gomorrah, fit backdrop for this bitter temptation. To the north the hills of Moab behind the poisonous mists rising out of the Dead Sea; sand and gravel casting up heat; torrid air and vicious smells, desolation.

To Jesus was offered now all the beguilements and blandishments and cajoleries that have, since Eden, plagued the human race—uttered more often than not in quotations from the Scripture; Satan is a great repeater of God's words.

Why not abandon his great mission to help the suffering people? Why not think, instead, of himself? After all, did the Son of God have to go on with this unnecessary farce? He who had the power to bring a feast ready to hand if he but gave the word! And another thing—why remain a lonely, obscure man, a carpenter about to turn wayside preacher? If the miraculous signs of his birth were to be trusted, then he had the power of God, and all the world would have to serve him, and he would know such titanesque glory as no conqueror in history had ever known—not Darius, not Alexander, not Caesar. All mankind would adore Him. Why not?

His answer he drew from Scriptures of long ago: "The Lord, your God, shall you adore and Him only you shall serve—not in bread alone does man live, but in every word that proceeds out of the mouth of God. Get you behind me, Satan!"

In his deliberately weakened condition evil had not been easy to resist. No temptation ever is. But now Jesus, who in addition to being God was also a real man, had experienced the torments that come to men. And he had banished the temptations by the example of sheer devotion.

When the torturing forty days were over, a haggard Jesus walked slowly back toward the Jordan River. It was good to come out again from the hot region where John had spent most of his life; good to feel the bracing, invigorating wind blowing on his perspiring face as he trudged nearer to the river. Dates in his sunburned hands, he walked as he broke the long fast.

THE WILDERNESS

Up from the Jordan straight His way He took
To that lone wilderness, where rocks are hurled,
And strewn, and piled—as if the ancient world
In strong convulsions seethed and writhed and shook,
Which heaved the valleys up, and sunk each brook,
And flung the molten rock like ribbons curled
In midst of gray around the mountains whirled:—
A grim land, of a fierce, forbidding look.
The wild beasts haunt its barren stony heights,
And wilder visions came to tempt Him there;
For forty days and forty weary nights,
Alone He faced His mortal self and sin,
Chaos without, and chaos reigned within,
Subdued and conquered by the might of prayer.

CAROLINE HAZARD, 1856–1945

Immediately following the revelation of his identity, which climaxed his baptism by John, Jesus withdrew into the wilderness, where he was tempted by the devil. Paolo Veronese (1528–1588) combined the two events in one painting.

Even today the jumbled mass of barren mountains in the Sinai is as inhospitable as it was in the days of Moses.

The Desert: A Place of Testing and Renewal

Jesus' withdrawal into the wilderness for 40 days of fasting after his baptism takes on added significance in light of ancient Jewish traditions and beliefs about desolate landscapes. To the Old Testament prophets, the 40 years during which the Israelites wandered through the desert wilderness of Sinai was a time of purification for the nation's sins. It was then that God made a covenant with his chosen people and revealed the laws and statutes of their religion. Other Old Testament writers, however, point out that the followers of Moses committed several grave sins in the desert, including the worship of a golden calf, and that these transgressions symbolized the sins of all succeeding generations and burdened them with guilt. Set against these religious and historical views of the wilderness was the actual day-to-day experience of ancient Hebrews, whose frontier land was vulnerable to raids by marauding desert nomads. For more than a thousand years before Jesus' birth, the Israelites needed to be ever vigilant in order to protect their villages, towns, and farmlands. Wholesale destruction of settlements was not uncommon. In addition, the wilderness itself was frightening to the settled Israelites — an "evil place," a land of "drought and deep darkness." It was a place where no one dwelled and intruders risked debilitating thirst, starvation, and the predations of wild beasts. Finally, on the supernatural level, the desert was thought to be the home of demons and evil spirits.

Perhaps for all of these reasons, religious mystics and others who wished to escape the distractions of civilization would sometimes go to the wilderness for seclusion, meditation, repentance, and renewal. There, although a solitary thinker faced dangers both natural and supernatural, he could also place himself closer to the Supreme Being. It was from a mountain in Sinai, for example, that God spoke to Moses. As for Jesus, his temptation by the devil was in keeping with the Jewish belief that one's faith in God can be proved by a test or trial of some kind. Possibly, it was the desert mountain near Jericho known as Djebel Quarantal, or "Mountain of the 40 Days," that Jesus climbed for his own retreat. From that dry, chalk-white peak, he would have overlooked the kind of desolation sought by mystics and ascetics throughout Jewish history.

TESTING THE STRENGTH OF AN UNCONQUERABLE WILL

Jesus' spiritual relationship to John, his motive for retreating to the desert following his baptism, and what was accomplished by the testing there are all probed in this selection from Jean Steinmann's A LIFE OF JESUS.

BY RECEIVING BAPTISM in the Jordan, Jesus had become a member of John's community. But John did not maintain among his friends that iron discipline which flourished among the Essenes; he thought of himself neither as a lawgiver nor as a Messiah. His spiritual family was a free association of those who awaited the imminent coming of God's Kingdom. By demanding baptism, Jesus had recognized the divine and inspired nature of the ceremony which John performed; and when he left the banks of the Jordan he did so with the same freedom the prophet allowed all his followers.

Never was Jesus to waver in his admiration and respect for John. He went so far as to declare him the greatest of the prophets, and to attribute the powers of the resurrected Elijah to him. He was to make baptism the ritual which specifically symbolized entry into the Kingdom. The word of John was a condensed summing-up of what the prophets had declared; and John's rite of baptism embodied, indeed transcended, all the virtues contained in other biblical ceremonies. Jesus saw more in it than a preparation for the Kingdom. It was indeed an act of enthronement, since in Jesus the Kingdom had found its King. As John had declared, this King was now living on earth. But how was he to make himself manifest? What laws would govern this new Kingdom of God? How were its ministers and their powers to be determined?

Faced with this Messianic mission, Jesus felt the need for a period of absolute solitude and retreat so that, by prayer and contemplation, he could achieve a condition of union and communication with God. The desert was the ideal setting for his task. During the day its sands were seared and scorched by a heat so oppressive that it seemed to annihilate every flicker of life: in this empty wilderness a man could feel himself lost indeed. The nights, on the other hand, were often icy-cold, and haunted by jackals prowling about in search of carrion. Under a full moon, the horizon was a faint silhouette of rock formations: the effect

Jesus dismisses the devil's order to turn stones into bread. A 15th-century German artist included a background scene in which Jesus admonishes the Samaritan woman at the well.

was uncanny, like the landscape of some dead star or deserted planet.

Jesus stayed there forty days and forty nights, fasting. By this act of self-deprivation he proposed to test the absolute quality of his mastery over himself, the strength of his unconquerable will. So long a fast gives the mind supranormal clarity, frees the body from its enslavement to the things of this life, and draws forth the soul from that cloudy opacity which is its normal condition. And now a grim struggle awaited Jesus, to be fought out under a blazing sun, by the Jordan's chalky cliffs, in the stony lifeless world of the desert.

All the great mystics assume the existence of certain intangible forces which strive to prevent God's ultimate victory. The Jews had a name for this spiritual enemy of God: they called him Satan.

Jesus never told his disciples that he saw Satan in human guise; it was only a voice that tempted him. "If thou be the Son of God," it said, "command that these stones be made bread." Here was the lure of mi-

raculous power, the dream of exercising control over the created world. To know that you, and you alone, were endowed with the power of reproducing the miracle of the manna in the wilderness, and thus, by a word and a gesture, of bringing nourishment to starving millions—would not that be a greater miracle still? It would mean the immediate realization here on earth of those words in the Lord's Prayer: "Give us this day our daily bread."

No need to wait for God's grudging bounty, harvest after slow harvest; all could now be had at will, and immediately. For Jesus himself this miraculous ability to transmute matter would mean the inauguration of the Kingdom, there and then, in the wilderness. With this bread, which one day would become the symbol of his Body and that Body's Presence, he could assuage his pressing hunger. Moreover, by transforming these loaf-shaped stones into real bread, he would cease to be the "Lamb of God," the Lamb whose blood must be spilt, who was doomed to be sacrificed and devoured. Instead he himself would become the devourer, the Lion of God, the Lion of Judah, the King whose coming every village awaited, the Messiah who would forge the Jews into a powerful, satisfied, well-fed nation—a horde, in other words, of splendid, and splendidly glutted, human animals.

But Jesus countered this temptation with a text from Deuteronomy: "It is written, 'Man shall not live by bread alone, but by every word that proceedeth out of the mouth of God.' "

Jesus resumed his trancelike meditation, and once again the voice of Evil assailed him, reinforced on this occasion by a most grand and resplendent vision.

The temple of Jerusalem was built on the ancient threshing floor of Araunah. Its southeast ramparts rose high above the Cedron Valley, a ravine used by the Jews as a burial ground. In his dream Jesus saw himself standing on the topmost point of these ramparts, the so-called pinnacle of the temple, which rose nearly five hundred feet above the Cedron gorge. From here he would have had a magnificent bird's-eye view of the crowded outer court before the sanctuary. To the south he could see the palace of the high priests, and to the west that of the Hasmonean kings. Northward lay the Antonia fortress. "If thou be the Son of God, cast thyself down: for it is written, 'He shall give his angels charge concerning thee: and in their hands they shall bear thee up, lest at any time thou dash thy foot against a stone.' " Satan's quotation from the Psalms was intended to make Jesus fulfill the popular dream of a Messiah.

If Jesus agreed to appear in this manner, as the heaven-sent leader, he would certainly be acclaimed by the crowds who haunted the streets of the Old City beneath the pinnacle; while the priests would acknowledge him as the Messiah, thus making their long-hoped-for revolt a fact. He would drive out the Romans. With his power behind it, the Jewish national army would wipe out the occupying legions. He would subdue Rome and rule an empire from the throne of the Caesars.

But Jesus was ready with another biblical quotation, once again from Deuteronomy. "It is written again," he declared, " 'Thou shalt not tempt the Lord thy God.' " God's hand was not to be forced, as the Israelites in the wilderness tried to do at the time of Moses. When the Messiah appeared for the last time there would be a sign from heaven. This Jesus knew.

Then the vision slid into fantasy. Jesus saw himself on the summit of a lofty mountain from where he could see "all the kingdoms of the world, and the glory of them." This inexhaustible power Satan now offered to place at his disposal, for the benefit of the Jewish race as a whole—on condition, naturally, that Jesus accepted the rules which such authority implied. The moral standard he would henceforth have to rec-

ognize would no longer be divine charity, but human power, a ruler's might. He must bow down and worship force, obey the aggressive instincts by which all great expansionist empires had been carved out. Then he would know the grandiose destiny of a Sargon, an Alexander, a Caesar. War and diplomacy would become his instruments of government. His empire would not be eternal, but in after time children would learn his name as the most fabulous conqueror the world had ever seen, the unknown, lowly Jew who triumphantly overthrew Tiberius.

Confronted by this dream of Jewish Messianism, Jesus replied: "Get thee hence, Satan: for it is written, 'Thou shalt worship the Lord thy God, and him only shalt thou serve.' " At once he was freed from his demonic obsession. He had rejected the power that did not derive from God. The Kingdom now at hand would be a spiritual regime, nothing to do with politicians in Jerusalem or the Emperors of Rome.

Adam, the first man, had been tempted in the Garden of Eden, and had succumbed. The second Adam, the first man of a new dispensation on earth, had been tempted in the wilderness—that garden which had been blasted and made desert by the curse upon his predecessor—and had triumphed over temptation. His victory became that of all humanity, since all humanity was embodied in him, as earlier it had been

The three temptations are depicted in a single panel from the 11th-century Codex Aureus of Echternach: a fearsome devil pointing to the stones he wants turned into bread; demanding that Jesus hurl himself from the pinnacle of the temple and summon angels to his rescue; and revealing the kingdoms that would be his if only Jesus would worship his demonic tempter.

embodied, to its own loss, in Adam, the first man.

But this was neither a simple nor a clear-cut victory. Jesus foresaw that everywhere, on the faces of princes and possessed idiots, rich and poor alike, he would find the same Satanic smile. As he made his way down the stony path that led to the Jordan, he knew he had a long and difficult struggle ahead of him; and this knowledge received prompt confirmation in the shape of the shattering news that John the Baptist had been arrested.

TEMPTATION

They took Him to a mountain-top to see
Where earth's fair kingdoms flung their golden net
To snare the feet and trick the souls of men.
With slimy craft and cynic guile they said:
If He but sees the glory and the pride,
The pomps and pleasures of this tinsel world,
He will forget His splendid futile dreams.
And so they took Him up and tempted Him.

They pointed far across their level earth,
East to the fabled empires of the Ind,
Whose rulers' power was as the power of gods,
Where caravans with tinkling camel-bells
Brought silks and perfumes, pearls and ivory,
And tribute from far humbled provinces;
South to the magic kingdom of the Nile,
To Nubia and Abyssinia,
Jungle and desert kingdoms, rude but rich
With slaves and gems and golden yellow sands;
Northward to barbarous lands but dimly seen,
Savage but surging with unmeasured strength;
West where Rome's empire sent her legions forth,
Conquering, building, ruling with wise force,
The mighty mother of an unborn brood
Of nations which should rise and rule the world.

All this they spread before Him, tempting Him,
And watched to see ambition light His eye,
The lust of power darken His bright face,
And avarice crook His hands to clutch the gold.

But from the mountain peak He raised His eyes,
And saw the deep, calm sky, the stars, and God.

WINFRED ERNEST GARRISON, 1874–1969

Eyes closed in prayer, Jesus is borne aloft to the pinnacle of the temple by a huge, ethereal devil. The watercolor painting is one of 300 scenes of the life of Jesus executed by French artist James Joseph Jacques Tissot following a visit to Palestine in 1887.

The next day again John was standing with two of his disciples; and he looked at Jesus as he walked, and said, "Behold, the Lamb of God!" The two disciples heard him say this, and they followed Jesus.

JOHN 1:35–37

MAKING THEM FISHERS OF MEN

According to the Gospel of John, the first two to be drawn to the newly baptized carpenter of Nazareth were originally followers of John the Baptist. François Mauriac, in his LIFE OF JESUS, described the attraction to Jesus as a spreading fire.

ONE OF THE TWO WAS ANDREW, the brother of Simon; the other was John, son of Zebedee. What did Jesus do to keep them? "Jesus turning round and seeing that they followed him, saith to them, 'What seek ye?' They said to him, 'Rabbi . . . where abidest thou?' He saith to them, 'Come, and ye shall see.' They went therefore and saw where he abode, and they abode with him that day."

What passed between them at that first meeting, in the dawn of Bethany, was the secret of a more than human love, love inexpressible. Already the lighted fire was catching from tree to tree, from soul to soul. Andrew told his brother that he had found the Christ, and brought Simon back to the desert with him.

The next day the conflagration spread, reached Philip, a native of Bethsaida, as were Andrew and Peter. The words and acts which attached him to Christ are not known to us. But the flame spread from Philip to Nathanael. This new tree did not take fire at once, for Nathanael was versed in the Scriptures and protested that nothing good could come out of Nazareth. His friend answered simply: "Come and see."

Was it enough for each of these chosen souls to see Jesus in order to recognize him? No, Jesus gave each a sign; and the sign he gave Nathanael was the same he was soon to use to convince the woman of Samaria. "Whence dost thou know me?" Nathanael had asked in a distrustful tone. "Before Philip called thee, when

Simon leaves his fishing to answer Jesus' call in this detail from a painting by Hans von Kulmbach (c. 1480–1522).

thou wast under the fig tree, I saw thee." Nathanael at once replied: "Thou art the Son of God."

During his mortal life Christ was prodigal of that sign which caused many a simple being to fall with his face against the earth. He replied even to the most secret thoughts of the scribes and the Pharisees; but they, far from striking their breasts, saw therein but a ruse of Beelzebub. The faith of the humble Nathanael surprised Christ more than their incredulity, and we may imagine his smile as he said: "Because I said to thee, 'I saw thee under the fig tree,' thou believest. Greater things than these shalt thou see."

Perhaps when this encounter with Nathanael took place, Jesus had already left the desert, where during forty days he had fasted and suffered the attacks of the Prince of Evil. Going up the Jordan, he had reached the Lake of Tiberias and the native country of the disciples who had left John to follow him. Not that the hour of total abandon had as yet sounded for them. They had had only the first call.

At Capernaum, his grip on them loosened for a little while; but they would never escape him again. Jesus, passing along the shores of the lake and seeing his friends cast down their nets, had need of only the words, "Come, follow me and I will make you fishers of men," for them, without so much as a turn of the head, to leave all and follow him. However, it was not without his having given them a new sign of his power, chosen from among all those which might most surely strike these simple minds.

He had first borrowed their boat in order to escape the people who pressed too closely upon him. Simon had rowed out a little way, and Jesus, seated in the stern, spoke to the multitude grouped about the water's edge, to a multitude in which feeling ran high, for already there was great division of opinion concerning him. In Nazareth, when he spoke in the synagogue, his commentaries on the prophets irritated the people who had known him from his earliest years. To them the carpenter Yeshua was of little importance, despite

the cures which were beginning to be laid at his door. Their irritation had reached its height when he had let them understand that the Gentiles would be preferred to them, and it was only by a miracle he had escaped their fury.

Now he no longer risked being alone: here he was in the boat with Simon and the sons of Zebedee. Since that day along the Jordan these boatmen had seen with their own eyes the miracle of Cana and Jesus' curing Simon's mother-in-law of fever. It remained for him to touch them in that which counted for most: to catch as many fish as they wished.

They had worked all that night without catching anything. And now Simon had to call James and John to his help to draw in the nets. The two boats were so full of fish they were almost sinking. Then Kephas fell to his knees. "Depart from me, for I am a sinful man, O Lord." Jesus' answer, like many of his words, contained a prophesy which we are still seeing fulfilled before our eyes: "Henceforth thou shalt catch men."

According to the Gospels of Matthew and Mark, Jesus encountered Simon and his brother Andrew as they were casting their nets in the Sea of Galilee, an event shown in the left background of Domenico Ghirlandaio's 15th-century painting. At center, the two disciples appear as elderly saints, while a third scene— perhaps the calling of James and John—is in the right background.

A medieval artist incorporated three sequential events from the life of Jesus in the letter "I" that he drew for an illuminated manuscript: the baptism (top), temptation (center), and calling of the disciples (bottom).

The next day Jesus decided to go to Galilee. And he found Philip and said to him, "Follow me.". . . Philip found Nathanael, and said to him, "We have found him of whom Moses in the law and also the prophets wrote . . ."

JOHN 1:43, 45

WHAT GOOD CAN COME FROM NAZARETH?

An early recruit to Jesus' entourage was Nathanael, thought by some to be the same person elsewhere called Bartholomew, one of the 12 apostles. In PECULIAR TREASURES, a witty who's who in the Bible, Frederick Buechner uses contemporary language to bring the elusive disciple to life.

HILIP COULD HARDLY WAIT to tell somebody, and the first person he found was Nathanael. Ever since Moses they'd been saying the Messiah was just around the corner, and now he had finally turned up. Who would have guessed where? Who would have guessed who?

"Jesus of Nazareth," Philip said. "The son of Joseph." But he could hear his words fall flat.

"Can anything good come out of Nazareth?" Nathanael said.

Philip told him to come take a look for himself then, but Jesus got a look at Nathanael first as he came puffing down the road toward him, near-sighted and earnest, no doubt with his yarmulke on crooked, his dog-eared Torah under his arm.

"Behold, an Israelite indeed, in whom is no guile," Jesus said. Nathanael's jaw hung open. He said, "How do you know me?"

"Before Philip called you," Jesus said. "When you were under the fig tree, I saw you."

It was all it took apparently. "Rabbi!" Nathanael's jacket was too tight across the shoulders and you could hear a seam split somewhere as he made an impossible bow. "You are the Son of God," he said. "You are the king of Israel."

"Because I said I saw you under the fig tree, do you believe?" Jesus said. There was more to it than parlor tricks. He said, "You shall see greater things than these." But all Nathanael could see for the moment, not daring to look up, were his own two feet.

"You will see heaven opened," he heard Jesus say, "the angels of God ascending and descending upon the Son of Man." When Nathanael decided to risk a glance, the sun almost blinded him.

What Nathanael did see finally was this. It was months later, years—after the Crucifixion of Jesus. One evening he and Peter and a few of the others took the boat out fishing. They didn't get a nibble between them but stuck it out all night. It was something to do anyway. It passed the time. Just at dawn, in that queer half-light, somebody showed up on the beach and cupped his mouth with his hands. "Any luck?" The answer was No. Then give it another try, the man said. Reel in the nets and cast them off the port beam this time. There was nothing to lose they hadn't lost already, so they did it, and the catch had to be seen to be believed, had to be felt, the heft of it almost swamping them as they pulled it aboard.

Peter saw who the man was first and heaved himself overboard. The water was chest-high as he plowed through it, tripping over his feet in the shallows so he ended up scrambling ashore on all fours. Jesus was standing there waiting for him by a little charcoal fire he had going. Nathanael and the others came ashore, slowly, like men in a dream, not daring to speak for fear they'd wake up. Jesus got them to bring him some of their fish, and then they stood around at a little distance while he did the cooking. When it was done, he gave them the word. "Come and have breakfast," he said, and they sat down beside him in the sand.

Nathanael's name doesn't appear in any of the lists of the twelve apostles, but there are many who claim he was known as Bartholomew, and that name does appear there. It would be nice to think so. On the other hand, he probably considered it honor enough just to have been on hand that morning at the beach, especially considering the unfortunate remark he'd made long ago about Nazareth.

They sat there around the fire eating their fish with the sun coming up over the water behind them, and they were all so hushed and glad and peaceful that anybody passing by would never have guessed that, not long before, their host had been nailed up on a hill outside the city and left there to die without a friend to his name.

ON THE ROAD

For road-mates and companions he chose twelve,
—All, like himself, of homeliest degree,
All toilers with their hands for daily bread,
Who, at his word, left all and followed him.

He told them of The Kingdom and its laws,
And fired their souls with zeal for it and him.

He taught a new sweet simple rule of Right
'Twixt man and God, and so 'twixt man and man,—
That men should first love God and serve Him well,
Then love and serve their neighbours as themselves.

They loved him for his gentle manliness,
His forthright speech, his wondrous winning ways,
His wisdom, and his perfect fearlessness,
And for that something more they found in him
As in no other.

For through the mortal the immortal shone—
A radiant light which burned so bright within
That nought could hide it. Every word and look,
And a sweet graciousness in all he did,
Proclaimed him something measurelessly more
Than earth had ever seen in man before,
And with him virtue went and holy power. . . .

Through all the land he journeyed, telling forth
The gracious message of God's love for man,—
That God's great heart was very sore for man,
Was hungering and thirsting after man,
As one whose dearly loved have gone astray,
As one whose children have deserted him.

The people heard him gladly, flocking round
To catch his words, still more to see his deeds,
The men all hopeful, and the women touched
By this new message and the messenger;
And everywhere the children drew to him
And found in him a sweet new comradeship.

Strange was his teaching, stranger still his deeds;—
He healed the sick and gave the blind their sight,
With his own hands cleansed lepers of their sores,
And raised the dead,—all in the name of God,
And for the love God's great heart held for them. . . .

JOHN OXENHAM, 1852–1941

In the silkscreen print at left by the contemporary Japanese artist Sadao Watanabe, the newly recruited disciples link hands with Jesus and are surrounded by a cloud of swarming fish. In Luke's Gospel, Jesus manifested his power by rewarding the unsuccessful fishermen with a miraculous catch of fish; the mosaic below, from the sixth-century basilica of San Apollinare Nuovo in Ravenna, Italy, includes the bursting net.

ARE YOUR SHOULDERS STRONG ENOUGH?

*Because the names Peter and Andrew are of Greek
origin, some scholars have speculated that they
were descended from the soldiers Alexander the Great led
through the area in the fourth century B.C. In the
following selection from* THE LORD JESUS, *Robert Payne
uses the Greek spelling of their names.*

THERE WAS ONLY A FAINT golden shimmering left in the air when Andreas thought he saw someone walking through a tamarisk grove along the shore. It seemed to be a man leading a donkey, but the donkey vanished, and soon there was only the fluttering of a ghostly white gown in the darkness. They were perhaps a hundred yards from the shore. The light faded, and the ghostly stranger vanished only to reappear further along the shore, where a solitary tamarisk tree shone against a patch of sky.

There came a voice over the lake, clear as a bell, but faint. "Come to me! Come to me!"

"He may be ill," Andreas suggested anxiously. "Or he may be a stranger who has lost his way."

"Or he may be a bandit," Petros commented.

It was very dark, for there was no moon and the stars were obscured by a floating mist. Petros dipped the oars lightly, making almost no noise. He rowed directly towards the dark spit of land with its solitary tamarisk tree, and once again they heard the voice coming over the waters. When they came close to the shore, Andreas held up a lantern.

He could see nothing: only the solitary tamarisk

The Significance of 12

In the opinion of many scholars, numbers in the Bible are not always meant to be taken literally. Often, they are rounded off or exaggerated for dramatic effect. The number 40, for example — the round number used most often throughout the Scriptures — is usually meant to represent an inexact but fairly long period of time. More important, however, numbers are frequently used as sacred symbols. The number 12 is especially significant: Jesus had 12 apostles and there were 12 tribes of Israel and 12 minor prophets.

The mystical aura surrounding the number 12 is of ancient origin. Long before biblical times, in China and in Sumer, the night sky was divided into the 12 signs of the zodiac. The Sumerian and Babylonian numerical systems were based on 12 rather than 10, the base of our decimal system today. Many ancient cultures divided the year into 12 months and the day into 12 hours. In addition, the number 12 itself combines other sacred numbers: It is the sum of 5 plus 7, and the product of 3 times 4. The Old Testament uses multiples of 12, as in the 24 classes of Levites and priests or the 24,000 servants assigned to King David. In the visions of Revelation, the number 12 abounds. The servants of God number 144,000, 12,000 from each of the 12 tribes. The new Jerusalem has 12 jeweled foundations and 12 gates of pearl, and in its center stands the tree of life, bearing 12 kinds of fruit for the healing of the nations.

*The 12 apostles
decorate the cup of this
13th-century chalice.*

*In this sixth-century ivory plaque,
an enthroned Jesus is surrounded by the 12
he chose as his inner circle of disciples.*

tree waving a little in the wind. "He has gone!" Andreas said in alarm, and he lowered the lantern.

"No, I am here—I am always here!" the voice said, and Andreas saw the man standing some distance away along the shore, almost at the very limit of the sulphurous yellow beam of the lantern.

The man came towards the boat. He was tall and well-built, and seemed to be holding his head a little to one side. He had a broad forehead, large deepset eyes, and a long nose. When he came closer Andreas saw that his beard and hair, which was parted in the middle and fell to his shoulders, were harvest-red, and his cheeks too were ruddy. He walked with extraordinary grace and authority, his spotless white gown pressed against his flesh by the wind.

When the stranger was some twenty paces from the boat, walking along the edge of the lake, Andreas called out: "Who are you?"

"I am Jesus," the man said, "and I come from Nazareth—and from Heaven."

For a few moments the man was silent. The tamarisks rustled in the wind, and there came to them the cry of distant wildfowl.

"I make you my companions for everlasting," the man said at last. "You are my chosen ones. The days of the earth are numbered, and the Kingdom of Heaven is at hand! Flames shall destroy the earth, the heavens will open out, and we shall see God in majesty on his white throne above the clouds! And you—you who are fishermen of the lake—you shall catch men alive, and bring them to Heaven for my sake!"

As Andreas listened to the voice, the silence and darkness of the lake thickened all round him. He was not on the lake; he was wheeling through the darkness of the night, and in all the universe there was only the face of a man lit by lantern-light.

"But our fishing, master?" Andreas murmured. "Shall we not fish any more? Shall we put our nets aside? Shall we let the poor people starve?"

Jesus answered: "Shall a man go hungry into the Kingdom of God? Nay, God has given the fish out of his bounty, and I, too, am given to men out of the bounty of God. See, I shall make you fishers of men and fishers of fish, until the time is fulfilled when there will be no more fishing."

He said the last words with a smile, lowering his voice, and then he beckoned to Petros and said: "I am the Son of God, and you are chosen by God, and therefore all the universe will weigh heavily on your

shoulders. Are your shoulders strong enough to bear the weight of the heavens?"

"They are the strongest shoulders to be found anywhere," Petros said proudly. "I can carry a fishing boat on them."

"And the heavens—could you carry the heavens on them?"

"The heavens are easier to carry than a fishing boat," Petros said stubbornly. He was still observing Jesus critically, standing a little away.

"Yes," Jesus said, "you shall be my fisherman for everlasting. To you shall be given the keys to the Kingdom of Heaven."

All this happened very quietly. No voices were raised. It was as though it had been decided long ago.

Among those Jesus summoned to be his disciples was the tax collector Matthew (called Levi by Mark and Luke). In this evocative canvas by Michelangelo da Caravaggio (c.1571–1610), the startled publican (as tax collectors were once called) points to himself in disbelief as Jesus beckons from far right.

There was a
marriage at Cana
in Galilee, and
the mother of Jesus
was there; Jesus
also was invited to
the marriage,
with his disciples.
When the wine
failed, the mother
of Jesus said to
him, "They have
no wine."

JOHN 2:1–3

Although he protested
that his "hour had not
yet come," Jesus acceded
to his mother's promptings
and performed his first
miracle, turning water
into wine at the wedding
feast at Cana. In
this early-16th-century
Flemish painting, Mary
fondly gazes at Jesus
as he directs the servant
to pour water into
empty jars.

ON THE EVE OF THE FIRST MIRACLE: A SACRED FIRE BURNING WITHIN

Following his baptism, Jesus returned to Galilee to gather his first disciples. In the novel ACCORDING TO THOMAS, *Ivan Nazhivin imagines Jesus at home in Nazareth—awaiting the moment to take up his mission. The author uses the Hebrew names Jeshua and Miriam for Jesus and Mary.*

EVERY TIME THAT JESHUA came back to visit Galilee, he had a feeling of relief, even of happiness. Judea, with its sun-scorched hills where life seemed withered and parched with suffering, lay behind him; and here he was surrounded by the wooded hills of his childhood, by the villages with their simple, hardworking population, by luxuriant gardens and vineyards.

But in spite of the extraordinary richness of nature and the diligence of the inhabitants, life here was far from being a Paradise. Taxation brought the people to the very limit of endurance: the Romans raised levies, the tetrarch Herod took enormous sums from them, the rulers of the temple demanded supplementary taxes, and the landlords skinned the peasantry. But nevertheless it was a great relief to come to Galilee, if only because here there were no haughty Sadducees, no Pharisees perpetually flying into raging passions, and no Romans with their heavy armor. The Galileans were pious and extremely superstitious, and were treated with contempt by the intellectuals of Jerusalem whenever they made their appearance in the city for the great festivals. They were accustomed to hearing themselves called blockheads, and their way of speaking brought endless ridicule.

Nazareth was then a small quiet town of some three or four thousand inhabitants. Its wretched clay-built houses, its tiny gardens, its silent barns, and its winepresses hewn in the rocks, and the great storks' nests at the tops of hoary trees, made it seem more like a village than a town. Its inhabitants did not disdain either a beaker of wine or a good joke or a merry song, and for that reason the scribes looked down with contempt on this frivolous people: they would say with a sneer—"Can anything good come out of Nazareth?"

The women with their washtubs were gathered as usual round the well under the venerable plane trees. Their faces were covered, as custom demanded, but

In a late-15th-century German woodcut, Mary—tapping at her empty beaker—stands behind Jesus as he blesses the water.

light and warmth lay in their beautiful dark eyes. Jeshua called a friendly greeting as he passed, and went on to his house, which lay hidden among fig trees and pear trees and clambering vines whose grapes were already filled with precious juice.

From the far side of the house, in the shadow of the trees, came the sound of planing. There one of the brothers was at work. "Shelom!" Jeshua greeted him.

His brother Jacob, working at the planing-bench, looked up. "Shelom!" he answered without a smile. He always thought that Jeshua, the eldest of them, abused his position and did too little work.

They had hardly exchanged a dozen words when their mother, Miriam, came out from the barn. She was now thin and faded, and her great black eyes were filled with sadness.

A wan smile lit up Miriam's face as she saw her son. She asked him about his affairs, what he was proposing to do, and how he was. Yet she felt that they had

really nothing to say to each other. Jeshua was a fragment that had been broken off; he lived in a world of his own, a world which seemed to the other members of the family to be not only inaccessible but even to some extent hostile.

Neighbors passed by and greeted Jeshua cheerfully over the low stone fence; many even stopped and exchanged a few words with him. But they too tended to regard him as a sheep that had broken away from the Nazareth flock. And when from time to time he spoke in their synagogue, they did not pay much attention to what he said—it would have been better if he had stuck to his own business; and now he wanted to teach them all. But people were talking about him, and so they called him "Rabbi"—sometimes in jest, but sometimes also in earnest.

After the humble meal, eaten in silence in the yard where everyone could see them, Jeshua went up to the

Mary, two haloed disciples, and other guests watch intently as Jesus blesses the water, which the servants then draw out as wine. The scene is from the celebrated altarpiece Duccio di Buoninsegna painted for the cathedral of Siena, Italy, between 1308 and 1311.

roof, anticipating a delicious sleep after such a long journey. A cool and gentle breeze was blowing as it always did in Galilee. The stars shone over his head. In the distant mountains he could hear the howling of jackals. Bats were circling over the flat roofs and the dark gardens, whistling softly, disappearing into the darkness and then returning, passing swiftly hither and thither. Everything was still and peaceful.

He fell asleep as the cocks crowed for the third time in the stillness of the night. But hardly had the East begun to redden beyond the mountains when Jeshua was up again, filled with a new readiness for life. And he felt an impulse now to take up the yoke of that peaceful hardworking life which he had led there as a child and which the Galileans around him were still living. After he had prayed, he came down into the house, turned back his sleeves, tied a string round his hair to prevent it from getting in his way while he was working, and then took up the saw, full of eagerness for work.

Those days of simple, quiet labor and nights of reflection, of exaltation, of struggle, passed without a break. He felt loneliness in these thoughts of his, a spiritual isolation. His firm determination to come forward among the people with the word of salvation was often weakened by anxious doubts. He felt the sacred fire burning within him; he heard the trumpets of the angels summoning him to battle. But how and where was he to begin? Who would listen to him, to an insignificant Galilean?

And now more frequently than in the past there would come into his mind those passages in the ancient writings which speak of the suffering and death of the one who was to make known the truth. There was particularly the well-known passage in Isaiah, where the prophet speaks—in mysterious words of sadness, which at the same time are filled with the promise of eternal happiness—of the "man of sorrows," the unknown, the despised and persecuted, the man, however, who through his fearlessly borne sufferings would win the right to set up the kingdom of truth and justice. This man is the servant of the eternal, the man who without fear will face destruction in order that he may bring happiness to men. . . .

"Are you coming to Simeon's wedding tomorrow?" his mother asked in a sleepy voice from the corner where she was sitting. "You must come."

"I will come," Jeshua answered, tearing himself away from Isaiah.

WATER INTO WINE

The festivities surrounding a Hebrew wedding in the time of Jesus would have required an abundant supply of wine and food for the guests. In this story from FAR ABOVE RUBIES, *Alice Sligh Turnbull imagines the hosts' panic as the wine supply ran out.*

ELIZABETH ROSE AND DRESSED CAREFULLY that morning. Soon would come the ceremonious entrance of the messengers from her betrothed, Philip, bearing her bridal dress and ornaments and the ointment and perfumes.

There was no breakfast to make, for she must fast until evening. But there were the prayers of atonement with which her mind must be occupied most of the day. She knelt facing Jerusalem and recited softly the solemn, stately words of the confession. When the messengers arrived, she spread the bridal gown with all its expensive ornaments upon the bed and smiled tenderly at Philip's extravagance.

In the early evening, while the neighbors swarmed about the rooms, trying to be helpful, Elizabeth stood before her mirror and let down her long black hair until it fell about her shoulders as a maiden bride's must hang. They helped her into her bridal dress, exclaiming at its beauty. With her own hands Elizabeth adjusted the attire about her waist and raised a crown of fresh myrtle leaves to her head. Then over all was thrown the long white veil of betrothal that would not be raised until Philip's own hands lifted it in the hush of the bridal chamber. Elizabeth was ready.

The early dusk had grown swiftly to darkness. The young girls who had been running in and out were gone hastily to their own homes to don their last bit of finery for the procession.

A shout came from the doorway. "Here they come! Look! Thou canst see the torches! And the flutes! Dost thou hear them? Oh, it will be a great procession. Call Elizabeth. Tell her they have started!"

The sounds came clearly through the night. Philip and his groomsmen were on their way to her. The neighbors were all thronging the streets. The maidens were waiting, ready to circle about her when she emerged from the house. All at once the shouting increased deafeningly. The torches again became a confused glare. They had reached her house. Elizabeth felt herself conducted through lines of laughing, bow-

Three episodes in the wedding feast story appear in this 11th-century ivory plaque: Jesus being greeted upon arrival (upper left); the servants approaching with empty beakers (upper right); and Jesus blessing the water at Mary's behest (bottom).

ing men and women on to the doorway, where Philip met her and drew her inside.

He led her proudly to the room reserved for the women and seated her on the soft-rug-covered dais prepared for her. The other women and maidens who were invited to the house crowded in and found seats on the floor and cushioned ledges. Through the door which led into the room where the feast was spread for the men, and where the singing and dancing would take place, Elizabeth could see the women who were to serve carrying food to the table and chatting importantly to each other as they worked. She watched the form of Mary of Nazareth as she came and went. So gentle in her movements, so quiet of speech, so tender and smiling as she looked upon the group that clustered round the bridegroom.

Then her servant Terenth came in with refreshments for the women. "There are many strangers," she commented, excitedly. "Four men are sitting with Nathanael, and he keeps calling one of them Rabbi. He is Mary's son from Nazareth, but I didn't know he was a rabbi! Philip's father is so excited. We can't bring things in fast enough to please him. He is mightily lavish with the wine. Philip will have to go clear to the new vineyards for more for tomorrow night. Thou shouldst see how the guests eat!"

She ran out, laughing, but it seemed only a moment until she was back with blanched face. "*The wine is gone!*" she gasped. "There isn't another drop and the feast but barely begun! We thought there were two more vats of it and they are empty! What can we do?"

At the first words Elizabeth had started in surprise. Now she sat tense with hands gripped together. No more wine! The feast begun in riotous plenty was to end in poverty and disgrace. "Tell Mary of Nazareth!" she whispered. "She is always calm and wise. She will know *how* to tell the steward of the feast when it has to be known."

When Terenth had rushed away and the chatter of awed comment and criticism and speculation was in full flow about her, Elizabeth sat speechless and stunned behind her veil.

This was no small calamity that was about to fall

An artist known only as the Master of the Catholic Kings (Spanish monarchs Ferdinand and Isabella) painted the solemn wedding feast at left.

upon them. It was a lifelong disgrace for Philip and his father. Never again could they hold up their heads in the village. No matter whose mistake it had been, the burden of reproach would rest upon them. And no one would ever let them forget it. This flagrant breach of hospitality, this unprecedented failure to make good the promise of their lavish invitations. No apology could be offered or accepted. There would be only the ugly fact to speak for itself. There would be a little while of forced merriment and then the guests would go. And Philip and his father would be left amid the ruins of the feast and the bitterness of their disgrace.

Suddenly she noticed that the women and maidens had stopped talking. A silence had fallen upon the feast-room, too. Elizabeth caught her breath. Someone must be telling Philip and his father now. For a long second the strange hush lasted. And then everything was as it had been before. The talking, the laughter, the women running to and fro with their platters and pitchers. And high above the other voices rose the strong tones of the steward.

"How is this, Philip?" he was demanding. "Every man when he maketh a feast doth first serve the good wine, and then when men have well drunk, he serveth that which is worse. But thou hast kept the *good* wine until now!"

The steward sounded well pleased. Then Philip replied, his voice vibrant with pride and joy: "But, steward, is the best not worth waiting for always?"

Then overwhelmingly rose the shouts: "To the bridegroom! Fill your cups and drink again to the bridegroom! Joy to Philip and his bride!"

One of the maidens leaned cautiously toward the door of the feast-room. "They *have* wine! They are drinking it now. Terenth is silly and excitable. Alarming us for naught. Wait till she comes again! We shall teach her a lesson."

But Terenth was already there. "There has been a *miracle*! There is a man of God in this house!" Then, before the excited gasps of wonder had become coherent, Terenth went on: "*There was no wine.* Any of the other servants will tell you that. I did as Elizabeth bade me. I asked Mary of Nazareth to break the news to Philip and his father. I was just behind her as she entered the room. Instead of going to the end of the table she stopped beside her son. I heard her whisper to him: 'They have no wine'—only that. But she looked at him beseechingly. Her son looked grave for a moment and then he smiled a little and said in the

gentlest voice: 'Woman, what have I to do with thee? Mine hour is not yet come.' But she smiled back at him and touched his shoulder—they must love each other deeply, those two—and signed to a servant. 'Do whatever he telleth thee,' she said.

"Then this Jesus told the servant to fill the six big water-jars in the hallway full of water. When it was done he said quietly: 'Draw out now and bear to the steward of the feast!'

"And as we drew, *the water was changed to wine!* They are drinking it now."

Elizabeth sat withdrawn, apart, trying to sense the awesome thing she had just heard. Under this roof, Philip's roof, which was now her home, that quiet guest in the other room had wrought a *miracle*! God was dwelling in this place.

The first miracle is depicted above on an ivory plaque from a sixth-century archbishop's throne (top) and a 16th-century French tapestry (bottom).

The ruins of a fourth-century A.D. synagogue at Capernaum

Synagogues in the Time of Jesus

The original Greek word synagogue means merely "a place of meeting," but in the Jewish world Jesus inhabited synagogues were second only to the temple in Jerusalem itself as religious institutions. In addition, they served as schools of religious instruction and communal halls for civic functions under the direction of a council of elders. Typically, a synagogue was a small structure built on a rise above the neighboring houses. Opposite the entrance, a portable ark contained the scrolls of the Law and the Prophets. In front of it, facing worshipers, were the "chief seats" for religious leaders. Men and women perhaps sat apart from each other in the congregation as they did in later times. For public worship, which was conducted on the sabbath, a minimum of 10 adult males had to be in attendance. The five-part service included prayers, psalm-singing, blessings, readings from the Scriptures, and commentaries on the sacred passages, but there were no sacrifices and no standard

liturgy. Although a rabbi might be recognized as the leader because of his distinguished teaching, there was no official clergy. In fact, any Jew who felt himself qualified could ask for permission to teach the Scriptures — as Jesus did at Nazareth. The first synagogues may have been built by Jews held captive far from the temple during the Babylonian Exile in the sixth century B.C., but synagogues were important religious and social institutions in the time of Jesus.

In more recent times, megillahs, the cylindrical containers for the scriptural scrolls read at synagogue services, became objects of beauty. This one of silver and gilt dates from the 18th century.

And he came to Nazareth, where he had been brought up; and he went to the synagogue, as his custom was, on the sabbath day. And he stood up to read; and there was given to him the book of the prophet Isaiah.

LUKE 4:16–17

A PROPHET WITHOUT HONOR IN HIS OWN COUNTRY

According to Luke, Jesus chose this solemn moment to announce his messianic mission, but his townsmen were unready to accept the revelation and turned in wrath against him. In his 1964 novel THE LORD JESUS, Robert Payne expands upon Luke's narrative to add a dramatic rescue by the apostles Matthew and Peter, to whom he gives the Greek names Matthay and Petros.

THERE WAS A DEATHLY SILENCE in the synagogue. They had expected the thunder of God; instead there was a tall, slight man with a red beard and heavily-lidded blue eyes gazing at them impassively, reserved and expressionless, seeming to have withdrawn into a proud and secret world of his own. And in a voice that was strangely cold he began to read the lesson for the day:

"*The Spirit of the Lord is upon me,*
Because he hath anointed me to preach
good news to the poor;
He hath sent me to heal the broken-hearted,
To preach deliverance to the captives,
And recovering of sight to the blind,
To set at liberty them that are bruised,
To preach the acceptable year of the Lord."

There was a silence when Jesus returned the scroll to the keeper of the books, but he did not sit down according to the custom of the synagogue. He remained standing, gazing quietly at the worshipers, and it was only after some moments, when the rabbi plucked him by the sleeve, that he took his place on the wooden bench beside the companions. All eyes were fastened on him. He had thought at first it was enough to read the passage from Isaiah, enough to be there, enough to withstand the silence that welled around him, his hands raised in a blessing, his eyes dark with suffering, for this was the moment when he assumed the heaviest responsibility of all, and he trembled at the thought of it. But it was not enough, and he rose again, with the light from an open window shining full on his face, and he said: "This day is the Scripture fulfilled in your ears!"

Someone shouted: "What is he saying? Is he saying he is the Messiah? Surely he is the son of Joseph!" And others shouted: "We brought our sick to him, and he has not healed them!"

Jesus said sternly: "I am He, of whom the Scripture speaks! Yet you tell me—do for us what you have done at Capharnaum, but how shall I do these things when there is no faith in me? I tell you of a truth there were many widows in Israel in the days of Elijah, when the heavens were covered over for three years and three months, when great famine was throughout the land, but Elijah did not go to them. He went only to Sarepta, a city of Sidon, to a woman who was a widow. And many lepers were in Israel in the time of Elisha the prophet, and none of them was cleansed save Naaman the Syrian, for the heathen were more faithful than the Jews!"

When he said this, a howl went up and the whole synagogue trembled with excitement. Who was he to praise the heathen? Why did he refuse to heal the people of Nazareth? This man, who looked like a prince, who spoke with a cutting edge to his voice, was too proud altogether. Away with him! Let him go to Gehenna! They began to shout and groan, and a moment later they rushed at him and dragged him out of the synagogue, amazed because he made no resistance and told his companions to remain silent.

It was a bright sunlit day with the dust trembling in the air when they led him through the narrow twisting streets and then out into the fields of the uplands and so to the Mountain of Horns, with its abrupt and precipitous cliffs. They threw a rope round his neck and dragged him as though he were a wild beast up the steep hill. Once, half way up the hill, they paused, pulled tightly on the rope, and said: "If thou art the Messiah, save thyself!" He answered: "It were better to save others." Some wanted him to be hurled head-long from the cliff and others, brandishing daggers, said it would be better to kill him while he was in their power, for the devil might give him wings. The

companions, led by Matthay and Petros, who were armed with clubs, hurled themselves into the crowd like a battering ram and carried Jesus off in triumph back to the synagogue where the sick, the blind and the lepers were still waiting for him. Later in the day he set out for Jerusalem. With him went two of the men he had healed from leprosy.

Some men from the synagogue followed him out of the town. From a safe distance they shouted: "He takes Greeks and lepers and a tax collector in the pay of Herod Antipas! No good can come from him."

American primitive artist Durs Rudy drew, colored, and lettered this scene of Jesus preaching to a rapt audience standing rigidly at attention; it dates from about 1810.

DROPPING PEARLS OF WISDOM IN PRODIGAL PROFUSION

And he went about all Galilee, teaching in their synagogues and preaching the gospel of the kingdom and healing every disease and every infirmity among the people. So his fame spread . . . . And great crowds followed him from Galilee and the Decapolis and Jerusalem and Judea and from beyond the Jordan.

MATTHEW 4:23–25

To remind late 19th-century readers that Jesus began his mission by preaching to the Jews, the English scholar Joseph Jacobs—himself a Jew—included the following tale in JESUS AS OTHERS SAW HIM. *Jacobs's work of fiction purports to be eyewitness accounts compiled in* A.D. 54. *In the following excerpt, a member of the Sanhedrin tells a Greek friend of the impression Jesus made when he appeared at a synagogue in Jerusalem.*

IT MUST HAVE BEEN A YEAR after I had first seen Jesus that I saw him again the second time in Jerusalem. It fell out in this wise: I was proceeding one morning to the meeting of the Sanhedrin, when, as I came near the Synagogue of the Galileans in the Fish-Market, I found a crowd of men entering in. I asked one of them what was going forward, and he said, "Jesus the Nazarene will expound the Law." So I determined to take the morning service in this synagogue rather than with my colleagues in the temple.

Now, this synagogue of the Galileans differed in naught from the rest of the synagogues of the Jews. In the wall at the west end was the cabinet containing the scrolls of the Law, with a curtain before it, for this is, as it were, the Holy of Holies of the synagogue. The men go up to this, on to the platform before it, by three steps. Then comes a vacant space, in the midst of which stands a dais, with a reading-desk whereon the Law is read. Then in the rest of the hall sit the folk, arranged in benches one after another.

Now, as I came in, they had said the morning psalms and most of the Eighteen Blessings, and shortly after the reading of the Law began. The curtain was drawn aside from the holy ark, the scroll of the Law was taken thence, to the singing of psalms, to the dais of the reading-desk. Then, as is customary, the messenger of the congregation summoned first to the reading of the Law a Cohen, a descendant of Aaron, one of the priestly caste. And after he had read some verses of the

Early Bibles taught with pictures like this one of Jesus in the synagogue.

Law in the holy tongue, the dragoman read its translation into Chaldee, so as to be understood by the unlearned folk, and by the women who were in the gallery outside the synagogue and separated from it by a grating. Then after the priest came a Levite, who also read some verses, and after him an ordinary Israelite. Then the messenger of the synagogue called out, "Let Rabbi Joshua ben Joseph arise."

Jesus the Nazarene went up to the reading-desk and read his appointed verses, and these were translated as before by the dragoman. And after the reading of the Law was concluded, the president of the congregation requested Jesus to read the *Haphtara*, the lesson from the prophets; and this he did, using the cantillation with which we chant words of Holy Scripture. Yet never heard I one whose voice so thrilled me and brought home to one the import of the great words; and this was strange, for his accent was, as I had before noticed, that of the Galilean peasantry, at which we of Jerusalem were wont to scoff. Then, after the Law had been returned to the ark with song and psalm, Jesus turned round to the people and began his discourse.

It is near five-and-twenty years since I heard him, and much have I forgotten in that long time. But many of his sayings still ring in my ears.

I cannot tell thee how deeply this discourse affected me. Just as the Greeks are eager to find each day some new beauty in man or the world, or some new truth about the relation of things, so we Hebrews rejoice in finding new ideals in the relations of men. Each of our sages prides himself on this—that he has said some maxim of wisdom that none had thought of before him, and so each of them is remembered in the minds of men by one or more of his favorite maxims. But it is rare if in a whole lifetime a sage sayeth more than one word fit to be treasured up among men. Yet was this man Jesus dropping pearls of wisdom from his mouth in prodigal profusion.

As each memorable word fell from his lips, a murmur of delighted surprise passed round the synagogue, and each man looked to his neighbor with brightened eyes. Some of the thoughts, indeed, I had heard from other of our sages but never in so pointed a form,

Two unknown 11th-century artists depicted Jesus reading from the book of Isaiah in the synagogue at Nazareth; the panel at left is from a Byzantine manuscript that once belonged to Eastern Roman Emperor Basil II and is now in the Vatican Library; the panel below is from the Codex Aureus of Echternach at the German National Museum in Nürnberg.

surely never in such profusion from a single sage.

And if what was said delighted us, the manner in which it was said entranced us still more. The voice of the speaker answered to the thoughts he expressed, as the lyre of David turned the wind into music. When he spoke of love, his voice was as the cooing dove; when he denounced the oppressor, it clanged like a silver trumpet. Indeed, his whole countenance and bearing changed in like manner, so that every word he uttered seemed to reflect his whole being.

But most of all it was the vividness of his eyes that impressed his words upon us. I had seen them flashing with scorn in the temple; I now saw them melting with tenderness in the synagogue. And there was this of strangeness in them, that they seemed to speak other and deeper words. As he gazed upon us, I felt as if all my inmost being was bare to the gaze of those eyes. They seemed to know all my secret thoughts and sins; and yet I felt not ashamed, for as they saw the sins, so they seemed to speak forgiveness of them.

A CHRONOLOGY OF JESUS' MINISTRY

The events of Jesus' ministry are listed below according to the sequence in the Gospel of Mark, generally considered the oldest of the four. Where Mark fails to include an incident, it is listed where scholars think it may have occurred—for example, Matthew alone tells of the Sermon on the Mount, which precedes the healing of the centurion's servant (an event not in Mark). John's Gospel, differing considerably from the other three, is the only one to include the first and last miracles: turning water into wine at Cana and the raising of Lazarus.

	Matthew	Mark	Luke	John
John baptizes Jesus	Then Jesus came from Galilee to the Jordan to John, to be baptized by him Matthew 3:13-17	In those days Jesus came from Nazareth of Galilee and was baptized by John in the Jordan Mark 1:9-11	When Jesus also had been baptized . . . the heaven was opened, and the Holy Spirit descended upon him Luke 3:21-22	
The temptation in the wilderness	Then Jesus was led up by the Spirit into the wilderness to be tempted by the devil Matthew 4:1-11	And he was in the wilderness forty days, tempted by Satan Mark 1:12-13	And Jesus . . . was led by the Spirit for forty days in the wilderness, tempted by the devil Luke 4:1-13	
Call of the fishermen; two disciples of John follow Jesus	As he walked by the Sea of Galilee, he saw two brothers . . . casting a net into the sea Matthew 4:18-22	And passing along by the Sea of Galilee, he saw Simon and Andrew the brother of Simon casting a net in the sea Mark 1:16-20	He saw two boats by the lake; but the fishermen had gone out of them and were washing their nets Luke 5:2-11	John . . . said, "Behold, the Lamb of God!" The two disciples heard him say this, and they followed Jesus John 1:35-43
The wedding at Cana				On the third day there was a marriage at Cana in Galilee John 2:1-11
Jesus cures Peter's mother-in-law	He touched her hand, and the fever left her Matthew 8:14-15	And he came and took her by the hand and lifted her up, and the fever left her Mark 1:29-31	And he stood over her and rebuked the fever, and it left her Luke 4:38-39	

See page 128

See page 146

	Matthew	Mark	Luke	John
Casting out many demons	*That evening they brought to him many who were possessed with demons* Matthew 8:16-17	*That evening, at sundown, they brought to him all who were sick or possessed with demons* Mark 1:32-34	*Now when the sun was setting, all those who had any that were sick . . . brought them to him* Luke 4:40-41	
Cleansing lepers	*A leper came to him and knelt before him, saying, "Lord, if you will, you can make me clean."* Matthew 8:2-4	*And a leper came to him beseeching him, and kneeling said to him, "If you will, you can make me clean."* Mark 1:40-45	*A man full of leprosy . . . fell on his face and besought him, "Lord, if you will, you can make me clean."* Luke 5:12-15 (See also 17:11-19)	
Curing a paralytic who takes up his bed and walks	*And behold, they brought to him a paralytic* Matthew 9:2-8	*And they came, bringing a paralytic carried by four men* Mark 2:2-12	*And behold, men were bringing on a bed a man who was paralyzed* Luke 5:18-26	
Call of Matthew (Levi)	*Jesus . . . saw a man called Matthew sitting at the tax office; and he said to him, "Follow me."* Matthew 9:9-13	*He saw Levi the son of Alphaeus sitting at the tax office, and he said to him, "Follow me."* Mark 2:14-17	*He . . . saw a tax collector, named Levi, sitting at the tax office; and he said to him, "Follow me."* Luke 5:27-32	
The Sermon on the Mount	*Seeing the crowds, he went up on the mountain, and when he sat down his disciples came to him* Matthew 5:1-7:27			
Healing the centurion's servant from a distance; healing an official's son	*A centurion came forward to him, beseeching and saying, "Lord, my servant is lying paralyzed at home"* Matthew 8:5-13		*Now a centurion had a slave who . . . was sick and at the point of death* Luke 7:2-10	*And at Capernaum there was an official whose son was ill* John 4:46-54
Raising the widow's son at Nain			*As he drew near to the gate of the city, behold, a man who had died was being carried out* Luke 7:11-17	

See page 165

See page 211

See page 169

	Matthew	Mark	Luke	John
Jesus teaches in parables	Then the disciples came and said to him, "Why do you speak to them in parables?" Matthew 13:10-15	And when he was alone, those who were about him with the twelve asked him concerning the parables Mark 4:10-12	And . . . his disciples asked him what this parable meant Luke 8:9-10	
Calming the storm at sea	And behold, there arose a great storm on the sea Matthew 8:24-27	And a great storm of wind arose Mark 4:37-41	And a storm of wind came down on the lake Luke 8:23-25	
Casting the demons into the Gadarene swine	And when they came to the other side, to the country of the Gadarenes, two demoniacs met him Matthew 8:28-34	And when he had come out of the boat, there met him out of the tombs a man with an unclean spirit Mark 5:1-20	And as he stepped out on land, there met him a man from the city who had demons Luke 8:26-39	
Raising Jairus's daughter	A ruler came in and knelt before him, saying, "My daughter has just died" Matthew 9:18-26	Then came one of the rulers of the synagogue, Jairus by name Mark 5:22-43	And there came a man named Jairus, who was a ruler of the synagogue Luke 8:41-56	
Curing the woman who comes from behind to touch his garment	And behold, a woman who had suffered from a hemorrhage for twelve years came up behind him Matthew 9:20-22	And there was a woman who had had a flow of blood for twelve years Mark 5:25-34	And a woman who had a flow of blood for twelve years . . . came up behind him Luke 8:43-48	
Casting the demon from a dumb man	As they were going away, behold, a dumb demoniac was brought to him Matthew 9:32-34		Now he was casting out a demon that was dumb Luke 11:14-23	
Preaching in the synagogue at Nazareth	Coming to his own country he taught them in their synagogue Matthew 13:54-58	And on the sabbath he began to teach in the synagogue Mark 6:1-6	And he came to Nazareth . . . and he went to the synagogue, as his custom was, on the sabbath day Luke 4:16-30	

See page 197

See page 172

See page 152

See page 206

	Matthew	Mark	Luke	John
Curing a man lying by the pool of Bethzatha		See page 195		*One man was there, who had been ill for thirty-eight years* John 5:2-9
Jesus feeds the multitude	*As he went ashore he saw a great throng; and he had compassion on them* Matthew 14:14-21 (See also 15:32-39)	*As he went ashore he saw a great throng, and he had compassion on them* Mark 6:34-44 (See also 8:1-10)	*When the crowds learned it, they followed him; and he welcomed them* Luke 9:11-17	*And a multitude followed him, because they saw the signs which he did* John 6:2-13
Walking on water	*And in the fourth watch of the night he came to them, walking on the sea* Matthew 14:25-33	*And about the fourth watch of the night he came to them, walking on the sea* Mark 6:48-51		*They saw Jesus walking on the sea and drawing near to the boat* John 6:19-21
Curing a man of deafness and a speech impediment	See page 191	*They brought to him a man who was deaf and had an impediment in his speech* Mark 7:32-37		
Restoring sight to a blind man at Bethsaida		*And some people brought to him a blind man, and begged him to touch him* Mark 8:22-26	See page 159	
The Transfiguration	*Jesus took with him Peter and James and John his brother, and led them up a high mountain apart* Matthew 17:1-8	*Jesus took with him Peter and James and John, and led them up a high mountain apart* Mark 9:2-13	*He took with him Peter and John and James, and went up on the mountain to pray* Luke 9:28-36	
Restoring sight to a blind man/two blind men near Jericho	*And behold, two blind men sitting by the roadside . . . cried out, "Have mercy on us"* Matthew 20:29-34 (See also 9:27:31)	*As he was leaving Jericho . . . Bartimaeus, a blind beggar . . . was sitting by the roadside* Mark 10:46-52	*And as he drew near to Jericho, a blind man was sitting by the roadside begging* Luke 18:35-43	See page 225
Jesus raises Lazarus		See page 218		*Now a certain man was ill, Lazarus of Bethany* John 11.1-44

And Jesus went about all the cities and villages . . . preaching the gospel of the kingdom, and healing every disease and every infirmity. When he saw the crowds, he had compassion for them, because they were harassed and helpless, like sheep without a shepherd.

MATTHEW 9:35–36

DOING GOOD, TEACHING LOVE

The miracles of Jesus astounded the people of his own time and have continued to fascinate thinkers ever since then. In THE LIFE OF OUR LORD—*a book written to be read to his own children but not published until 1934, 64 years after his death—Charles Dickens simply but eloquently summarized these wonders.*

JESUS BEGAN TO CURE sick people by only laying his hand upon them; for God had given him power to heal the sick, and to give sight to the blind, and to do many wonderful and solemn things which are called the miracles of Christ.

The first miracle which Jesus did was at a place called Cana, where he went to a marriage feast with Mary his mother. There was no wine; and Mary told him so. There were only six stone water-pots filled with water. But Jesus turned this water into wine, by only lifting up his hand; and all who were there, drank of it.

Jesus did such wonders that people might know he was not a common man, and might believe what he taught them, and also believe that God had sent him. And many people, hearing this, and hearing that he cured the sick, did begin to believe in him, and great crowds followed him wherever he went.

One day there came to him a man with a dreadful disease called leprosy. It was common in those times, and those who were ill with it were called lepers. This leper fell at the feet of Jesus, and said "Lord! If thou wilt, thou cans't make me well!" Jesus, always full of compassion, stretched out his hand, and said "I will! Be thou well!" And his disease went away, immediately, and he was cured.

Being followed, wherever he went, by great crowds of people, Jesus went, with his disciples, into a house, to rest. While he was sitting inside, some men brought upon a bed, a man who was very ill of what is called the palsy, so that he trembled all over from head to foot, and could neither stand, nor move. But the crowd being all about the door and windows, and they not being able to get near Jesus, these men climbed up to the roof of the house, which was a low one; and through the tiling at the top, let down the bed, with the sick man upon it, into the room where Jesus sat. When he saw him, Jesus, full of pity, said "Arise! Take up thy bed, and go to thine own home!" And the man rose up and went away quite well; blessing him, and thanking God.

There was a centurion too, an officer over the soldiers, who came to him, and said "Lord! My servant lies at home in my house, very ill."—Jesus made answer, "I will come and cure him." But the centurion said "Lord! I am not worthy that Thou shoulds't come to my house. Say the word only, and I know he will be cured." Then Jesus, glad that the centurion believed in him so truly, said "Be it so!" And the servant became well, from that moment.

But of all the people who came to him, none were so full of grief and distress as one man who was a magistrate or ruler over many people, and he wrung his hands, and cried, and said "Oh Lord, my daughter—my beautiful, good, innocent little girl is dead. Oh come to her, come to her, and lay Thy blessed hand upon her, and I know she will revive, and come to life again, and make me and her mother happy. Oh Lord we love her so, we love her so! And she is dead!"

Jesus went out with him, and so did his disciples, and went to his house, where the friends and neighbours were crying in the room where the poor dead little girl lay, and where there was soft music playing. Jesus, looking on her, sorrowfully, said—to comfort her poor parents—"She is not dead. She is asleep." Then he commanded the room to be cleared of the people that were in it, and going to the dead child, took her by the hand, and she rose up, quite well, as if she had only been asleep. Oh what a sight it must have been to see her parents clasp her in their arms, and kiss her, and thank God, and Jesus his son, for such great mercy!

And because Jesus did such Good, and taught people how to love God and how to hope to go to Heaven after death, he was called *Our Saviour.*

*A luminous Jesus stands among the sick and infirm who have been brought to him for healing.
The richly detailed etching is the work of the 17th-century Dutch master Rembrandt van Rijn, whose vast
artistic output includes many scenes from the life of Jesus.*

Lifting one hand in blessing, Jesus gently starts raising the paralytic to his feet. The 16th-century tapestry, executed from a design by Raphael, who set the scene in what appears to be a Renaissance cathedral, hangs in the ducal palace in Mantua, Italy.

HOW HE CAME

When the golden evening gathered
    on the shore of Galilee,
When the fishing boats lay quiet by the sea,
Long ago the people wondered,
    tho' no sign was in the sky,
For the glory of the Lord was passing by.

Not in robes of purple splendor,
    not in silken softness shod,
But in raiment worn with travel came their God,
And the people knew His presence
    by the heart that ceased to sigh
When the glory of the Lord was passing by.

For He healed their sick at even,
    and He cured the leper's sore,
And sinful men and women sinned no more,
And the world grew mirthful-hearted,
    and forgot its misery
When the glory of the Lord was passing by.

Not in robes of purple splendor,
    but in lives that do His will,
In patient acts of kindness He comes still;
And the people cry with wonder,
    tho' no sign is in the sky,
That the glory of the Lord is passing by.

W. J. DAWSON, 1854–1928

> *And they came, bringing to him a paralytic carried by four men. And when they could not get near him because of the crowd, they removed the roof above him; and when they had made an opening, they let down the pallet on which the paralytic lay.*
>
> MARK 2:3–4

THE POWER THAT FLOWED FROM HIM

Mark's description of the healing of the paralytic includes—as does Luke's but not Matthew's—the colorful incident of the man's litter being lowered through the roof. In his book JESUS, Edmond Fleg cast the story as a first-person narrative.

HE INN WAS FILLING UP. Crowds arrived from Judaea and Idumaea, from the borders of Tyre and Sidon, from Decapolis, and other countries from beyond the Jordan. You can imagine how the inn-keepers put up their prices!

One morning, Baruch and Reuben carried me out of the town on my litter in the direction from which we had come. Were they taking me home? I raged helplessly. But Aunt Sephora, who was following with my uncle, said softly: "You are going to see him."

Could it be true? Now I understood why the road was almost impassable. There were crowds in front of me, crowds behind me—all were moving towards him. "Whom will he heal?" I asked myself.

We halted in the plain, just beyond the peak near the seven springs. I could not see a single blade of grass; wherever I looked there were bodies—upright, seated, recumbent—wedged closely together. Beside me, a figure shook with palsy; a little way off, I caught sight of a face that was a running mass of sores. "I wonder how many paralytics there are," I thought.

From the moment that Jesus appeared between two of his disciples, there was a frenzied scramble and a wild outburst of cries and entreaties. Women touched his robe and kissed it frantically. Halt, lame, hunchbacks and bandy-legged flung themselves at his feet, and licked the dust. The scrofulous exposed their scabs, the ulcerous their running sores; the blind fumbled in the air, and sought his eyes.

Suddenly a demoniac hurled them all aside, with a hideous howl. He jostled, scratched, and struck out with clenched fists, from which hung the rattling links of the chains he had snapped. He foamed at the mouth, his teeth chattered, and his knees knocked together with the sound of a hammer against an anvil. Beneath his tattered garment, shudders rippled up and down his body like waves on the sea.

"Let us alone," he shrieked. "What have we to do with thee, thou Jesus of Nazareth? Thou art come to destroy us! I know thou art the Holy One of God!"

But Jesus rebuked him, saying: "Hold thy peace, and come out of him!"

Consecutive episodes in the healing of the paralytic at Capernaum are depicted above: lowering the afflicted man through the roof (left), a 16th-century Flemish stained glass panel; and Jesus telling him to rise, take up his pallet, and go home (right), a 6th-century mosaic from Ravenna, Italy.

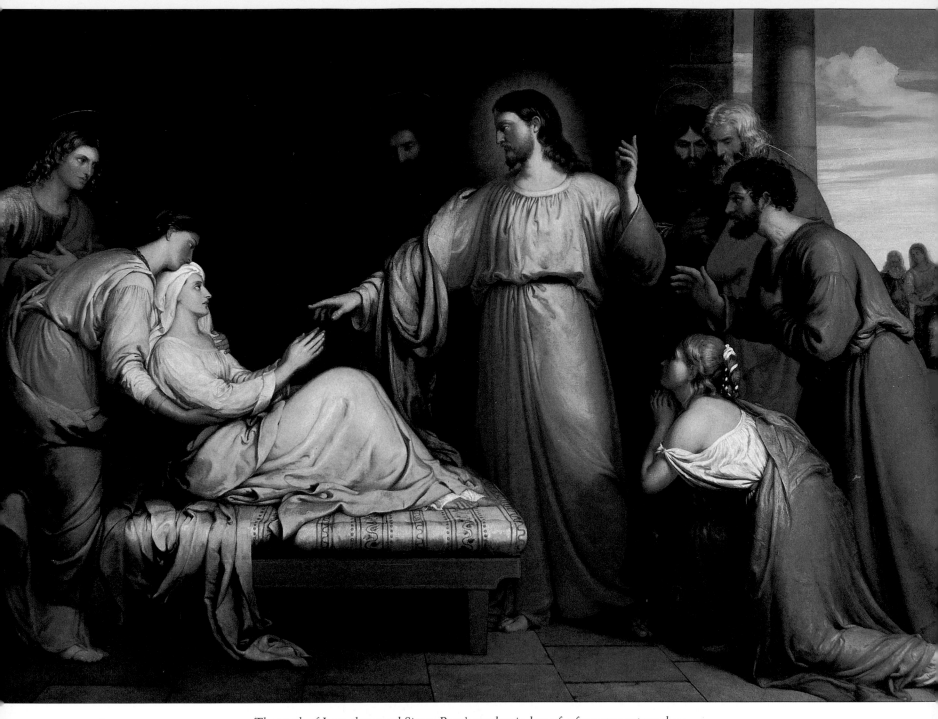

The touch of Jesus that cured Simon Peter's mother-in-law of a fever was captured on canvas by J. Bridges, a British painter who flourished between 1818 and 1854. Although Matthew places the event after the Sermon on the Mount, both Mark and Luke mention it as one of Jesus' first healings, taking place immediately after he drove out an unclean spirit from a man in the synagogue at Capernaum.

The demoniac flung himself backward, bending his body like a bow till it touched the ground. A convulsion shook him from head to foot, something leapt from his mouth with a final howl, and he rose, fell on his knees, and with a voice that was the voice of angels said: "Blessed art thou, Jesus of Nazareth!"

As I lay on my litter, I thought: "How shall I ever draw near to the Rabbi through such a crowd, when even those with the full use of their limbs cannot draw near him? Shall I alone remain unhealed?"

Suddenly I felt my litter sway. By the four cords that were fastened to it, it was being hoisted up above the heads of the crowd. Baruch, Reuben, and two others uncovered the roof where he stood. I could hear the voice of Jesus. Slowly, my litter was lowered until I lay at his feet.

"Be not afraid," he said. "Son, thy sins be forgiven thee. . . ."

Something, I knew not what, stirred softly in my bones. I was conscious of a warm tide that streamed through my veins—the warmth of my own blood. I felt the life-blood pulse through me. "I am forgiven! If I am forgiven, I shall be healed!"

Power emanated from Jesus; it flowed towards me, filled me, flooded me. In a corner, voices were raised in complaint. Sternly, he said: "Why reason ye these things in your hearts? Whether it is easier to say to the paralytic: 'Thy sin be forgiven thee,' or: 'Arise! Take up thy bed, and walk'? But that ye may know that the Son of Man has power on earth to forgive sins . . ."

He turned to me and commanded: "Arise! Take up thy bed, and walk!"

The power that flowed from him tugged softly at my arms and legs, whose rigidity relaxed; I felt it under my ribs, my back, my neck; it was raising me up!

Suddenly, I was transformed into another being; I knew this other being was on his feet, knew that he was walking, moving away from the litter, knew he was coming back to lift it! And this other being was myself! It was I who stooped, raised the litter and bore it away! I was walking! I was walking! The power of Jesus was in every step I took!

Naturally, a discussion immediately arose—"Who can forgive sins but God alone?"

But I had no mind to question and doubt him in the new joy of using my limbs. I came and went, strode up and down, and to and fro; I never paused, but walked tirelessly in the courtyard of the inn. I little thought a time would come when I should long to stand still!

THE MASTER'S TOUCH

"He touched her hand, and the fever left her."
  He touched her hand as He only can,
With the wondrous skill of the great Physician,
  With the tender touch of the Son of Man,
And the fever pain in the throbbing temples
  Died out with the flush on brow and cheek;
And the lips that had been so parched and burning
  Trembled with thanks that she could not speak;
And the eyes, where the fever light had faded,
  Looked up—by her grateful tears made dim;
And she rose and ministered to her household—
  She rose and ministered unto Him.

"He touched her hand, and the fever left her."
  Oh blessed touch of the Man Divine!
So beautiful then to rise and serve Him
  When the fever is gone from your life and mine;
It may be the fever of restless serving,
  With heart all thirsty for love and praise,
And eyes all aching and strained with yearning
  Toward self-set goals in the future days;
Or it may be a fever of spirit anguish,
  Some tempest of sorrow that dies not down
Till the cross at last is in meekness lifted
  And the head stoops low for the thorny crown;
Or it may be a fever of pain and anger,
  When the wounded spirit is hard to bear,
And only the Lord can draw forth the arrows
  Left carelessly, cruelly rankling there.

Whatever the fever, His touch can heal it;
  Whatever the tempest, his voice can still;
There is only joy as we seek His pleasure;
  There is only a rest as we seek His will—
And some day after life's fitful fever,
  I think we shall say in the home on high:
"If the hands that He touched but did His bidding
  How little it matters what else went by!"
Ah, Lord! Thou knowest us altogether,
  Each heart's sore sickness, whatever it be.
Touch Thou our hands! Let the fever leave us—
  And so shall we minister unto Thee!

AUTHOR UNKNOWN

And when Jesus entered Peter's house, he saw his mother-in-law lying sick with a fever; he touched her hand, and the fever left her, and she rose and served him.

MATTHEW 8:14–15

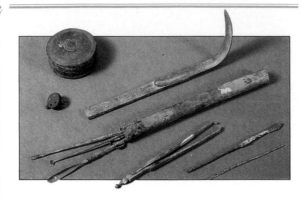

Simple and crude by modern standards, these copper medical instruments date to the Roman period.

Illness: A Sign of God's Displeasure

To the Hebrews, there was a single explanation for all disease and bodily affliction: God was wreaking punishment for sin. To be healed, therefore, the sufferer should look to the priest or prophet, not the physician. The cure, if any, would come from repentance, fasting, sacrifice, and sincere prayers for forgiveness, not from earthly medicines — or so Jewish leaders contended, citing numerous scriptural injunctions. Simpler folk, influenced by the superstitions of the neighboring Canaanites, believed that their ills might be the cruel work of demons and occasionally sought relief in charms and incantations, though magic was strongly denounced in the Old Testament. More practical treatments included the use of oils, bandages, and poultices, the anodyne known as the balm of Gilead, and various healing herbs. And, unique in ancient times, the law of Moses laid down strict rules of public hygiene that protected the purity of the water supply, removed excrement and waste, and imposed 40-day quarantines for specific diseases.

Jesus, who attracted a huge following by his healing of the physically and mentally ill, repudiated the traditional view of disease as retribution for wrongdoing or as a test of faith. Showing compassion for the emotional turmoil as well as the physical suffering of the afflicted, he sought to demonstrate the power of faith and hope in the restoration of well-being.

On the way to Jerusalem he was passing along between Samaria and Galilee. And as he entered a village, he was met by ten lepers, who stood at a distance and lifted up their voices and said, "Jesus, Master, have mercy on us."

LUKE 17:11–13

ONE WHO CAME TO BRING LIFE

Although Matthew and Mark also write of Jesus' cleansing of lepers, only Luke tells the story of the ten who were healed. In a short story based on Luke's account, Manuel Komroff sets the scene in a forbidding wilderness but retains the central point: the ingratitude of all except one.

THE LONG JOURNEY led him through that wild rocky wilderness, the black and sorrowful valley between the lands of Galilee and Samaria. Here in the shadow of a great jagged rock Jesus rested. The air was still; not an insect, not a bird and no rivulet broke the silence. The stillness seemed deep as death. And here in this quiet and in the purple shadow of a great rock, he looked out into the desolate and hopeless valley.

Suddenly he heard the sharp snap of dried branches and the crunch of sandals on the hard stone. A voice which seemed to come from above him cried out: "Unclean!" It was a cry filled with terror.

He looked up and there, almost directly over him on top of the great rock, stood an old man in rags. His twisted figure, supported by a staff, was silhouetted against the clear sky.

"Unclean!" he repeated. "Tarry not here. We are outcasts and this valley of rocks belongs to us."

"Praise the Lord in Heaven," Jesus said. "He watches over all men."

"The Lord in Heaven," cried the old man, again raising his deathly white arms, "has brought this upon us. The one you would have us praise is not here."

"Where man is, there is the Lord also."

"Go!" the old man cried. "What we have here we

will share with no one. The thorns, the cinders, the burning heat, the rocks, all that you see belongs to us. And our sorrows and wretchedness are also our own. Go, stranger! We will divide with no one."

"I ask nothing. But I am ready to give. How many are you?"

"Four are men; two are women; two are boys and two are girls. Altogether we are ten."

Soon voices were heard, and the unclean outcasts emerged slowly from secret grottoes dug out of rock. Their curious large eyes gazed hard at Jesus. They were certain that the sheer horror of their faces would drive him off. But he did not move.

"You fear not?" the old man asked.

"I fear not. I choose those who suffer. They are my people."

The old man gazed hard at Jesus, then he sank to his knees and bowed his head. "Forgive me," he said. "I did not understand. But one thing I know. You come to us as a friend and not as an enemy. This wilderness is our home. But were it a green valley and rich we would still welcome you; for no one has yet come out of the world to speak with us. Only one thing. Do not ask us to praise the Lord. Would you have us thank him for our wretchedness?"

Then one of the women spoke up boldly. "He has forsaken us. He has turned a deaf ear to our prayers." And the second woman, with skin as white as that pillar of salt that was once Lot's wife, spoke: "The Lord is an evil Lord."

Then one of the four men spoke and said: "We do not need to pray. The beasts of the forests do not pray. The fish in the ocean do not pray. We are creatures lower than the beasts. So why should we pray?"

"There are those," said another, "who live in palaces, and others in huts. Even the oxen are given a shed for the night. But what have we?"

"I bring you life," said Jesus, "and nothing more."

He held out his arms and two of the children ran toward him. He embraced them and stroked their heads. Suddenly the children burst into tears.

Various of Jesus' miracles are represented on a fifth-century ivory diptych, a hinged tablet that may have been placed on the altar during services. From top to bottom, left and right, feeding the 5,000, restoring a blind man's sight, curing the paralytic; raising Lazarus, changing water into wine at Cana, and cleansing a leper.

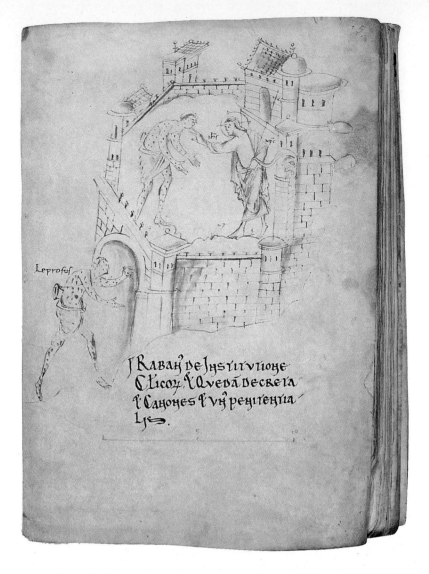

The leper who beseeched Jesus to make him clean is depicted with the spots of his malady in a pen-and-ink drawing from the ninth-century book above and in the tenth-century manuscript illumination at right.

"Tell me why you are weeping," he asked.

"I do not know," said one.

But the other looked into his face and said: "A strange feeling, almost frightening, came over me. It was as though a million needle points were rushing through my veins. And every toe and finger had inside it a little heart which was beating hard. And in my head, before my eyes, the heavens seemed to open. And your words were true. He who sits on the throne in heaven watches over everyone. Even we who are poor and sick and have nothing: He loves even us. And I will pray to Him."

The child sank to her knees and clasped her hands in prayer. And as she prayed the blood seemed to return to her hands and face. And those who stood about looked on with wonder and astonishment.

"He loves you all," Jesus said. "And you who are poor and sick and have nothing: you are no longer poor and no longer sick, and the world that belongs to all people now also belongs to you. Go, show yourselves unto the priests, and let them see that you have been cleansed."

All who were standing now sank to their knees and held their white arms up toward heaven. And slowly, very slowly, the red of life returned to their limbs and inch by inch crept upward, glowing, warm, throbbing, until it had reached their fingertips.

The outcasts lost no time. One by one they rose and walked away silently between the great rocks of the wilderness. But the old man, the one who had stood over Jesus on the great rock and waved his staff in the air, fell down at his feet.

"Forgive me," he pleaded. "I have done more than the others. It was I who forbade you to tarry. It was I who threatened you. And it was I who gathered the other nine to frighten you away. Envy and hate were in my heart. Forgive me."

"You are forgiven. But will you forget that one passed here by chance?"

"Master, I am ashamed. We will forget this great thing that you have done for us. It is not that our hearts are evil. But there is a blindness in the nature of man and gratitude melts with time. We are not worthy. Send a curse after us and let us return to our wretchedness."

"I have come to bring you life. Go. Hurry. Join the others and live once more. Forget or remember, it matters little. Only one thing matters. Believe and have faith."

BLIND BARTIMEUS

Blind Bartimeus at the gates
Of Jericho in darkness waits;
He hears the crowd—he hears a breath
Say, "It is Christ of Nazareth!"
And calls in tones of agony,
"Jesus, have mercy now on me!"

The thronging multitudes increase;
Blind Bartimeus, hold thy peace!
But still, above the noisy crowd,
The beggar's cry is shrill and loud;
Until they say, "He calleth thee!"
"Fear not, arise, He calleth thee!"

Then saith the Christ, as silent stands
The crowd, "What wilt thou at my hands?"
And he replies, "O give me light!
Rabbi, restore the blind man's sight."
And Jesus answers, "Go in peace
Thy faith from blindness gives release!"

Ye that have eyes yet cannot see,
In darkness and in misery,
Recall those mighty Voices Three,
"Jesus, have mercy now on me!"
"Fear not, arise, and go in peace!"
Thy faith from blindness gives release!"

HENRY WADSWORTH LONGFELLOW, 1807–1882

*Matthew's account of
Jesus restoring sight
to two blind men outside
Jericho is the subject
of a painting by Nicolas
Poussin (1594–1665),
a French artist working
in Rome. Mark and
Luke speak only of one
blind man at Jericho,
whom Mark calls
Bartimaeus.*

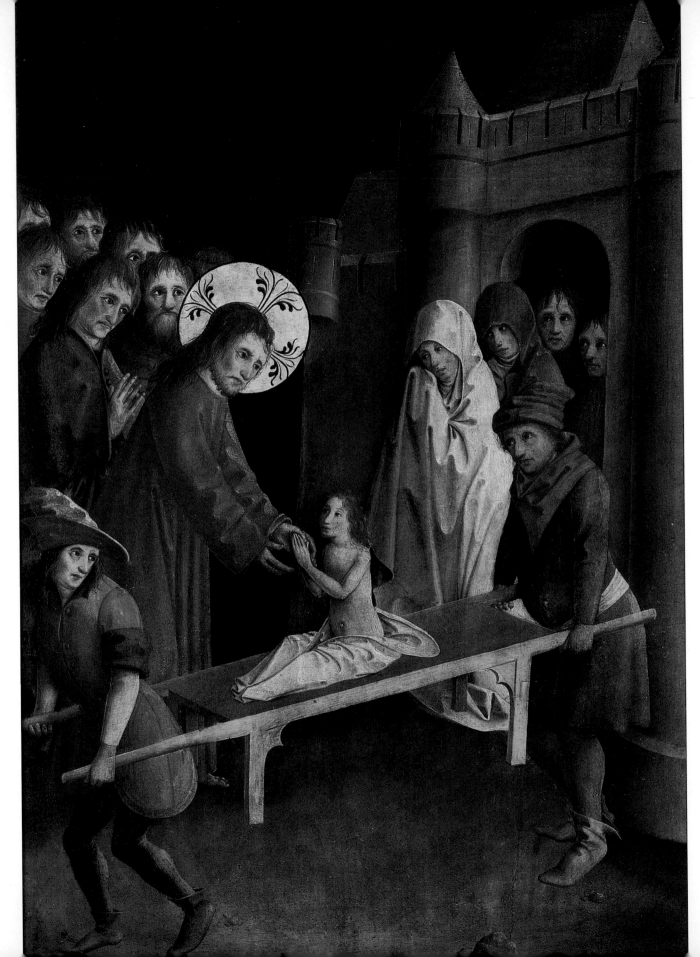

As he drew near to the gate of the city, behold, a man who had died was being carried out, the only son of his mother, and she was a widow . . . . And when the Lord saw her, he had compassion on her and said to her, "Do not weep."

LUKE 7:12–13

A 15th-century German artist known only as the Master of the Darmstädter Passion depicted the son of the widow of Nain as a child rather than the young man mentioned in Luke. He clothed the grieving mother in white.

IF THE PROPHET ELISHA COULD COME AGAIN

Only Luke tells of Jesus' sympathetic concern for the widow of Nain that prompted him to bring her only son back from the dead. In the following selection from THESE SHARED HIS CROSS, Edwin McNeill Poteat describes the village in which the woman lived, invents a past for her as the impoverished widow of a dismissed schoolteacher, and draws a comparison between Jesus' miracle and that of Elisha as related in 2 Kings.

THE VILLAGE OF NAIN, long since lost in the dust of ancient Galilee, is still held in place in the memory of the years by the frail hands of a nameless widow and her son.

Under the shadow of the proud summit of Mount Tabor, refreshed by the fertile and fragrant plain of Esdraelon, and beckoned toward the Great Sea by the white finger of Mount Carmel, the villagers of the simple town spent their indifferent days in shop, field and market, and came home at dusk to rest from their weariness in simple homes. Nain could boast no ancient episode such as gave fame to the neighbor town of Shunem. Jeremiah had once said boldly that the might of Jehovah advancing against the King of Egypt would be as Tabor and Carmel; but though Nain nestled nearest the base of the great mountain, she could claim little celebrity from the prophet's daring words. And so her people passed their lives undisturbed by great hopes, and undismayed by little fears, destined to pass out of time unknown save for the recollection of a casual visit hidden in a desultory record.

Two years had lightened the burden of the widow's grief as she realized with each passing day the likeness of her growing son to his dead father. He looked like him, had that eager passion for learning, and the courage and persuasiveness in argument that the villagers, however they had deprecated it in his father, had never been able to forget. His mother, given to works among the needy, endeared herself by the simplicity and gentleness of her bearing, and there were many who, recalling the injustice of her husband's dismissal, sought in subtle ways to expiate it. There was much, indeed, to mitigate the loneliness of the days, and as she thought of the future, she saw her son entering into the career his father had only dreamed

of, some day a great scribe perhaps, or even a great ruler among his people.

"Mother," the young man said to her as they finished their evening meal.

"Yes, my son."

"I wonder if the days are not soon to be fulfilled in which the sorrows of our people will be ended. Listen to these words of Jeremiah." He unrolled a scroll and, laying his hands down flat on its surface, read: "In those days they shall say no more, the fathers have eaten sour grapes and the children's teeth are set on edge. But everyone shall die for his own iniquity: every man that eateth sour grapes, his teeth shall be set on edge."

"But what says that word to us?" the mother asked.

"This: if we are not punished for the sins of our fathers, we will be rewarded for our own righteousness. Rome is not the penalty for the sin of any but ourselves. Had we a leader from among our own people to stir us with a sense of our moral obligations and promise us a destiny which our deeds can win . . ." He was excited at the prospect, and as he lifted his hands to emphasize his words, the scroll furled itself with a shudder. He looked at it and laughed. "That's the way the mind of a Pharisee acts."

During the spring there were many times when his nimble mind picked up a word of wisdom from the ancient books, and lighted it with new understanding and promise, and ever the heart of his mother was

Two miraculous cures of Jesus described in Matthew 8:2–13 are depicted in this 11th-century illumination for a Gospel book made for Holy Roman Emperor Henry III: cleansing a leper as he came down from delivering the Sermon on the Mount (left) and healing the centurion's servant (right).

THE WOMAN WHO CAME BEHIND HIM IN THE CROWD

Near him she stole, rank after rank;
    She feared approach too loud;
She touched his garment's hem, and shrank,
    Back in the sheltering crowd.

A shame-faced gladness thrills her frame:
    Her twelve years' fainting prayer
Is heard at last! She is the same
    As other women there!

She hears his voice. He looks about,
    Ah! is it kind or good
To drag her secret sorrow out
    Before that multitude?

The eyes of men she dares not meet—
    On her they straight must fall!
Forward she sped, and at his feet
    Fell down, and told him all.

To the one refuge she had flown,
    The Godhead's burning flame!
Of all earth's women she alone
    Hears there the tenderest name!

"Daughter," he said, "be of good cheer;
    Thy faith hath made thee whole."
With plenteous love, not healing mere,
    He comforteth her soul.

GEORGE MACDONALD, 1824–1905

The woman who came up behind Jesus in the crowd believed that she had only to touch his garment to be cured of her 12-year flow of blood. Her act of faith is shown in the sixth-century mosaic above, right. On another occasion Jesus rewarded a Canaanite woman's similarly strong belief in his powers by healing her demon-possessed daughter, a scene included in a 15th-century devotional book, above.

glad, and the future brightened whenever she dared to anticipate it.

And then the portent of death invaded the little house again. One evening the young man complained of a throbbing agony underneath his heart, and all through the ominous night his mother tended him, brewing homely medicines, and cooling his burning forehead with wet napkins. But in the morning, as the top of Tabor picked up the first signal of the day and flashed it on to Carmel by the sea, the boy grew limp and silent, and his breathing as gentle as the utter motionlessness of death.

His mother stood up and walked bravely to the door. The stillness of dawn pervaded the village. She would not rouse the neighbors; it was too late for help. She remembered the ancient story, endlessly told in Nain, of the widow of Shunem, the village less than a mile distant, and she wondered for the moment, why in her day no prophets were abroad, prophets who could lay themselves upon a cold body and warm it back to life. When, she wondered, would Elisha come again?

She was surprised that so many shared her grief. And when, the next day, they carried her beloved dead through the Horse Gate on the east side of the village, she found herself thronged with mourners. Over and over in her mind the words of Jeremiah repeated themselves: "A voice is heard in Ramah, lamentation and bitter weeping, Rachel weeping for her children; she refuseth to be comforted because they are not." She said to herself that she must not weep, that loyalty to the boy and his father demanded strong, silent grief. But in spite of the reminiscence and the resolution, she gave way to an irresistible convulsion of tears, leaning momentarily against the bier to support herself.

"Weep not." She heard a strange voice, firm, commanding, and infinitely tender. She looked through the mist of tears. A man was standing by the bier. He searched deftly among the grave clothes and put his hand firmly upon the young man's wrist. There was a convulsive shudder, and she heard the voice, firm, commanding, and infinitely tender, say, "Young man, I say unto thee, Arise."

The boy sat up, livid with the pallor of death, looked at his mother and smiled weakly. When she reflected on it in later years she invariably remembered that she was neither terrified nor astonished at the restoration of the boy.

Then came one of the rulers of the synagogue, Jairus by name; and seeing him, he fell at his feet, and besought him, saying, "My little daughter is at the point of death. Come and lay your hands on her, so that she may be made well, and live."

MARK 5:22–23

The Daughter of Jairus

The second of the three miracles in which Jesus raises a person from the dead appears in the Gospels of Matthew, Mark, and Luke—and each Evangelist interrupts his narrative to include the incident of the woman suffering from a hemorrhage who comes up behind to touch Jesus' garment. Elizabeth Stuart Phelps's retelling is from THE STORY OF JESUS CHRIST.

JESUS WAS AT HOME once more, but he was not permitted to rest. Crowds larger than he had left received him. He was surrounded and overwhelmed. It seemed as if all the invalids in Galilee were moaning after him. In his busiest and weariest hour an urgent demand came.

An officer of the Jewish church, an important person, Jairus by name, had a little daughter, dearly cherished. She was scarcely twelve years old, just at the lovely age, not yet past her play-days, but already with the dainty airs of a little woman—a winsome maid, her father's darling. She lay at the point of death, and messengers had been sent for the Nazarene.

At the feet of Jesus, Jairus flung himself down like a slave, and such an agony went up in his face and attitude as even a cold man could not easily have resisted. Jesus, melting with sympathy, tenderly reassured the father, and started without delay in the direction of the ruler's house.

But what a throng! When he tried to pass through the people, they closed like a round wall about him. Such a mass of humanity pressed upon him that it was impossible to move. At that moment, stealing past the push and rush of the thoughtless throng, a timid

Jesus confounds those bewailing the death of Jairus's daughter by saying that she is only sleeping. The drawing below is by Giovanni Domenico Tiepolo (1727–1804). In the more restrained version of the scene at right, an illumination from a 10th-century Gospel book, Jesus greets the parents outside the synagogue over which Jairus presides and commands their daughter to rise.

hand touched the fringe of his garment, then, terrified, withdrew instantly.

"Who touched me?" Jesus asked quickly. No person in the crowd replied. "Strength goes out of me," insisted the Master. "Who was it?" And the crowd marveled that he even felt the gentle touch, so great was the press of the multitude.

Jesus and Jairus walked together to the ruler's house. The father did not speak again. He was afraid of offending the rabbi. After those first hot words, the first wild moment, what could he do? When the servant came, weeping, and told him that it was too late, not to trouble the Master, for the little maid was gone—his heart was broken in one mad outcry. This great healer, this mysterious man, so famous for his tenderness, so marvelous for his pity, must needs fail him, *him*, Jairus, out of all Palestine, and that in the hour of his terrible need! For the fact could not be denied that Jesus had stopped on the way to a dying patient to cure an old, chronic case.

That woman could have been healed just as well tonight, tomorrow, or next week. But he had lingered. And the child was dead.

"Do not be afraid," said Jesus, tenderly; "only believe!" But his face was very grave. And by a single motion of his expressive hand he ordered all his disciples back but three—Peter, James, and John, his dearest. The group entered the ruler's house.

The house was not silent. Mourners had already taken possession of it. Obtrusive wails and groans, mingled with genuine sobs and tears, filled the place. Jesus seemed surprised at the condition in which he found the family.

"The child is not dead," he said, decidedly. Some of the neighbors, who did not altogether believe in the famous healer, began to laugh. It was a derisive laugh, a cold sound in that house of woe, and it did not please him. A keen rebuke shot from his mild eyes at the unseemly scorn.

"Nay," he repeated, "she is not dead. She is asleep." He spoke in the tone of a man who was not to be gainsaid. He went into the sick room and looked at the child.

"This is sleep," he persisted. The father's sobs had ceased. The mother lifted her face, discolored with tears, worn with watching, and piteously raised her hands. The three friends of the rabbi stood at his side, reverently wondering.

Jesus silently regarded the little maid. She lay un-

conscious and was quite rigid. Jesus looked at her with a strange expression. His eyes seemed to say: "It is between me and thee. We understand."

He looked at the little girl with the tenderness that is only to be expected of those in whom the love of children is profound and genuine. She seemed to quiver beneath his look, but her color and her attitude did not change. Then he took her by the hand.

Her little wasted fingers lay for a few moments in his vital grasp; then he felt them tremble. Who sees the instant when the lily blossoms? Who could have detected the moment of time in which the child be-

gan to stir? Was it his hand that moved, or hers that directed his slowly upward till it reached her pillow and so came upon a level with her face?

It did not seem sudden or startling, but only the most natural thing in the world, when the little girl laid her cheek upon his palm.

"Give her something to eat," said the healer, quite in an ordinary tone. This commonplace order restored the senses to the excited household. But Jairus remembered how he had thought of Jesus, perhaps how he had spoken to him when the Nazarene stopped to cure the chronic case. And the father felt ashamed.

Believing that Jesus has arrived too late to save the girl, mourners jostle for a view of him at the bedside of Jairus's daughter. The painting is the work of George Percy Jacomb-Hood (1857–1927).

The woman from whom seven demons were driven, perhaps also the contrite sinner who washed Jesus' feet with tears, Mary Magdalene is shown at prayer in this 17th-century Flemish embroidered textile enriched with silver gilt thread and seed pearls.

He went on through cities and villages, preaching and bringing the good news of the kingdom of God. And the twelve were with him, and also some women who had been healed of evil spirits and infirmities: Mary, called Magdalene, from whom seven demons had gone out . . . and many others, who provided for them out of their means.

LUKE 8:1–3

A STRANGER IN HER GARDEN

Luke alone among the Evangelists introduces Mary Magdalene early in his narrative, the others first mentioning her as a witness at the Crucifixion. Among the many authors who have speculated on Mary's past is Kahlil Gibran, from whose book JESUS *the following excerpt is taken. Mary is responding to a question of how she came to know and love Jesus.*

IT WAS IN THE MONTH OF JUNE when I saw him for the first time. He was walking in the wheat-field when I passed by with my handmaidens, and he was alone.

The rhythm of his step was different from other men's, and the movement of his body was like naught I had seen before. Men do not pace the earth in that manner. And even now I do not know whether he walked fast or slow.

My handmaidens pointed their fingers at him and spoke in shy whispers to one another. And I stayed my steps for a moment, and raised my hand to hail him. But he did not turn his face, and he did not look at me. I was swept back into myself, and I was cold as if I had been in a snowdrift; and I shivered.

That night I beheld him in my dreaming; and they told me afterward that I screamed in my sleep and was restless upon my bed.

It was in the month of August that I saw him again, through my window. He was sitting in the shadow of the cypress tree across from my garden, and he was as still as if he had been carved out of stone.

My slave, the Egyptian, came to me and said, "That man is here again; he is sitting there across from your garden."

And I gazed at him, and my soul quivered within me, for he was beautiful. Then I clothed myself with the raiment of Damascus, and I left my house and walked toward him. Was it a hunger in my eyes that desired comeliness, or was it his beauty that sought the light in my eyes? Even *now* I do not know.

I walked to him in my golden sandals and when I reached him, I said, "Good-morrow to you."

And he said, "Good-morrow to you, Miriam."

And he looked at me, and his night eyes saw me as no man had seen me before. And suddenly I was shy. Yet he had said only, "Good-morrow to you."

Then I said to him, "Will you not come to my house? Will you not have bread and wine with me?"

And he said, "Yes, Miriam, but not now."

"Not now, not now," he said. And the voice of the sea was in those two words, and the voice of the wind and the trees. And when he said them unto me, *life* spoke to *death*.

For mind you, my friend, I was dead. I was a woman who had divorced her soul. I was living apart from this self which you now see. I belonged to all men, and to none. They called me harlot, and a woman possessed of seven devils. I was cursed, and I was envied.

But when his dawn eyes looked into my eyes all the stars of my night faded away and I became Miriam, only Miriam, *a woman lost to the earth she had known, and finding herself in new places.*

And now again I said to him, "Come into my house and share bread and wine with me."

And he said, "Why do you bid me to be your guest?"

And I said, "I beg you to come into my house." And it was all that was sod in me and all that was sky in me, calling unto him.

Then he looked at me, and the noontide of his eyes was upon me, and he said, "You have many lovers, and yet I alone love you. Other men love themselves in your nearness. I love you in yourself. Other men see a beauty in you that shall fade away sooner than their own years. But I see in you a beauty that shall not fade away, and in the autumn of your days that beauty shall not be afraid to gaze at itself in the mirror, and it shall not be offended. I, alone, love the unseen in you."

Then he said in a low voice: "Go away now. If this

WERE NOT THE SINFUL MARY'S TEARS

Were not the sinful Mary's tears
  An offering worthy Heaven,
When o'er the faults of former years
  She wept—and was forgiven?

When bringing every balmy sweet
  Her day of luxury stored,
She o'er her Saviour's hallowed feet
  The precious perfume pour'd;

And wiped them with that golden hair
  Where once the diamonds shone:
Though now those gems of grief were there
  Which shine for God alone.

Were not those sweets, though humbly shed—
  That hair—those weeping eyes—
And the sunk heart that inly bled—
  Heaven's noblest sacrifice?

Thou that hast slept in error's sleep,
  Oh, wouldst thou wake in Heaven,
Like Mary kneel, like Mary weep,
  "Love much," and be forgiven?

THOMAS MOORE, 1779–1852

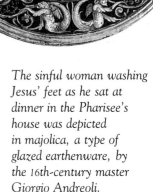

The sinful woman washing Jesus' feet as he sat at dinner in the Pharisee's house was depicted in majolica, a type of glazed earthenware, by the 16th-century master Giorgio Andreoli.

cypress tree is yours and you would not have me sit in its shadow, I will walk my way."

And I cried to him and I said: "Master, come to my house. I have incense to burn for you, and a silver basin for your feet. You are a stranger, and yet not a stranger. I entreat you, come to my house."

Then he stood up and looked at me even as the seasons might look down upon the field, and he smiled. And again he said: "All men love you for themselves. I love you for yourself."

And then he walked away. But no other man ever walked the way he walked. Was it a breath born in my garden that moved to the east? Or was it a storm that would shake all things to their foundations?

I knew not, but on that day the sunset of his eyes slew the dragon in me, and I became a woman—I became Miriam, Miriam of Migdel—Mary, the Magdalene, a *slave* in *his kingdom of love.*

And behold, a woman of the city, who was a sinner, when she learned that he was at table in the Pharisee's house, brought an alabaster flask of ointment, and standing behind him at his feet, weeping, she began to wet his feet with her tears, and wiped them with the hair of her head, and kissed his feet, and anointed them with the ointment.

LUKE 7:37–38

In painting this fresco for a chapel in Florence, the 14th-century Italian artist Giovanni da Milano clearly linked the tearful woman come to wash Jesus' feet in the Pharisee's house with Mary Magdalene by showing the flight of seven demons driven from her.

Washing His Feet with Tears

*Although there is no evidence in the Gospels that
Mary Magdalene is the sinful woman who came weeping
to Jesus as he sat at the Pharisee's table, many
writers have thought it so. The following selection
is from an anonymous 14th-century Italian novel.*

MARY THE MAGDALENE had already begun to give a boundless love to Jesus, hearing that he ate with publicans and sinners and that he forgave them their sins. And she recalled too well all the things that she had ever done, weeping and lamenting for each one and for all.

The devils who molested her took counsel together and said: "We must no longer tempt her with sins as before, since we see that she is repenting them bitterly. But rather we must do thus: let us aggravate these sins in her sight, as greatly as we can; and then also let us do another thing: let us praise this Jesus for his great power, his virtue, his rare excellence, so that she may not dare even think of going to him."

And when these thoughts came to the Magdalene, she perceived the ugliness of her sins and was abashed. But while she was being thus molested, behold a divine light shone in her room, and said: "Mary, do not fear to go to Jesus, for he is the best and the most gentle physician that has ever been seen in this world. And the greater the illness, so much the more the physician, if he be good, stays beside him who is ill, and so much the more strives to heal him."

And the Magdalene began to cry aloud, saying: "I will place all my hope in him as if I were ill, for I perceive and acknowledge that he is the supreme physician for soul and body."

So the devils were defeated and said to each other: "In this also we have gone from bad to worse. And thus he knows how to discomfit us, when he will."

And rising up with fervour she lit a lamp, and began to take ointments that she possessed, and she chose the most precious from amongst them, filling thereof an alabaster box, all the while sighing and shedding tears. Then she went to the window and saw that day was breaking. Waiting no longer, she took her cloak and covered her face so as not to be recognized by all she met as usual. And she took the box under her cloak; and thus she went out all alone to seek Jesus, the desire of her soul.

Now it happened according to Jesus' will, and the Magdalene came at last to the house of the Pharisee, and, entering, she asked no word of any there, but went up the stairs; and the guests were already seated at the table. And when the Magdalene saw him, she instantly recognized the good Jesus, and she went behind him, and threw herself on the ground at his feet.

Mary spoke thus: "Master, my sins are such and so many that I could not count them, and my life is so hateful in mine own eyes that, while so close to thy purity and touching thy sweet feet, I have not the courage to remember it. But I know and believe that thou knowest all things better than I could tell thee, and therefore I ask nothing else but that thou shouldst take away from me all that displeases thee in me."

And with this she wept so violently that I think her heart would have broken had not God strengthened her, for he reserved her for greater works.

And Jesus turned towards her and said: "Woman, thy faith hath made thee whole. Thy petitions are granted, and thy desire shall be fulfilled. Go in peace." And then all the devils were cast out from her, and all the guilt of sin taken from her, and she was filled with great gladness.

After washing Jesus' feet with her tears, the repentant woman dried them with her hair, kissed them, and anointed them with ointment brought in an alabaster flask. A follower of the Flemish master Dirk Bouts (c. 1410–1475) painted the scene early in the 16th century.

*In this detail from a page of a medieval picture Bible,
Jesus tells Nicodemus that he must be born of water and the Spirit—
that is, baptized—in order to enter the kingdom of God.*

**Now there was a man of the Pharisees,
named Nicodemus, a ruler of the
Jews. This man came to Jesus by night
and said to him, "Rabbi, we know
that you are a teacher come from
God; for no one can do these signs that
you do, unless God is with him."**

JOHN 3:1–2

MEETING JESUS BY NIGHT

*For much of his brief public ministry Jesus would be
at odds with the Jewish hierarchy. But early on he seems to
have made at least one convert from among the members
of the Sanhedrin. Eleanor Stock recreates Jesus'
nocturnal meeting with the Pharisee Nicodemus in her
short story "The Hill Road."*

OD HAD A SONG he wanted to sing, and when
he had finished it he created a man to sing
it. And the man was Jesus, a carpenter of
Nazareth. He went up to Jerusalem, and as
he walked up and down its narrow, crowded streets,
God's song swept across the hearts of people. Some
ran to meet it, it was so full of strength and beauty.
But others ran from it, trembling with fear.

When the rulers of Israel—priests, scribes, and
Pharisees—heard it, they shuttered the windows of
their souls and barred the gates of their mind against
it; that is, all of them except Nicodemus and one or
two others who, when they heard it, stopped to listen.

Nicodemus was no longer a young man, and at first
he listened with the gentlemanly indifference of one
who is tired of life. But a day came when the swift,
clean words cut through the mist of indifference and
with a lightning flash revealed Nicodemus to himself.

That night he took the hill road to the Mount of
Olives. He had heard that Jesus was in the habit of
spending his nights there. The road ended abruptly
among a clump of olive trees.

As he stood looking down upon Jerusalem, he felt
the presence of long-forgotten memories, and the tall,
broad-shouldered dreams of his boyhood seemed to

rise from the city of pinnacles and towers lying there so quiet and clean in the white radiance of the Eastern night. Unconsciously he lifted his face toward heaven and stretched out his hands, palms upward, in prayer. In the light of the moon and stars his thin, tired face was like an exquisite cameo of old ivory, carved against the onyx shadows of the olive trees.

Jesus saw him thus. The beauty and pathos of the old man tugged at his heart and quietly, lest he break in upon the prayer, Jesus came and stood beside him. He watched the labored rise and fall of the old man's breathing, the throbbing pulse in the thick veins on his forehead, and at once sensed the courage and endurance it had cost Nicodemus to come out alone and by night up the hill road.

Nicodemus looked up. "You are here."

Now that he was face to face with the young teacher, Nicodemus was at a loss for words. How could he tell Jesus that for a member of the Sanhedrin to have any dealings whatsoever with a Sabbath-breaking Nazarene was not only flagrantly undignified, but dangerously unconventional. At last he spoke slowly, hesitatingly: "You are a teacher come from God. . . ."

"Are you sure, Nicodemus?"

"You may well ask that. We priests and Pharisees have so often tried to bait you with those very words, but I speak them in all sincerity. Only *you* can tell me, and my need is too great to be denied—how I, an old man, may find life, *eternal life*. . . ."

Jesus put his hand on that of the old man. "By knowing the God within you, by catching a vision of His Kingdom."

"But it is so long since I have felt God within me— and the eyes of my soul have grown too dim to see so divine a thing as His Kingdom. Surely you realize that I cannot do these things. And if I could—how?"

"There is only one way; you must be born anew."

Nicodemus shook his head and answered with bitter irony: "How can a man be born when he is old? Can he enter his mother's womb again?"

"Do not wonder, Nicodemus, at my telling you that you must be born again, spiritually. The wind blows

Jesus greeting Nicodemus the Pharisee is among the 76 woodcuts Virgil Solis executed for a 1562 edition of Martin Luther's translation of the Bible into German.

wherever it chooses, and you hear the sound thereof, but you do not know where it comes from or where it goes. This is the way with everyone who owes his birth to the Spirit."

"But how can that be?" Nicodemus asked.

"You are a teacher of Israel and yet ignorant of this? I speak of that which I know, and of that which I have seen. You remember how it is told that Moses in the desert lifted the serpent up in the air—even so the Son of Man must be lifted up, so that everyone who believes in him may have life. Don't you see, Nicodemus? You said your soul seemed to you like a barren, hemmed-in plain. Break down its barriers, widen its horizons, let God's light flood it, and even as the spring sunshine makes the fields blossom, so his light will make your soul alive with new interest, new hope, new joy, new life, life in its fullest sense. Lift up the Son of Man within you, and this new life will be life eternal. That's what it means to be born again, not once, but every day and every hour."

As Jesus spoke these words, night gave place to dawn. The untrammeled song of a lark swept over the hillside and lost itself in the immensity of waking life.

"It is as though that song had come out of my heart," Nicodemus began. He wanted to say more, to make some expression of gratitude, but he could not find the right words. "I came to you in the night," he hesitated, "a soul seemingly without life; now in the dawn I go back—reborn."

WHOM HE GIVES TO DRINK WILL THIRST NEVERMORE

Best known for his play CYRANO DE BERGERAC, *the French dramatist Edmond Rostand turned to a biblical theme for* THE WOMAN OF SAMARIA, *written expressly for the celebrated actress Sarah Bernhardt in 1897. Following is an excerpt from a scene in which the woman, whom Rostand has named Photine, encounters Jesus at the well of Sychar (or Sichem). Alone by the well, Jesus is speaking.*

I AM WEARY. Yes, but therefore was I born.
My hands are torn by many a wayside thorn;
My feet are blistered by the rocks they pressed,
But from my bruised body is exprest
Some wine of healing, as from trodden grapes,
In the winepress poured, the purple juice escapes.
From willing weariness some help will flow
To these, my brethren. While I walk below,
Each pang I bear has some result divine,
And I, O Father, conquer by this sign.
Now that I almost faint from weariness,
Thy love will send some token of success . . .
Straight fall the sunbeams. 'Tis the bright sixth hour.
A flute-like voice drifts like a breeze-tossed flower.
A woman comes from Sichem. Past the turn,
Hither she comes to draw. . . . The sun's rays burn.

Three panels from a 13th-century church lesson book illustrate the story of Jesus and the Samaritan woman (top to bottom): their discourse at the well, the surprise of his disciples; her departure to summon fellow Samaritans.

So near she is that I can see her plain,
The silken girdle and the golden chain,
The veil enshadows, but hides not her grace,—
My Father's gift to all the Hebrew race.
I hear her silvern anklets softly ring.
Jacob, thy daughters, coming to this spring,
Always, advancing with unhurried tread,
Poising the jar on nobly lifted head,
Come, with grave smiles and half mysterious air;
Conforming to the graceful urns they bear,
Their bodies slender vases; handle-wise
Their curved arms lifted to the brooding skies.
    [*At this moment, the Samaritan woman appears at the top of the hill, on the footpath.*]
Immortal splendour of this gesture free!
Always it seems most beautiful to Me,
This gesture every Hebrew woman learns,
Bearing to wayside wells the heavy urns,
For with that very gesture,—Ah, I know,—
A Hebrew maid came, thirty years ago,
The little, gentle handmaid of the Lord,
As yet untroubled by the wondrous word
That Gabriel bore her, in the Almighty's name.
So with her cruise my lovely Mother came.
This woman is a sinner. Carelessly,—
A vase that knows not the divinity
Her bare arms raised to Heaven yet dimly proves,—
She sings, while dreaming of unworthy loves.
    PHOTINE [*coming down the footpath*]
*O take ye the foxes that ravage the vines.
    This love is a weight on the heart.
    Bring me grapes, O my love . . . We will perish, apart.
All gifts are my true lover's signs.*
    [*Photine has reached the well, and, without seeing Jesus, she fastens the amphora to the windlass and slowly lets it down.*]
    JESUS
Not for a moment has she turned to Me.
    [*Photine turns the heavy wooden windlass that draws up the rope, lifts her water jar, and moves up the footpath, humming her broken song.*]
She is going. If I make no sign,
She too will go away. Yet all are mine—
    [*Photine is nearly out of sight.*]
O Woman,—I am athirst. The sun is very hot!
Give me to drink, I pray.
    PHOTINE
    The Jews deal not
—He is a Jew, this thirsty, wayworn man,—

With Sichemite or with Samaritan.
Little or large, all dealings they decline.
Our bread, they say, smells of the flesh of swine.
Honey from Sichem hives the Jews refuse;
They say it tastes of blood. My dripping cruise
Came from Samaria's tainted well but now.
A heathen bears it on her unclean brow.
You should refuse it, finding it to stink,
Instead of asking for . . .
 JESUS
 Give me to drink!
 PHOTINE
Has your great thirst your teaching so refuted?
Know, Jew, that you would be the less polluted
Handling foul vermin, reptiles poisonous,
Than being succoured so by one of us.
Stay till tomorrow. Either sit or stand.
I'll not let down my pitcher to my hand.
'Tis on my shoulder. There it will remain.
Ho, Eleazar, lacking gifts and train!
I'm not Rebecca, as you seem to think.
Be thirsty if you will. You shall not drink.
 [She comes back a little way.]
You see this water,—clear, so pure, so clear,
The cruise seems empty, though I filled it here,
So cool one sees the moisture on the cruise;

Silver and pearl this draught—which I refuse.
O Beggar, hear the thirst-provoking sound,
The tinkle, tinkle, in its depths profound,—
Light as a draught distilled of summer air!
No water is so cool, so clear, so fair.
Ah, well for you, the Law, be very sure,
Says that this purest water is impure!
 JESUS
 If you but knew the gift of God,
And Who brings light when in the dark you shrink—
And Who He is that says Give me to drink;
Who sitteth here upon the well's wide rim,
He would not ask of thee, but thou of Him.
 PHOTINE
You speak in riddles just to make me heed.
 JESUS
I would give living waters to thy need.
 PHOTINE
Stranger, I listen, for I have no choice,
Some Influence masters me,—your eyes, your voice.
You speak of living waters. Yet you keep
Nothing to draw with, and the well is deep.
Whence hast thou then that water, wondrous Jew?
—It must be false and yet I think it true,—
Is there, in all the sources of Judea,
Water as limpid as this water here?

Jesus and the Samaritan
woman are the subject
of etchings by a
19th-century artist,
J. Schnorr von Carolsfeld
(above, left), and a master
of the 17th century,
Rembrandt van Rijn (right).

People an hour away come here to draw.
Our father Jacob built it, when he saw
The land athirst. Here drank his mighty sons,
Their wives, their servants, and their little ones.
Most famous of all famous springs and wells.
What is it this mysterious stranger tells?
Here Jacob's cattle ages since were fed,
Art greater then than Jacob?

> JESUS
> Thou hast said.

> PHOTINE

In your cupped hands a little I will pour
Then you will see . . .

> JESUS
> He thirsteth nevermore

Whom I have given to drink. With how much pain
You come to draw again and yet again,
But whoso drinks the living draught I give
Within himself shall welling fountains live,
And life eternal from those waters brim,
If he but drink the draught I bring to him.

> PHOTINE

What! For eternity to have no thirst?
A good thing to believe,—if one but durst.
Elijah's draught lasted a wondrous while

While he was in the desert. Ah, you smile?
Some learning to this woman you must grant—
He went for forty days and did not want.
You've learned his secret in your wandering?
O Master, lead me to that hidden spring.
Show me this wonder, that your wanderings saw,
That I thirst not, nor hither come to draw.
Give me this water. Stranger, I implore,—
This living water, that I thirst no more.

> JESUS

Go call thy husband and return to me.

> PHOTINE

I have no husband.

> JESUS
> Verily,

Thou saidest truly. Five men by that name
Were called, and thou would call a sixth the same.
Thou saidest truly, yea, and well
Thou hast no husband, it is truth you tell.
That holy name thou hast no right to speak.
Five men have had thee. Didst thou seek
God's blessings, or the blessings of God's priest?
Troops of young friends, and wholesome marriage feast?

> PHOTINE

Lord, Lord! a prophet surely . . .

Who Were the Samaritans?

When Samaria, the capital of the northern kingdom of Israel, fell to the Assyrians in 721 B.C. and its citizens were carried off into captivity, other Jews considered the destruction to be God's punishment for the northerners' idolatry, witchcraft, and sorcery. In Jesus' day, people living in the area were known as Samaritans, but no one really knows who they were or where they came from — though it has been suggested that they were descendants of the Israelites who escaped deportation and had intermarried with non-Jewish settlers. They believed in one God, Jahweh, whom they worshiped in a temple on Mount Gerizim.

Jews regarded the Samaritans as contemptible heretics and outcasts. On several occasions noted in the New Testament, Samaria was inhospitable to Jesus and his ministry; even so, individual Samaritans are praised for their goodness or their faith, including the Good Samaritan of Jesus' parable and the woman he encountered at the well.

Although acknowledging only the first five books of the Hebrew Bible as Scripture, Samaritans read from scrolls similar to those of the Jews.

All that remains of the Samaritan temple atop Mount Gerizim are these foundation stones.

In this representation of the story told in the Gospel of John, the Italian artist Giovanni Domenico Tiepolo captured the Samaritan woman's wonderment upon learning she had met the Messiah.

JESUS
Thou callest me prophet since I know thy heart.
It is but part, and such a little part,
If thou wilt learn, of things that I can show.
    PHOTINE
O Master, canst thou tell?
    JESUS
    What wouldst thou know?
    PHOTINE
'Tis then: You Jews our whole religion spurn
Because we worship here, and yet we learn
That your forefathers,—who are also ours,—
Worshipped here only. Have the heavenly powers
So changed?
    JESUS
Be of good comfort, for the hour is nigh
When all will worship God, both low and high,
Wherever any humble soul finds space

To speak to God. He dwells not in one place.
God is a Spirit. They who worship Him
Will never reach Him at the horizon's rim.
The Spirit goes where never foot has trod.
Nowhere, and Everywhere, man finds his God.
    PHOTINE
I have lived far from God. I can receive
Only a little, but I do believe
Three things: the dead will some day come again;
Angels have visited this mortal plain,
And—fairest, surest hope beneath the sun,—
I wait the coming of the Promised One,
Await and love him, L'Ha-Schaab, Christ, Messiah!
    JESUS [*lifting his eyes to heaven*]
Hear her, O Father. Woman, have no fear.
Thou sayest the words that I have longed to hear.
Lift up thy head. Behold thy soul's Desire.
I—I that speak—am He. I am Messiah.

The French artist Gustave Moreau (1826–1898) made Salome a demure maiden about to begin a provocative dance before Herod Antipas. The tetrarch is seated on an ornate throne in a cavernous, opulent, and highly imaginative palace.

WHEN A YOUNG GIRL DANCED

According to the Gospels of Matthew and Mark, John's execution by order of Herod Antipas is a result of the vengeance of his wife Herodias. In the following selection from THE GREATEST STORY EVER TOLD, *Fulton Oursler recreates the infamous party at which Antipas's stepdaughter and niece Salome danced.*

BY NOW JOHN THE BAPTIST had been kept in prison at the palace in outlying Machaerus for so many months that his friends no longer lived in daily fear of his being put to death. There was really only one person who desired his blood: the queen, Herodias. She had never softened her scolding hatred; day and night she seethed in secret with an unyielding fury that poisoned all her thoughts.

In celebration of his birthday, Herod Antipas had invited all the bigwigs of Galilee—princes, tribunes, important officials—to come and sup. At the appointed time they came, smiling their superior Roman smiles, flattering themselves as being sybarites and voluptuaries in a barbaric colony, making clear to one another with nudges and glances their contempt for this arrant provincial kingling, but making no secret, either, of their appreciation for his savory meats and well-aged wines.

The night was hot, moist, and still. The tall banquet hall was lit with torches and long tapers and the sultry air was thick with the smell of roasts and heady liquors. The voices of the feasters rampaged above the sinuous, devious songs of the minstrels. There was hardly one sober head at Herod's table when, at the height of the feast, the damask curtains parted and the king's stepdaughter came mincing in for the principal performance of the evening.

She was the daughter of Herodias, this Salome, and the daughter also of Philip, Herod's brother. For an instant the damsel stood poised with outstretched hands—her fingers moist with oils pressed from rare petals, attar in her hair, and the exact purpose of seduction in her brain.

The players of the harps, the strokers and incessant beaters of the drums began their rhythmic motions, and Salome in the transparency of a diaphanous robe began to dance. Forward and back she moved in barefoot steps. At a final *chassé* movement, across to right and back to left, there was let loose a very hell of noise, bellows of praise, and the clapping of hands, the stamping of feet! Salome, a little scared at such incendiary success, would have run off, but Herod drew her to him.

"Ask me whatever you want, Salome, and I will give it to you," he whispered hoarsely. "Whatever you shall ask, Salome, my sweet, I'll give you—though it be half my kingdom."

Salome remembered her instructions and ran off to the queen, who waited in another apartment.

"Mother, Mother, what *shall* I ask for?"

The mother told the girl quickly enough. The kingly boon must not be anything Salome might want for herself, but what the mother desired with all her vengeful soul. The man John! The desert preacher with his pale face and cavernous eyes. That prude Baptist who had condemned her to the people for her new marriage. That insensible Baptist who, of all men she had known, was untroubled by her voluptuous beauty, unkindled by her fire. That water-splashing, locust-chewing, honey-sipping giant who would not yield to the natural passions of a man.

The beheading of John is among 20 scenes from the Baptist's life created in bronze for the doors of the cathedral baptistery in Florence, Italy, by Andrea Pisano (c. 1270–1348); other of his panels appear on pages 34 and 123.

"John the Baptist!" Herodias commanded intensely. "Ask for his head!"

A little disappointed, now bored and languorous, Salome ran back into the banquet hall, back to the king. He chuckled at sight of her. "Well, Salome, what will it be?"

"I will that immediately you give me in a dish the head of John the Baptist."

The king's eyes were sobered with unexpected horror. A moment of incertitude and then he realized that his wanton vow must now be paid in blood. The Romans watched him with sheer gloating delight; in his quandary he was making good sport for them. They made bets on whether he would dare fulfill his own oath or be forsworn before them all. How, they sniggered, would he dare invoke by murder the ill-will of the crowds who had been baptized by John? Yet how perjure the royal word?

Those Romans knew that the pampered Queen Herodias, indulged in all her wishes, had long desired this very thing. And they suspected that she had coached her child in that bawdy dance and waited for this drunken opportunity. A captain, who commanded a thousand Roman soldiers, told his neighbor: "Herod is in a box. He will be wrong now no matter what he does."

None could guess that there was something more than political concern in Herod's heart, that the conscience of the king had been beleaguered by this rugged giant from the wilderness. John was strong, where the king was weak; John believed, where Herod was always in doubt; John was positive, and Herod loved him for it.

But the king knew there was no excuse even for a reprieve, no chance for a temporary delay. "Fetch the executioner!" he said miserably.

Hurrying to the prison, the executioner, shoving aside guard, keeper, and warden, woke John from a peaceful sleep. He ordered the prisoner, clad in his long, sleeveless garment of haircloth, to kneel and lay his head on a butcher block. With one expert swing the axman cut the head from the long, muscular neck. By the untidy hair he lifted the dripping head and let it fall in a deep dish of gold, then carried it to Herod. And the king gave it to the hands of the child.

Now, as Salome started back toward the damask curtains, at her very first step the harpists smote their strings and the drummers beat with their sticks, and almost unconsciously the girl fell into the old writhing of her dance. Her hips swayed again as she passed through the curtains, the lifted dish with the dead man's head held high in her little-girl arms. She laid the bloody thing at the feet of her mother and then, like a sleepy crosspatch, had to be put to bed.

A servant woman holds the platter for its grisly offering in Michelangelo da Caravaggio's painting of the beheading of John dated 1608 (below, left). Herod is clearly horrified by the gift Salome requested in the gilt bronze relief (below, right) that Donatello (c. 1386–1466) made for the baptismal font in the church of San Giovanni in Siena, Italy.

Named after the Roman Emperor Tiberius, Herod Antipas's capital on the western shore of the Sea of Galilee was a center of Jewish learning from the second to the sixth century. The modern town on the site was founded in 1922.

Herod Antipas, the Fox

The most politically gifted of Herod the Great's sons, Herod Antipas inherited only part of his father's kingdom at the death in 4 B.C. of the tyrant who had ordered the massacre of the innocents. Although he was not a Jew by ancestry, Antipas reigned for 43 years as tetrarch of principally Jewish Galilee, firmly keeping the peace and respecting the religious beliefs of his subjects. His presence in Jerusalem at the time of Jesus' arrest and trial, for example, indicates that he celebrated the Passover feast with a pilgrimage to the Holy City. Ambitious and luxury-loving, Antipas built the beautiful seaside town of Tiberias. (Ironically, the construction work uncovered an ancient cemetery, making the site ritually impure to observant Jews, and Antipas was forced to populate his new capital with foreigners and people of the lower classes.) On the international stage, he won the respect of Rome as a skilled and loyal diplomat.

Antipas's downfall began when he fell in love with Herodias, who was both his niece and sister-in-law. His enraged wife, the daughter of a Nabatean king, escaped to her native land, and her father punished his errant son-in-law with a disastrous military defeat. In the New Testament, Jesus calls Antipas "that fox," perhaps referring to his cleverness, but the tetrarch is also shown giddily succumbing to the wiles of Herodias when he orders the execution of John the Baptist. She was also responsible for his final, fateful error. Jealous that her brother Agrippa had been elevated to a kingship, she urged Antipas to go with her to Rome to ask Caligula for a crown, too. The emperor, convinced by letters from Agrippa that Antipas was a traitor, banished the tetrarch to Gaul in A.D. 39. The proud Herodias was offered sanctuary in Rome, but she chose exile with her husband instead.

To avoid offending his Jewish subjects' distaste for graven images, Herod Antipas put neither his own portrait nor that of the Roman emperor on the coins of his realm.

None Greater Than the Baptist

Herod Antipas's arrest and imprisonment of John the Baptist, according to Matthew and Mark, took place during the 40 days Jesus spent in the desert following his baptism. In his book A LIFE OF JESUS, Edgar J. Goodspeed summarizes John's influence on Jesus.

THE FEW MONTHS of Jesus' active ministry are strangely interwoven with the work and fate of John the Baptist. It was the fame of John's preaching that had drawn Jesus from his carpenter's bench at Nazareth down to the Jordan thickets where John, a wilderness prophet whose clothes and ways made people think of Elijah, was thundering repentance and proclaiming a mightier one to come in judgment after him.

Jesus found John all he had anticipated and more. He said afterward to his own disciples, "I tell you, among men born of women no one has ever appeared greater than John the Baptist."

He had made the greatest friends of his life there in John's camp meetings by the Jordan—the men who afterward became his own first disciples and then the inner circle within the chosen band of the twelve. He found his own message and mission at his baptism, and in the succeeding weeks of moral struggle in the wilderness. The initial impulse to begin to preach came to Jesus when on returning to the scene of John's meetings, he had found the Baptist's followers gone, and John himself hurried off to prison.

John had aroused the anger of Antipas when in his denunciation of the evils of the day he had pointed to the action of Antipas in putting away his lawful wife, the daughter of King Aretas of Arabia, and marrying Herodias. Even in prison Herodias wanted him put to death for this, but Antipas stood in awe of John and occasionally listened to what he had to say, though he found it very disturbing.

Herodias found her opportunity when in his birthday revels Antipas was entertaining his officers and courtiers, probably at his palace in Tiberias, which he had rebuilt in some splendor. In the course of this celebration, Herodias' daughter came in and with entire disregard of her rank gave a dance before the governor and his friends that so delighted him that he offered to give her anything she wanted.

After going out to consult her mother, she came back to the banquet hall and said to the governor, "I want John the Baptist's head on a platter!"

This horrible request sobered Antipas, but with all his boon companions about him he had not the courage to refuse, and he gave her what she asked.

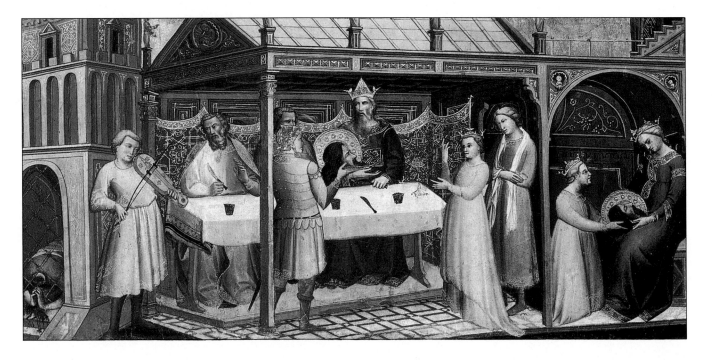

This depiction of Herod's banquet by Lorenzo Monaco (c. 1370–c. 1422) contains sequential scenes in the drama: a headless John, hands still clasped in prayer (left); a soldier bringing the Baptist's head on a platter (center); Salome presenting the trophy to her mother, Herodias (right).

Demanding John's Head on a Platter

Salome, the daughter of Herodias, gained enduring notoriety for her dance before Herod Antipas and for the outrageous request she made at her mother's prompting. In this entry from PECULIAR TREASURES, a whimsical who's who in the Bible, Frederick Buechner puts the tale in contemporary language.

ONE OF THE LESS OFFENSIVE acts of King Herod Antipas was to walk off with his brother's wife, Herodias—at least there may have been something like love in it—but it was against the law, and since John the Baptist was a stickler for that sort of thing, he gave Herod a hard time over it. Needless to say, this didn't endear him to Herodias, who urged her husband to make short work of him. Herod said he'd be only too pleased to oblige her, but unfortunately John was a good man with a strong following, and it might lead to unpleasantness.

Then one day he threw himself a birthday party, and one of the guests was Herodias' daughter by her former marriage. Her name was Salome, and she was both Herod's stepdaughter and his niece. As it happened, she was also a whiz at dancing. Sometime during the evening she ripped off a little number which so tickled Herod that, carried away by the general hilarity of the occasion, he told her he'd give her anything she wanted up to and including half of his kingdom.

Since she already had everything a girl could want and was apparently not eager for all the headaches that taking over half the kingdom would undoubtedly involve, she went out and told her mother, Herodias, to advise her what she ought to ask for.

It didn't take Herodias twenty seconds to tell her. "The head of John," she snapped out, so that's what Salome went back and told Herod, adding only that she would prefer to have it served on a platter. No sooner was it brought to her than she got rid of it like a hot potato by handing it over to her mother.

Salome disappears from history at that point, and you can only hope that she took the platter with her to remind her that she should be careful when she danced that particular dance in the future, and that she should never ask her mother's advice again about anything, and that even when you cut a saint's head off, that doesn't mean you've heard the last of him.

Although the look on her face is one of smug satisfaction, Salome's stance reveals her repugnance for the prize she has won. This painting is the work of the Italian master Titian (c. 1490–1576).

Jesus blesses the kneeling boy's loaves and two fish in the foreground of this fresco from a church in Poggibonsi, a small town near Siena, Italy. In the middle ground, the disciples marvel at a basket of leftovers after the crowd (right rear) has been fed. The artist, Gerino da Pistoia, added figures romping with dogs in the background.

AS HE WALKED WITH US

Calm, strong and gentle Man of Galilee,
Whose heart by every human woe is stirred;
By whom are plaintive cries of creatures heard;
Whose eye escapes no tracery of tree,
Or modest wayside flower; alert to see
The fantasy of cloud, the flight of bird;
Whose ear can catch the faintest note and word
Of wind and stream, and distant western sea;
When I am treading on the open space,
Or threading slowly through the crowded marts,
Skilled Craftsman of the woods and market-place,
Companion to all life and human hearts,
I crave, Thou unseen, understanding Guide,
To find thee, silent, walking by my side.

HARRY WEBB FARRINGTON

Lifting up his eyes, then, and seeing that a multitude was coming to him, Jesus said to Philip, "How are we to buy bread, so that these people may eat?" This he said to test him, for he himself knew what he would do. . . . Andrew, Simon Peter's brother, said to him, "There is a lad here who has five barley loaves and two fish; but what are they among so many?"

JOHN 6:5–6, 8–9

A LAD WITH LOAVES AND FISH

Although all four Gospels relate the miracle of Jesus feeding the 5,000, only John says that it was a boy who provided the five loaves and two fish. Agnes Sligh Turnbull seized on this detail for the following story taken from her book FAR ABOVE RUBIES.

IT WAS LATE SUNSET beside the Sea of Galilee. Peace and beauty lay all around, but there was no peace in the heart of the woman who walked hurriedly past Bethsaida and Capernaum to a rock commanding a view of the sea. For Miriam, the wife of Jonas the fisherman, was hopeless and bitter to the point of despair. She was still a young woman, but her youth showed only occasionally in her dark eyes. She threw herself upon the rock and began to weigh the years of her life in the balance.

Her home was a rudely built house of two rooms, the only furniture being a battered clay lamp, the mill at the doorway, a table, a pallet, and a stool. Miriam kept the hut clean, but her work was endless—water to carry, meal to grind, fish to clean for the market.

So time had passed, and before Jonas could buy his own boat there had been hungry mouths to feed and grim, biting poverty had come. The children were sound and strong; Jonas looked upon them with pride, but Miriam had but a weary, passive affection for them. As soon as Mark, the eldest, was old enough, Jonas took him in the boat; and when he was twelve, he was allowed to go to Capernaum to sell fish.

One evening the boy had come running home quite excited. "I could hardly sell my fish. Nobody was at home. And then all at once I saw the crowd before Simon's house. They were standing away out in the street. I tried to get in, but no one else could get near the door. And just then I saw four men carrying a pallet. They went close to me and I could see the sick man upon the bed. He had palsy. They tried to get in to the rabbi, but they could not get through the crowd, so the bearers went up the outside stairs to the roof and lifted some tiles and let the sick man right down in front of the rabbi. In a few minutes he came out, walking. The rabbi had healed him."

"Come, eat your supper, Mark," Miriam said, wearily. But Jonas was curious. "What does the rabbi look like?" "I could not see him," Mark replied.

Only this day, at noon, little Mark had again come running in and had thrown his basket down. "Mother," he cried, "the rabbi I told thee of—the one who healed the palsied man—is over there, across the sea on the mountainside, and everyone from Capernaum and Bethsaida is going over to see him and hear him teach. Mother, wilt thou let me go? I must see him." His voice was passionate with eagerness.

"Thou must eat first," said Miriam.

"But I am not hungry. If I tarry I may miss him!"

"Still, thou must eat," Miriam replied, firmly. "Here," taking a handful of the barley cakes she had just baked and two of the small fish on the table, "take these with thee. Thou canst eat them on the way. But be not later than sundown returning."

The afternoon passed, the sun began to go down, and Mark had not returned. She started to find him, and came to the shore where the boats were for crossing, and asked for help. Soon she was on the eastern bank and went up the way directed, where the boatman said there must have been thousands following the rabbi. At last she reached the crest of the hill and stopped, for she saw a great multitude seated, listening to a man who stood before them.

The sunset light rested upon his face as he spoke. She crept closer and saw suffering there, longing, a lonely sorrow that does not speak. Also love and sympathy, infinite strength. Stronger than all, there was the rare light of sublime and holy joy, of the peace that passeth understanding.

He stopped speaking and several men drew near him and they talked together. Miriam could not hear what they said. Suddenly one of them turned and pointed behind him. It was then she saw Mark. He sat in the front row of people, his dark eyes riveted on the rabbi's face. In one hand he absently clutched his open basket. Miriam could see that the food she had placed there was still in it. The eager, foolish lad; he had taken no time to eat. But all at once Miriam's eyes grew large with wonder.

The young men were going among the people, separating them into groups, making paths between them. Then one of them went up to Mark and after a word took the basket from the boy's willing hand and, turning, gave it to the rabbi. The Master gazed steadfastly toward heaven, then beckoned to the men. They came bearing large empty baskets. There was a sudden straining forward on the part of the multitude, for out of Mark's tiny basket, held directly in their view, he was filling the others. Heaping them with loaves and fish.

The disciples went among the people, distributing the food, and returned to have the baskets refilled again and again. Miriam was on her knees, trembling. This man, the Master, had taken her poor food from the hands of her own little lad, and with it had wrought a miracle. It was as if God, himself, had reached down from his heavenly place to touch her humble hand.

At last she raised her head. The Master was watching her with clear, searching, asking eyes. With a cry she stretched forth her hands. "Master," she whispered, "thou hast opened my eyes. I will be faithful." He smiled and turned to look upon Mark, who still sat rapt, his eyes raised to the Master's face in worship. Her own little lad! And she had never seen the beauty of his soul.

She rose and ran quickly to Mark. She listened lovingly to his passionate talk of wonder and the child, warmed by her new interest, showed her the adoration of his heart.

Miriam knew that out of the common daily elements which her heart had so despised, there would come to her evermore now the miracle! She knew that in each day of lowly, wearing, faithful toil, she would see again the face of the Master of Men.

Framed by the letter "L" in this detail from a choral book in the cathedral library of Siena, Jesus blesses the food he is about to provide for the 5,000. Below, the same scene from the devotional book illuminated for the duc de Berry by the Limbourg brothers early in the 15th century.

The multiplication of the loaves and fish was fashioned in high relief for a cathedral in Holland.

BARLEY BREAD

As I was going down the street to sell my loaves of barley,
A crowd of men were following the man from Nazareth,
And I in wonder followed too,
Outside the town where lilies grew,
And cyclamen, and bells of blue, —
I ran till out of breath.

"Barley bread, barley bread! Who will buy my barley?
Sweet and crisp as any from the oven in the square,
Buy my loaves of bread, and fish
Freshly caught as one could wish"—
I followed them beyond the town and found him waiting there.

A hollow place among the hills was filled with many people,
And there upon the trodden grass he made the men sit down,
A long way from the gates it was, and we were tired and hungry,
A crowd of hungry people big enough to fill a town.

They came with jingling silver then and bought my bread and fishes;
He broke them there in sight of all, and lifted up his hands.
And everyone had food to eat—
My fish as good as any meat,
And barley bread, so brown and sweet,
Enough for his demands.

My heart was strangely stirred within, to see him feed the people;
I looked and loved him, standing there, the sunlight on his head;
And as the sun set on the hill,
And all the men had had their fill,
We gathered up the fragments, and went home at last to bed.

O Teacher out of Nazareth, if I have aught to give you,
Take, take the little that I have, just as you took my food,
For till today I never heard
A thing so moving as your word;
So take my loaves of barley bread and feed the multitude.

HILDA W. SMITH, c. 1889–1984

*And when evening came, the boat was
out on the sea, and he was alone on the land.
And he saw that they were making headway
painfully, for the wind was against them.
And about the fourth watch of the
night he came to them, walking on the sea.*

MARK 6:47–48

"DON'T BE AFRAID. IT IS I."

*Following the miracle in which he fed 5,000 with
only five loaves of bread and two fish, Jesus dismissed
the crowd, sent his disciples by boat to the other side
of the Sea of Galilee, and withdrew into the hills
to pray alone. His subsequent appearance to the
tempest-tossed disciples was dramatized
by Dorothy L. Sayers in one of a series of plays
she wrote for radio, published in 1943 as
THE MAN BORN TO BE KING. At the beginning of
this scene, Simon Peter is speaking.*

ULL HARDER BOYS—there's a nasty storm coming up. Look at those black clouds driving across the moon. It'll be a dirty night. I hope the Master got away from the crowds safely.

JUDAS: I hope he did. And I only hope—never mind!

ANDREW: What, Judas?

JUDAS: I only wondered. Was he getting rid of the people—or of us? They may be making him king now.

SIMON: What, without us? He wouldn't let us down like that. If there are any crowns going, we shall be there.

PHILIP: Sitting on thrones, judging the twelve tribes of Israel. He said so.

JUDAS: Did he indeed?

JAMES: One day when we were arguing about the kingdom. But I think he was making fun of us. Anyway, he wouldn't go and do anything behind our backs.

JUDAS: Are you quite sure?

JAMES: Of course, I'm sure. What a beastly idea.

JOHN: I don't think Jesus wants to be made a king. Not that sort of king anyway.

JUDAS: No? Well, he was rather asking for it, wasn't

he? All those people, and a miracle like that! What did he expect?

JOHN: The people don't understand.

THOMAS: Do any of us understand?

JOHN (*vaguely*): When I held the bread in my hands—so little—and yet enough and to spare for all that multitude—God's plenty, multiplying itself in my hands—I don't know! It was as though we had touched the very source of life—as though—

(*Storm increases*)

SIMON: Don't dream! Keep her head to the waves!

ANDREW: Whereabouts are we?

SIMON: Not more than three miles out, with this wind. Put your backs into it!

ANDREW: Look out! There's a squall coming.

(*Crash of waves breaking over the boat*)

All right, there?

JAMES: We've shipped a lot of water.

MATTHEW: I don't like this. Give me the dry land.

JOHN: Poor Matthew! Here, take this bowl and bale out.

MATTHEW: Oh, well—we can only die once. They that go down to the sea in ships see the wonders of the Lord—yes, I don't think. It's all very well for you chaps, you're used to it, but if ever I—(*with a yell of very real terror*) Ow! Ow! Look there!

ANDREW: What is it?

MATTHEW: There! There! Something coming along—walking on the top of the waves—

JUDAS: Nonsense!

JAMES: I can't see anything.

MATTHEW: Wait for the moon—there! Over there! Look! It's a spirit or something!

DISCIPLES (*crying out together*): Heaven defend us! It's a demon! An angel! The ghost of a drowned man! How fast it comes! It's catching us up!

SIMON: Row for your lives!

MATTHEW (*rapidly*): God forgive me, God forgive me. I've been a great sinner—

PHILIP: If only the Master were here!

JAMES: Speak to it, somebody.

SIMON: In the name of God, what are you?

JESUS: I AM.

SIMON: It spoke the great name of God.

JESUS: Don't be afraid. It is I.

JOHN: It is the Master.

SIMON: Is it really you, Lord? Don't go! Wait for me.

JESUS: Come then, Simon.

SIMON: Yes, yes, I'm coming.

*Jesus steps lightly over
the waves to grasp
an obviously foundering
Peter in this 13th-
century manuscript
illumination.*

Spying Jesus across the water, Peter steps from the wave-buffeted boat to join his Lord. This panoramic canvas is the work of the 16th-century Venetian master Jacopo Tintoretto.

ANDREW: Simon—what are you about? Stay in the boat. You're mad.

SIMON: Let me go!

ANDREW: Trim the boat. Take care. Hold her! Back her! Catch him, somebody.

JAMES: He's gone. . . . He's walking on the water. . . .

PHILIP: The waves bear him up. . . .

JOHN: His eyes are on the Master—O great and merciful God! . . .

THOMAS: He's looking back at us—he's waving to us.

DISCIPLES (*together*): He's gone under.

SIMON: Help, help! I am drowning. Help, Lord!

JESUS (*quite close*): Hold on. I am here. I've got you. Why did you lose faith all of a sudden?

SIMON: I was afraid—I looked back—

JESUS: You were all right till you stopped to think about yourself. Into the boat with you!

ANDREW: Pull him in, boys! . . . Look out there! (*Wind and waves*)

JESUS: Well, children? Is there room for me?

DISCIPLES: Yes, Master. Yes, of course.

JESUS: You're not afraid of me, are you?

JOHN: Master, when you are here we are afraid of nothing. . . . Shift over, Matthew. . . . Dear Master—

JESUS: Peace be unto you. (*The wind drops instantly*)

SIMON: The storm is over.

JESUS: Row on now, for we are nearly at the land.

*Remonstrating with Peter for his lack of faith,
Jesus grasps the disciple as he is about to
sink beneath the waves. This 19th-century
etching is the work of J. Schnorr von Carolsfeld.*

WALKING ON THE SEA

When the storm on the mountains of Galilee fell,
    And lifted its waters on high;
And the faithless disciples were bound in the spell
Of mysterious alarm—their terrors to quell,
    Jesus whispered, "Fear not, it is I."

The storm could not bury that word in the wave,
    For 'twas taught through the tempest to fly;
It shall reach his disciples in every clime,
And his voice shall be near in each troublous time,
    Saying, "Be not afraid, it is I."

When the spirit is broken with sickness or sorrow,
    And comfort is ready to die;
The darkness shall pass, and in gladness to-morrow,
The wounded complete consolation shall borrow
    From his life-giving word, "It is I."

When death is at hand, and the cottage of clay
    Is left with a tremulous sigh,
The gracious forerunner is smoothing the way
For its tenant to pass to unchangeable day,
    Saying, "Be not afraid, it is I."

When the waters are passed, and the glories unknown
    Burst forth on the wondering eye,
The compassionate "Lamb in the midst of the throne"
Shall welcome, encourage, and comfort his own,
    And say, "Be not afraid, it is I."

NATHANIEL HAWTHORNE, 1804–1864

The Sea of Galilee

At 680 feet below sea level, the Sea of Galilee is the world's lowest freshwater lake, with a length of about 13 miles, a width of up to 8 miles, and a depth of as much as 150 feet. Also known in ancient times as the Lake of Gennesaret, the Sea of Tiberias, and the Sea of Chinnereth (the name of an important shore town), this normally calm body of water shimmers deep blue in a semitropical climate, fed by the Jordan River in the north and surrounded by the verdant fields and orchards of Galilee. Often, however, fierce storms abruptly rise up and toss the waters about — as happened when Jesus lay asleep in his disciples' boat. In the north, there is scant protection from strong winds; southward, turbulence can spring up without warning because of temperature shifts between the low-lying lake and the hills around it.

In Jesus' day, the fishing industry contributed to the enviable wealth of the region. Dried, salted fish were exported throughout Palestine and to lands beyond. Simon Peter and Andrew were working their nets here when Jesus called them to become "fishers of men." The headquarters for his Galilean ministry was the seaside town of Capernaum; Mary Magdalene came from the nearby hamlet of Magdala. In this idyllic Galilean setting, Jesus fed the 5,000 with five loaves and two fish and exorcised the demons from a possessed man, driving them into a herd of swine. Here, too, Jesus appeared to his disciples after the Resurrection, ending his earthly mission by charging Peter to feed his sheep.

*Still pure enough to drink, the water of the Sea of Galilee
is home to approximately 40 different species of fish.*

And when he got into the boat, his disciples followed him. And behold, there arose a great storm on the sea, so that the boat was being swamped by the waves; but he was asleep.

MATTHEW 8:23–24

With their boat about to be swamped in a storm on the Sea of Galilee, the disciples hasten to rouse Jesus, asleep in the stern. The maritime scene is by Rembrandt van Rijn.

EVEN THE WINDS AND SEA OBEY

*Awakening Jesus, the disciples beg him to save them
from the storm—a plea that leads him to rebuke
them for having so little faith. Nonetheless, he quells the
storm, causing them to marvel at his power.
Marjorie Holmes's version of the story is from her
novel* THE MESSIAH, *published in 1987.*

THE STORM STRUCK SWIFTLY. The water, at first like a bolt of silver cloth covering the gently heaving body of a sleeping woman, was suddenly seething, as if the woman herself had risen up in a violent temper, screaming and yanking at the sails. Peter, steering the ship in a diagonal course across the lake, was not at first concerned.

He grinned, as Judas came reeling toward him, pale with alarm, grabbing at the rails. "Don't worry, I know these squalls. We can ride this one out and be on shore within the hour," Peter yelled into the wind. But a blast of wind nearly tore the rudder from his hands, and he began to bark orders.

The waves, swollen to glistening monsters, were bearing down upon them, snarling at the fragile craft. James and John were already darting about like monkeys; the other men, drowsing below or on the deck, threw off their cloaks and came running to help. Even Judas, who knew little of wind and canvas, sprang to the task, obediently following commands.

Thunder crashed, lightning nearly split the sky, whipping fire across the black heaving water. The wind roared; there was the steady lash of the waves. Where is Jesus? Peter worried. James had reported that he was sleeping. How could anyone lie peacefully sleeping, as if this were a night of calm seas?

Judas, drenched to the skin and terrified now, was suddenly at Peter's elbow. "Where is our Master? Why isn't he up here with us?"

"Say no word against him!" Peter bellowed. Yet his own fear had begun to poison his heart. Why am I out on such a night when the lightning strikes at us like flaming spears and the waves snarl? What am I doing following this man who has promised us the kingdom, yet lies sleeping while the waves are like whales threatening to devour us?

A glassy mountain, huge, dark, glistening, was suddenly upon them, bashing the boat, its white crest exploding over the bow; all were sent skidding and crashing into one another and against the rails. At the same instant there was another flash of lightning. Half blinded by the light, stunned by a blow on his head, Peter found himself on his hands and knees. "I will go fetch him," he panted. "He will save us."

Peter began fighting his way toward Jesus, Andrew and Philip just behind him. Another flash of light revealed the still white form, the curly head propped peacefully against the wooden pillow. So utterly still he lay, undisturbed by the pitching and rolling, he might have been a statue—or a corpse. New terror struck Peter. "Master, wake up, wake up!" he screamed.

Jesus sat up, blinking, and gazed at them, for an instant bewildered. Then he, too, felt the pitching and rolling, heard the furies. Springing to his feet, he pushed past them and strode to the rail.

They saw him standing there for a moment, feet apart, bracing himself with his hands. His head was back, his chin outthrust, his face lifted to the storm, as if to welcome its cold wet torrents and the wind that so wildly blew his hair. There was power and dignity in his stance, as if he were embracing its very assault. He lifted his arms in a gesture of both authority and release. "Peace, be still!" he cried out.

The men could feel the boat shuddering under their feet. They staggered and clung to each other as it gave a final lurch. Looking up in amazement, they realized the avalanche of rain had stopped. Only a few scattered drops still fell. The wind had ceased. The angry sea calmed, the very skies began to clear until only a few clouds remained, scudding across the face of a placid moon.

Jesus turned and beckoned to them. "It grieves me that you were so troubled," he said kindly. "But oh, Peter, don't you remember the night you first rowed me away from the shore? Have you forgotten the great haul of fish where there had been no fish for days? And the boat that was sinking? You too, James and John," he addressed them—and all the others who stood shivering and astonished. "Have you not yet learned there is nothing to fear so long as you are with me? Why does it take you so long to believe in the Father who sent me? Where is your faith?"

Awed, they went back to mop up the deck, repair the battered sails. The night was far gone. They discussed it among themselves until morning. Marveling at this man who could not only heal the sick and raise the dead but command the storm. Who was he that even the winds and the raging seas obeyed him?

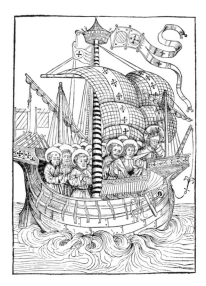

*Jesus asleep during
the storm at sea is the
subject of the 1491
etching above and the
medieval manuscript
illumination below.*

CHRIST STILLING THE TEMPEST

*And when he had
ceased speaking,
he said to Simon,
"Put out into the
deep and let
down your nets
for a catch." And
Simon answered,
"Master, we toiled
all night and took
nothing! But at
your word I will let
down the nets."*

LUKE 5:4–5

Fear was within the tossing bark,
　　When stormy winds grew loud;
And waves came rolling high and dark,
　　And the tall mast was bowed:

And men stood breathless in their dread,
　　And baffled in their skill—
But One was there, who rose and said
　　To the wild sea, "Be still!"

And the wind ceased—it ceased!—that word
　　Passed through the gloomy sky;
The troubled billows knew their Lord,
　　And sank beneath his eye.

And slumber settled on the deep,
　　And silence on the blast,
As when the righteous falls asleep,
　　When death's fierce throes are past.

Thou that didst rule the angry hour,
　　And tame the tempest's mood,
Oh! send thy spirit forth in power,
　　O'er our dark souls to brood!

Thou that didst bow the billows' pride
　　Thy mandates to fulfill,
Speak, speak, to passion's raging tide,
　　Speak and say—"Peace, be still!"

FELICIA DOROTHEA HEMANS, 1793–1835

THE FISHERS

Yea, we have toiled all night. All night
　　We kept the boats, we cast the nets.
Nothing avails: the tides withhold,
　　The Sea hears not, and God forgets. . . .

So, stricken with the cold that smites
　　Death to a dying heart at morn,
We waited, thralls to hunger, such
　　As the strong stars may laugh to scorn.

And while we strove, leagues out, afar,
　　Returning tides—with mighty hands
Full of the silver!—passed us by,
　　To cast it upon alien lands.

Against the surge of hope we stood,
　　And the waves laughed with victory;
Yet at our heartstrings, with the nets,
　　Tugged the false promise of the Sea.

So all the night-time we kept watch;
　　And when the years of night were done,
Aflame with hunger, stared on us
　　The fixed red eye of yonder sun.

Thou Wanderer from land to land,
　　Say who Thou art that bids us strive
Once more against the eternal Sea
　　That loves to take strong men alive.

Lo, we stood fast, and we endure:
　　But trust not Thou the Sea we know,
Might of bounty and of hate,
　　Slayer and friend, with ebb and flow.

Thou hast not measured strength as we
　　Seafaring men that toil. And yet—
Once more, once more—at Thy strange word,
　　Master, we will let down the net!

JOSEPHINE PRESTON PEABODY, 1874–1922

Another example of Jesus' mastery of nature is recounted in Luke 5:4–10. After having sat teaching from Simon Peter's boat, Jesus told him to put out into the deep and lower the nets even though he had fished all night without success. Peter's compliance was rewarded with a remarkable draft of fish that threatened to sink his boat and that of his partners who came to the rescue. Raphael (1483–1520) drew the cartoon on which this tapestry was based; it now hangs in the Vatican.

In this painting by Jan Brueghel the Elder (1568–1625), Jesus stands—not sits, as the Gospel of
Matthew says—in a boat along the shore of the Sea of Galilee to speak to the people in parables. The Flemish artist,
noted for his landscapes, added a homely detail in the left foreground: fishermen cleaning their catch.

LESSONS FROM A BOAT

From his unique, waterborne pulpit Jesus taught in parables that helped explain the kingdom of heaven to his eager audience. In the following essay from her anthology CHRIST AND THE FINE ARTS, *Cynthia Pearl Maus retells two of them.*

THE POPULARITY OF JESUS as a teacher grew very rapidly, not alone because of the simplicity and directness of his address, but also because of the poetic beauty of the stories he told and the homely, familiar illustrations he used.

Crowds came pouring in from all sides to hear this new and comparatively unknown rabbi from despised Nazareth. So much so that he was forced to get into a boat belonging, no doubt, to one of his disciples, and to push out into the lake. Along the shore of the Sea of Galilee, eastward from Capernaum, there is a lovely little bay shaped like a horseshoe. Many thousands of people can sit on the shore at this spot and hear clearly a man speaking from a boat in the middle of this curve in the bay.

From this vantage point, one day, Jesus began to say to the multitude that gathered on the shores: "Behold, a sower went forth to sow. And as he sowed some seed fell along the path, and the birds came and soon pecked it up. Other seed fell on rocky ground, where there was but little soil. It shot up quickly, but because there was no depth of soil, it soon withered away under the scorching rays of the noonday sun. Still other seed fell among the thorns and brambles and they stifled it so that it yielded no crop."

Every growing lad on the beach could understand that kind of teaching; for had not they seen, many times, the thorny little plants, whose names are legion in Palestine, crowd out the good seed?

"But," continued Jesus, "some seed fell on good ground, and yielded a bountiful crop. It grew and increased and gave for the labor of the sower sometimes thirty- or sixty- or even a hundredfold." Then he added, "All of you that have ears to hear, listen! and profit by the wisdom of the careful sower."

Again we find Jesus using simple, wayside, growing things by which to illustrate what God's kingdom of love is like. His listeners knew that the mustard seed was one of the smallest and most bountiful of all seeds. It grows in abundance around the Sea of Galilee and along the Jordan Valley. One day he said to them, "The Kingdom of God is like the mustard seed, which is the smallest of all seeds."

The mustard plant, particularly in the Jordan Valley, where it is often cultivated, is very pungent and penetrating, and when crushed makes not only seasoning for foods, but healing for the skin as well. It grows annually to a height of from eight to ten feet, often towering above the smaller herbs; and the birds—goldfinches and linnets—flock to perch on its branches and to feast on its tiny seed. It is a wonderfully productive plant, not only beautifying the garden with its rich yellow blossoms, but also producing each year tens of thousands of black seeds.

Doubtless because of both its beauty and its productiveness, and certainly because of its familiarity, Jesus used this plant to illustrate for his disciples, and the multitude gathered on the shores of Galilee, what God's kingdom of love is like. Just a little of the spirit of God hidden deep in the soil of the human heart leavens and makes beautiful and useful the whole of one's life. But stony hearts, hard hearts, hearts that are interested in the trivial things of life, are unproductive soil for God's kingdom of love. Again and again we find Jesus using homely, familiar things with which his hearers were well acquainted to picture for them what God's kingdom of love was like.

It is small wonder that his disciples liked to sit with him in a boat at the end of a busy day of teaching, now and then rowing off to the other side of the lake, to listen to the rich cadences of his voice as he explained to them the deeper meaning of his parables and sayings often lost by the multitudes who in increasing number flocked to hear this teacher who "taught with authority"—the authority of sincerity and truth—"and not as the scribes."

Giving an example his rustic listeners could easily understand, Jesus likened himself to the good shepherd who lays down his life for his flock. Jesus was depicted as a shepherd from at least as early as the third century, the date of this sculpture.

> **"There was a man who had two sons; and the younger of them said to his father, 'Father, give me the share of property that falls to me.' And he divided his living between them. Not many days later, the younger son gathered all he had and took his journey into a far country."**
>
> LUKE 15:11–13

THE PRODIGAL SON

Thus Jesus began one of his most famous parables, a tale used to explain how God's love prompts forgiveness whereas mortal selfishness withholds it. James Weldon Johnson, a prolific author and a longtime leader of the National Association for the Advancement of Colored People, cast the parable as an old-fashioned revivalist's sermon in verse.

Young man—Young man—
Your arm's too short to box with God.

But Jesus spake in a parable, and he said:
A certain man had two sons.
Jesus didn't give this man a name,
But his name is God Almighty.
And Jesus didn't call these sons by name,
But ev'ry young man,
Ev'rywhere,
Is one of these two sons.

And the younger son said to his father,
He said: Father, divide up the property,
And give me my portion now.
And the father with tears in his eyes said: Son,
Don't leave your father's house.
But the boy was stubborn in his head,
And haughty in his heart,
And he took his share of his father's goods,
And went into a far-off country.

There comes a time, there comes a time
When ev'ry young man looks out from
   his father's house,
Longing for that far-off country.

And the young man journeyed on his way,
And he said to himself as he travelled along:
This sure is an easy road,
Nothing like the rough furrows behind
   my father's plow.

Young man—Young man—
Smooth and easy is the road
That leads to hell and destruction.
Down grade all the way,
The further you travel, the faster you go.
No need to trudge and sweat and toil,
Just slip and slide and slip and slide
Till you bang up against hell's iron gate.

And the younger son kept travelling along,
Till at night-time he came to a city.
And the city was bright in the night-time like day,
The streets all crowded with people,
Brass bands and string bands a-playing,
And ev'rywhere the young man turned
There was singing and laughing and dancing.
And he stopped a passer-by and he said:
Tell me what city is this?
And the passer-by laughed and said: Don't you know?
This is Babylon, Babylon,
That great city of Babylon.
Come on, my friend, and go along with me.
And the young man joined the crowd.

Young man—Young man—
You're never lonesome in Babylon.
You can always join a crowd in Babylon.
Young man—Young man—

You can never be alone in Babylon,
Alone with your Jesus in Babylon.
You can never find a place, a lonesome place,
A lonesome place to go down on your knees,
And talk with your God, in Babylon.
You're always in a crowd in Babylon.

And the young man went with his new-found friend,
And brought himself some brand new clothes,
And he spent his days in the drinking dens,
Swallowing the fires of hell.
And he spent his nights in the gambling dens,
Throwing dice with the devil for his soul.
And he met up with the women of Babylon.
Oh, the women of Babylon!
Dressed in yellow and purple and scarlet,
Loaded with rings and earrings and bracelets,
Their lips like a honeycomb dripping with honey,
Perfumed and sweet-smelling like a jasmine flower;
And the jasmine smell of the Babylon women
Got in his nostrils and went to his head,
And he wasted his substance in riotous living
In the evening, in the black and dark of night,
With the sweet-sinning women of Babylon.
And they stripped him of his money,
And they stripped him of his clothes,
And they left him broke and ragged
In the streets of Babylon.

The young man joined another crowd—
The beggars and lepers of Babylon.
And he went to feeding swine,
And he was hungrier than the hogs;
He got down on his belly in the mire and mud
And ate the husks with the hogs.

And not a hog was too low to turn up his nose
At the man in the mire of Babylon.

Then the young man came to himself—
He came to himself and said:
In my father's house are many mansions,
Ev'ry servant in his house has bread to eat,
Ev'ry servant in his house has a place to sleep;
I will arise and go to my father.

And his father saw him afar off,
And he ran up the road to meet him.
He put clean clothes upon his back,
And a golden chain around his neck,
He made a feast and killed the fatted calf,
And invited the neighbors in.

Oh-o-oh, sinner,
When you're mingling with the crowd in Babylon—
Drinking the wine of Babylon—
Running with the women of Babylon—
You forget about God, and you laugh at Death.
Today you've got the strength of a bull in your neck
And the strength of a bear in your arms,
But some o' these days, some o' these days,
You'll have a hand-to-hand struggle with bony Death,
And Death is bound to win.

Young man, come away from Babylon,
That hell-border city of Babylon.
Leave the dancing and gambling of Babylon,
The wine and whiskey of Babylon,
The hot-mouthed women of Babylon;
Fall down on your knees,
And say in your heart:
I will arise and go to my Father.

Working in watercolor and ink on paper around 1800, an American primitive artist named Frederich Krebs illustrated the parable of the prodigal son in the panels above (from left, opposite page): the departure; loose living in a far country; forced to work among the swine; welcomed home.

Then the disciples came and said to him, "Why do you speak to them in parables?" And he answered them, ". . . because seeing they do not see, and hearing they do not hear, nor do they understand."

MATTHEW 13:10–11, 13

THE TELLER OF TALES

The Gospels are replete with parables, the disarmingly simple tales Jesus used to get his message across to the humble folk who flocked to hear him. In THE POET OF GALILEE, *a work published in 1909, William Ellery Leonard examined Jesus as an unsurpassed storyteller.*

In response to the lawyer's question, "And who is my neighbor?" Jesus spoke the parable of the good Samaritan. In an illustration from the renowned sixth-century Gospel manuscript in the cathedral library at Rossano, Italy, the Samaritan finds the half-dead robbery victim (left) and takes him on his own beast to an inn (right).

THE STORIES OF JESUS bear witness to a teeming, creative brain. With wonderful economy of effort he sets his characters before us as living men and women. His device is not to describe, but to show them doing or speaking, whether it be the good Samaritan binding up the wayfarer's wounds, or the shepherd coming home rejoicing with the lost sheep on his shoulder, or the woman sweeping her house in search of a lost coin, or the unjust steward with his account books.

With the realistic exactness of one reporting an incident out of his own experience, he mentions now one, now another characteristic detail, such as only a poetic imagination would emphasize. With him it is not simply a grain of mustard seed, but a grain of mustard seed that a man took and cast into his garden, and it grew and became a tree and the birds of the heavens came and lodged in the branches thereof. Even in the brief mention of the woman making bread, he tells us she hid the leaven not simply in the meal, but in three measures of meal—and that makes her an actual housewife. These apparently trivial touches reveal the born storyteller.

Again, his people are always represented as occupied with something interesting, something in which they are themselves vitally interested—whether it be buying land to make sure of a treasure buried there, or hunting for a lost sheep, or building a house, or guiding the plow—usually something that his peasant companions or groups of chance listeners would have found particularly interesting as a part of their own world. Though Jesus tells the story of a king and his army, and of a rich merchant and his pearl, most of his inventions concern the homely activities of fisher or vine-dresser or shepherd or the familiar, if learned, scribe and judge.

The merciful Samaritan ministers to the wounded man who lies stricken at the roadside in this work by the 19th-century German artist Carl Julius Milde.

Near to the folk also was his constant use of what our grammar calls "direct discourse." He reports the householder, who went out at different hours of the day to hire more laborers for his vineyard, as in actual conversation in the market-place; he does not tell us the prodigal said he would arise and go to his father, but he lets us overhear the prodigal speak.

Near to the folk, again, are his repetitions, like those familiar in ballad poetry and in all primitive recitals: as "Enter thou into the joy of thy Lord" in the parable of the talents; and "I have sinned against heaven" of the prodigal son; and "I pray thee have me excused" in the parable of the invitations: each repeated with the simple directness of an old folk tale.

The background is but lightly drawn, even in such a vivid scene as the prodigal feeding the swine; or it is omitted altogether, where, however, the convincing reality of the actors suggests it so truly that we are surprised to find on rereading that our imaginations have supplied so much. Here again is seen the magic of the artist: it is not what his imagination does for us, so much as what it is able to make our imaginations do.

But these stories exist not for themselves alone; like all great art, they have a meaning beyond themselves. Each exists for an idea; they all illustrate the ethical or religious principles that fired the imagination of the Poet of Galilee. It seems indubitable that no other body of poetry so slight in quantity ever contained teachings of equal loftiness and equal scope.

Teaching in Parables

Among them, Matthew, Mark, and Luke record 39 parables of Jesus, representing about one-third of all his teaching. Many of these overlap, although each Evangelist has unique stories. (There are no parables in the Gospel of John, who quotes Jesus as saying, "I shall no longer speak to you in figures but tell you plainly of the Father.") Evidently, Jesus believed that these simple, straightforward tales about familiar situations would most effectively communicate God's message to his largely uneducated, unsophisticated listeners. *Parabole*, the original Greek word, implies a comparison or parallel. Jesus usually drew a clear parallel between an imagined incident in daily life and an ethical or religious concept. Often, he gave his stories a surprising twist, as when he sympathetically portrayed a despised Samaritan or the repentant prodigal son, but most of his tales concluded with a clearly stated moral.

The parables as a whole, however, sometimes raise difficult issues. In particular, why did Jesus once explain to his disciples that he used parables so that outsiders "may indeed see but not perceive and may indeed hear but not understand"? Some suggest that he was hiding his message from his enemies, including the Pharisees. Others believe that he was merely acknowledging the sad fact that many who heard him would resist the truth expressed in his parables or lack the spiritual depth to understand. Other problems include different interpretations sometimes given to the same parable in different Gospels, and occasional mismatching of a story and moral. But these apparent inconsistencies are easily explained by the vagaries of oral tradition. Jesus spoke the parables aloud; then they were passed down by word of mouth. Perhaps four decades or more after the Resurrection, the early Christians began to collect and write down the parables, obviously working from many different versions. Even so, the major theme of the parables still comes through strongly: mankind must prepare through sincere repentance and loving faith for the great spiritual joy that will characterize the coming of the Kingdom of God.

One of the most beloved images created by Jesus is the good shepherd, here adorning an early Christian baptismal font.

The loops of the letter "B" encircle two scenes of Jesus casting out demons. The manuscript illumination is from a 12th-century Bible in the cathedral library at Winchester, England.

They came to the other side of the sea, to the country of the Gerasenes. And when he had come out of the boat, there met him out of the tombs a man with an unclean spirit.

MARK 5:1–2

The Unclean Spirit Whose Name Was Legion

Unlike the Jews who ate no pork, the Gerasenes living southeast of the Sea of Galilee kept herds of swine. And one such herd was unfortunate enough to become the refuge of demons fleeing Jesus' power. The central section of Sholem Asch's novel THE NAZARENE, *from which the following passage comes, is cast in the form of a long-lost memoir of Judas Iscariot.*

THE PLACE WAS EMPTY and forlorn and without inhabitants. And wild stones were sown upon the hill, the head of which hung straight above the water. And the stones were like unto a stairway hanging falsely above an abyss. And a damp green moss grew upon the stones, and herbs such as are not seen in inhabited places, thick and thorny and grasping like the claws of beasts at our garments and tearing at our flesh, making it to bleed.

And we beheld ourselves enclosed among the spearlike growths upon the hanging steps, and great terror fell upon us as though we had been set beyond the bounds of God's grace. For the place was such as seemed in no wise to pertain to the creation of the Lord—though it be forbidden to think that there can be a place beyond the bounds of grace.

As we stood there it seemed that the forbidden thought was confirmed. For there arose soon a mighty cloud of dust which veiled the light of the sun; and in the darkness there was a tumult, and the tumult was not of the storm, but as of the oncoming of evil hosts. And in the tumult there was a yelling, but not as of beasts but as of tormented spirits. And the dust and yelling came from hordes of wild swine, which like demons descended from unknown heights.

After them, there came running the swineherds; and they cried in fear, for they were pursued by a wild man, a giant for size, naked and covered with growth like a beast of the field. And he had not a face in human likeness, but in that of a beast, and his eyes shed fire, and his nose was like a mighty, twisted trumpet, and from his mouth, which was as the gateway of hell, looked forth his teeth like unto spears.

But when the wild man beheld us, then he ceased from pursuing the swineherds and turned his path toward us. But ere he reached us he perceived the white robe of the Rabbi, who stood among the wild growths with arms outstretched as though to receive him. And the wild man paused in his flight and looked upon our Rabbi, who stretched out his hands and cried: "Come to me, thou lost son!"

And we saw the wild man start, and flee toward our Rabbi, at first as it seemed to us in fury, and as if to fall upon him. But when he came close he halted, as if the look of our Rabbi had calmed him, as the look of the trainer calmeth a wild horse. And they two stood over against each other, the wild man and our Rabbi with outstretched arms. And behold, it was like the wrestling of Jacob with the angel; even so our Rabbi wrestled with the evil one, but not with his hands, only through his eyes. And our Rabbi spoke to him with compassion: "Calm thyself, my son. I know thy father's house, and I know whence thou comest. Return, for thy father awaiteth thee."

And when the wild one heard this, he lifted up a mad voice and cried: "And how shall I return to my father's house, seeing that my father's house is clean and I am unclean? Demons have made their nest in my flesh, and they smite me continually with a thousand sicknesses. Legions dwell within me and my name is legion."

And he threw himself to the earth and yelled with a thousand voices, as though armies of wild cats were within him and coursing through his body, seeking a way out and finding it not. And he shook and trembled in all his limbs.

And my Rabbi laid his hands upon him and bade the demons depart from the man, and to torment him no more; but that they should enter into the swine, which rolled upon the stones and fell into the sea. And my Rabbi said unto him: "Legion is no more thy name, but Israel, as thy father hath called thee. And no more a wild man art thou, but a child of thy father, a lost son that returneth home."

SWINE RUSHING TO THE SEA

*Jesus' casting of the demons into the Gerasene swine
dismayed and terrified the local inhabitants.
The anonymous author of BY AN UNKNOWN DISCIPLE,
from which this excerpt comes, describes the scene.*

THE DAWN WAS BREAKING when we reached the land after a stormy passage across the lake, and I followed Jesus up the slope of the shore to the brow of the headland. There a herd of swine was slowly rooting its way towards us.

The swineherds had turned aside to eat their morning meal, and, as they ate, pigs of all sizes and colors, of all ages and shapes, moved on alone, occupied only with filling their bellies. Here a small pig grunted in anger as he was pushed aside by a gaunt sow. There a great boar, with tusks pushed up under his lip, thrust himself out from the crowd with sidelong blows of his heavy head to seize the portion of some smaller pigs, who fled, squealing.

Jesus stood still to watch, and, as he watched, he smiled. When he spoke, it was to answer the question that had remained unspoken in my mind. "No," he said, "why should we call them unclean? They are God's creatures as we all are."

He turned as a man came forward out of the group that stood behind and said, "Rabbi, it is not safe to be here. There are madmen amongst the tombs. They are possessed by demons. They can be heard screaming day and night. Though they have been bound with chains and fetters, one that I saw plucked the fetters from him as a child might break a chain of field flowers. Then he ran, foaming, into the wilderness, and no man dare pass by that way now."

Jesus lifted his eyes to the man's face. "Have men tried only this way to tame him?" he asked.

"What other way is there, Rabbi?" asked the man.

"There is God's way," said Jesus. "Come. Let us try it." And he went towards the tombs. The swineherds joined us, leaving their pigs rooting and grunting.

*Nearly a thousand years separate these two versions
of Jesus driving the unclean spirits into the Gerasene swine:
a 19th-century watercolor by the French artist James
Joseph Jacques Tissot (top) and a 10th-century manuscript
illumination (bottom, foreground detail).*

As a friend restrains the possessed man, Jesus exorcises the evil spirit. This illumination is from the duc de Berry's 15th-century devotional book, other scenes from which appear on pages 71, 191, and 232.

It was not many cubit lengths to the tombs, but the others were far behind when we reached that desolation. I caught sight of the madman at the moment that he first saw us, for, as I touched Jesus to point to his naked figure, he began to run towards us shrieking and cutting his flesh with sharp stones. The men behind us fled down the hillside, but Jesus stood still and waited.

"Be at peace!" he said, reaching out to touch the man. And Jesus put his own cloak upon him and led him apart amongst the tombs to where he could wash the blood from his limbs.

It was then that the swineherds, who with the others devoured by curiosity had drawn near again, remembered their swine, and turning saw them on the edge of the cliff.

"See!" cried one to the other, "the swine are in danger. We shall lose some of them."

They ran warily, one to each end of the cliff, meaning to get between the swine and the sea. Some bystanders, being ignorant and unskillful, yet wishing to help, ran swiftly down the hillside in the face of the swine, who, seeing them come in haste, turned quickly and rushed in a mass towards the sea.

"Stand back!" shouted the swineherds. "You will drive them over the cliff." But it was too late. The swine had rushed one upon another, and the slope was steep, and in a moment they were swept over the edge of the cliff into the sea. The swineherds ran to the cliff edge and looked over to see where the swine were drowning in the deep water below.

"It is the devils!" one of the bystanders said. "They went into the swine. Did you not see how they left the madman? They talked with the Rabbi, and he gave permission for them to enter into the swine."

"It must be so," said one swineherd to the other. "We will go and tell our master. He will surely see that it was not our fault."

When the swineherds returned with their master, and he saw the madman sitting clothed, he, too, was afraid. And he talked with the crowd, and some of them came forward, and he asked if they might speak, and when Jesus gave them leave, they begged him to go away out of their country, for they had fear of him. And Jesus, looking at them, saw that it was true, for they trembled as they spoke, and he had compassion on them, and said that he would go.

The Persistent Belief in Demons

Demonology, or belief in demons, was pervasive throughout the ancient Near East from the time of Sumer in the third millennium B.C. Dwelling near cemeteries or in the desert wilds, evil demons might be the ghosts of people who died violently. They were thought to cause diseases and other human suffering but were considered less powerful than pagan gods. Occasionally, good demons intervened in human affairs.

The Hebrews, unlike the neighboring Canaanites and other peoples of that era, tended to dismiss demonology. When evil spirits torment a sinner's mind or inflict disease, the Scriptures make clear that they are servants of the Lord's will, not independent agents. The Old Testament prohibitions against magic were, in effect, warnings against demonology, since pagan magic was principally aimed at warding off demons.

In Jesus' day, belief in disease-causing demons, or unclean spirits, persisted among the common people, but the ancient superstitions took on new meanings. In the last centuries before Jesus, Jewish theorists had begun to picture demons as tempting humans into wickedness rather than merely bearing physical affliction. These evil spirits followed the dictates of a prince known by such names as Belial, Mastemah, or Satan. In other words, Jewish thinkers — perhaps under the influence of Persian beliefs in a continuing cosmic war between good and evil — saw God and his angels in conflict with demonic forces for control of heaven and earth and for the souls of men and women.

The work of a contemporary American folk artist, this devil treats his victim as a puppet.

Rushing to drown themselves in the sea, the Gerasene swine trample one herdsman and send another fleeing in terror. This 1883 painting is by the British artist Briton Riviere.

"And when you pray,
you must not be
like the hypocrites;
for they love to
stand and pray in
the synagogues
and at the street
corners, that they
may be seen by
men. . . . But when
you pray, go into
your room and shut
the door and pray
to your Father who
is in secret; and
your Father who
sees in secret
will reward you."

MATTHEW 6:5–6

*Fra Angelico (1387–1455)
placed Jesus in a stark
landscape to deliver
the Sermon on the Mount
to his 12 disciples. As
Matthew reported, Jesus
sat for the lesson—the
usual position for a rabbi
when teaching his followers.*

The Lord's Prayer

Among the many revolutionary injunctions contained in the Sermon on the Mount is Jesus' instruction on prayer. Roger L. Shinn analyzed the Lord's Prayer in THE SERMON ON THE MOUNT, *which he subtitled "A Layman's Guide to Jesus' Most Famous Sermon."*

IMMEDIATELY AFTER WARNING his hearers not to "heap up empty phrases," Jesus went on to give them a prayer that has been muttered as empty phrases more times than anyone can count. Evidently men still need to learn about prayer.

In approaching the Lord's Prayer notice again what Jesus says about the reasons for praying, especially the wrong reasons. In addition to one wrong motive—to "be seen by men"—Jesus describes a second. The motive for prayer is not to provide God with information that he lacks. Critics often remark that they see no value in prayer, because if there is a powerful, personal God, he knows already what we tell him in prayer. Those who say that do not usually realize that Jesus said it first. But Jesus drew a different conclusion.

After rejecting the false motives for prayer, Jesus does not go on to say why men should pray. Perhaps he felt that if people do not know the reasons for prayer, there is no use telling them. Perhaps he saw that good reasons cannot be stated so neatly and glibly as bad reasons. His hearers are left to decide for themselves why anyone should pray. But they are not left without any clues. They have all of Jesus' life and teaching as a help. They have especially the accounts about his own praying—most notably that night of prayer in the garden of Gethsemane.

Jesus' prayer was often solitary prayer, and he recommends praying "in secret." Jesus points to the value—yes, the necessity—of the solitary approach to God. But he sees the need of both solitude and community. The pronouns of the Lord's Prayer are ours, us, we—not my, me, I. This prayer is for the community of disciples, united by the same Spirit.

Few prayers are shorter or use simpler language than the Lord's Prayer. The whole prayer can be read aloud in seconds. Yet the simplicity may be deceptive. The understanding of the prayer involves all of Jesus' message and the depths of our own spirits. The words carry a weight of meaning from the whole gospel. We see this when we examine the petitions.

"Our Father who art in heaven." Augustine says that the opening words are already the answer to the prayer, for we can ask nothing greater than to approach the Lord of the universe as Father. There is still something breathtaking in the idea. Think of the universe of modern physics and astronomy, a universe of uncounted galaxies and mysterious cosmic rays, a universe of distances measured in light years. Then address the creator, "Our Father."

"Thy kingdom come, thy will be done." The phrases are both petitions and expressions of trust. They call on God, who alone can establish his kingdom. And they call on the praying person to conform to the will of God.

The heart of the prayer, "Thy kingdom come," is the heart of Jesus' whole message. He bids his disciples pray for that work of God, already beginning but not yet complete.

Although the kingdom is a gift of God, its practical significance for us is clear in the petition, "Thy will be done, on earth as it is in heaven." The citizens of God's heavenly kingdom are called to live by God's will on earth. That should be the normal expectation of any religious commitment. But here, set in the midst of the Sermon on the Mount, it is a call to daring life. Purity of heart and mercy, persecution for righteousness' sake, men lighting the world for God's glory, love for enemies—all this is the will of God. For this we pray whenever we join Christ in his prayer.

"Give us this day our daily bread." Immediately the prayer turns from the exalted and the strenuous to the commonplace. What is so common as daily bread? Here in the midst of language about the holiness of God and the wonder of his kingdom is the prayer for bread—one of man's ordinary needs. To pray for bread—for oneself and the world—is as basic to the Christian as to pray, "Hallowed be thy name."

When the disciples first learned this prayer, they did not know that the day was coming when their Lord would offer them bread, saying, "This is my

In this 12th-century manuscript illumination, Jesus incorporates the lessons contained in the Sermon on the Mount in a scroll handed down to his 12 apostles.

body." In Christian faith it is as natural to pray for bread as to use this same commonplace bread in the sacrament of the Lord's Supper.

"Forgive us our debts." Anyone who has read the Sermon on the Mount up to this point will not be surprised by the prayer for forgiveness. Once again we see that the New Covenant is a covenant of grace. We meet its terms not by perfect compliance with God's will, but by accepting in faith his forgiveness.

This faith will prompt us to forgive. In Matthew's account, the prayer is followed by the foreboding words of verses 14-15. The idea is not that God is only as generous as we are. The gospel often refutes that idea. But if we refuse to forgive, we lack the faith that can accept forgiveness.

"Lead us not into temptation." Does a good God deliberately tempt us? If he wants to test us, should we pray that he not do so?

Here, as in some other sayings of Jesus, we can get help from the scholars who translate the Greek back into the probable Aramaic words of Jesus. Then the sentence means this: "Do not allow us to be led into temptation." Or: "Do not let us be tested beyond our capacity to endure." God is not the tempter; but he has put us into a world of temptations.

In this world we may prayerfully seek to avoid temptations. But what is more important, we pray that we shall not yield to them, that God will deliver us from the evils into which we might be tempted.

Christians often conclude the Lord's Prayer with the words: "For thine is the kingdom and the power and the glory, for ever. Amen."

This final doxology or paean of praise does not appear in the oldest manuscripts of the New Testament. By the second century, we know, Christians were using it widely. It echoes earlier themes in the prayer: it hallows God's name and it ascribes to him lordship in his kingdom. Probably Jesus did not include these words; the early church added them, in accord with the general liturgical practice of ending public prayers with an expression of praise.

Amen means *truly, verily,* or *may it certainly be so.* When Christians end this prayer with a genuine Amen, they glorify God. While the church has often drawn up creeds to define loyalty, Christ gave his followers a prayer rather than a creed. Christians, separated by doctrines and ecclesiastical authorities, are able to unite in this prayer. That is appropriate, since the prayer comes from Christ himself.

THE LORD'S PRAYER

Our Father which art in heaven,
Hallowed be thy name.
Thy kingdom come.
Thy will be done,
    in earth, as it is in heaven.
Give us this day our daily bread.
And forgive us our debts,
    As we forgive our debtors.
And lead us not into temptation,
    but deliver us from evil:
For thine is the kingdom,
    and the power, and the glory,
    for ever. Amen.

MATTHEW 6:9–13 (King James Version)

THE BEATITUDES

Blessed are the poor in spirit:
    for theirs is the kingdom of heaven.
Blessed are they that mourn:
    for they shall be comforted.
Blessed are the meek:
    for they shall inherit the earth.
Blessed are they which do hunger
    and thirst after righteousness:
    for they shall be filled.
Blessed are the merciful:
    for they shall obtain mercy.
Blessed are the pure in heart:
    for they shall see God.
Blessed are the peacemakers:
    for they shall be called the children of God.
Blessed are they which are persecuted
    for righteousness' sake:
    for theirs is the kingdom of heaven.
Blessed are ye when men revile you,
    and persecute you, and shall say all manner
    of evil against you falsely, for my sake.
Rejoice and be exceeding glad:
    for great is your reward in heaven:
    for so persecuted they the prophets
    which were before you.

MATTHEW 5:3–12 (King James Version)

Jesus' original 12 disciples, flanking him on the mountain, are the first to receive the words of the Lord's Prayer, but lesser folk below await the instruction. Exceptionally rich colors, including gold applied as paint, were used in this manuscript illumination dating to the second half of the 13th century.

*And as he sat at table in his house,
many tax collectors and sinners were sitting
with Jesus and his disciples; for there
were many who followed him. And the
scribes of the Pharisees . . . said
to his disciples, "Why does he eat with
tax collectors and sinners?"*

MARK 2:15–16

WE ARE SICK; HE ALONE IS WELL.

*The sick, not the well, need a physician, Jesus
responded; he came to call to repentance not the righteous
but the sinners. W. Russell Maltby imagined how Jesus'
friendship changed the lives of two outcasts in the
following "story-letters": the first from Johanan, collector
of taxes at Magdala, to his superior Zacchaeus,
commissioner of taxes at Jericho; and the second
(opposite page), Zacchaeus's reply.*

I HAVE JUST HAD JESUS, the prophet of Nazareth, to dinner today, and a number of our friends came to meet him. As you know, dear Zacchaeus, I was rather nervous about the whole affair. First thing this morning I would have given a good deal to stop the dinner altogether. You and I often say that our sort of people are no worse than other folk; but when I went over the invitations in my mind, I couldn't help feeling that we were a queer company for such a man as this Jesus.

Well, Jesus came. What is he like? If you had asked me halfway through the dinner, I should have said he was the nicest man I had ever met. But now I think— oh, I don't know what to think, except that I am not fit to touch the latchet of his shoes.

I cannot tell you all the things we talked about. They were much the same kind of things you and I might speak of, but there was a difference. I found myself talking to him as though I had known him all my life. I began telling him—I can't think how I did it, now—about how I got into this business of ours, and I was explaining our difficulties and how impossible it is always to keep straight when everybody is try-ing to take advantage of you; and especially in these times when the future is so uncertain and one must make provision while one can for wife and family.

He just listened, and looked straight into my face as though he understood all I said—and all I didn't say, as well—and as though he were sorry for us. He didn't interrupt, or argue with me, but the more I looked at him, the more I wished I had never got into this cursed business, and the more I wished I could get out and begin again.

You will think it ridiculous, but as he sat there, I wondered why we were not all like him. We are all sick; he alone is well. If I had been alone with him, I think I should have made a clean breast of it and asked him what to do. He could see that my feelings were getting out of hand—they say in the town that Johanan has no feelings, and I half believed them un-til today. But really the tears were in my eyes, and I had such a longing, and felt so helpless. And Jesus said to me, as though he understood everything, "Don't be afraid, Johanan. Think it all over again, and remember your heavenly Father knows what you need. Don't lose your life trying to save it."

Well, the meal ended, and, after bidding him good-bye at the door, I watched him till he was out of sight. He is on his way to Jerusalem and is to pass through Jericho. I mentioned you to him. Be sure you see him. Don't let anything stop you.

*Short of stature, the tax collector Zacchaeus—according
to Luke 19:3–4—climbed a tree to see Jesus as he
passed through Jericho. Virgil Solis's woodcut dates to 1562.*

We have missed our way, Zacchaeus. But I think, since Jesus was here, that God has not altogether cast us off. Do you think that we two could begin again?

YOU HAVE MADE Zacchaeus a poor man, dear Johanan. The half of all that I had gathered these many years went at one stroke, and the rest seems likely to follow. It was your letter that did it, and I shall leave you to do the repenting, for I cannot. I am too contented for any grieving.

You told me that I must not miss seeing Jesus, but I nearly did. It was seven days ago when I heard that he had entered Jericho, and I made off to see the man who had made such a difference to you. But there was already a great crowd about him, and I could not get near. So I ran on ahead, clambered on to the bough of a tree, and waited there, sure of a good view.

I saw him in the distance and watched as he came near, thinking he would pass and leave me behind. He came within three paces of me and stopped. He looked me in the face and said, as though I were a friend, "Zacchaeus, make haste and come down. You must give me a home today."

Was I glad? I have asked myself a hundred times why those words quivered all through me. But is it nothing, Johanan, after so long a time, to be treated like a man? He gave me his friendship. Outcasts must make friends with outcasts, for we have no others, but what need had he of me?

I lost no time. I tumbled from my perch, gave him the best welcome I knew how, and turned to lead the way to our house. The chatter of the crowd ceased. There was a horrible silence. The light went out of men's faces and I saw round me nothing but anger and contempt. It seemed as though he had lost all his friends at one stroke, and lost them all for me.

I wondered whether he repented of having involved himself with me, and while I was wondering he drew a little nearer to me as we walked, and said, "You will have room for these other friends of mine?" and he pointed to the young men who were with him. I answered, "Yes," but I was at my wit's end and could no longer play my part. Indeed, Johanan, all my armor was gone. If I could have turned upon them and said, "These men slander me. Publican as I am, my hands are clean!" But I could not say so. For once they spoke the truth when they said that my house was no place for him. I looked at him and my eyes were opened. Beside him, we are all common and un-

Allowing his disciples to pluck and eat grain as they passed through a field on the Sabbath also brought Jesus into conflict with the Pharisees. Abel Grimmer (c. 1570–1640) set the incident in a fanciful northern European landscape complete with a windmill and castles on the river Rhine.

clean. My ears were burning and my thoughts were in a maze; but still I found myself saying, "He must not come to my house in vain"; and just as we reached the house the light broke on me and I knew what to do.

"Listen," I cried, "I will give half of my fortune to the poor, and if I have defrauded any man of anything, I will pay him back fourfold." Then my tongue failed me and I looked to him to see if he could help me out. I could not read his thoughts, but there was a smile upon his face. He lifted his hand as though to bless my house, and said, "Salvation has entered this house today. Zacchaeus, too, is a son of Abraham."

As an enraptured Mary sits at his feet, Jesus turns to admonish Martha, who has interrupted his teaching to complain that her sister has left the serving to her. The painting is one of only about 40 attributed to the Dutch master Jan Vermeer (1632–1675).

TO MARTHA

Martha, his rebuke was gentle;
    Do not grieve
The wasted year that won but disapproval;
    Just believe
Above the disappointment of thy careful day
There glows the selfsame star that shines on
    Mary's way.

MABEL MUNNS CHARLES

He entered a village; and a woman named Martha received him into her house. And she had a sister called Mary, who sat at the Lord's feet and listened to his teaching. But Martha was distracted with much serving.

LUKE 10:38–40

CHOOSING THE BETTER PART

The story of Mary and Martha occupies only a few short sentences in Luke, yet it teaches a universal lesson: the spiritual takes precedence over the temporal. In "Sisters" Eleanor B. Stock allows Mary to take the lesson a step further.

MARY'S LOVELINESS WAS TWIN SISTER to the dawn. She took the road to the village well, and as she walked, life sang in her heart. Life—she saw it all about her—in the sun, whose strong hands pushed the mist aside and clutched the little white houses standing in huddled groups along the road, and in the very road itself stretching so comfortably before her.

Life—she felt it within her—filling her with complete and unshadowed happiness. Life was so splendid a thing! Did it not hold Martha, and Lazarus, and Jesus, their friend, who even now would be taking the road to Bethany that he might break bread with them at sundown?

As she pondered these things she lifted her face with a little gesture of expectancy, and as though she had received a command, she stood perfectly still, poised and attentive. Soon a smile of welcome illumined her face. They had come—the great unseen wings! She felt their gentle touch upon her cheeks. Always, when she thought of the Master and his kingdom, they came. Sometimes they flew past, brushing against her lightly and quickly, leaving her filled with a great buoyancy, a great radiance of spirit; but at other times, when she was tired, when in the early evening she sat in the doorway and watched the stars, they folded and upheld her and filled her with peace.

Jesus at dinner with Mary and Martha is one of many religious engravings produced by the English artist, poet, and visionary thinker William Blake (1757–1827).

She had never spoken about them to Martha. Dear, practical Martha would not understand. But the Master—*he* would understand. Very shyly, she had told him. "It is as the wings of a dove, covered with silver, and her pinions of yellow gold," he had answered her, quoting the words of the Sweet Singer of Israel. "God has gifted you with the sense of His presence."

This morning Mary felt their touch more vividly than ever, and her walk to the village wayside well became a pilgrimage to the Source of Life.

Noon came out of the dawn. Yet Mary lingered. Time slipped by unheeded, *and Martha waited.*

When at last Mary lifted the latch of her door, the crisp fragrance of freshly baked loaves silently reproached her tardiness. She smiled ruefully. "I'm so sorry; I forgot it was our day to use the public oven." Mary put her arms around Martha. "But life's so big and, after all, tasks are so little—like ants, hundreds and hundreds of them, one after another, in a long line from morning until night. Oh, Martha, you ought to step over them once in a while and just forget them, the way I do. But you're tired. Go and rest now, and don't worry about preparing the evening meal; just leave it all to me."

Martha smiled dubiously and patted her younger sister in much the same manner as one pets a charming but willful child.

With the first shadows of evening, Mary stood in the doorway, watching for Jesus. It was not long before she saw him coming along the road. Mary felt a sudden sense of awe. This man, in whom life was so vital, so unfettered and free, this great man with the simple, courteous manners, this poet of a kingdom that lay hidden within the human heart, was Lazarus's friend, and Martha's friend, and hers!

Her tasks unheeded, her resolution forgotten, Mary sat in the doorway, talking with the Master.

"The wings of a dove—have you felt them today?" he asked.

"Yes; they seemed nearer than ever before. But how did you know?"

"The story of their coming is written in your eyes."

Mary and Jesus talked on and on. Busy Martha caught the hum of their voices. Now and then, passing the doorway as she went about her tasks, her eyes grew wistful. A whole radiant world lay open to them that somehow was barred to her. The ache in her heart became unbearable. "Master," she said, her voice almost a sob, "don't you care that I do all the work alone? Tell Mary to come in and help me."

Mary was about to answer Martha, to make the usual excuses, when Jesus said, his voice full of compassion: "Martha, you are troubled with many things. Mary has chosen the better part, that shall not be taken from her."

Instantly the cloud that crossed Mary's eyes gave way to an expression of relief. "That's just what I keep telling Martha. Why, if I always remembered to do the things Martha says need to be done, I would be stirring up such a noisy business, clattering pots and swishing brooms, that the beautiful wings would fly by, ever so softly, far off, in some quiet place on a little pathway, or a hillside open to the sky."

Jesus laughed. "Yes, Mary, you have chosen the better part, but there is only one way to keep it."

"How?"

"I need not tell you, for you already know."

Mary scanned his face, that of a seer and a poet; then she looked at his hands, strong and brown from having worked at countless tasks in the carpenter shop in Nazareth; and she caught a glimpse of the working life, ever creating through dreams, and dreaming through deeds. "I believe I understand now," she said. "They are sisters, not strangers."

"Who?"

"Being and doing," she said, then rose and went in.

The Resurrection and the Life

Now a certain man was ill, Lazarus of Bethany, the village of Mary and her sister Martha. It was Mary who anointed the Lord with ointment and wiped his feet with her hair, whose brother Lazarus was ill. So the sisters sent to him, saying, "Lord, he whom you love is ill."

JOHN 11:1–3

In the painting below, by an anonymous artist, the raising of Lazarus is given a period and setting more appropriate to 15th-century France.

Only John among the four Evangelists tells the story of Jesus raising Lazarus from the dead, and he places it at the climax of the public ministry. It is this miracle, John reveals, that prompts the chief priests and Pharisees to plot Jesus' death. In the following excerpt from Dorothy L. Sayers's play-cycle THE MAN BORN TO BE KING, *John as narrator sets the scene.*

WHEN JESUS CAME TO BETHANY he found that Lazarus had already lain in the grave for four days. And many Jews had come from Jerusalem to comfort Martha and Mary for the loss of their brother. Then Martha, as soon as she heard that Jesus was coming, went and met him on the road, but Mary sat still in the house.

MARTHA: O Rabbi, Rabbi! You've heard the trouble we're in. Lazarus is dead. Oh, if only you had come earlier, you would have healed him and he wouldn't be lying there cold in his grave. Even now, I know that God will give you anything you ask. . . . Yet what can prayers do for one who is dead and buried?

JESUS: Take comfort, dear Martha; your brother shall rise again.

MARTHA: Yes, Rabbi. I know that he will rise again—in the resurrection at the last day.

JESUS: I am the resurrection and the life. They that believe in me shall live, even though they were dead,

Jesus raising Lazarus from the dead is the appropriate decoration of this fifth-century cylindrical box from Syria; the box, called a pyx, was used to carry the host to the sick.

and the living that believe in me shall never die . . . do you believe this?

MARTHA (*puzzled, but sticking to the thing she really does believe*): Yes, Master, I do believe in you. I believe you are the Christ, the Son of God, sent into the world as the prophets foretold.

JESUS: So much at least you believe. Where's Mary?

MARTHA: At home. I'll run and fetch her.

SEQUENCE 2: INSIDE THE HOUSE (*Sound of lamenting*)

MARTHA (*in a low, urgent tone*): Mary, Mary!

MARY: What is it, Martha?

MARTHA: The Master is here and is asking for you. Come quick! He's waiting out there on the road.

MARY: Thank God he has come at last!

MARTHA: Here's a cloak. We'll slip away quietly.
   (*Lamenting continues*)

1ST MOURNER: What has become of Mary?

2ND MOURNER: She has left the house with Martha.

3RD MOURNER: They have gone to weep at their brother's grave.

4TH MOURNER: Let us go and mingle our tears with theirs.

MARTHA: Oh, Mary—our friends have followed us.

MARY: It can't be helped now. We must hurry to the Master's feet.

1ST MOURNER: See! There is somebody waiting for them at the turn of the road.

2ND MOURNER: Who is it?

3RD MOURNER: Mary has fallen down and kissed his feet.

4TH MOURNER: It is Jesus of Nazareth.

MARY: Oh, Rabbi! Oh, dear Master! You are welcome to our sad hearts. Alas! If you had come earlier, our brother would never have died.

JESUS: Are you sure of that, Mary?

MARY: Oh, yes, I am sure. For I heard him tell you so.

And indeed I believe that death itself could never abide your presence.

JESUS (*troubled*): O my sisters! O my children! If only the world had faith enough, that would be true indeed. . . . Where have you laid Lazarus?

MARY: He lies in a cave a little way from here.

JESUS: Show me the place.

1ST MOURNER: The prophet is troubled.

2ND MOURNER: He is weeping.

3RD MOURNER: He must have loved Lazarus very much.

4TH MOURNER: He opened the eyes of the blind— couldn't he have prevented his friend from dying?

1ST MOURNER: Alas! No man is strong enough to deliver the world from death.

(*Lamenting renewed*)

SEQUENCE 3: AT THE GRAVE

MARTHA: Here is the place, dear Master. He lies in that quiet tomb, hewn out of the rock, with the great stone laid across it.

MARY: Lazarus, our brother, who had no love for life, let the burden slip from his shoulders and now is troubled no longer.

MARTHA: He carried his life as a condemned man carries his cross. But now he has laid it down.

JESUS: If any man love me, let him take up his cross and follow me. Roll away the stone from the tomb.

MOURNERS: Roll away the stone?

MARTHA (*horrified*): Master . . . he has been four days dead! The stench of corruption is on his flesh.

JESUS: Did I not tell you that if you believed you should see the glory of God? Roll back the stone.

MARY: Will none of you men do as the Rabbi says? . . . Oh, John, they are afraid.

JOHN: We will do it for you, Mary. Peter and James, come—set your hands to the stone.

1ST MOURNER: Here is a crowbar.

PETER: Lift all together.

(*The stone is heaved off with a crash*)

1ST MOURNER: The grave is open.

2ND MOURNER: What will he do?

3RD MOURNER: Something fearful is going to happen.

4TH MOURNER: Look! He is praying.

JESUS: Father, I thank Thee that Thou hast heard me. And I know that Thou hearest me always. But I give Thee thanks aloud, that these people that stand by may hear it and believe that Thou hast sent me. . . . (*loudly*) Lazarus!

1ST MOURNER: Oh, God! He is calling to the dead.

JESUS: Lazarus, come forth!

(*A fearful pause*)

1ST MOURNER (*in a thin, strangled gasp*) Listen! . . . Listen! . . . A-ah-ah!

2ND MOURNER (*in a quick babble of terror*): Oh, look! Oh, look! Out into the daylight . . . blind and bound . . . moving—with its feet still fast in the grave bands!

JESUS: Unbind him. Take the cloth from his face.

3RD MOURNER: No—no! What will it look like! The face of the four-days-dead?

MARY: Oh, Martha, come and help me. . . . Lazarus— dear brother—speak if you can!

LAZARUS: Lord Jesus!

MARY: You are smiling—you are laughing—you are alive!

LAZARUS (*joyfully*): Yes, I am alive!

MARTHA: Where have you been?

LAZARUS: With life.

MARY: Do you know who called you back?

LAZARUS: Life. He is here and he has never left me.

JESUS: Loose him and lead him home.

The 15th-century Italian friar known as Fra Angelico added a touch of realism to his version of Lazarus's resurrection: the woman at left recoiling from the stench of a man dead four days.

LAZARUS AND MARY

A pupil of Rembrandt, and the teacher of Vermeer, Carel Fabritius (1622– 1654) copied a work of his master in painting this Resurrection scene— and made Rembrandt (man with mustache at lower left) an eyewitness.

        Now as Christ
Drew near to Bethany, the Jews went forth
With Martha mourning Lazarus. But Mary
Sat in the house. She knew the hour was nigh
When He would go again, as He had said,
Unto his Father; and she felt that He,
Who loved her brother Lazarus in Life,
Had chose the hour to bring him home thro' Death
In no unkind forgetfulness. Alone—
She could lift up the bitter prayer to heaven,
"Thy will be done, O God!" But once more
Came Martha, saying, "Lo! the Lord is here
And calleth for thee, Mary!" Then arose
The mourner from the ground, whereon she sat
Shrouded in sackcloth, and bound quickly up
The golden locks of her dishevel'd hair,
And o'er her ashy garments drew a veil
Hiding the eyes she could not trust. And still,
As she made ready to go forth, a calm
As in a dream fell on her.
        At a fount
Hard by the sepulchre, without the wall,
Jesus awaited Mary. Seated near
Were the way-worn disciples in the shade;
But, of himself forgetful, Jesus lean'd
Upon his staff, and watch'd where she should come,
To whose one sorrow—but a sparrow's falling—
The pity that redeem'd a world could bleed!
And as she came, with that uncertain step,—
Eager, yet weak, her hands upon her breast,—
And they who follow'd her all fallen back
To leave her with her sacred grief alone,—
The heart of Christ was troubled. She drew near;
Then, with a vain strife to control her tears,
She stagger'd to the midst, and at His feet
Fell prostrate, saying, "Lord! hadst thou been here,
My brother had not died!" The Saviour groan'd
In spirit, and stoop'd tenderly, and raised
The mourner from the ground, and in a voice
Broke in its utterance like her own, He said,

"Where have ye laid him?" Then the Jews who came,
Following Mary, answer'd through their tears,
"Lord, come and see!" But lo! the mighty heart
That in Gethsemane sweat drops of blood,
Taking from us the cup that might not pass—
The heart whose breaking cord upon the cross
Made the earth tremble, and the sun afraid
To look upon his agony—the heart
Of a lost world's Redeemer—overflowed,
Touched by a mourner's sorrow! Jesus wept.
Calm'd by those pitying tears, and fondly brooding
Upon the thought that Christ so loved her brother,
Stood Mary there; but that lost burden now
Lay on His heart who pitied her; and Christ,
Following slow and groaning in Himself,
Came to the sepulchre. It was a cave,
And a stone lay upon it. Jesus said,
"Take ye away the stone!" Then lifted He
His moisten'd eyes to heaven, and while the Jews
And the disciples bent their heads in awe,
And, trembling, Mary sank upon her knees,
The Son of God pray'd audibly. He ceased,
And for a minute's space there was a hush,
As if th' angelic watchers of the world
Had stayed the pulse of all breathing things,
To listen to that prayer. The face of Christ
Shone as he stood, and over Him there came
Command, as 'twere the living face of God,
And with a loud voice, he cried, "Lazarus!
Come forth!" And instantly, bound hand and foot,
And borne by unseen angels from the cave,
He that was dead stood with them. At the word
Of Jesus, the fear-stricken Jews unloosed
The bands from off the foldings of his shroud;
And Mary, with her dark veil thrown aside,
Ran to him swiftly, and cried, "Lazarus!
My brother Lazarus!" and tore away
The napkin she had bound about his head—
And touched the warm lips with her fearful hand—
And on his neck fell weeping.

NATHANIEL PARKER WILLIS, 1806–1867

The amazement and awe of the bystanders as Lazarus returns from the dead was captured on canvas by French artist Jean Baptiste Corneille (1646–1695).

And after six days Jesus took with him Peter and James and John his brother, and led them up a high mountain apart. And he was transfigured before them, and his face shone like the sun, and his garments became white as light.

MATTHEW 17:1–2

Flanked by the Old Testament prophets Moses and Elijah, Jesus soars above the mountaintop upon which his awestruck disciples sprawl. Raphael added a number of other witnesses unrecorded in the Gospels.

"THIS IS MY BELOVED SON"

*The moment for supreme revelation had arrived,
and Jesus selected only three of his disciples
to witness it. In her novel* THE MESSIAH, *Marjorie
Holmes placed the event on snowcapped
Mount Hermon, from the base of which flow the
headwaters of the river Jordan.*

UP AND UP THEY CLIMBED, Peter, James and John, rejoicing, seeing no one except for a few shepherds, grazing their flocks of sheep in the foothills. No preaching and healing today, no crowds to be kept at bay, no sights of human misery, no sounds of wailing and pleading or the horrible hiss that demons sometimes make, spewing from a tortured mouth.

All was clear, clean, still, the rocks glittering like diamonds in the sun and snowlight, the very trees and shrubs as crisp as if cut from embroidered silk, before they fell away. Their leaves and thorns and sparkling branches cast shadows on the frosty ground, for in these heights it was winter always.

The air was like chilled wine, to be drunk in glorious drafts, making the head light, then even lighter the higher they ascended. They drank it deeply into their lungs, free and young and a trifle giddy, as at a joyous banquet. Peter was soon panting, though beaming as he tried to keep up with James and John.

Jesus was already far ahead. Though he had invited them to go with him, after his first cordial greeting he had set off, with a pace they could not match. At first, looking up, they could see his long legs leaping rocks, or striding along as if on a special mission, his white garments blowing. Then he disappeared.

Halfway to the broad white cone, Peter paused to wrap his cloak around him. "Master, wait, we must rest!" he bellowed, shielding his eyes to the glare. His voice was loud from years of trying to outshout the sea; it boomed back at him now in repeating echoes. But Jesus was too far above them to be seen.

"Do you suppose he's going straight on to the summit?" James, too, was searching the white expanse. "It's a long way and we're tired already, and cold." He hoisted himself nimbly onto a rock and began to massage his wet feet. John joined him and they sat discussing it, puzzled but accepting. Their delicate, fine-boned faces were untroubled, if a little surprised.

"There is something on his mind," they agreed. "Jesus has said almost nothing; he hasn't even looked back."

"Jesus knows we will follow him and find him—wherever he is," Peter said. All three were gazing upward toward the truncated cone, divided into three peaks. "It will probably be the highest summit," they decided.

Meanwhile, catching their breath, they gazed in wonder at the magnificent panorama spread before them in every direction below. West, the valleys and hills of Lebanon, green-striped but bronzing with summer; the cities of Tyre and Sidon, looking like fragile doll villages that might topple right into the blue Mediterranean. South soared Mount Tabor, Mount Hattin and the whole range of violet-blue mountains that encircled the shining harp-shaped lake they knew so well.

Refreshed, they climbed on, and soon were relieved to discover the slightly drifted tracks of the one they were following. It was hard going now, the snow deeper, the air even more thin. Everything glistened and sparkled with an intensity Peter had never seen before, even on the water. And it flashed through his mind, in a humble marveling, how his life had changed. From a dull, stolid fisherman, routinely muttering his prayers, seldom even attending his local synagogue—to this! The very dangers of following Jesus, the terrible possibilities, had added a reckless color and sense of purpose to his life. And to be so close to him—*one of the chosen three.* Selected to be with Jesus whenever the occasion seemed important. A sudden awareness of that honor struck him afresh.

At last, breathing hard, light-headed, nearly exhausted but filled with anticipation, they reached the place where Jesus must surely be, and stood blinking and looking about for a moment, their eyes first half blinded with the sun and snow. Grad-

*The Transfiguration is
the central image of the
so-called Dalmatic of
Charlemagne. The richly
embroidered liturgical
garment is among the
treasures of St. Peter's
Basilica in the Vatican.*

Snowcapped Mount Hermon, Israel's highest peak, is a possible site for the Transfiguration of Jesus.

Where Jesus Communed with Moses and Elijah

The "high mountain apart" where Jesus was transfigured is not named in the Gospels, but as early as the sixth century, pilgrims were honoring the physically isolated Mount Tabor southeast of the Sea of Galilee as the sacred spot. Despite this tradition, however, triple-peaked Mount Hermon in northern Israel, known by local Arabs today as "Chief of the Mountains," is a more likely candidate. While Tabor is only 1,843 feet tall, Hermon rises to 9,166 feet, a huge mass some 5 miles wide and nearly 20 miles long. Also, Tabor does not lie near Caesarea Philippi, where Jesus and his disciples had withdrawn to discuss his dwindling ministry, but a ledge of Hermon directly overlooks the city from about 8,500 feet.

Venerated since ancient times by various pagan religions, the majestic Hermon could have been seen from almost every part of Palestine. Its melting snows feed the river Jordan, and its huge shadow falls 30 to 40 miles westward upon the Mediterranean Sea at sunrise, eastward past Damascus at sunset. The "dew of Hermon" (Psalms 133:3) is heavier than anywhere else on Earth.

Supporting a centuries-old tradition, the Church of the Transfiguration stands atop Mount Tabor.

ually their vision cleared; they saw that it was a broad and level spot, surprisingly covered with green grass, for the sun poured down upon it like a golden funnel. Overhead the sky seemed close enough to touch, a pure cloudless blue. And now they realized they had been led to sacred ground, and even then were witnessing something profound. For at last their eyes began to focus on the one they sought.

And they knew him and knew him not, for he was standing in radiance at the center of the circle, his white garments shimmering beyond even the radiance of the sunlit snow. Jesus' head was thrown back as if in prayer, his countenance utterly changed—effulgent, transfigured. And awe and terror smote them, so that James and John covered their eyes for an instant, and stifled the cries in their throats.

Then they saw, to their further astonishment, that two men were with him. Whence they came and how they got there, the apostles could not fathom. Their eyes sought confirmation from each other, to make sure they were not dreaming. For now, in the stillness, they could hear the men speaking in low tones. And Jesus turned to the strangers and answered them, though it was impossible to hear what was being said. What were they discussing? Could it be perhaps what Jesus was to accomplish in the time he had left? For suddenly they realized—with a shock of recognition it came to Peter, James and John—these two figures were not of this world.

"*Moses! Elijah!*" Peter tried to moisten his dry lips. Silently he whispered their names. The prophets had returned. Surely with a message straight from heaven.

Peter swayed, he had to fight for control. He must stand fast, he must not faint. He dared not fall prostrate either in awe or in terror, as James and John had done. Why should any miracle overcome him now? After all the miracles he had witnessed! Had he not helped Jesus steady the man climbing down from his bier on his way to the grave? Stood beside Jesus when with a word and a touch of his hand, he drew life back into a little girl? . . . He needs me, he has made that clear. He has a reason for allowing me to be here with him now. I was the first to acknowledge him as the Christ. He has promised me the keys to heaven!

Oh, to prolong this moment, fix it in time forever, mark it with his zeal! Staggered before the vision, light-headed from the climb, yet he was gripped by sublime conviction, given the courage to step forward. He heard his own voice saying, "Jesus, Master, we are here. We have followed you through the snows to be with you. Now I know why: we must build three tabernacles—one for you, one for Moses and one for Elijah! Only say the word."

But even as he spoke, Peter realized, to his dismay, that a bright cloud was coasting over the face of the sun, casting a shadow upon the strangers, so that he could see them less clearly. They were dissolving, vanishing before his eyes. And as Peter stood frozen in bewilderment, a voice spoke from the cloud in tones both reassuring and yet astounding: "This is my beloved son, with whom I am well pleased. Hear him."

Now Peter, too, hurled himself prostrate upon the ground. In a moment he felt Jesus' hand, warm and firm on his shoulder. "Come, Peter, rise, don't be afraid." One by one Jesus bent over them, touching each in turn. And looking up in awe and wonder, they were relieved to find themselves staring at the same dear familiar face. Jesus was smiling, their friend unchanged. The dazzling white raiment was once more a simple homespun tunic.

"Moses and Elijah have gone," Jesus said simply. "Though they were here. You saw them. It is one reason I wanted you with me. That your faith in the Son of Man might be confirmed. But only to strengthen you for what is to come."

ACCORDING TO ST. MARK

The way was steep and wild; we watched Him go
    Through tangled thicket, over sharp-edged stone
    That tore His Feet, until He stood alone
Upon the summit where four great winds blow;
Fearful we knelt on the cold rocks below,
    For the o'erhanging cloud had larger grown,
    A strange still radiance through His Body shone
Whiter than moonlight on the mountain snow.

Then two that flamed amber and amethyst
    Were either side Him, while low thunder rolled
    Down to the ravens in their deep ravine;
But when we looked again, as through a mist
    We saw Him near us.—Like a pearl we hold
    Close to our hearts what we have heard and seen.

THOMAS S. JONES, 1882–1932

Almost too terrified to look at the glorious vision, the disciples witness Jesus talking to Moses and Elijah. The painting is by Giovanni Bellini (c. 1430–1516), a master of the Venetian school.

The Final Days

The Evangelists recount the events leading to Jesus' execution in considerable detail, and Christians throughout the world annually commemorate the incidents of that first Holy Week with great solemnity.

Six days before Passover, during a quiet supper at Bethany, Mary the sister of Lazarus anointed Jesus' feet with a costly ointment and dried them with her hair—as if in preparation for his burial. The next day Jesus entered Jerusalem in triumph, expectant pilgrims greeting him as the Messiah. But he did not seize power as many hoped. Instead, he brought the message of his heavenly kingdom to the temple precincts, thus fatefully challenging the Jewish establishment. With the aid of Judas, these leaders seized Jesus at prayer in Gethsemane shortly after the Passover meal, brought false witnesses against him, and quickly secured his death sentence from the Roman procurator, Pontius Pilate. Jesus' excruciating and ignominious death on the cross followed, leaving his disciples in despair and his opponents satisfied that the upstart rabbi from Galilee had been expeditiously eliminated.

At Jesus' announcement that one among them will betray him, the beloved disciple swoons on his breast as the others react with disbelief. The 16th-century Flemish craftsman added a servant pouring wine to his tapestry version of the Last Supper.

THE PRESENTIMENT OF AN APPALLING FATE

Six days before the Passover, Jesus came to Bethany . . . . There they made him a supper; Martha served, and Lazarus was one of those at table with him. Mary took a pound of costly ointment of pure nard and anointed the feet of Jesus and wiped his feet with her hair; and the house was filled with the fragrance of the ointment.

JOHN 12:1–3

The dramatic incident during the supper at Bethany on the eve of Jesus' entry into Jerusalem served to reveal the tragedy in store for him. In the historical novel ACCORDING TO THOMAS, *Ivan Nazhivin used Hebrew versions of the names of the principals: Jeshua, Eleazar, and Miriam.*

ON SATURDAY JESHUA and his disciples arrived at Bethany: only an hour's journey still separated them from Jerusalem. Eleazar's family greeted them as usual with joy and reverence, but there was a shade of anxiety in their greeting. The air was full of some hidden excitement, something intangible and at the same time disquieting. The crowds streaming from every direction to take part in the festival were growing steadily more numerous. The dust-covered pilgrims passing on their way to Jerusalem all seemed to be aware that something unusual was in the air, something wonderful and joyful, and they were chatting excitedly as they walked.

The crowd's excitement infected even those who lived in Eleazar's modest cottage. It was not very long since Eleazar himself had left his couch after a severe illness, and he was now still more emaciated than he used to be. Helped by both his sisters, he was in the courtyard getting ready the Sabbath meal which his beloved guests were to share. Jeshua, who wanted to hide from the insistent curiosity of the crowd, was sitting with his closest disciples inside the house. When Miriam's velvety black eyes fell on Jeshua's clouded face, her heart seemed to congeal with the terrible presentiment of an appalling fate.

And when Khazzawn had trumpeted for the third time from the roof of the synagogue, and the sparkling Ishtar rose in the still bright sky like a pure light burning before the throne of God, Eleazar in a weak voice invited them all to take their places round the lighted lamps under the old fig tree. Miriam glanced at him questioningly, and he nodded approvingly and with a touch of ceremony.

The girl disappeared into the house, and came back bringing an alabaster box. Then she approached Jeshua, and anointed his head with the costly ointment. As she was doing it she noticed his gray hairs for the first time: her heart contracted with pain and her hand trembled. She poured the rest of the ointment over his feet and, as custom demanded, smashed the alabaster container on the ground.

Jeshua was deeply moved. "I thank you, my friend," he said in a shaking voice.

Tears rose in his eyes and shone like gold in the glare of the lamps. Miriam fell down at his feet and with a quick movement of her delicate hand she loosed her gloriously soft and silky hair, and carefully and lovingly wiped his feet with it.

Judas frowned. "This ointment was worth perhaps three hundred denarii," he said, in his usual clumsy and halting voice. "Rather than waste money like that, it would have been better to sell the ointment and give the money it brought to the poor."

The other disciples murmured. There was probably some truth in what Judas had said: but this truth was one of those that are better left unspoken. Jeshua felt aggrieved. "The poor you will always have with you," he said, trying to repress a feeling of annoyance. "Perhaps she has already anointed me against my burial."

They all looked askance at Judas, who was always the scapegoat. But his heart was already poisoned, as if he had been bitten by a snake. Jeshua, seeing his face contorted with passion, felt pity for him.

Eleazar and Martha did their best to cover up the unpleasant incident as quickly as possible. Gradually the company settled down, although the strong aromatic smell of the costly myrrh hung for a long time in the evening air and kept reminding them of what had passed at the supper table.

Mary anoints Jesus' feet in this panel from a 15th-century altarpiece.

Two unrelated events from Jesus' last week appear in this 13th-century French bas-relief: Mary anointing Jesus' feet and the scourging of Jesus at the pillar.

She Who Came Beforehand to Anoint Him for Burial

Matthew and Mark also write of the anointing at Bethany, though they place it in the house of Simon the leper, a figure otherwise unidentified, and leave the woman unnamed. Martin Luther's sermon on the event is from LUTHER'S MEDITATIONS ON THE GOSPELS.

ON THE EVE PRIOR TO PASSION WEEK, Jesus was in Bethany. We read that Mary took ointment. It was an old custom to wash with perfumed water not only the face but also the hands and the feet. Mary had purchased a very costly vessel. In our day we have wild nard, but not the kind mixed with balsam of that time, which was very precious. It was not an ointment but a sweet-smelling perfume with herbs. She poured it over his head and raiment. It spoiled nothing but made everything pure and of a sweet smell.

The Lord suffered it. He took no pleasure in the perfume, for his heart was full of heaviness and thoughts of death. In six days, he would die. He who knows certainly that he will die a shameful death on a particular day will take no delight in gold, pearl necklaces, and clothes, for his spirit is in deep anguish because he must shed his blood. Piping, singing, and dancing do not help here. But Christ permitted what she did. Mary believed him to be a prophet and meant it well. He was wrestling with death and took no delight in this of itself.

Then Judas Iscariot thought to himself: "Mary wastes money. She pours out the perfume even on his feet and this rose water costs so much. Why did she not use lye or soap? This perfume might have been sold for three hundred groschen and given to the poor. That is too much. With this amount of money I could have fed twenty-four people and could indeed have cared for sixty persons for a month, and now it is all gone in one hour."

Christ said: "Let her alone. She is come beforehand to anoint my body to the burying." He pointed to his death, though she did not understand it. These three hundred groschen, he would say, are a farewell, a gift given for the last time.

The next day a great crowd who had come to the feast heard that Jesus was coming to Jerusalem. So they took branches of palm trees and went out to meet him, crying, "Hosanna! Blessed is he who comes in the name of the Lord, even the King of Israel!"

JOHN 12:12-13

THE TRIUMPHANT ENTRY

Come, drop your branches, strow the way,
    Plants of the day!
Whom sufferings make most green and gay.
The king of grief, the man of sorrow
Weeping still, like the wet morrow,
Your shades and freshness comes to borrow.

Put on, put on your best array;
Let the joyed road make holy-day,
And flowers, that into fields do stray,
Or secret groves, keep the high-way.

Trees, flowers, and herbs; birds, beasts, and stones.
That since man fell, expect with groans
To see the Lamb, come, all at once,
Lift up your heads and leave your moans!
    For here comes he
    Whose death will be
Man's life, and your full liberty.

Hark! how the children shrill and high
    "Hosanna" cry;
Their joys provoke the distant sky,
Where thrones and seraphim reply;
And their own angels shine and sing
    In a bright ring;
    Such young, sweet mirth
    Makes heaven and earth
Join in a joyful symphony.

HENRY VAUGHAN, 1622–1695

Jesus riding into Jerusalem is one of several scenes Duccio di Buoninsegna painted for an altarpiece of the cathedral at Siena, Italy, between 1308 and 1311.

One More Important Than a King

*Jesus chose the week before Passover to enter Jerusalem,
a time when the city's streets were teeming with
pilgrims arriving for the holiday feast—and, in fulfillment
of the prophecy in Zechariah 9:9, he came seated on
the foal of an ass. To an outsider such as the Greek slave
Demetrius, in this passage from Lloyd C. Douglas's
1942 novel THE ROBE, the scene was unsettling.*

THERE WAS NO LAUGHTER in this pilgrim throng that crowded the widening avenue today. This was a tense, impassioned, fanatical multitude; its voice a guttural murmur, as if each man canted his own distresses, indifferent to the mumbled yearnings of the others. On these strained faces was an expression of an almost terrifying earnestness and a quality of pietistic zeal that seemed ready to burst forth into wild hysteria.

Suddenly, for no reason at all that Demetrius could observe, there was a wave of excitement. It swept down over the sluggish swollen stream of zealots like a sharp breeze. Men all about him were breaking loose from their families and racing forward toward some urgent attraction. Up ahead the shouts were increasing in volume, spontaneously organizing into a reiterated cry; a single, magic word that drove the multitude into a frenzy.

Demetrius set off after the crowd, forcing his way with the others until the congestion was too dense for further progress. Wedged tight against his arm and grinning into his face was another Greek slave, easily recognizable as such by the slit in his ear-lobe.

"Do you know what is going on?" asked Demetrius.

"They're yelling something about a king. They keep howling another word that I don't know—Messiah. The man's name, maybe."

Demetrius impulsively turned about, thrust a shoulder into the steaming mass, and began pushing through to the side of the road, followed closely by his countryman. All along the way, men were recklessly tearing branches from the palms that bordered the res-

Celebrating Palm Sunday

When Jesus entered Jerusalem on the Sunday before his death, he joined devout Jewish pilgrims on their way to observe Passover, the commemoration of God's deliverance of the Israelites from bondage in Egypt. Since Passover was also associated with the early spring barley harvest, many would have been carrying bundles of palm branches and other plants as prescribed for such agricultural festivals in Leviticus. From these bundles, no doubt, the pilgrims drew their spontaneous tribute. Although the Gospel of Matthew implies that they cut the branches on the spot for this purpose, palm trees did not grow in the vicinity of Jerusalem.

In fulfillment of the biblical prophecy, Jesus came seated on a colt, the foal of an ass, while the crowds, echoing the psalmist, cried, "Blessed is he who comes in the name of the Lord! Hosanna in the highest!"

The Christian Holy Week — the commemoration of the events culminating in the death and Resurrection of Jesus — begins on Palm Sunday, which celebrates his triumphal entry into Jerusalem.

A throng of the faithful carrying palm branches reenacts Jesus' triumphal entry into Jerusalem. The tradition dates to the early centuries of the Christian era, as reported by pilgrims to the Holy Land. Right, a date palm decorates a capital from the fourth-century synagogue at Capernaum.

idential thoroughfare, indifferent to the violent protests of property-owners. Running swiftly among the half-crazed vandals, the two slaves arrived at the front of the procession.

Standing on tiptoe for an instant in the swaying crowd, Demetrius caught a fleeting glimpse of the obvious center of interest, a brown-haired, bare-headed, well-favored Jew. A tight little circle had been left open for the slow advance of the shaggy white donkey on which he rode. It instantly occurred to Demetrius that this coronation project was an impromptu affair for which no preparation had been made. Certainly there had been no effort to bedeck the pretender with any royal regalia. He was clad in a simple brown mantle with no decorations of any kind.

It was difficult to believe that this was the sort of person who could be expected to inflame a mob into some audacious action. Instead of receiving the applause with an air of triumph—or even of satisfaction—the unresponsive man on the donkey seemed weighted with an insupportable burden of anxiety.

Now there was a temporary blocking of the way, and the noisy procession came to a complete stop. The man on the white donkey straightened, as if roused from a reverie, drew a deep sigh, and slowly turned his head. Demetrius watched, with parted lips and a pounding heart.

The meditative eyes, drifting about over the excited multitude, seemed to carry a sort of wistful compassion for these helpless victims of an aggression for which they thought he had a remedy. Everyone was shouting, shouting—all but the slave, whose throat was so dry he couldn't have shouted, who had no inclination to shout, who wished they would all be quiet, quiet! It wasn't the time or place for shouting. Quiet! This man wasn't the sort of person one shouted at, or shouted for. This moment called for quiet.

Gradually the brooding eyes moved over the crowd until they came to rest on the strained, bewildered face of Demetrius. Perhaps, he wondered, the man's gaze halted there because he alone—in all this welter of hysteria—refrained from shouting. His silence singled him out. The eyes calmly appraised Demetrius. They neither widened nor smiled; but, in some indefinable manner, they held Demetrius in a grip so firm it was almost a physical compulsion. The message they communicated was something other than sympathy, something more vital than friendly concern; a sort of stabilizing power that swept away all such negations as slavery, poverty, or any other afflicting circumstance. Demetrius was suffused with the glow of this curious kinship. Blind with sudden tears, he elbowed through the throng and reached the roadside.

"See him—close up?" asked the other slave.

Demetrius nodded.

"King?"

"No," muttered Demetrius, soberly—"not a king."

"What is he, then?" demanded the other.

"I don't know," mumbled Demetrius, "but he is someone more important than a king."

*Like many other artists who painted this scene, Pietro Lorenzetti (1280–1348)
included men climbing trees to cut branches for strewing on the road before Jesus. Judas is
distinguished among the disciples (left) by his lack of a halo.*

An Upstart Named Jesus

*Tension undoubtedly mounted in the days immediately
following Jesus' entry into Jerusalem, as he
returned to dispute with the religious authorities
in the temple. In this selection from his historical novel
THE UPPER ROOM, R.A. Edwards describes the day
Pontius Pilate left his usual post in Caesarea
for Jerusalem, only to find the city rife with rumor.*

ALL THROUGH THE WEEK Jerusalem had talked nationalist politics, and the city was alive with speculation about a new Messiah, who had begun the week with a spectacular entry into the city and with what might have been a dangerous riot; but who had then seemed to slip out of the center of the picture, and all that could be heard of him was that he was in and about the temple doing nothing more than argue theology with the Jewish leaders, and going off for the night to Bethany. But even if he had no intention of setting himself up as a national champion, the city went on talking about him.

What Jerusalem was saying Rome knew well enough; for it was Rome's business to know; and all day long spies moved in and out of the crowd collecting news for the procurator. From Caesarea, Pilate was watching for something that never happened, was never meant to happen; watching for the moment just before the proclamation of the pretender from Galilee as king. Then Rome would strike, and this Passover would become a bloody scrawl on the year's history.

Word had come to Pilate that the moment would assuredly come before the week ended; and with the news had come a cringingly haughty message from Annas, the high priest emeritus, asking why Rome garrisoned the country if they were not to have security from any upstart who cared to threaten a national rising. The message had added that the particular upstart's name was Jesus.

So Pilate sent to the city to find if his own sources of information confirmed the disturbing message. The confirmation came. It seemed to be a fact that some

*This carved wood panel of Jesus being greeted in
Jerusalem, from the church of St. Jakob in Rothenburg,
Germany, dates to the 16th century.*

sort of riot had taken place in the temple precincts on the Sunday, and, much as he disliked the whole business of dealing with Jews, his somewhat blown reputation demanded that he should be on hand if any more than usual trouble developed. He gave orders for the change of quarters to Jerusalem.

As he rode into the city, Pilate's military eye saw how certainly one of his war engines could breach its walls, and he marvelled at the serene childishness that could imagine the Empire being seriously troubled by the Jews' nationalist aspirations. He rode flauntingly erect, ignoring the hostile faces of the folk who trudged beside the white road toward the gate; but wished that he dare give the order for massacre, or the better one to ride back and leave the enigmatic people to their fate. So the pagan gods rode into the city for their last battle, championed by a man eager only to wash his hands of everything.

A curious crowd, wondering why Pilate had come, hung about the Tower of Antonia, and was gradually shepherded away by the Roman guards. Another crowd swayed round the temple main entrances, eagerly trying to learn whether the high priest—for Caiaphas, with his father-in-law Annas, was known to be bitterly opposed to Jesus—intended any move; whether the Sanhedrin was or was not sitting; whether contact had already been established with Pilate; canvassing every kind of possibility, and arguing nearly to blows for and against Jesus. He had said this, he had said that; he would be at the head of a rising tomorrow in spite of the rumor that he had several times refused the messiahship; he had said that he was the Messiah; he was already under arrest in the temple prison; Pilate had him in Antonia . . . Talk, talk, endless talk; and all that an impartial observer could have said was that, though the crowd was dreadfully dangerous, the bulk of opinion seemed to be against Jesus and against violence, and that the fear of Rome was just about strong enough to see the weekend through without serious bloodshed.

A more acute observer might have commented that the moment was ripe for a bold stroke at Jesus, an arrest, or even an execution. In fact, spies were already flitting in and out of the crowd, gathering evidence upon which exactly that action would be based before morning; while other spies, in the pay, not of Rome, but of the temple authorities, fostered the sentiment against Jesus. The authorities knew that he was in the city. The gates were closed. He was doomed.

Precious stones set in gold frame the 11th-century enamel of the entry at left, a treasure of the cathedral of San Marco in Venice. Jesus' sidesaddle position on his mount reveals a Byzantine, or eastern, influence on the artist. Jesus depicted astride his colt, as in the 16th-century carved and painted limewood figure below, indicates a west European origin.

THE DONKEY

When fishes flew and forests walked
  And figs grew upon thorn,
Some moment when the moon was blood
  Then surely I was born.

With monstrous head and sickening cry
  And ears like errant wings,
The devil's walking parody
  On all four-footed things.

The tattered outlaw of the earth,
  Of ancient crooked will;
Starve, scourge, deride me: I am dumb,
  I keep my secret still.

Fools! For I also had my hour;
  One far fierce hour and sweet:
There was a shout about my ears,
  And palms before my feet.

G. K. CHESTERTON, 1874–1936

236   CLEANSING THE TEMPLE

And Jesus entered the temple of God and drove out all who sold and bought in the temple, and he overturned the tables of the money-changers and the seats of those who sold pigeons. He said to them, "It is written, 'My house shall be called a house of prayer'; but you make it a den of robbers."

Like the Coming of a Storm on a Cloudless Day

Immediately following his triumphal entry into Jerusalem, according to Matthew and Luke, Jesus went to the temple and took the drastic action described in the following passage from Robert Payne's novel THE LORD JESUS. *Mark places the event on the following day, while John puts it earlier in Jesus' ministry, soon after the wedding feast at Cana.*

As a priestly group in the right background looks askance, Jesus wreaks havoc among the money changers. Rembrandt's etching is dated 1635.

H E DID NOT LOOK A KING coming in triumph, yet people were continually spreading their garments in his path, and as soon as the ass had trodden on the garments, they would run back, pick up the garments and try to lay them before him again; and it was the same with the palm branches. And with the noise of the shouts there came the strange crackling sound of palm branches being trodden underfoot.

If anyone had thought of taking a census of the people following Jesus, they would have discovered that the crowds came from all walks of life, and there were many who were sick or had sick relatives and hoped for a miracle. Just in front of Jesus and just behind him were ruddy-faced Galileans, shepherds and fishermen, strong-shouldered, blue-eyed, many of them possess-

ing a Greek cast of features, while a surprising number of them had reddish hair. But these Galileans were outnumbered by the mass of poor Jews from all the provinces of Palestine, all struggling to approach closer to him, all shouting at the top of their voices, all delirious with joy because they had seen him with their own eyes and recognized in that strange brooding figure the presence of divinity.

When they came in sight of the temple, a great shout went up. Louder and louder came the voices of the pilgrims until at last they seemed to be shouting with a single voice, which echoed and re-echoed off the glistening white marble walls of the temple. "Glory to the Highest!" they shouted. "Glory to the Son of David! May he be blessed, now and in all the generations to come!"

The vast procession, now numbering more than four thousand, entered the outer courts of the temple in a seething and uncontrollable mass; only around Jesus himself was there a small area of peace. Nothing could prevent them from taking possession of these outer courts. The temple guards had received no in-

The tense, elongated figures in this scene of Jesus driving the money changers from the temple identify it as a work of the great 16th-century Spanish painter known as El Greco ("the Greek," for his land of origin).

THE FINAL DAYS 237

structions and were undermanned. Nor was there any sign of the Roman legionaries, who were usually called to assist the guards when trouble broke out.

Most of the companions expected Jesus to make his way into the inner courts. In their minds' eyes they saw him striding past the Altar of Sacrifice and penetrating into the Holy of Holies, to emerge in the robes of the high priest and from the steps proclaim the new dispensation of Israel.

But in fact nothing of the kind happened. He stood alone in the outer courts, no longer subdued, no longer with bowed head. His eyes flashed. He seemed taller than anyone around him. He raised his arms in a majestic command for silence and said in a voice that seemed to rise like a huge wave and fall with a deafening crash against the marble pavements: "Shall my Father's house be given over to the shopkeepers?"

And saying this, he strode towards the booths of the merchants and money changers, and taking a whip of cords from one of the temple guards, he brought the whip down on the startled heads of the dazed men who had spent their lives selling the sacrificial sheep and pigeons to the pilgrims. He poured the coins of the money changers onto the marble floor and overturned the tables. He threw open the doors of the cages where the pigeons were suffocating in the heat. He threw open the gates of the pens housing the sheep. He stormed from one booth to another, majestic and imperious, giving no quarter; and the only sound came from the cracking of the whip.

Jesus continued to go among the merchants and money changers until he was assured that not a sheep remained in the pens, nor a single dove in a cage. There were doves flying everywhere and sheep pouring through the gates in a mad rush for freedom.

No one had ever seen him in such a rage. The veins throbbed at his temples, his face shone with the glittering light beating down from the marble walls, his eyes blazed. He strode across the temple courts like a man possessed, his arms flaying; and sometimes the whip whistled on the empty air.

There was in his rage something elemental and terrible, like the sudden coming of a storm on a cloudless day. They had expected miracles; they saw instead a vast outpouring of naked energy. It was time to sweep the temple clean of all the encrustations of the ages; and the whip, which he wielded with a kind of maniacal fury, was the sign of his determination to purify the sacred precincts.

The English painter J.M.W. Turner (1775–1851), best known for his landscapes in watercolor, placed Jesus (above, right background) amid a swirl of figures in an exotic temple. The pre-Renaissance Italian painter Giotto de Bondone (c. 1276–1337) added animals freed from pens to his more restrained version of the incident.

As a money changer cringes before the onslaught of Jesus, two purveyors of sacrifical animals scurry away; this German etching is dated 1491.

THE ANGER OF CHRIST

On the day Christ ascended
    To Jerusalem,
Singing multitudes attended,
And the very heavens were rended
    With the shout of them.

Chanted they a sacred ditty,
    Every heart elate;
But he wept in brooding pity,
Then went in the holy city
    By the Golden Gate.

In the temple, lo! what lightning
    Makes unseemly rout!
He in anger, sudden, frightening,
Drives with scorn and scourge the whitening
    Money-changers out.

RICHARD WATSON GILDER, 1844–1909

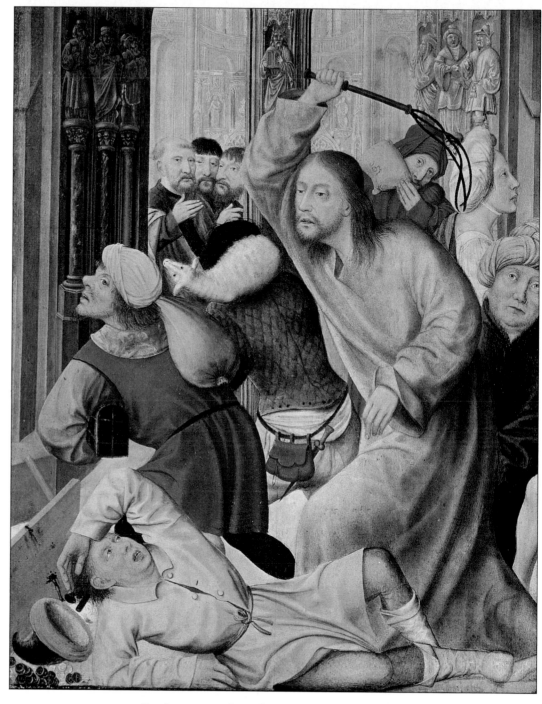

Resolute yet somehow aloof, Jesus raises a whip to a fallen money changer in this scene by a follower of the Flemish painter Quentin Massys (c. 1466–1530).

FOR SOMEONE WITHOUT FEAR, ONE PLACE IS AS SAFE AS ANOTHER

*Although Luke names Peter and John as the disciples sent
to prepare the Passover feast in the upper room, Mark
does not identify them. In this selection from
THESE SHARED HIS PASSION, a work published in 1940,
Edwin McNeill Poteat takes the liberty of assigning
the task to the brothers James and John—and uses the
incident to reveal the uncertainty and apprehension
of Jesus' followers as the final confrontation
with the religious authorities approached.*

EARLY THURSDAY AFTERNOON Salome raised herself
on her couch and listened to what she
thought was a rap on the outer door. She had
been resting during the hot two-hour period
that stifled the crowded city as the sun began its slow
descent from the meridian; and her room, carefully
shuttered against the glare, had been quiet and cool.

The rap was repeated outside, impatiently. She
slipped her feet into her sandals and was on the point
of answering the summons when she heard the shuf-
fling feet of a servant girl crossing the court. Moving
to the window, she swung the heavy wooden shutter
half open and looked out into the white sunlight.

As the outer portal creaked open, a tall man, his

*The 16th-century artisan who carved this Last Supper out of
limestone has the beloved disciple nestled under Jesus' left arm
and Judas clutching his money bag in the right foreground.*

head protected against the heat by a looping fold of his tunic, entered the yard. He balanced a large water jar on one shoulder, and as he stooped slightly to avoid a low lintel, a few drops of the water spilled and spattered in a silver cascade over the servant girl. The water carrier laughed as he set the jar down, quite undisturbed by the sharp words of the young woman who, flicking uselessly at the dark spots that mottled her robe, turned to close the gate. A sharp knock and the noise of voices stopped her. She opened the gate slightly again, and looking suspiciously through the narrow crack, saw two men.

"We were told," said one of them, somewhat out of breath, "to follow the man with the water jar, and to ask the master of the house where the room is, in which we are to prepare the Passover."

She scrutinized the faces of the men for a moment, and then slowly drew the gate open again, wide enough to allow their entrance. "Come in," she invited; "you are from Galilee?"

"Yes," they answered, and stepped quickly inside.

Through the half-opened shutter, Salome had seen her two sons, James and John, step inside the gate, and was waiting at the low door of the house when they reached it. She touched her lips with her finger to warn them lest their surprise at seeing her there betray them into noisy talk.

"The mother of the Teacher is sleeping in there," she said. "We must not disturb her. She has been very tired, and sleeps fitfully. Come into my room." She led them back to her cool chamber, and bade them sit on the long couch near the window.

"We did not know you were here," John said mysteriously. "He said nothing of Mary's being here either. Only the command to follow the man with the water jar. Is it here that we shall eat the feast?"

"Yes, and it is nearly prepared. All that lacks is getting the food. The room is ready; it is a large and comfortable place." She raised her eyes and pointed to the ceiling as she spoke. "An upper room, where you can sup in quietness and in safety."

"You say his mother rests not well?" asked James solicitously.

"Nay, she scarcely sleeps at all," replied Salome. "Since Monday she has been afraid. Last night at midnight, she cried out, and when I went into her room she was sitting up, her hands gripped tightly over her heart, and a look of terror in her eyes. 'A pain, like to the sharp thrust of a sword, racks me here,' she said. I gave her a breath of camphor leaves to smell, and she quieted at length."

"Yes," said James, "we are all afraid, all except him. If he is afraid, he betrays it by no word or sign."

"Tell me," Salome demanded gently of them, "what is he going to do?"

"After the supper tonight, he will return to the Mount of Olives," answered John.

"Can he not stay here; is it not safer here?"

"To one who has no fear, one place is as safe as another," laughed James.

"But, I was thinking not of tonight," corrected Salome, "but of—well, of the years ahead. Those who are his followers expect so much of him; and they that hate and fear him— they will

Symbolically removed from the other disciples, Judas sits at the foot of the table in this 15th-century painted wood carving from Germany.

As the beloved disciple sinks on his breast, Jesus hands Judas (figure without halo at left in Lorenzetti's fresco, right) the morsel dipped in wine. Duccio's version of the same incident (below) curiously omits halos from all the disciples seated opposite Jesus.

surely not suffer him forever. His mother is full of misgivings. She would have him return with her to Nazareth. I—I would see him seize the power that waits but for his grasp."

"Nay, good mother," warned James. "Do you forget his word to you when you sought positions for us on his left and right when he was to grasp—as you put it now—his kingdom?"

"I forget nothing," she answered animatedly. "He promised you a cup to drink and a baptism to undergo. Did that not mean that after our cup was drained, you would be rewarded?"

"I think it was not thus that he intended," John answered. "He promised us nothing. He reminded us that rewards and positions were not his to give."

"So you have not urged him to seize power, and promised your support to him?" asked Salome. "And is there still bitterness to drain from new cups; and must this baptism of his engulf us all, his weary mother and me and . . . ?"

James took the hand that had been stressing her fretful words with brisk, impatient gestures, and his touch quieted her. "I do not know," he answered wearily. "I do not think he will abandon us to danger, but I do not think he will endanger the gospel by seizing power. We have talked much with him of late. He talks of wars and rumors of wars, of broken homes and divided families, of friends who prove false, and of faithfulness to the end."

"And yet he will not stop it with a sign, or avert it by proclaiming himself as King? There is nothing he cannot do . . ."

"Nothing, indeed, except those things which his love forbids. There is much I do not understand; but this I know: he will not fight for power."

As Salome looked from one face to the other, searching her heart for some intimation of ministry she might bring to her sons, she heard a sound at the door. Turning, she saw Mary the mother of Jesus standing, framed by its rough outlines. Her eyes, somber and dark with weariness and the intuitions of tragedy, lighted for a moment as she recognized the two men; and her greeting was cordial.

"The feast," she said, looking toward Salome, "the feast. Must we not put it in readiness? He will be here at the set of sun, and wishes not to be delayed. He says that he will have other business after supper, beyond the brook. He will meet someone in the garden. I hope it is a friend."

THE LAST SUPPER

Perhaps at first they talked of little things
At supper-time that evening in the spring—
The upper room was dim with candle-shine
As Jesus sat with twelve, remembering.
Then quietly He said, "There is one here
Whose kiss will bring betrayal by and by."
They did not look at Judas curiously,
But each man murmured, "Master, is it I?"

Each one looked inward, frightened lest he find
A shoddy place where he had dreamed of steel.
None placed the guilt on any other guest
Who had partaken of that gracious meal. . . .
When they are hungry on my little street,
When I see tears or hear a heart's hurt cry
Because some one has failed to keep high faith,
May I, too, murmur, "Master, is it I?"

HELEN WELSHIMER

The noted Belgian portraitist Philippe de Champaigne (1602–1674) gave distinct personalities to each one of the 12 disciples in his Last Supper—including Judas (left foreground), grasping his telltale money bag.

An Underlying Tension at the Passover Feast

The precise instructions to the two disciples, recorded by Matthew and Luke as well as by Mark, suggest that Jesus had made arrangements in advance for the Passover feast and wished to keep the meeting place a secret from potential enemies. Jim Bishop's account of the preparations is from THE DAY CHRIST DIED, *a dramatic, hour-by-hour reconstruction of the final 24 hours, published in 1957.*

An *18th-century stained glass panel from the Victoria and Albert Museum in London*

T HE ASSIGNMENT WAS SIMPLE. Peter, a big impetuous man who carried a short Roman sword at his side, led young John on the two-and-a-half-mile journey to Jerusalem. Inside the Fountain Gate they identified their man easily because, in Judea, men seldom carried water. It was women's work to go to the pool daily with a tall narrow pitcher on their heads, draw water and bring it home. Jesus had not mentioned the name of the man, but both apostles recognized him at once as the rich father of the young disciple Mark.

He had led them up the big Roman steps, across the town to his home, through the courtyard, and up a flight of outside stairs to a room which occupied all the second floor. A roasting oven was already there, and so were the lamb, herbs, and spices and bread necessary to a dinner for thirteen men.

The two hurried to build the fire and roast the lamb. It was forbidden to break any bone in the animal because it symbolized Israel, whole and undivided. Peter and John divided the tasks. While Peter, because he had more experience, spitted the lamb down the middle and set it in the brick and tile oven so that no part of its skin would touch the sides, the other fashioned the round, thin, unleavened bread into little cakes. This was the matzoth, ritually prepared bread, so called because the Jews ate it as they followed Moses and he had made of the tribes a holy nation, beloved

In this Italian ivory carving dating to about the year 1100, eleven look-alike disciples are flanked by Jesus (left) and, most likely, Judas. Though not mentioned in the Gospels, the fish on the table became a common symbol for Jesus in early Christian art.

by God. It was also called the bread of affliction because the Israelites had left Egypt in such haste that their women had no time to leaven the bread.

They also made a salad from one of five kinds of bitter-tasting plants, to remind the diners that the bondage in Egypt was bitter. The two men filled a bowl with vinegar, in which the bitter leaves would later be dipped. Red wine was made ready—the poor were able to buy it at the temple at cost price—and this would later be mixed by the host in the measure of one part of water to four parts of wine. Finally Peter and John made charoseth, a dish consisting of almonds, figs, dates, wine and cinnamon.

Their work was not finished when Jesus walked upstairs and into the room. The greetings were subdued. Jesus studied the room carefully. This was, to him, an important night. He did not discuss his feelings; to the apostles he seemed abnormally introspective. They looked for signs of despair, or even of elation— a sign of sorts would have guided their feelings, much as, when lightning flashes and thunder rolls, the sheep look not at the sky but at the shepherd.

The twelve seemed to be composed, but there was an underlying tension in the room. Their greetings were whispered; a group of bearded men, averaging about thirty years of age, simple men who were certain, now and then, that they were in the presence of the Son of God, although at other moments they became frightened and their belief wavered. Their faith in Jesus was full so long as it was not overburdened. Though they had, of course, withstood trial in the past, this was a moment of great strain. They had heard Jesus discuss his impending death with obvious sadness. And each feared to ask the question they all wanted to ask: "Can you not call upon your father's angels and destroy the city and the world and then let us sit with you today and judge the souls of men?" No one asked it.

They stood in twos and threes near the pillars supporting the roof and they looked at him and whispered and wondered and worried. Mark's father sent two men servants up to serve the Pasch and the smoke of the roasting lamb hung blue over their heads and undulated as they moved.

The servants set the table in the middle of the room. It was shaped like a U about twelve inches above the floor. The open end of the U was nearest the entrance—in this case, the top of the staircase.

The couches from which Jesus and the twelve ate

The unknown German artisan who fashioned the early-14th-century embroidery above reduced the Last Supper participants to Jesus, the beloved disciple, Judas, and one other, possibly Peter. Jesus blessing and distributing bread at the Last Supper is the central image on the liturgical ivory comb at left.

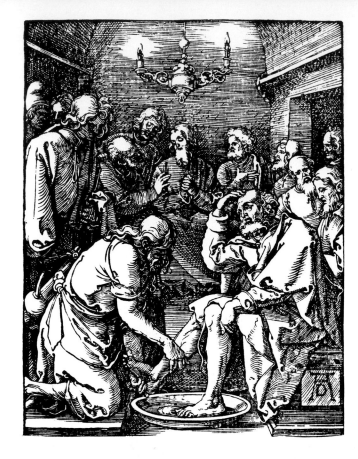

Unwilling at first to submit to Jesus' ablutions, Peter asked him to wash his hands and head as well when he learned the importance his master placed on the ceremony. At right, an etching by Albrecht Dürer (1471–1528); below, a painting by an unknown artist dated about 1390.

were called triclinia. They came in different sizes, from about seven feet in length to twelve. Among the Jews, the curved part of the U was considered the side of special favor, and three places were set on that side. As host, Jesus would be in the middle. The place of honor was to his left, and Peter would recline there. The place of second honor was to the right of Jesus, and this normally was the place of Judas, the treasurer, though on this night it would be taken by young John. The three would eat from a single low couch, the edge nearest the table being about the same height as their plates and the back edge much lower and open, so that the diner approached the couch from the rear, lowered himself into it, propped loose cushions to suit his comfort, and then leaned on his left elbow, keeping the right hand free for eating.

At seven o'clock the lamb was ready. As it was taken tenderly from the oven, Jesus and the apostles shouted: "There is no God but one!"

The men in that room with Jesus were called, among themselves, "the twelve." In many ways, they were average—representative of the mankind that Jesus had come to save. They were pious men in an age when piety was common. For the most part, they were not men of exceptional intellect or training; some may not have even been able to read or write, but all had studied the oral law at the knees of their mothers and fathers. They were emotional and loving and given to arguments, and in a dispute they would usually answer a question with another.

Before the feast began they stood in groups, washing their hands in the ceremony of purification. Peter and John were busy with the lamb, and the odor of it sweetened the room.

The apostles moved toward the tables. The dishes of herbs were in place. The two servants walked in and out of the inverted U table, setting ritually clean dishes in place and standing metal goblets, or chalices, before the places for the thirteen diners.

The chill of early evening could be felt in the room and the servants set about lighting braziers. The whole lamb had been set, brown and sizzling, on snowy cloths on the low table. The spices and wild herbs and the fruits had been set, along with the bowls. Now the apostles looked to Jesus and he looked around the room at them and said: "I have greatly desired to eat this Passover with you before I suffer; for I say to you that I will eat of it no more, until it has been fulfilled in the kingdom of God."

The celebrant on this 17th-century
Passover cup holds unleavened bread.

The Passover Seder

According to most experts, the Last Supper reflects and reinterprets the annual Passover feast — the seder — instituted in Exodus 12 to symbolize God's deliverance of his people from their Egyptian bondage. Traditionally, this ritual meal, which took place after sundown, included roasted lamb, unleavened bread, and bitter herbs, accompanied by no less than four cups of wine. Celebrants were supposed to slaughter their own lambs at home, but in later times priests ritually killed the sacrificial animals in the temple at Jerusalem. The unleavened bread, made from several varieties of grain, may have recalled the tale of the Jews being forced to leave Egypt in haste, thus allowing no time to bake ordinary bread. The herbs, meant to invoke the bitterness of exile, might include

horseradish, pepperwort, lettuce, dandelion, chicory, marjoram, and basil. The cups of wine stood for the years of sorrow and the subsequent years of freedom, and also affirmed the joy of the feast.

*Left, the seder ritual
is recorded in a 15th-
century manuscript.*

*And during supper, when the devil had
already put it into the heart of Judas
Iscariot, Simon's son, to betray him, Jesus,
knowing that the Father had given all
things into his hands, and that he had
come from God and was going to God, rose
from supper, laid aside his garments, and
girded himself with a towel.*

JOHN 13:2–4

MINISTERING TO THOSE IN THE UPPER ROOM

*The Gospels give few details about the actual Passover
supper that Jesus shared with his disciples on the eve of his
arrest, trial, and condemnation, except to say it was held
in an upper room. In the following scene from his
novel* BEHOLD THE MAN, *Toyohiko Kagawa describes
the Last Supper from the viewpoint of Mary of Bethany,
who is serving the meal.*

MASTER! IS SOMETHING LACKING?" Mary asked, for Jesus had quietly entered the kitchen. "I would have a basin of water," he said. "My disciples are weary and their feet dusty."

"I will wash them," Mary said eagerly.

Jesus smiled slightly, shook his head. "Nay, Mary, tonight that is my task."

She started to protest, astonished, but could not speak against the gentle determination in his manner. Yet all the way upstairs with the basin she rebelled at the thought of Jesus ministering to those who rightfully should have ministered unto him.

She returned to the kitchen to find young John Mark entering from the street with a large keg of wine. "I will carry it upstairs, lad," she said.

It was heavy, but she took no thought of that. Little enough burden to bear for Jesus, who continually bore so much for others. In the upper room, she set the keg down with a bump. Jesus was indeed washing the disciples' feet. Bewilderment, even consternation, sat on every face—but they were permitting it!

Jesus finished with the drying of the feet of Judas

John alone among the four Evangelists fails to include the incident during the Last Supper in which Jesus blesses bread and wine and gives it to the disciples; this reverent version is by Fra Angelico (1387–1455).

Leonardo da Vinci's fresco for the monastery Santa Maria della Grazie in Milan, executed from about 1495 to 1498, is one of the world's most celebrated paintings. Unfortunately, the artist's experimental mixture of oil and tempera did not adhere well to the wall. The work soon began to deteriorate, and efforts to preserve it have not been entirely effective—leaving the modern viewer with only a vague impression of its original beauty.

Now as they were eating, Jesus took bread, and blessed, and broke it, and gave it to the disciples and said, "Take, eat; this is my body." And he took a cup, and when he had given thanks he gave it to them, saying, "Drink of it, all of you; for this is my blood of the covenant, which is poured out for many for the forgiveness of sins."

MATTHEW 26:26–28

and turned to Peter who was next. Unable to control himself, Peter said violently: "Master, you shall never wash my feet."

Jesus' answer was swift. "If I wash you not, you have no part with me."

On Peter's face the inner struggle was written in line and muscle. At last he said humbly: "Lord, not my feet only, but also my hands and my head."

As Mary picked up the water jug and basin to take them down to the kitchen, Jesus was speaking gravely to the disciples. "If I, then, your Lord and Master, have washed your feet; you also ought to wash one another's feet. For I have given you an example, that you should do as I have done to you."

Mary went downstairs, grateful that she had heard these words, and came back shortly with vinegar for the herbs. This time, she became aware of a change in Jesus' tone. "He who eats bread with me has lifted up his heel against me," he said sorrowfully.

The disciples looked around the table at one another, and back at Jesus, uneasily. There was silence—thick and impenetrable. No voice ventured into the dark stream of it. Then Jesus lifted his eyes upward, away from them all. "Verily, verily, I say unto you, that one of you shall betray me."

Immediately, there were protestations. But Mary saw that each looked doubtfully at the others, suspicion and incredulity mingling in his countenance. While all talked, while all remonstrated, filling the room with words as if to drown foreboding, Mary saw the Master, after a moment when he seemed to be in prayer, break off a piece of unleavened bread and, dipping it into the vinegar, hand it to Judas.

"What you do, do quickly," Jesus said.

None seemed to know what Jesus meant, save John alone, upon whose face a strange expression dawned, unbelief struggling against apprehension. Mary, trying to evolve some clear thought from her chaotic emotions, argued that no doubt Judas had neglected some important errand for the Master, as lately he was wont to do, for Judas rose at once and, brushing by her without a word, went down the stairs.

In this detail from a late-10th-century situla, or holy water bucket, Judas receives the 30 pieces of silver from one of the chief priests.

Then one of the twelve, who was called Judas Iscariot, went to the chief priests and said, "What will you give me if I deliver him to you?" And they paid him thirty pieces of silver. And from that moment he sought an opportunity to betray him.

MATTHEW 26:14–16

A PLEA FOR ACTION REJECTED

Since the Evangelists do not reveal a motive for Judas's betrayal of Jesus other than greed, writers have not hesitated to invent more complex reasons for his heinous act. Judas's discontent with Jesus' failure to lead a political rebellion against Rome, it has been suggested, led to his great treachery. In the following excerpt from BY AN UNKNOWN DISCIPLE, *an anonymous work of fiction published in 1919, a frustrated Judas urges a course of action on his master.*

IT WAS FULL SUMMER before the disciples returned to Capernaum. Judas Iscariot was the last to come in. When I greeted him he stopped and looked at me half-bewildered, as if he had never seen my face before, and then suddenly he seemed to fit me into a place in his memory, for he called out eagerly, "Is Jesus at Capernaum?"

And when I said that he was, he forged forward again as if his purpose so filled his mind that there was room for nothing else. At Capernaum, Judas made for the beach, and here we found Jesus with three or four others. The men, bent on their daily tasks, were about to launch a boat when Judas, travel-worn and thin, his beard and every line of his weary face heavy with dust, burst into their peace. They stopped their work and stared at him as if something in his aspect struck fear into them.

"I have something to say to you," Judas said. "Where can we talk?"

"I was going to the other side of the lake. Come apart with me and rest awhile," said Jesus, and he put his shoulder to the gunnel of the boat, and I helping, we pushed her off. As she took the water I jumped in to steady her, and Judas followed. So it came about that I heard what Judas had to say.

"Master," he said, "I have preached the kingdom as you told me. Throughout all Galilee I have found the same misery and slavery. Everywhere the hold of the Romans is tightening. Our statesmen do not care. They will never win us back our freedom. In a short time it will be too late."

His voice broke, and he covered his eyes with his hands; but the tranquillity that lay in the eyes of Jesus did not waver. He sat patient, helping Judas with silence till he should recover himself.

In a moment Judas had mastered himself. He uncovered his eyes and looked Jesus straight in the face. "When I asked you before, you turned a deaf ear to me. But now I have seen the misery of the people, their oppression and starvation. Will you not listen? You alone can free them. You have but to lift your

The blood money is counted out in Judas's hands; this illuminated manuscript page dates to about 1190.

hand and thousands will flock to you. Never has there been such a ferment. The people will follow you anywhere, even to death. You have seen their misery. Will you not restore to us our nation?"

A great compassion shone in the eyes of Jesus, and there was reverence in his voice as he answered. "Judas, it is not the way. Listen. Once before this temptation came upon me. When the message first came to me, when I looked round on the world and saw men as they are, and God told me to tell them what they might be, then I was driven into the wilderness, and there I fought with devils. God gives the message. It is for the Messenger to learn how to deliver it. Your question was before me, Judas, and to find an answer I wrestled with the powers of evil. All the kingdoms of this world and their splendour seemed to pass before me, and a voice within me said, 'These will all acknowledge your kingdom, and the rule of the God who sent you. But you must first unite the people and drive out those who stop them from living as God would have them live. Then will God have the kingdom, the power, and the glory.'

"In my soul I pondered, and then I saw the meaning of the devil that spoke within me, and I said, 'Oh, Satan, if I by your evil help drive out evil, then will you, not God, be Ruler? I will not fall down and worship you. For if I by force drive out force, will not the strong reign? And if I by cruelty drive out cruelty, will not the cruel be master?' I tell you, No, Judas, I will never hand this world over to the Master of cruelty and force. It is not the way."

There was silence. Judas frowned as if his mind was working hard. "Master," he said, "if you will not lead in Galilee, will you go to Jerusalem? You have never preached the kingdom in Jerusalem."

A long look passed between the two, and then Jesus said, "I will go to Jerusalem."

Judas stared at him.

"You will go to Jerusalem?" he asked, as if amazed at his own success.

"I will go to Jerusalem," Jesus repeated, and half to himself he added, "It is not meet that a Prophet should die out of Jerusalem."

Judas caught the words and answered hastily, "You will not die. You will go to a triumph"; and, suddenly, as if seized with suspicion, he cried, "You have promised? You will not fail me?"

Jesus turned and said, "I will never fail you, Judas." And with that the talk ended.

Two incidents of the final days appear on this page from a 13th-century English Psalter: Judas receiving the silver (top) and Jesus expressing displeasure with his dozing disciples in the garden of Gethsemane.

THIRTY PIECES OF SILVER FOR JESUS

I think you know, Annas, the price is low
    For such a man; there is not in Judea
So fair a face to rest your eyes upon,
    So smooth a breast to shatter with a spear.

Besides He's young and has been well-beloved;
    There was a woman once who left the street,
And followed Him into a hostile house,
    And knelt and pressed her lips against His feet.

He has no wealth, yet men have gone with Him,
    And left their homes and worldly goods behind,
Because His voice was gentle when He spoke,
    And when He looked at them His eyes were kind.

Admit the price is low; for thirty coins
    One buys a plot of ground, a harlot's kiss,
A cask of wine, perhaps, a Negro slave,
    But seldom such a comely man as this.

HELENE MULLINS, 1899–

And they went to a place which was called Gethsemane; and he said to his disciples, "Sit here, while I pray." And he took with him Peter and James and John, and began to be greatly distressed and troubled.

MARK 14:32–33

Jesus' agony as he contemplates his approaching ordeal is etched on his face in this detail from a painting by Andrea Mantegna (1431–1506).

IF NOT TREMENDOUS DELUSION, THEN THE GRANDEST AFFIRMATION

Although divinely aware of the torture and death awaiting him, Jesus responded unmistakably as a human. In this extract from THE STORY OF JESUS CHRIST, *published in 1897, Elizabeth Stuart Phelps re-creates the lonely, wrenching experience in the garden on the Mount of Olives.*

I T WAS NOT QUITE DARK IN GETHSEMANE, for a full moon, contesting with a stormy cloud, peered through. The still, cool spot, secure from disturbance, was a favorite with Jesus; he had spent many solitary nights there. His feet turned to it instinctively.

The eleven followed him, disturbed and subdued. Eight fell back when he signified, by a gesture, his wish for the society of the three whom he preferred. They walked apart with Jesus into the most secluded portion of the olive garden. It was darker here, and strangely still. Jesus stretched out his arms with a groan. He who had suffered so much and so long, and who never complained of the worst that happened, suddenly appealed to them by the most piteous words: "My soul is exceedingly sorrowful . . . even to death. Tarry, and watch with me!"

Before any one of the three could reply, he had disappeared into the heart of the grove. At the foot of a thick tree, with knotted hands, and with face upon the ground, a solitary figure sank.

Human endurance has gone to the limits of pain, shame, and death for all the causes that can torment the souls and bodies of men. But here was a man who carried a burden so isolate that the imagination almost refuses to hold it. Here was a man who believed that the salvation of the human race rested upon himself alone.

Defeat, disgrace, and approaching death shook his convictions to the foundation. He cried out against it: "Father! Father!"

He was so young, so vigorous. Even the torment of prolonged vigil had not conquered him. He was alive to the last red drop of blood in his fair, pure body. He was alive to the last energy of his unshaken brain. And his heart?—why, the life of his heart seemed something great enough to supply the forces and the fountains of the world!

Death!—at the top of vigor, at the brim of existence! Slow torture, and tomorrow shameful death!

The stillness startled him. Smitten with a sudden sense of his loneliness, he staggered up and gazed about him, looking for his friends. He had spent himself in prayer, had shut himself in to the society of God. Yet such a yearning for human sympathy rushed upon him that it seemed as if he would drown in it. He pushed the olive branches apart, and called the names dearest to him—"Peter, James, John!"

But the tired men, sore with trouble, were all asleep. They turned stupidly at the sound of his voice. Peter sprang up. The lips of Jesus quivered: "Could ye not watch *one* hour with me?" he said gently.

He went back to the thick olive trees; there on the ground he fell again. The drama of his life returned before him, swiftly as scenery shot in flame and smoke. The devout docility of his childhood, the pure dreams of his boyhood, and the first surprise of his extra-consciousness. He heard the voice on the river Jordan when his kinsman, the prophet, baptized among the reeds. He listened to the message of the clouds that enveloped him: *"My beloved son!"* He had staked everything, he had suffered everything, on the conviction that he was in some supreme sense different from that which governed the personality of any other man, the Son of his God; chosen for a transcendent mission; des-

In this 14th-century colored woodcut from the Bibliothèque Nationale in Paris, one of the disciples (lower left) forces an eye open to peer at Jesus praying to his left.

His three disciples lost in sleep below, Jesus accepts the bitter cup from which he must drink; the scene decorates a late-16th-century Italian dish.

tined to lift a world of men out of the doom of life.

If this was not the most tremendous delusion which ever visited a human brain, then it was the grandest affirmation. For such was not the task of a man. It was the privilege of a divinity. He had begun life by wondering why he was not like other men; he ended it by understanding.

As naturally as manhood develops from infancy, so Christhood had developed from manhood. Gradually, quietly, he had come to perceive that it was his to live the divine life in human form. But this was not all. It was the conviction of Jesus that it depended upon himself whether men should possess the privilege of personal immortality. He believed that he held in his own hands the gift of eternal life to the human soul. He believed that upon the facts of his life, and upon the facts of his death, this responsibility rested.

In Gethsemane it seemed to Jesus of Nazareth that he had achieved nothing. He was a defeated man. He had missed his Father's errand. Through the blind gates of death, in a few hours, he must be pushed, to hold up his trembling, empty hands and say: "Father, I trusted Thee—but I have failed!"

There in the olive garden lay his poor friends, asleep again. Even they could not understand enough to give him the little common, human sympathy that love saves for the emergency of the beloved. He stole out and watched them, and returned with his head sunken on his breast. He had bared it to the night air for very anguish, and he perceived now that heavy drops were falling from his face and body and streamed upon his heart. He looked at them. In the faint light it could be seen that they were red.

By the subtle law which may convert the most sacred private experiences into world-wide value, and which governed every event in the life of Jesus, there have been given to us certain records of an hour known only to himself and God. The utterance of a prayer: "Father, not as I will, but as Thou wilt!"

As his white lips framed these words, the olive branches stirred above his head, and there, as in the Jordan desert when his troubled life was at its morning, the mystical did visit him. Men called that presence an angel's, not understanding what an angel is.

Fra Angelico emphasized the three drowsy disciples in his depiction of the agony in the garden; an angel attends Jesus at prayer in the left background.

With human terror and divine resignation, Jesus contemplates the proffered cup in this detail of a painting by the Spanish master Goya (1746–1828).

'TIS MIDNIGHT; AND ON OLIVE'S BROW

'Tis midnight; and on Olive's brow
    The star is dimmed that lately shone:
'Tis midnight; in the garden now
    The suffering Saviour prays alone.

'Tis midnight; and from all removed,
    The Saviour wrestles lone with fears;
E'en that disciple whom He loved
    Heeds not his Master's grief and tears.

'Tis midnight; and for others' guilt
    The Man of Sorrows weeps in blood;
Yet He that hath in anguish knelt
    Is not forsaken by His God.

'Tis midnight; and from heavenly plains
    Is borne the song that angels know;
Unheard by mortals are the strains
    That sweetly soothe the Saviour's woe.

WILLIAM B. TAPPAN, 1794–1849

DEEP IN THE REALM OF AGONY

According to early Christian tradition, the Evangelist Luke was the "beloved physician" mentioned by Paul in his letter to the Colossians. Luke's account of Jesus praying in the garden says that his sweat became blood— a detail omitted from some manuscripts but incorporated in Jim Bishop's THE DAY CHRIST DIED.

THE WORK WAS FINISHED. There was an end to the preaching; an end to the miracles; an end to the instruction of the apostles; and even an end to prophecy. Jesus had publicly audited his accounts to the Father in the presence of the chosen ones, and in these prayers he had prayed for himself first—as all good priests should do—and then he prayed for the men who would carry his story of love to the people. He had closed with a prayer for all the faithful of all times.

As he knew when he had told the Father that he would consent to be born and to live as a man, and to die *as a man*, the moment of trial would be slow and terrifying. His Godside would not be able to save him a bit of pain, a shred of shame, or even shield him from the horror of anticipating the awful things that were to come.

It was a time for waiting. He might have walked through the little grove in the full light of the waning moon; he might have sat with the eleven and talked of the time when they had first met, of the time when many Jews up and down the land had come forward convinced that this was indeed the Messiah; he might have talked about the time, only last Sunday, when hundreds of his people in a festive mood had acclaimed him as the son of David, and their hosannas had rung up and down the road to Jerusalem, the echoes dying against the gleaming pillars of the temple.

Instead, Jesus motioned to Peter and James and John. These three, in whom he reposed special trust, followed him into the shadows of a little olive garden. He stopped under the trees. In the pattern of the foliage which blotted part of the moonlight, they saw the face of Jesus and it held fear and horror. The long slender hands shook. The features seemed to be gray, tinged with blue. The mouth was slack. The eyes were huge with a vision the others could not see. *As a man* he was able to sustain the fullness of suffering; as the Son of God he had a knowledge of what was to come.

Intent in prayer, his disciples lost in sleep below him, Jesus seems unaware of the arresting party approaching across a surreal landscape; the painting is by Giovanni Bellini (c. 1430–1516).

THY WILL BE DONE

Thy Will be done. No greater words than these
Can pass from human lips, than these which rent
Their way through agony and bloody sweat,
And broke the silence of Gethsemane
To save the world from sin.

G. A. STUDDERT-KENNEDY, 1883–1929

To the apostles, he seemed to be immeasurably weary. They fell mute and turned their eyes away because they did not think that it was right to look upon the face of the Messiah in weakness and fear.

He doubled his hands into fists and held them against his breast. "Stay here and keep awake," he said with entreaty.

They nodded in silence and watched him make his way through the low-branched trees for a short distance. There, he paused beside a big flat rock, knelt for a few moments, then, abandoning himself to overwhelming mortal fear, threw himself full length on the rock, face down. In a loud voice he said: "My Father, if it is possible, let this cup be spared me!" The lament came, almost involuntarily, from the lips. "And yet," he said, as though afraid to be afraid, "not as I will, but as You will."

No one knew better than Jesus that if he died as the Son of God the gesture would be small, the sacrifice negligible. From this moment until the hour when he expired he knew that he would have to suffer much more than anyone else who might travel the same path and endure the same things; the mere waiting was almost beyond him. Every minute of every hour must now be borne as a man with extraordinary courage in order to achieve the victory of the one God.

The three who reclined against olive trees in the garden fell asleep, as had the eight on the other side of the road. Thus in the little grove was the incongruous sound of the Son of Man beseeching mercy and, mingled with it, the sleep-borne noises of healthy men whose faculties had been short-circuited by fatigue.

And so, in a real sense, Jesus was alone in the garden. As he prayed, his anguish deepened and became unbearable. He stood, and close to a stupor of fright at the visions he had seen, came back to the three, perhaps to seek human solace.

He looked down and his heart ached as he saw the three sleeping. As Peter half opened his eyes, Jesus whispered: "Simon, are you sleeping? Were you not able to stay awake one hour? Keep awake and pray, all of you, that you may not succumb to temptation." He sighed. "The spirit is willing, but the flesh is weak."

Jesus went back to pray, now even further into the realm of agony than before. As he knelt again to tell his Father that he would accept the cup, the salty sweat, gleaming on his face and forehead, began to change color. It reddened and deepened in hue until, in his agony, he knew that it was blood.

Sandro Botticelli (c. 1444–1510) envisioned Jesus on a tufted mount above an appropriately ominous tomb, set off by a picket fence.

In his illumination for a book of hours, Jean Fouquet (c. 1416–1480) included a soldier ripping a garment from a young man in flight (left rear). The incident, reported only by Mark, suggests to some that Mark was an eyewitness and was himself that young man.

There came a crowd, and the man called Judas, one of the twelve, was leading them. He drew near to Jesus to kiss him; but Jesus said to him, "Judas, would you betray the Son of man with a kiss?"

LUKE 22:47–48

ABANDONED BY HIS FRIENDS, DENIED BY THE WORLD

The seizure of Jesus in the garden of Gethsemane, betrayed by one of his inner circle, is the turning point in the drama of the final days. The hero of Lew Wallace's novel BEN-HUR is an eyewitness, crossing paths with the Nazarene at this moment as he does several times in the course of the epic tale.

THE STREETS WERE FULL OF PEOPLE going and coming, or grouped about the fires roasting meat, and feasting and singing, and happy. And as this was the occasion when every son of Israel was full brother to every other son of Israel, and hospitality was without bounds, Ben-Hur was saluted at every step, while the groups by the fires insisted, "Stay and partake with us. We are brethren in the love of the Lord." But with thanks to them he hurried on.

The pious celebration was at its height, when looking up the street, he noticed the flames of torches in motion streaming out like pennons. He observed that the singing ceased where the torches came. His wonder rose to its highest, however, when he became certain that amidst the smoke and sparks he saw the keener sparkling of burnished spear-tips, arguing the presence of Roman soldiers. What were they, the scoffing legionaries, doing in a Jewish religious procession?

An unknown miniaturist incorporated the principal elements of Jesus' arrest in the limited space available.

The moon was shining its best; yet, as if the moon and the torches, and the fires in the street, and the rays streaming from windows and open doors, were not enough to make the way clear, some of the processionists carried lighted lanterns; and fancying he discovered a special purpose in the use of such equipments, Ben-Hur stepped into the street so close to the line of march as to bring every one of the company under view while passing. The torches and the lanterns were being borne by servants, each of whom was armed with a bludgeon or a sharpened stave. Their present duty seemed to be to pick out the smoothest paths among the rocks in the street for certain dignitaries among them—elders and priests; rabbis with long beards and heavy brows; men of the class potential in the councils of Caiaphas and Annas. Where could they be going? And their business—if peaceful, why the soldiers?

As the procession began to go by Ben-Hur, his attention was particularly called to three persons walking together. They were well toward the front, and the servants who went before them with lanterns appeared unusually careful in the service. In the person moving on the left of this group he recognized a chief policeman of the temple; the one on the right was a priest; the middle man was not at first so easily placed, as he walked leaning heavily upon the arms of the others, and carried his head so low upon his breast as to hide his face. His appearance was that of a prisoner not yet recovered from the fright of arrest, or being taken to something dreadful—to torture or death. The dignitaries helping him on the right and left, and the attention they gave him, made it clear that if he were not himself the object moving the party, he was at least in some way connected with the object—a witness or a guide, possibly an informer. So if it could be found who he was the business in hand might be shrewdly guessed. With great assurance, Ben-Hur fell in on the right of the priest and walked along with him. Now if the man would lift his head! And presently he did so, letting the light of the lanterns strike full in his face, pale, dazed,

A 15th-century Italian painter balanced Peter's brief display of bravado with the panic-stricken flight of the other disciples; the soldier at center wastes no time in binding Jesus, identified for him by Judas's infamous kiss of betrayal.

pinched with dread; the beard roughed; the eyes filmy, sunken, and despairing. In following the Nazarene, Ben-Hur had come to know his disciples as well as the Master; and now, at sight of the dismal countenance, he cried out, "The 'Scariot!"

Slowly the head of the man turned until his eyes settled upon Ben-Hur, and his lips moved as if he were about to speak; but the priest interfered.

"Who are thou? Begone!" the priest said to Ben-Hur, pushing him away roughly.

Waiting an opportunity, the young man fell into the procession again. Thus he was carried passively along down the street, down the gorge and over the bridge at the bottom of it. There was a great clatter on the floor as the crowd, now a straggling rabble, passed over beating and pounding with their clubs and staves. A little farther and they turned off to the left in the direction of an olive orchard enclosed by a stone wall in view from the road.

Ben-Hur knew there was nothing in the place but old gnarled trees and a trough hewn out of a rock for the treading of oil. While, yet more puzzled, he was thinking what could bring such a company at such an hour to a quarter so lonesome, they were all brought to a standstill. Voices called out excitedly in front; a chill sensation ran from man to man; there was a rapid falling-back, and a blind stumbling over each other. The soldiers alone kept their order.

It took Ben-Hur but a moment to disengage himself from the mob and run forward. There he found a gateway without a gate admitting to the orchard, and he halted to take in the scene.

A portentous shooting star streaks toward a crescent moon in the sky above the garden where Jesus is being seized; the 14th-century painting is the work of Pietro Lorenzetti.

A man in white clothes, and bareheaded, was standing outside the entrance, his hands crossed before him—a slender, stooping figure, with long hair and thin face—in an attitude of resignation and waiting. It was the Nazarene!

Behind him, next to the gateway, were the disciples in a group; they were excited, but no man was ever calmer than he. The torchlight beat redly upon him, giving his hair a tint ruddier than was natural to it; yet the expression of the countenance was as usual all gentleness and pity.

Opposite this most unmartial figure stood the rabble, gaping, silent, awed, cowering—ready at a sign of anger from him to break and run. And from him to them—then at Judas, conspicuous in their midst—Ben-Hur looked, and the object of the visit lay open to his understanding. Here was the betrayer, there the betrayed; and these with clubs and staves, and the legionaries, were brought to take him.

Presently the clear voice of the Nazarene arose. "Whom seek ye?"

"Jesus of Nazareth," the priest replied.

"I am he."

At these simplest of words, spoken without passion or alarm, the assailants fell back several steps, the timid among them cowering to the ground; and they might have let him alone and gone away had not Judas walked over to him. "Hail, master!"

With this friendly speech, he kissed him.

"Judas," said the Nazarene, calmly, mildly, "betrayest thou the Son of man with a kiss? Wherefore art thou come?"

Receiving no reply, the Master spoke to the crowd again. "Whom seek ye?"

"Jesus of Nazareth."

"I have told you that I am he. If, therefore, you seek me, let these go their way."

At these words of entreaty the rabbis advanced upon him; and, seeing their intent, some of the disciples for whom he interceded drew nearer; one of them cut off a man's ear, but without saving the Master from being taken. And yet Ben-Hur stood still! Nay, while the officers were making ready with their ropes the Nazarene was doing his greatest charity—not the greatest in deed, but the very greatest in illustration of his forbearance, so far surpassing that of men.

"Suffer ye thus far," he said to the wounded man, and healed him with a touch.

Both friends and enemies were confounded—one side that he could do such a thing, the other that he would do it under the circumstances.

"Surely he will not allow them to bind him!" Thus thought Ben-Hur.

"Put up thy sword into the sheath; the cup which my Father hath given me, shall I not drink it?" From the offending follower, the Nazarene turned to his captors. "Are you come out as against a thief, with swords and staves to take me? I was daily with you in the temple, and you took me not; but this is your hour, and the power of darkness."

The posse plucked up courage and closed about him; and when Ben-Hur looked for the faithful they were gone—not one of them remained.

Over the heads of the crowd about the deserted man, between the torchsticks, through the smoke, Ben-Hur caught momentary glimpses of the prisoner. Never had anything struck him as so piteous, so unfriended, so forsaken! Yet, he thought, the man could have defended himself—he could have slain his enemies with a breath, but he would not.

Directly the mob started in return to the city, the soldiers in the lead. Ben-Hur became anxious; he was not satisfied with himself. Where the torches were in the midst of the rabble he knew the Nazarene was to be found. Suddenly he resolved to see him again. He would ask him one question.

The Nazarene was walking slowly, his head down, his hands bound behind him; the hair fell thickly over his face, and he stooped more than usual; apparently he was oblivious to all going on around him. In advance a few steps were priests and elders talking and occasionally looking back. When they were all near the bridge in the gorge, Ben-Hur took the rope from the servant who had it, and stepped past him.

"Master, master!" he said, hurriedly, speaking close to the Nazarene's ear. "Goest thou with these of thine own accord? I am thy friend. Tell me, I pray thee, if I bring rescue, wilt thou accept it."

The Nazarene never so much as looked up or allowed the slightest sign of recognition. "Let him alone," Ben-Hur said to himself; "he has been abandoned by his friends; the world has denied him; in bitterness of spirit, he has taken farewell of men; he is going he knows not where, and he cares not."

Among the scenes from Jesus' final days decorating this late-10th-century situla *(also seen on page 250) is Judas's kiss of betrayal (top center).*

The 16th-century artist who fashioned this enamel plaque shows Jesus appearing before Caiaphas in mock regal attire. In three of the Gospels, Pilate's soldiers clothe Jesus in this manner later; Luke identifies Herod's soldiers as the ones responsible.

Then those who had seized Jesus led him to Caiaphas the high priest, where the scribes and the elders had gathered. . . . Now the chief priests and the whole council sought false testimony against Jesus that they might put him to death, but they found none, though many false witnesses came forward.

MATTHEW 26:57, 59–60

DETERMINED TO HAVE HIS LIFE

In the minds of his enemies, Jesus' guilt was already established and his punishment set. The elaborate procedure by which their wish was fulfilled is described by Ernest Renan in his LIFE OF JESUS, one of the most widely read books of the 19th century.

THE COURSE WHICH THE PRIESTS had determined to take against Jesus was in perfect conformity with the established law. The procedure against one who seeks to corrupt purity of religion, however, amounts to a judicial ambush.

When a man was accused of being a "corrupter," two witnesses who had been induced to commit perjury were hidden behind a partition. It was then arranged that the accused be brought into an adjoining room, where he could be heard by these two witnesses without his perceiving them. Two candles were lighted near him, so that it might be conclusively proved that the witnesses "saw him." He was then forced to repeat his blasphemy, and urged to retract it. If he persisted in it, the witnesses who had heard him took him to the tribunal, and he was stoned to death.

The scheme of the enemies of Jesus was to convict him by the testimony of the witnesses and by his own avowals of blasphemy and outrage on the Mosaic religion, to condemn him to death according to law, and then to have the sentence confirmed by Pilate. The whole priestly authority was for all practical purposes in the hands of Annas. The warrant of arrest probably came from him. It was before this powerful man that Jesus was brought in the first instance.

Annas examined him as to his doctrine and his disciples. Jesus, with just pride, declined to enter into long explanations. He referred Annas to his teachings, which had been public; he declared that he had never held any secret doctrine; and he asked the ex-high priest to question those who had listened to him. This response was perfectly natural; but the exaggerated respect with which the old priest was surrounded made it seem audacious, and one of the bystanders is said to have replied to it by a blow.

Annas, although the real author of the judicial murder about to be done, had no power to pronounce sentence on Jesus; he sent him to his son-in-law Caiaphas, who bore the official title. This man, the blind instrument of his father-in-law, naturally had to ratify all that had been done. The Sanhedrin was assembled at his house, and the inquiry began. Several witnesses, prepared beforehand, appeared before the tribunal. The fatal words which Jesus had actually uttered: "I am able to destroy the temple of God and to build it in three days," were reported by two witnesses. To blaspheme the temple of God was, in Jewish law, to blaspheme God himself. Jesus remained silent, and declined to explain the incriminating speech. The high priest then adjured him to say if he were the Messiah. Jesus avowed that he was, and even proclaimed before the assembly the near approach of his heavenly reign.

The sentence was already decided and his accusers only sought for pretexts. Jesus felt this, and did not attempt a useless defense. From the point of view of orthodox Judaism, he truly was a blasphemer, a destroyer of the established worship; and these crimes were punished by the law with death. With one voice, the assembly declared him guilty of a capital crime. The members of the council who secretly leaned to him were absent or refrained from voting. The frivolity, characteristic of long-established aristocracies, did not permit the judges to reflect much on the consequences of the sentence they had passed. Human life was at that time lightly sacrificed; the condemnation was delivered with careless disdain.

The Sanhedrin had not the right to carry out a sentence of death. But in the confusion of powers which then reigned in Judaea, Jesus was nonetheless condemned from that moment. He remained for the rest of the night exposed to the ill-treatment of an infamous pack of servants, who spared him no indignity.

In the morning the chief priests and the elders met once more. The point was to get Pilate to ratify the sentence pronounced by the Sanhedrin, which, since the Roman occupation, was no longer sufficient.

The agents of the priests therefore bound Jesus and led him to the Praetorium, which had once been the palace of Herod, near the Tower of Antonia. It was the morning of the day on which the Paschal lamb had to be eaten. The Jews would have been defiled by entering the judgment hall of the Roman procurator and would have been unable to share in the sacred feast. They accordingly remained outside.

In a gesture of outrage at what he considers Jesus' blasphemy, the high priest Caiaphas tears his garments. Giotto's early-14th-century fresco is in the Scrovegni Chapel in Padua, Italy.

Peter followed at a distance; and when they had kindled a fire in the middle of the courtyard and sat down together, Peter sat among them. Then a maid, seeing him as he sat in the light and gazing at him, said, "This man also was with him." But he denied it, saying, "Woman, I do not know him."

LUKE 22:54–57

In a courtyard below the room where Jesus is being interrogated, Peter waves away the maid who has identified him as a companion of Jesus. Duccio included the scene in the altarpiece he painted for the cathedral at Siena (also seen on pages 230 and 242). All four Gospels record Peter's triple denial of Jesus.

> **When Judas, his betrayer, saw that he was condemned, he repented and brought back the thirty pieces of silver to the chief priests and the elders, saying, "I have sinned in betraying innocent blood."**
> **. . . And throwing down the pieces of silver in the temple, he departed; and he went and hanged himself.**
>
> MATTHEW 27:3–5

A SINNER ONLY IN HIS OWN INNOCENCE

Judas's repentance, the unsuccessful attempt to undo his treachery, and his abysmal death are recounted only in Matthew's Gospel—though a different story about his end is attributed to Peter in the first chapter of The Acts of the Apostles. In the climax of their novel I, JUDAS, Taylor Caldwell and Jess Stearn describe the traitor fleeing to the temple after witnessing Jesus' death on Calvary.

THE STREETS WERE DESERTED, the inhabitants taking shelter from the storm and marking the holiday. In every home they were preparing the paschal feast, doubly sacred because it was joined with the Sabbath. In a hundred windows I saw the candlelights. The sky was almost pitch black now, the thunder close and ominous. I ran through the dark streets, stumbling in my confusion, until the temple ramparts loomed dimly in front of me. It was so dark I could barely see the towers.

I stood alone before that vast complex and felt an urge to cry out against those who had sent him to be slaughtered. They would be judged as they judged him, cursed till the day of the final judgment.

"Annas, Caiaphas," I shouted to the rooftops, "this temple shall be pulled down over your heads. You shall wander homeless until the days of retribution, for you have slain him by whom there was salvation. May God pity you and yours for the generations to come. For no others shall."

My voice rang out in the silence, and the echo came back hauntingly in the words of the prophet Isa-iah, in a voice like that I had heard long before on the banks of the river Kedron: "He is despised and rejected of men, a man of sorrows . . ."

There was a tremor under my feet. The stones shook, and the temple, revealed in a brilliant flash of lightning, rocked a moment, then settled back with a groan. I drew closer to the great wall, thinking to be buried under its ruins. But the trembling of the earth stopped, the heavens opened up, and the rain fell as if the skies themselves were weeping.

There was still no life. It was almost as if the temple priests and the soldiers cowered in their corners, to escape a just retribution. But there must be somebody there, for it was the custom for certain favored priests to take the Passover feast at the temple. Looking up, I saw a feeble light flickering in a window. I bounded up the steps, past the room where I had sat with the high priests, and stopped before a door guarded by two soldiers. I showed my credentials. "I am expected," I said haughtily.

The suicide of Judas is graphically portrayed in this painted glass panel dating to about 1520; a spotted devil prepares to devour the traitor's soul escaping from his body.

As the lifeless body of Judas dangles from the tree on which he has hanged himself, a devil makes off with his soul. The manuscript in which this illumination appears is in the Pierpont Morgan Library in New York.

dignation. "What is it to us how innocent you proclaim yourself? We all know what you have done, and your reasons matter not, for actions speak more than words. But this money shall never go back to the treasury. For it is blood money, and it is not lawful to keep this reminder of your perfidy."

"My perfidy," I shouted, matching his rage. "I am innocent, I swear it to the world. He wanted to die, to fulfill the prophecies of old. He said so himself."

As the guards came to drag me off, I fled down the stairs and kept running until I came to the Golden Gate, which enters onto the Garden of Gethsemane.

The trees creaked and groaned in the wind, but otherwise nothing broke the grave-like stillness. I could hardly breathe. I found myself in the very olive grove, under a gnarled old tree, where I had last kissed him. I looked up at the strong branches. What can a man do but die when an encompassing dream is destroyed in one moment? How can a man endure when his life has lost its meaning and there is nothing but a trackless desert remaining all of the years of his life?

But, as I stand here below the tree under which I will die, I cannot help but wonder. Is he indeed the Messiah? Is he indeed the hope of man, the Promise of God? Have I deceived myself, or is he the Truth?

In death only is the answer. My question may be answered. It may not. In any event, I will be at peace.

As I moved, my hand rubbed against my tunic, and I recalled the scrap of parchment that had dropped out of his hand at Calvary. In the light of a candle, by which I had been feverishly writing, I saw, with a feeling of disappointment, that it was but one of the psalms. I would have wanted more to remember him by. Even as I looked up again at the tree, and tied my tunic into a knot, I wondered why he had carried these words to the cross with him.

"The Lord is my shepherd," I read, "I shall not want. He maketh me to lie down in green pastures, he leadeth me beside the still waters. He restoreth my soul, he leadeth me in the paths of righteousness for his name's sake. Yea, though I walk through the valley of the shadow of death, I will fear no evil, for thou art with me. . . ."

They looked at me doubtfully, taking in my wet and bedraggled appearance. "It will go badly with you if you do not admit me. I bear an urgent message."

Boldness won out.

I saw first the surprised countenance of the crafty Annas, who sat at the head of the table. I could see they had not yet begun the feast. I looked around the table, thinking of another supper, and counted thirteen. It seemed a fit number for such an occasion.

My hand reached into my tunic, slid over the parchment that had slipped out of his fingers, and then found the pouch with the thirty pieces of silver.

"How dare you give me this blood money? I have sinned only in my own innocence. I will have no part of this filthy lucre." I flung the pouch across the table to where Caiaphas sat scowling blackly.

Some of the silver pieces flew out of the bag and rattled across the floor.

"Out with you," shouted Caiaphas in fury and in-

And as soon as it was morning the chief priests, with the elders and scribes, and the whole council . . . bound Jesus and led him away and delivered him to Pilate. And Pilate asked him, "Are you the King of the Jews?"

MARK 15:1–2

THE ACCUSED:
BOLD, RESOLUTE, DEFIANT

Were it not for his trial and condemnation of Jesus, the first-century Roman procurator of Judea would most likely be forgotten to history. In this extract from his fictional LETTERS OF PONTIUS PILATE, the British journalist W. P. Crozier shows how little the event meant to Pilate—who even apologizes to his correspondent, the essayist Seneca, for the length of his letter.

JESUS WAS ARRESTED late last night. I provided a troop of soldiers who accompanied the officials of the Sanhedrin. The advantage is that, as the news spread through the city this morning, it was known that Procurator and Sanhedrin had acted jointly. The Sanhedrin is not popular with the most zealous Jews, but the general impression would be that if all the authorities, Roman and Jewish, were acting together, this must be a troublesome fellow who was better out of the way.

The prisoner was taken to the high priest's quarters until this morning when he was handed over to my people. I believe Caiaphas got a few of the leading priests together and they examined him for themselves. The case is a perfectly simple one, from my point of view, and will give no difficulty. Since Antipas will not handle the matter, I shall execute Jesus as a maker of sedition against Caesar.

But these priests have always to remember that sedition against Caesar is usually a merit in the eyes of the populace, and they will want to make out a good case for themselves. They will insist, I suppose, on Jesus' defiance of the Law, attacks on the ritual and outbreak in the temple. Probably they will say that he

In a symbolic gesture absolving himself of guilt for the death of Jesus, Pilate washes his hands. The artist, Mattia Preti (1613–1699), emphasized his subject's resolution by having him stare directly at the viewer.

Having had Jesus scourged, Pilate brought the prisoner, garbed in purple and crowned with thorns,
before the mob to ask what further punishment was sought. The resounding answer: death by crucifixion.
Antonio Ciseri, a 20th-century Italian artist, included Pilate's troubled wife in the scene.

regarded himself as the expected Messiah, and the people have no use for a Messiah who cannot keep himself out of the hands of the despised Romans. That is not the kind of deliverer the Jews want.

I gave orders for Jesus to be taken to Antipas, as I said I would, with a polite statement that as the disturber of the peace was a Galilean, he would perhaps consider the matter came within his jurisdiction. I received a reply, equally polite, that Antipas recognized my courtesy but waived any right that he might have over an offender in my city of Jerusalem. A touching exchange of courtesies!

Afterward I tried and condemned the prisoner. The trial was short but in due form and order. Jesus was accused of disturbing the peace, stirring up disaffection and claiming to be King of the Jews. There was evidence both from our side and from that of the Jews, both from Galilee and from this city. Caiaphas, Annas and the leading Sadducees were prominent and so were some but not all of the chief Pharisees; some of the Pharisees would lend no assistance in convicting a rebel against Caesar however much they desired his death as a rebel against themselves.

However, that did not help him. The priests had much to say of his attacks on their religion, but I cut them short on that. They cannot have it both ways. If we are not allowed to interfere in their religion, they cannot appeal to us when their observances are attacked; as soon as the offense becomes political, directly or indirectly, then we take note of it. When a man brawls in the temple he tends to provoke a general explosion and that concerns us closely. The charge against Jesus of disturbing the peace was proved to the hilt and he could not deny it.

I inquired of the prisoner whether he admitted the more serious accusations. The Jews alleged that he regarded himself as the destined deliverer of the nation, which involves the end of both their authority and ours. They cited both the public utterances in which Jesus had spoken of a new kingdom as being imminent and also certain admissions about himself which they said he had made to his own followers.

I put the question to him. I asked him whether he considered himself to be the deliverer. "So *they* say," he answered, indicating the High Priest and his neighbors, with a curt gesture of contempt. I pointed out to him that he was accused also of representing himself as King of the Jews. I asked him whether he considered himself to be that king. He made nearly

the same answer: "So *you* say," meaning, I suppose, that in neither case was there anything in his own conduct or motives to support the accusation, but that he knew well enough that we meant in any case to fix the charge upon him. He realized that he was trapped, and there was no way of escape, but he was bold, resolute, defiant, almost insolent.

I condemned him to death. I could, of course, do nothing else. All roads lead to that conclusion. I am sure that if he was not a dangerous rebel yesterday, he would have been one tomorrow. For either he would have succeeded in his assault on the priesthood or he would not. If he had not, how long would a man of his temperament, so passionate, headstrong and bold, have abstained from making that appeal to the patriotic feelings of these Jews which always—always—meets with a quick response, even when made by men of much less powerful character than his?

Allow me one word about the inscription announcing the offense of Jesus. It was "King of the Jews," set up over the cross. The Pharisees were indignant. They themselves want a King of the Jews. It would give them the greatest pleasure to see Caesar overthrown tomorrow and a Jewish king installed—not a half-Jew like Herod—who would rule the country through them and suppress their Sadducean rivals. But it angered them to see the precious title "King of the Jews" held up to ridicule; it was too plain a reminder of their servitude. Besides, they thought it an insult that a crucified criminal, a presumptuous and defiant countryman, should be labeled "King."

I took a short way with them. "What I have written I have written," said I, and bade them begone.

I run on so, my dear Seneca. The subject carries me away. I must apologize to you again; I am afraid that even you will find the subject tedious. For, after all, what does it matter—one Jew more or less?

Rembrandt's Jesus seems removed from the turmoil swirling about him as Pilate asks the crowd's judgment against his prisoner.

BY ORDER OF PONTIUS PILATE: THIRTY-NINE STROKES

Although he found Jesus guilty of no crime, Pilate turned him over to his soldiers for a brutal whipping prior to the carrying out of the death sentence. In the following excerpt from THESE SHARED HIS CROSS, Edwin McNeill Poteat depicts a cruelly tormented Jesus whose compassion extends to his tormentor.

Bound to a pillar, Jesus endures the whips of the Roman soldiers; the stained glass panel dates to the 13th century.

THE RAVEN, SO NAMED by his fellow legionaries because his voice was singularly rasping, stirred lazily in the straw. The men of his company lay about him in various attitudes and degrees of sleep. The sun was only just high enough to have begun pouring its lazy warmth into the open court, and as the light began its slow trespass across the sprawling figures, there was a sound at the gate. As a messenger accompanied by an orderly bearing the ensign of the Procurator entered, every soldier in the court struggled briskly to his feet.

The messenger unrolled a parchment and read: "Order of criminal death to Jeshua of Nazaret. Strokes Thirty-nine by Scourge. Death by Crucifixion. Pontius Pilate Procurator." He handed the parchment to his attendant, who in turn handed him a smaller scroll which he proceeded to intone: "Marius known as the Raven, Master of the Scourge. Thirty-nine strokes, no more no less. Error by scourge-master punished by twice the margin of mistake." He turned sharply and disappeared through the gate.

The Raven was not a little pleased at his appointment, though he had seen many men shrink from applying the lash. He plucked the sleeve of a young guardsman and started to obey the summons of the messenger. No one else moved toward the door;

Who Was Pontius Pilate?

Outside the New Testament, references to Pontius Pilate and his 10-year procuratorship in Judea are rare. The Roman historian Tacitus mentions him only in passing when noting "the execution of Christus, author of that sect, by the procurator Pontius Pilate in the reign of Tiberius." But the Jewish historian Josephus recounts three incidents involving his rule. On one occasion, Pilate deliberately offended Jews by sending soldiers into Jerusalem carrying images of the Roman emperor, but called them back after an angry crowd demonstrated in the streets. Next, he sought to win favor by improving the Holy City's water supply, but Jews were outraged when he tried to use temple funds for the project. In the rioting that followed, several citizens were killed because Pilate's soldiers disregarded his orders to use batons rather than swords. Finally, Pilate was ordered by his superior Lucius Vitellius, the governor of Syria, to go back to Rome for an investigation after his forces ambushed and killed a gathering of religious fanatics in Samaria. According to tradition, he was tried and condemned to exile in France at Vienne-sur-Rhône, where he committed suicide during the reign of Caligula. The New Testament's authors were not unsympathetic to Pilate, and early Church fathers even thought of him as "a Christian by conscience."

A rare artifact dating to Pilate's procuratorship: a stone inscription bearing his name from Caesarea, the Roman capital of Judea

scourgings were routine matters, to be attended to as a duty, not as a spectacle. And as the Raven and his somewhat bewildered companion made their exit, he stopped and picked up a handful of loose straws, while the rest of the men indifferently made themselves comfortable again.

The scourging that preceded the death of condemned felons took place in a small enclosure at the rear of the praetorium. There was only room enough for the guard of six lictors who acted both as witnesses and as precaution against any possible act of violence by the prisoner. The regimental doctor stood by to interfere if the victim seemed likely to die under the lash, and to administer a restorative if needed during the ordeal. When it was over he applied an unguent of camphor oil to staunch the bleeding.

The scourge-master was allowed, if he wished, a counter whose duty it was to stand and tell the strokes after they fell. The law that provided that an error must be doubly recompensed allowed the penalty to be laid on by the counter. The Raven had never been sure of his ability to count. Once before he had failed by two strokes to administer the full thirty-nine, and he had not forgot the four blows applied to his own back by a fellow soldier with whom, as ill-luck would have it, he had quarreled two days previous. It was quick thinking on his part that called the youthful guardsman out as his aid. He was new to the legion and afraid of him. At least so the Raven thought. If an error occurred, the consequences therefore would cause him a minimum of discomfort.

When they reached the court of scourging, the victim had already been trussed up on a post the thickness of his own torso, and as high as his waist. He was bent forward over the post; his hands extended downward and were bound with leather thongs that tightened about his arms above the elbows and his legs above the knees. The Raven and his counter stopped a moment outside the gate.

"Take these straws," said the Raven. "As each stroke falls, break off a length of straw and lay it on the stone, like this." He broke off an inch and stooped and with the heel of his hand brushed clean a

The third-century martyr St. George endured tortures similar to those inflicted on Jesus. A 15th-century Italian artist surrounded his saint with a crowd that could be taken for the Roman soldiers and Jewish elders who persecuted Jesus.

spot on the flagstone and put down the piece of straw. Then he broke off another length, and another, until ten lengths were set in a row before him.

"Make three rows, like that," he said, straightening himself up. "But the fourth row must have only nine. And if you count wrong, carrion, I'll break your back." He shoved the boy viciously through the gate and followed him into the enclosure.

The Raven saluted the little company, threw off his tunic, rolled up the sleeves of his leather jacket and took the scourge that was handed him. The doctor nodded, and the officer in charge lifted his hand as a signal to begin.

After a second of uncomfortable suspense, the scourge fell in a whistling circumflex and creased the back with three white lines. As the Raven raised his arm for a second blow, the wales oozed with blood.

After the involuntary convulsion at the first blow, the victim did not move. His body was limp with relaxation; the thongs thumped pitilessly against ribs weirdly resonant, but there was no outcry. The scourger breathed noisily as he cut the air and the reddening flesh. Blood began to run in little trickles down the sides of the whipping post; they started along the shoulders, ran under the armpits, down the arms and into the limp hands. Once the doctor raised his hand and stopped the torment of lead and leather

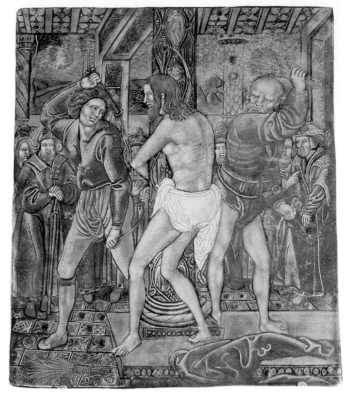

The flagellation of Jesus,
a Limoges plaque created before 1520

As the Roman soldiers apply their whips, two angels with basins to catch his blood kneel at Jesus' feet, and a third hovers above with a cloth to wipe his brow. Jaime Huguet painted the scene between 1450 and 1460.

to examine the culprit. He was alive and aware. The blows began again.

But not before the Raven had cast an oblique glance at the straw fragments on the flagstone over which the boy was bending. He had meant to count the strokes himself, but the patterns his blows had cut in the white flesh before they became a confused and bloody laceration had disturbed his figures. The boy, he feared, might also be confused. So when the doctor had assured himself his patient was still conscious and signaled for continuance, the Raven speeded up the tempo of his rhythmic lashing. At the end of what he vaguely thought was about thirty strokes he stopped and looked toward the boy, but his vision was blurred.

Edging toward the lad, he stepped carelessly into a pool of black blood and slipped, and before he could catch his balance, his foot had left a smear across the spot where the counter's scattered straws had been. He stood up angrily and raised his lash above the boy. The doctor moved toward him and, placing himself between the two, pointed significantly to the victim. The Raven turned. Nine times more he laid the rending whip across the motionless back.

"Thirty-nine," he croaked excitedly.

"Forty-two," the lad replied, quietly.

"You dog," snarled the scourger. "You kept no count; show me your straws."

"Nay," said the lad. "I needed no help to keep the tally; have I not two good eyes and ten good fingers?"

The centurion in charge ordered the Raven to stand aside and took the bloody lash from him.

"Take off your shirt," ordered the officer brusquely. "There is more important business here than listening to your arguing." And to the lad: "Will you pay his score, or shall I ask another?" By the way of answer the boy reached for the whip the officer held.

Two guardsmen were helping the scourged man to his feet. "I know not the laws of Rome," Jesus said. "But God's laws are the ways of mercy and forgiveness. Cannot the wounds I suffered through this man's error be atonement for his sin?"

The Raven straightened himself in astonishment and looked at Jesus. The centurion laughed gruffly, shook his head, and pointed toward the exit.

Jesus felt his arms seized by his escort. They helped him through the gate that swung shut behind them. As they started toward the praetorium, he heard over the wall the whistle of a lash, a heavy thud, and the sharp, convulsive cry of a man torn by pain.

A Man Who Bled Like Everyone Else

The vicious scourging at the pillar was followed by the humiliation of being mocked by Roman soldiers. Though suffering intensely, Jesus remained stoic and compassionate—being rewarded, Robert Payne suggests in this extract from his novel THE LORD JESUS, with a vision of his heavenly Father.

OUT OF THE BLAZE OF SUNLIGHT, along dim passageways, up steps and over a kind of bridge, he was led by two legionaries into a courtyard, a dark, evil-smelling place where the moisture clung to the walls. All the sounds of Jerusalem ceased on the threshold of the courtyard.

The soldiers looked at him with awe. He was in their power, but they were still afraid of him, of the strange remoteness which he carried with him, wearing strangeness like a garment. They took sidelong glances at him, and then turned away, ashamed of something they had seen. As always when he entered a strange place, he paused and made a sign of blessing.

The guards waited patiently until the blessing was over. They knew they had to scourge the prisoner, and this punishment in an obscure courtyard where the sun rarely penetrated was almost worse than crucifixion, for there were no laws regarding scourging.

Unless a commanding officer had given instructions for a certain number of blows to be delivered, they gave as many as they pleased, at whatever intervals they pleased, in whatever manner seemed most suitable. If for some reason they took a dislike to the prisoner—if he screamed too much or too little; if he showed too much courage or none at all—they would continue to lacerate him long after he lost consciousness. But if it happened that the prisoner was later to be crucified, they would generally be lenient with him, giving him no more than twenty or thirty blows.

The scourging pillar was set against the wall near a fig tree. It was about seven feet high, stained with rust-colored blotches, and was evidently the broken column of some long-abandoned temple. Behind the column lay a tangle of thorn bushes, which at this season of the year were beginning to flower.

Jesus was limping a little as he crossed the courtyard. He knew he was to be scourged, but he had expected it would happen in some public place, in the

Although the arms of the soldiers flanking Jesus have been damaged in this late-13th-century ivory carving, scholars identify the work as representing the mocking of the scourged prisoner.

sunlight, in full view of the members of the Sanhedrin and the jeering mob. He had imagined there would be an officer in charge, and perhaps a doctor. He had not expected a small, evil-smelling courtyard thick with horse dung and flies. His guards had not spoken to him and gave the impression of being indifferent to him; and he was grateful for their silence.

Standing beside the pillar, he shivered a little in the damp air. For a moment he allowed his gaze to fall idly on the dark and empty windows of the barracks, which were like blind eyes looking down on the courtyard. Then he turned, laid his head against the pillar in weariness and despair, and for some reason kissed the column and ran his hands along the edges.

The young soldiers went about the task deftly, expertly, like machines. They removed his gown, bound him with thin cords to the pillar, and then stepped back smartly, each grasping a ten-foot bullhide whip studded with small splinters of bone. There were so many pieces of bone set in the leather that the whips gleamed white when they whistled in the air.

They took turns whipping him. The first blow cut across his shoulders and curled round his face. He groaned and locked his teeth, while the waves of pain broke over him and drowned him, so that he felt he was suffocating under the weight of the immense burden of pain. He writhed and twisted against the cords. He could feel the breaking of the flesh, the bony claws, the wet warm blood pouring out through the cracks in the skin. And as the blows increased in fury, coming with ever greater frequency, he became no more than a quivering nerve-end, jumping and jerking feverishly.

As the pain grew more intense, spreading over his whole body, as he sucked in his breath, as the air around him turned to fire, as the earth gave way under his feet and as he hung to the pillar by the thin cords, he was aware that he was entering another landscape. The walls of the terrible courtyard fell away as he entered the world of the whip and the little sharp edges of bone inserted in the leather thongs.

He heard laughter, but the sound of his own blood falling on the stone base of the column was louder. He lost count of the blows. He lost all power to pray. He was nothing. He was pain. He was dead.

But he was not quite dead, for although there came a time when he no longer felt the whips because he had lost consciousness, there were curious intervals of lucidity in which he saw strange gaps of brightness breaking through the surrounding dark.

The sky shivered and trembled like a curtain in a high wind, and suddenly he found he was able to look through the curtain at the indistinct shapes of things moving across a golden field. Music came from them, the music of youthful voices and of trumpets. The shapes assumed form and substance. There was a high throne, dazzling like a waterfall, and the wings of angels were perpetually beating on the throne. The voices grew more triumphant; and there was such a storm of singing that he could not distinguish the words, and the movement about the throne was so furious that he could not distinguish the angels, but he knew he was in the presence of God. And when at last the sound of singing died, he heard the voice he had been expecting for so long, saying: "Thou art my Son, my beloved Son—"

They had ceased whipping him. They had cut down the ropes which bound him to the column, and were pouring water on him.

"So this is the man who calls himself the King of the Jews!" they exclaimed, not without astonishment. "It is all wrong to leave him here. He should be dressed like a king, surely!"

They propped him up at the foot of the column, threw a red military cloak round his shoulders and fastened the clasp; and then a branch of a thorn bush was placed in his right hand for a scepter, and a crown of flowering thorns was placed on his head. Then, still jostling one another, they knelt before him and declaimed in chorus: "Hail, King of the Jews!"

High up in one of the towers of the Antonia fortress, Pontius Pilate looked out of a window at the small courtyard far below. For some moments he gazed in silence, and then he turned to the centurion by his side. "I am afraid," he said, "that this Messiah of theirs suffers like everyone else. He bleeds when he is cut. It is a great pity. I had hoped to see a miracle."

Angels bear such symbols of Jesus' suffering as (clockwise from lower left) the reed given him as a mock staff, the pillar on which he was scourged, a veil with the image of his face, the cross, and a ladder and hammer; they are set in a rosewood and ebony frame for this 17th-century silver and silver-gilt plaque of the humbled Jesus.

Ecce Homo, Latin for "Behold the man"—Pilate's words in presenting Jesus for judgment by the crowd—is the title given this painting by Michelangelo da Caravaggio (1565–1609).

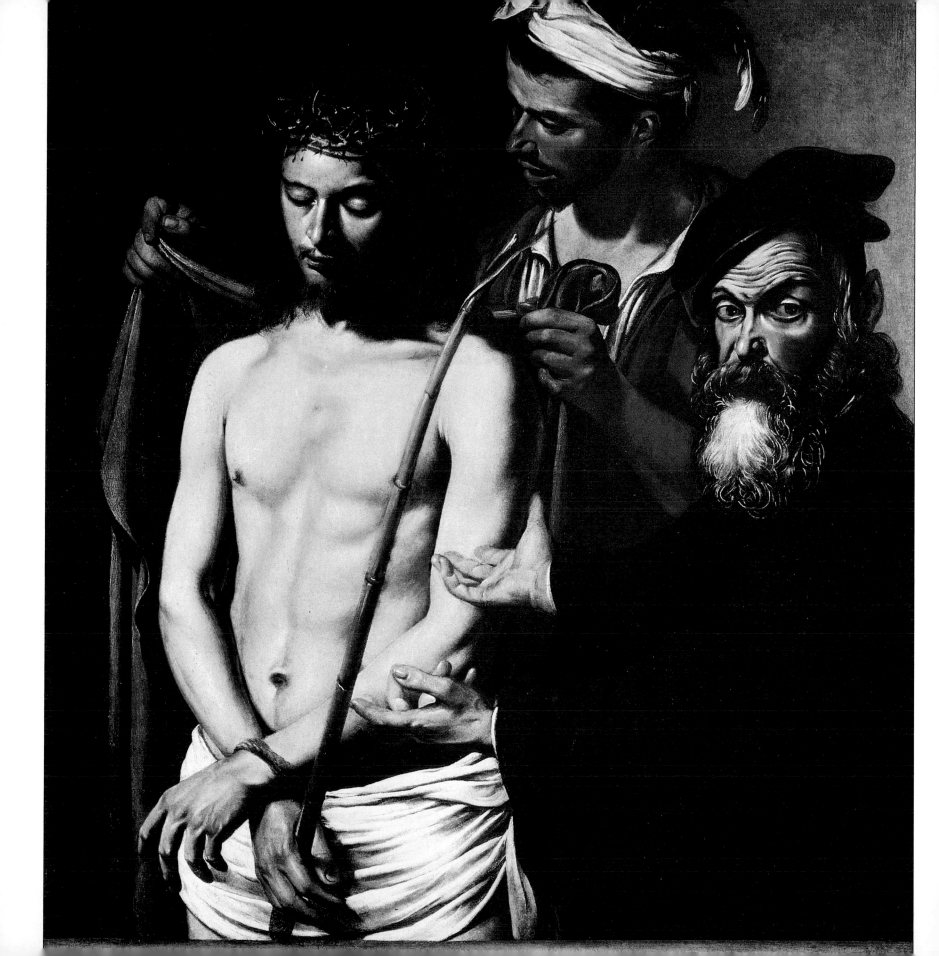

ALBERTVS · DVRER · SVPER · TABVLA · HAC · COLORIS · CINERICII · FORTVITO · ET · CITRA · VLLAM · A · VERIS ·
IMAGINIBVS · DELINIATIONEM · FACIEBAT · ANNO · SALVTIS · M · D · XXVII · AETATIS · VERO · SVAE · LVI

In this crowded panorama of the road to Golgotha, Albrecht Dürer included the lamenting women rudely
pushed by soldiers (far left), the two near-naked thieves also being led to their execution,
and Jesus, stumbling beneath the weight of his cross. The artist appended a legend attesting that he created
the work in 1527 and added his distinctive monogram, "AD."

And as they led him away, they seized one Simon of Cyrene, who was coming in from the country, and laid on him the cross, to carry it behind Jesus. And there followed him a great multitude of the people, and of women who bewailed and lamented him.

LUKE 23:26–27

THE MAN WHO SHARED HIS BURDEN

Simon of Cyrene, suggests Frank Harris in his play THE KING OF THE JEWS, *was en route from his fields in the country to apply for a job as a temple doorkeeper when he was pressed into service by the soldiers leading Jesus to his Crucifixion. That evening Simon returned home to tell his wife, Hushim, of the remarkable encounter. Hushim is speaking in the following excerpt.*

WELL? HAVE YOU GOT THE POST? You have been a time. Are you a doorkeeper of the temple; have we a house in the inner court?

SIMON [*passing his hand over his forehead*]. I don't know.

HUSHIM. Don't know? You must know. Was Joad there? He promised to speak for you. Did you see him?

SIMON. I didn't see him. [*Sits down wearily.*]

HUSHIM. Didn't see him? What did you do?

SIMON. I did nothing. I'm tired, Hushim.

HUSHIM. Tired? What happened? Are you ill?

SIMON. I'm not ill, I'm only tired.

HUSHIM. What's the matter with you? Can't you speak?

SIMON. If you knew—

HUSHIM. If I knew what? Oh, you make me mad. [*She takes him by the shoulder and shakes him.*] What's happened? Now tell me everything that

Jesus carrying the cross, left panel of a 14th-century carved ivory diptych

happened since you left. You went out to the field?

SIMON [*nods while drinking the wine she has given him*]. I was at the field till nearly the second hour working, then I came into the city. When I reached the street which leads from the temple to Golgotha I could not cross it, there was such a crowd. All had come to see some prisoners who were going to be crucified.

HUSHIM. But didn't you push through?

SIMON. I got through to the first file, but there soldiers kept the passage. I had to wait. No one was allowed to cross. They told me there were three criminals. The people were talking about them. Two were thieves and one was a rebel from the north who had tried to make himself king. It was to see him the people had run together. Some said he was a holy man.

After a little while the prisoners came by. The two thieves first, and then slowly the man, whom some called a prophet. He looked very ill. They had platted a crown of thorns and pushed it down on his head, and the thorns had torn the flesh and the blood ran down his face. When he came opposite to me he fell and lay like a dead man; the cross was heavy. The centurion ordered some of the Roman soldiers to lift the cross from him and he got up. He seemed very weak and faint; he could hardly stand. The centurion came across to me and pulled me out and pointed to the cross and told me to shoulder it and get on.

HUSHIM. But why you?

SIMON. I suppose because I looked big and strong.

HUSHIM. Didn't you say you had to be at the temple?

SIMON. Of course I told him, but he thrust me forward and warned me if I didn't do as I was told, I'd have to go to the temple without feet.

HUSHIM. Oh, what luck! Why didn't you run away?

SIMON. I didn't think—

HUSHIM. Well, you carried the cross? And then—

SIMON. I went to lift the cross; it seemed as if I were helping to punish the man. While I stood hesitating, he looked at me, Hushim. I never saw such eyes or such a look. Somehow or other I knew he wanted me to do it. I lifted the cross up and got my shoulder under it and walked on.

Women sympathizers offer succor to Jesus on the way to Golgotha in this 16th-century painting by Giovan Battista Naldini.

The faithful bear a cross through the streets of Jerusalem during a Holy Week commemoration.

The Way of the Cross

As early as the fourth century, pilgrims to Jerusalem began trying to retrace Jesus' footsteps to Calvary. Because much of the city had been destroyed and buried, the actual pathway of his ordeal was unknown, but it was believed that the Romans purposely built temples on Christian holy places. Calvary, for example, was supposed to be beneath a temple to Aphrodite. By the 14th century, Franciscan monks had established a devotional walk in the Holy City with eight stopping points, or stations, that commemorated critical moments of the Passion. Some 200 years later, the 14

Stations of the Cross represented on the walls of Roman Catholic churches throughout the world today had been identified as follows: (1) Jesus is condemned to death; (2) takes up the cross; (3) falls; (4) meets Mary, his mother; (5) Simon of Cyrene is forced to help him; (6) Veronica wipes Jesus' face; (7) Jesus falls again; (8) meets the women of Jerusalem; (9) falls for the third time; (10) is stripped of his garments; (11) is nailed to the cross; (12) dies; (13) his body is taken down; (14) he is buried.

According to legend, the imprint of Jesus' face was left on the veil offered by Veronica; Francisco de Zurbarán (1598–c. 1664) recreated the anguished visage.

I did not seem to notice the weight of it. I was thinking of his look. And so we went through the crowd past Golgotha to the hill of Calvary. On the top I put down the cross.

HUSHIM. When was that? It must have been about the third hour. Why didn't you go to the temple then?

SIMON. I forgot all about the temple. I could think of nothing but the holy man. He stood there so quiet while the priests and people jeered at him.

When they were getting ready to nail him to the cross, I went over to him and said, "O Master," and he turned to me, "forgive me, Master, for doing what your enemies wished." And he looked at me again, and my heart turned to water, and the tears streamed from my eyes, I don't know why.

He put his hands on my shoulders and said, "Friend, friend, there is nothing to forgive." [*Lays his head on his arms and sobs.*]

HUSHIM. Don't cry, Simon, don't cry. He must have been a prophet!

SIMON [*choking*]. If you had seen him.

HUSHIM [*beginning to cry*]. I know. I know. What else did he say?

SIMON. He *thanked* me, and though I was a foreigner and a stranger to him, and quite rough and common, he took me in his arms and kissed me. . . . I was all broken before him.

He was wonderful. When they nailed him to the cross, he did not even groan—not a sound. And when they lifted the cross up—the worst torture of all—he just grew white, white. All the priests and the people mocked him and asked him, if he could save others, why couldn't he save himself. But he answered not a word. Instead, he prayed to God to forgive them, and he comforted one of the thieves who was sobbing in pain. Oh, he was wonderful. Even in his anguish he could think of others.

And then the storm burst, and I stood there for hours and hours in the darkness. I could not leave him. Later some of his own people came about the cross, weeping, his mother and his followers, and took him down, and they called him Master and Lord, as I had called him. They had all loved him. No one could help loving him, no one.

Above his head on the cross they had written, "King of the Jews." They did it to mock him. But he was a king, king of the hearts of men.

HUSHIM. What was his name?

SIMON. Jesus of Nazareth.

Known for his representations of deformed, monstrous figures, the Dutch painter Hieronymus Bosch (1450–1516) emphasized the maniacal cruelty of Jesus' tormentors.

SIMON THE CYRENIAN SPEAKS

He never spoke a word to me,
  And yet He called my name;
He never gave a sign to me,
  And yet I knew and came.

At first I said, "I will not bear
  His cross upon my back;
He only seeks to place it there
  Because my skin is black."

But He was dying for a dream,
  And He was very meek,
And in His eyes there shone a gleam
  Men journey far to seek.

It was Himself my pity bought;
  I did for Christ alone
What all of Rome could not have wrought
  With bruise of lash or stone.

COUNTEE CULLEN, 1903–1946

Attended by other holy women, Jesus' mother stretches to support her fallen son on the way to the hill of execution (distant background) in this dramatically intense painting by Raphael (1483–1520).

Soldiers strain to hoist the third cross atop Golgotha in this panoramic canvas, probably the work of a 17th-century Flemish artist, as crowds continue to surge up the hill from a town reminiscent of those along northern Europe's Rhine River.

AT NOON: A TWILIGHT OUT OF TIME

The terrible suffering of Jesus on the cross has captured the pity and stirred the imagination of countless writers. Among the many who placed their fictional characters at the scene is Lew Wallace. The following selection is from BEN-HUR, *one of the best-selling novels of the 19th century.*

THE GUARD TOOK THE NAZARENE'S CLOTHES from him, so that he stood before the multitude naked. The stripes of the scourging he had received in the early morning were still bloody upon his back; yet he was laid pitilessly down, and stretched upon the cross—first, the arms upon the transverse beam. The spikes were sharp—a few blows, and they were driven through the tender palms. Next, they drew his knees up until the soles of the feet rested flat upon the tree; then they placed one foot upon the other, and one spike fixed both of them fast. Such as could not hear the dulled sound of the hammering yet saw the hammer as it fell, shivered with fear. But not a groan, or cry, or word of remonstrance from the sufferer: nothing at which an enemy could laugh.

The workmen put their hands to the cross, and carried it, burden and all, to the place of planting. At a word, they dropped the tree into the hole; and the body of the Nazarene also dropped heavily, and hung by the bleeding hands. Still no cry of pain—only the divinest of all recorded exclamations, "Father, forgive them, for they know not what they do."

The cross, reared now above all other objects, and

standing singly out against the sky, was greeted with a burst of delight; and all who could see and read the writing upon the board over the Nazarene's head made haste to decipher it. Soon as read, the legend was adopted and communicated, and presently the whole mighty concourse was ringing the salutation from side to side, and repeating it with laughter, "King of the Jews! Hail, King of the Jews!"

The sun was rising rapidly to noon, when suddenly a dimness began to fill the sky and cover the earth— at first no more than a scarce perceptible fading of the day; a twilight out of time; an evening gliding in upon the splendors of midday. But it deepened, and directly drew attention; whereat the noise of the shouting and laughter fell off, and men, doubting their senses, gazed at each other and turned pale.

The dimness went on deepening into obscurity, and that into positive darkness, but without deterring the bolder spirits upon the knoll. One after the other the two thieves were raised on their crosses, and the crosses planted. The guard was then withdrawn, and the people set free closed in upon the height and surged up it, like a converging wave. A man might take a look, when a newcomer would push him on, and take his place, to be in turn pushed on—and

there were laughter and ribaldry and revilements, all for the Nazarene.

"Ha, ha! If thou be King of the Jews, save thyself," a soldier shouted.

Others wagged their heads wisely, saying, "He would destroy the temple, and rebuild it in three days, but cannot save himself."

The second hour after the suspension passed like the first one. To the Nazarene they were hours of insult, provocation, and slow dying. When the third hour was about half gone, some men of the rudest class—wretches from the tombs about the city— came and stopped in front of the center cross. "If thou be King of the Jews, or Son of God, come down," they said, loudly.

The breathing of the Nazarene grew harder, his sighs became great gasps. Only three hours upon the cross, and he was dying! A tremor shook the tortured body; there was a scream of fiercest anguish, and the mission and the earthly life were over at once. The heart, with all its love, was broken.

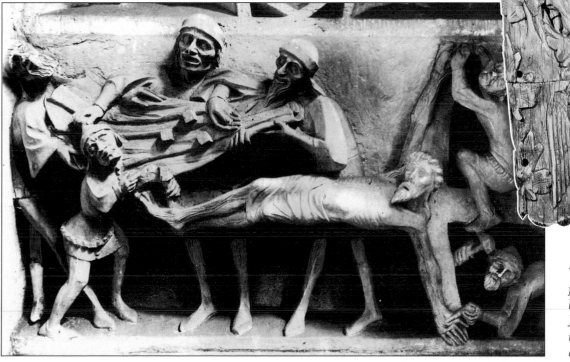

The Crucifixion carved in ivory formed the top of a 14th-century bishop's staff (above); at left, Jesus is nailed to the cross in this detail from a German choir screen relief.

A devil (upper left) perches on the cross of the thief who mocked Jesus in this Crucifixion scene by Lorenzo Monaco (c. 1370–1425), an Italian monk who taught or influenced such other painters as Fra Filippo Lippi and Fra Angelico (see opposite page).

THERE IS A GREEN HILL FAR AWAY

There is a green hill far away,
   Without a city wall,
Where the dear Lord was crucified,
   Who died to save us all.

We may not know, we cannot tell,
   What pains He had to bear;
But we believe it was for us
   He hung and suffered there.

He died that we might be forgiven,
   He died to make us good,
That we might go at last to heaven,
   Saved by His precious blood.

There was no other good enough
   To pay the price of sin;
He only could unlock the gate
   Of heaven and let us in.

O dearly, dearly has He loved,
   And we must love Him, too,
And trust in His redeeming blood,
   And try His works to do.

CECIL F. ALEXANDER, 1823–1895

When the soldiers had crucified Jesus they took his garments and made four parts, one for each soldier; also his tunic. But the tunic was without seam, woven from top to bottom; so they said to one another, "Let us not tear it, but cast lots for it to see whose it shall be."

JOHN 19:23–24

A TOSS OF THE DICE FOR A SEAMLESS GARMENT

It was a Roman custom for soldiers carrying out an execution to divide the victim's clothing among them; and all four Evangelists include the incident, a fulfillment of Psalms 22:18. Lloyd C. Douglas's novel THE ROBE tells what happened to the tunic. In the following passage, the slave Demetrius joins his master, the tribune in charge of the execution, at Golgotha.

THERE WAS NOT AS LARGE A CROWD as he had expected to see. There was no disorder, probably because the legionaires were scattered about among the people. It was apparent, from the negligence of the soldiers' posture, as they stood leaning on their lances, that no rioting had occurred or was anticipated.

Demetrius moved closer in and joined the outer rim of spectators, most of them poorly dressed, many weeping. There were several women, heavily veiled and huddled in little groups, in attitudes of silent, hopeless grief. A large circle had been left unoccupied below the crosses.

Edging his way slowly forward, occasionally rising on tiptoe to search for Marcellus, his master, Demetrius paused beside one of the legionaires who, recognizing him with a brief nod, replied to his low-voiced inquiry. The commander and several other officers were on the other side of the knoll, at the rear of the crosses, he said.

Demetrius made a wide detour around to the other side of the knoll. Marcellus, the centurion Paulus, and four or five others were lounging in a small circle

In addition to the women bewailing Jesus' death, Fra Angelico placed the founder of his monastic order, Saint Dominic, and other clerics at the foot of the cross.

on the ground. A leather dice-cup was being shaken negligently, and passed from hand to hand. As Demetrius slowly approached the group of officers, Marcellus shook the cup languidly and tossed out the dice.

"Your lucky day!" growled Paulus. "That finishes me." He stretched his long arms and laced his fingers behind his head. "Demetrius," he said, nodding toward a rumpled brown mantle at the foot of the central cross, "hand me that coat. I want to look at it."

Demetrius picked up the garment and gave it to him. Paulus examined it with idle interest.

"Not a bad robe," he remarked, holding it up at arm's length. "Woven in the country; dyed with walnut juice. He'll not be needing it any more. I think I'll say it's mine. How about it, Tribune?"

"Why should it be yours?" asked Marcellus, indifferently. "If it's worth anything, let us toss for it." He handed Paulus the dice-cup. "High number wins."

There was low mutter of thunder in the north and a savage tongue of flame leaped through the black cloud. Paulus tossed a pair of threes, and stared apprehensively at the sky.

"Not hard to beat," said Vinitius, who sat next to him. He took the cup and poured out a five and a four. The cup made the circle without bettering this cast until it arrived at Marcellus.

"Double six!" he called. "Demetrius, you take care of the robe." Paulus handed up the garment.

Demetrius rolled up the robe and thrust it inside his tunic, pressing it tightly under his arm. Turning about, he started down the hill. It was growing so dark now that the narrow path was indistinct. He flung a backward look over his shoulder, but the descending gloom had swallowed up the knoll. By the time he reached the city, night had fallen on Jerusalem, though it was only mid-afternoon.

Another slave was waiting at the entrance to his master's quarters. "What have you there?" he asked.

"The Nazarene's robe," said Demetrius.

"How do you happen to have it?"

"It belongs to the Tribune. The officers tossed for it. He won it."

"I shouldn't think he'd want it," remarked the slave. "It will probably bring him bad luck."

"Why *bad* luck?" demanded Demetrius. "It belonged to a brave man."

Roman soldiers toss dice for Jesus' robe in this 17th-century painting of the school of Novgorod, seat of an important medieval principality in northern Russia.

And when they came to the place which is called The Skull, there they crucified him . . . . And Jesus said, "Father, forgive them; for they know not what they do."

LUKE 23:33–34

When Jesus saw his mother, and the disciple whom he loved standing near, he said to his mother, "Woman, behold, your son!" Then he said to the disciple, "Behold, your mother!" And from that hour the disciple took her to his own home.

JOHN 19:26–27

One of the criminals . . . . said, "Jesus, remember me when you come into your kingdom." And he said to him, "Truly, I say to you, today you will be with me in Paradise."

LUKE 23:39, 42–43

And about the ninth hour Jesus cried with a loud voice, "Eli, Eli, lama sabach-thani?" that is, "My God, my God, why hast thou forsaken me?"

MATTHEW 27:46

Jesus, knowing
that all was now
finished, said (to
fulfil the scripture),
"I thirst." A bowl
full of vinegar stood
there; so they put
a sponge full of the
vinegar on hyssop
and held it to
his mouth.

JOHN 19:28–29

When Jesus
had received
the vinegar,
he said, "It is
finished";
and he bowed
his head and
gave up his
spirit.

JOHN 19:30

There was
darkness over the
whole land until the
ninth hour, while
the sun's light failed;
and the curtain of
the temple was torn
in two. Then Jesus,
crying with a loud
voice, said, "Father,
into thy hands I
commit my spirit!"
And having said this
he breathed his last.

LUKE 23:44–46

The works of art accompanying the
so-called seven last words of Jesus, as
quoted by three of the Evangelists,
are (opposite page, clockwise from
top left) a cast metal relief by
Donatello (c. 1386–1466); the central
panel of an altarpiece by Matthias
Grünewald dated about 1515; a
late-13th-century painting by
Giovanni Cimabue; and a sixth-
century Syrian manuscript
illumination; (this page, also
clockwise from top left) a 9th- or 10th-
century ivory plaque; a cast
metal crucifix by Donatello; and a
14th-century processional banner.

When the centurion and those who were with him, keeping watch over Jesus, saw the earthquake and what took place, they were filled with awe, and said, "Truly this was the Son of God!"

MATTHEW 27:54

CATACLYSMS OF NATURE ANNOUNCE HIS DEATH

The death of Jesus—occurring at the very moment the Sabbath observance was being announced in Jerusalem's temple—was accompanied by a number of strange phenomena. Although many in the city remained indifferent, at least one acknowledged the significance of these signs. The French writer Daniel-Rops comments in this selection from his JESUS AND HIS TIMES.

IT WAS THREE O'CLOCK, the legal hour of sunset, and in the temple the opening ceremony of the Passover was about to commence. Three blasts, short, long, short, from the sacred trumpets and the high priest in a blue cope ascended the steps. The sound of a flute rose up before the altar of sacrifice. On Golgotha, three further words came down from the cross: "It is finished," and then a last prayer: "Father, into thy hands I commend my spirit," the final exhalation of a life now completed.

The message which Jesus had sought to give the world came to its consummation. Many times he had said that the price of salvation was blood; now that price was paid. An ungrateful Israel was at the very moment absorbed in its rites—at the very moment when these rites were to change in meaning. All that had for centuries uplifted the heart of Israel, all the prophecies, had passed out of the domain of prophecy and had become history. For the last cry of the victim was in itself an echo of the faith of the Psalmist: "Into thy hand I commend my spirit: thou hast redeemed me, O Lord God of truth." The son of David echoing the words of his ancestor; everything was mysteriously bound together according to the divine plan; everything was completed.

Probably none of the Jews engaged at that moment in chanting the *Hallel* realized the unique importance of the drama of Calvary. They may not even have regarded the greenish darkness brooding over the city as a warning sign. But nature again reacted dramatically, for at the moment Jesus expired the veil of the temple was torn in two, from top to bottom, the earth shook, and the rocks were split.

There were other strange phenomena; dead men came out of their graves and appeared to many; fear swept across Jerusalem. The hour of judgment had come, but how many in the city knew it?

There was one man, however, who felt that there was some connection between the convulsions of the earth and the last cry of the crucified. This was the centurion whose duty it was to remain with the sufferers until the end. He had heard the Jews say to Pilate that this man "ought to die because he made himself the Son of God." At the time he had paid no attention to the words but the cataclysms of nature, the cramping sense of dread which had spread over the city and the groaning in the very bowels of the earth brought him revelation. On the darkened hillside, by the three gibbets, light came to him. "Truly this was the Son of God," he said. We know no more of this honest soldier, the first of countless millions who were to believe in Jesus crucified.

CALVARY

Friendless and faint, with martyred steps and slow,
Faint for the flesh, but for the spirit free,
Stung by the mob that came to see the show,
The Master toiled along to Calvary;
We gibed him, as he went, with houndish glee,
Till his dim eyes for us did overflow;
We cursed his vengeless hands thrice wretchedly,—
And this was nineteen hundred years ago.

But after nineteen hundred years the shame
Still clings, and we have not made good the loss
That outraged faith has entered in his name.
Ah, when shall come love's courage to be strong!
Tell me, O Lord—tell me, O Lord, how long
Are we to keep Christ writhing on the cross!

EDWIN ARLINGTON ROBINSON, 1869–1935

In his starkly realistic depiction of the Crucifixion, Andrea Mantegna included the soldiers tossing dice for Jesus' tunic at the foot of the cross. The initials on the central cross are those of the Latin words for "Jesus of Nazareth, King of the Jews," the cynical and contemptuous inscription dictated by Pilate.

And when evening had come, since it was the day of Preparation, that is, the day before the sabbath, Joseph of Arimathea, a respected member of the council, who was also himself looking for the kingdom of God, took courage and went to Pilate, and asked for the body of Jesus.

MARK 15:42–43

EXPLAINING THINGS TO PILATE

Named in all four Gospels as the man who claimed Jesus' body from Pilate for burial, Joseph of Arimathea is mentioned nowhere else in the New Testament—though he is identified, variously, as a rich man, a dissenting member of the Sanhedrin, and a secret disciple of Jesus. In the following extract from her novel KING OF THE JEWS, Mary Borden imagines the interview at which Joseph asked for the body.

THE GREAT ROOM WAS FILLING with shadow when the councillor was shown in; the last rays of the sun coming through the narrow slits of windows lay in gold bands across the floor.

A world divided the Jew in his rich robes and the Roman soldier in Caesar's harness. They did not speak the same language, acknowledge the same ruler or worship the same God. They had, in fact, almost nothing in common, save their deep mutual racial antagonism, and they faced one another in the great stone-flagged room of the fortress through a fog of prejudice. But they were both honest men, and it was this that made an understanding between them possible. This and one other thing. They had both seen and talked to Jesus of Nazareth while he was alive.

Pilate spoke with cold formality to the dark shrouded figure; there was scarce a tinge of sarcasm in his voice: "You have come to me, Councillor, to ask

In his painting of Jesus being taken down from the cross, Peter Paul Rubens (1577–1640) included Hebrew, Greek, and Latin versions of Pilate's inscription as specified in John's Gospel.

leave, so I understand, to bury the body of a traitor."

"I do not believe him to have been a traitor, your Excellency."

"Naturally, otherwise you would not be here. Still, your friend is a traitor in the eyes of your law and mine. You come as his friend. Am I right?"

"Quite right, my lord."

"Hum." Pilate stroked his chin. "He didn't seem to have many friends when he came before me this morning. Where were they all, Councillor?" The Roman watched the Jew's face closely, as if a deal hung on the answer, and it did. Had Joseph of Arimathea attempted at that moment to minimize the importance of Jesus, hoping to gain his end by so doing, the result of the interview might have been very different. But he spoke the truth.

"Jesus of Nazareth has many friends, but they are amongst the poor. They could not hope to make their voices heard in the Sanhedrin or before your tribunal. They had no spokesman."

"What of yourself?"

"I was not warned about the proceedings. The priests kept the trial quiet until it was over."

"Still, there were Pharisees present in plenty in the courtyard, before my judgment seat. Don't they represent the common people in your senate? I thought your learned men were the leaders of the poor."

"Not of the very poor, your Excellency. There is a large part of our people who are considered outcasts, unfit to be represented in the council. They are little better than slaves. They have no leader."

"Save this Jesus?"

The Jew bowed. Pilate scowled, then spoke again. "What did this miserable class believe their leader would do for them?"

"They believed he would save them."

"And how was he to do this without bringing about a revolution? You said that he was no traitor."

The Jew waited a moment before answering, but when he did it was with his head up, and a glint of defiance in his sombre eyes.

"It would be impossible for you, my lord, a Roman, to understand the power or the purpose of this man. Had he accomplished what he willed to accomplish, a revolution would undoubtedly have taken place within our nation, but not of a kind that would be of im-

The 16th-century craftsman who fashioned this pendant for an enamelware figurine of Mary holding her dead son adorned his work with gold, rubies, and pearls.

The Shroud of Turin

Angels bearing the miraculously imprinted shroud in a 16th-century Italian painting

Although never authenticated by the Roman Catholic Church, the so-called Shroud of Turin has been venerated as the burial cloth of Jesus since it came to light in 1357. The blood-stained linen, about 3.5 feet wide by 14 feet long, bears the front and back negative images of a bearded man whose body has been wounded by scourging and crucifixion. Devotees have argued that the imprints were scorched upon the shroud in a holy fire that accompanied the miraculous disappearance of Jesus' body from his tomb. In 1988 three separate research institutions were given stamp-sized samples of the shroud for laboratory analysis. Using a procedure known as carbon dating, which can date animal and vegetable materials within 100 years by measuring radioactive decay, the scientists all agreed that the flax used to make the linen was grown in the 14th century. The method by which the unknown forger produced the image is still not fully understood. But, whatever its true origins, the shroud's impact on generations of believers transcends the realm of science and scholarship.

The image long alleged to be that of Jesus, a detail from the Shroud of Turin

among the many devout people of decent position."

And Pilate was silent again. Joseph of Arimathea had told him what he wanted to know. It wasn't clear, nothing was clear that had to do with the Jews, but it was the vague, exasperating, nebulous truth.

That there was a superstitious feeling in some quarters about this man Jesus was evident. Where superstition came into play among the Jews, there were always numerous unpleasant possibilities. It would be best to have the man's body safely out of the way.

"One more thing, Councillor." Pilate spoke quickly now, biting off his words as if impatient to be rid of the Jew and all that he stood for. "If I give you the body, where will you bury it, and how will you manage the matter? It must be done tonight and your people do no work on holidays."

"The place is ready. I own a piece of land near the execution ground where I have built a new tomb. I would put the body there."

CRUCIFIXION TO THE WORLD BY THE CROSS OF CHRIST

When I survey the wondrous Cross
Where the young Prince of Glory died,
My richest gain I count but loss,
And pour contempt on all my pride.

Forbid it, Lord, that I should boast
Save in the death of Christ, my God;
All the vain things that charm me most,
I sacrifice them to his blood.

See from his head, his hands, his feet,
Sorrow and love flow mingled down;
Did e'er such love and sorrow meet?
Or thorns compose so rich a crown?

His dying crimson like a robe
Spreads o'er his body on the Tree,
Then am I dead to all the globe,
And all the globe is dead to me.

Were the whole realm of nature mine,
That were a present far too small;
Love so amazing, so divine,
Demands my soul, my life, my all.

ISAAC WATTS, 1674–1748

As faithful followers lower Jesus' body from the cross, a mourning woman kisses his feet and a man at right claims the crown of thorns and the nails driven through the victim's hands and feet. Fra Angelico inserted Resurrection panels above his central painting.

portance to Caesar. He had no interest in politics, would have nothing to do with armed insurrection. He purposed to change the hearts of the nation and those hearts he touched believed in him."

"Why didn't they rise up then to defend him? Why didn't they storm my tribunal this morning? If they believed in him, why didn't they run through the city and rouse these many followers of his?"

The councillor of Arimathea was disturbed by the question. His labored breathing was audible. "I do not know why his disciples did nothing. They may have lost hope or they may have expected him to save himself by a miracle."

"And there was no miracle?"

"No. There was no miracle."

"And now they are all gone happily to their homes to make holiday."

"No. There is mourning tonight in many a house in this city, not only in the homes of the outcasts, but

A Seed for the Fostering Earth

*The hasty burial of Jesus to meet the Sabbath deadline is
described in the following passage from Daniel-Rops's
JESUS AND HIS TIMES. To his objective skill as an
historian, the French author adds a novelist's flair to draw
a poignant lesson from Jesus' death.*

THE MOSAIC LAW commanded that the body of an
executed man "shall not remain all night
upon the tree." It was, therefore, in accordance with the Law to ask for permission to
bury him. But, on the evidence of the Talmud, it
seems that the bodies of condemned criminals were
put in pits belonging to the judicature and remained
there until the flesh rotted away and only then could
their bones be returned to their families. So it would
be asking a favor of Pilate. In Roman custom, to refuse to give the body of an executed man to his family,
or to demand money for doing so, was regarded as exceptional severity and Pilate had no reason to be un-
merciful. He allowed Joseph's request.

At the same time he received another request.
Some of the more orthodox Jews, fearing that the
Passover might commence before the crucified men
were dead and removed—which would constitute a
legal impurity of the whole town—asked that death
might be hastened by breaking the dying men's legs.
Pilate sent a picket for this purpose.

The *crurifragium*, or breaking of the legs, was recognized Roman punishment, a cruel supplement to other tortures, but in the case of men already dying on
the cross it was normally used to shorten their sufferings. In Jesus' case, it was not necessary; he was already dead. The soldier's lance thrust was probably
only a routine gesture to make absolutely sure that the
man was dead. The soldiers could go back and reassure Pilate that the execution had been accomplished.

The body, removed from the cross, was prepared for
the grave in some haste since the hour of the Sabbath
was near. It is not correct to state, however, that the
funeral rites were curtailed, for the Law permitted the

*A man, possibly Joseph of Arimathea, helps support the body
of Jesus taken down from the cross; the sculptor Michelangelo
also carved the famous Pietà, or Mary holding her son's body,
which is a treasure of St. Peter's basilica in the Vatican.*

Search for the True Cross

Not until A.D. 350, when St. Cyril of Jerusalem said that the cross of Jesus was in the Church's possession and pieces "had already been scattered throughout the land," is there any known reference to the fate of the instrument of torture on which Jesus died. The New Testament is silent on the subject but a popular tradition holds that the crosses of Jesus and the two thieves crucified with him were discovered in an excavation in Jerusalem just to the east of Calvary by St. Helena. A former innkeeper and

A ninth-century reliquary for a fragment of the true cross

concubine of a Roman official, she had been converted late in life by her son Constantine, the Roman emperor who himself had converted and legalized Christianity in the empire after seeing a vision of the cross in the heavens. Revered for her piety and compassion, Helena built many churches and decided to make a pilgrimage to the Holy Land in 324, when she was in her eighties. In one version of her discovery, she was inspired to distinguish the true cross from those of the two thieves by having all three brought to the body of a dead man. The one that restored him to life was venerated as the cross of Jesus. Described as being in pieces, the cross was widely distributed throughout the Christian world and is said to survive in numerous reliquaries.

washing and embalming of the dead even on the Sabbath. So, even if the six blasts on the silver trumpet had already announced the holy day, the disciples were at liberty to finish their pious work.

Joseph of Arimathea had close by a new grave of the type usual in Palestine, similar to that from which Lazarus arose. There would be two chambers hollowed out of the rock, the first a kind of vestibule with a door at the end opening into the tomb proper. This would be almost square, just about two yards each way, and against the wall was a kind of shelf for the reception of the corpse. The tomb was closed by a very heavy stone, something like a millstone, which rolled up to the sloping recess of the outer chamber where it was held by a wedge. If this were removed the stone would roll forward blocking the entrance to the tomb itself.

The tomb was opened. Jesus was wrapped in the grave clothes, which consisted of at least two pieces. There was the winding sheet, the *sindon*, and a smaller piece of linen, the *soudarion* or grave cloth, a kind of handkerchief placed over the face. The head was raised on the mound of stones which was provided in all Jewish tombs for this purpose. The devoted women from Galilee assisted in the last rites.

Nicodemus, who had first come to Jesus by night, brought a mixture of myrrh and aloes "about a hundred pounds' weight." It was a pathetic gesture from a pathetic man who had more good will than courage. Nicodemus could not stand up for Christ living but he made a sumptuous offering to his remains.

The light was fading; they must make haste to finish, to remove the wedge and let the stone roll up and close the tomb. Then they went away, leaving the body in the silence of the tomb.

In the darkness of the grave, Jesus was now no more than other men, a body of flesh awaiting corruption. So his unhappy disciples must have thought. And yet, corruption, which in the natural order must follow inevitably, was not to be. "Except a corn of wheat fall into the ground," said Jesus, "it abideth alone. But if it die it bringeth forth much fruit." The seed lay in the fostering earth; the fruit would spring forth from the seed and the harvest was at hand.

This scene of Jesus being placed in his tomb, the work of an unknown artist, is from the Victoria and Albert Museum in London.

And Joseph took the body, and wrapped it in a clean linen shroud, and laid it in his own new tomb, which he had hewn in the rock; and he rolled a great stone to the door of the tomb, and departed. Mary Magdalene and the other Mary were there, sitting opposite the sepulchre.

MATTHEW 27:59–61

Joseph of Arimathea and Nicodemus are the only men mentioned in the Gospel accounts of Jesus' burial; Pieter Lastman (1583–1633) included the traditional holy women in his version of the event.

Savior and Redeemer

From Friday to Sunday, Jesus lay in his sepulcher—his mission
of peace and salvation ended in disgrace, the hopes of his
followers for a new kingdom of God on earth shattered. Then
the women who came to anoint his body made the
astonishing discovery that the tomb was empty; angels watching
there asked why they sought the living among the dead.

Jesus had conquered death and shortly thereafter the risen Christ
appeared to Mary Magdalene, to Simon Peter, to two disciples
walking to Emmaus, to his fearful disciples gathered in
Jerusalem, to unbelieving Thomas, to the fishermen in Galilee,
and last of all to Saul on the road to Damascus. Though
he was taken up to heaven in full view of the disciples,
he left the promise that he would return. The story of Jesus
was to be without end.

*A penumbra of red and
white cherubs encases
Jesus as he steps
out of his sarcophagus.
Although Andrea
Mantegna (1431–1506)
set the Resurrection
in a fanciful grotto, he
adroitly captured the
fear that made the
guards tremble and
become like dead men.*

Bearing such symbols of Jesus' death as the pillar on which he was scourged, angels make ready the tomb—its lid displaying the coins of Judas's betrayal. The crowded deposition scene is the work of French court painter Jean Fouquet (c. 1416–1480).

Next day . . . the chief priests and the Pharisees gathered before Pilate and said, "Sir, we remember how that impostor said, while he was still alive, 'After three days I will rise again.' Therefore order the sepulchre to be made secure until the third day, lest his disciples go and steal him away, and tell the people, 'He has risen from the dead.' "

MATTHEW 27:62–64

DEAD—AND YET ALIVE AGAIN

Counting the Friday of his Crucifixion, the intervening Jewish Sabbath (Saturday), and the first day of the week (Sunday) on which he arose from the dead, Jesus lay in his tomb three days. In the following excerpt from THE GREEN BOUGH, *a work published in 1913, Mary Austin attempts to recreate Jesus' thoughts and feelings as he struggled toward consciousness.*

IT WAS THE SEASON of the green bough. On into the night emanations from the warm, odorous earth kept the chill from the air, and the sky, steeped in the full spring suns, retained, almost until dawn, light enough to show the pale undersides of the olive branches where they stirred with the midnight currents. It was not until the hours fell into the very pit of the night that he awoke.

For more than an hour past he had swung from point to point of consciousness on successive waves of pain; now he was carried almost to the verge of recovery, and now he felt the dragging clutch of the Pit from which hardly he had escaped. By degrees, as he was borne toward life, his passages in and out of insensibility began to approach more nearly the normal phases of waking and sleeping; the pangs of his body separated from the obsessions of spiritual distress, and recurrent memory began to ply.

It began with the agony in the garden and the uncomprehending sleep of his companions. Could ye not watch one hour!

He remembered the futility of trial, the scoffings and the betrayals. Pain by pain, his body picked out for him other memories of the way, the cross, the tearing nails—more than all else the impotence of purely human impulses under the larger vision which kept him, even in the midst of anguish, profoundly aware of how little they knew the thing they did. It came back upon him as the stiffness of his wounds, the burden of understanding that loses even the poor human relief of bitterness and blame. As he fell away again into the trough of bodily pain it was to measure the full horror of that drop, which when the racked consciousness that had sustained him in the knowledge of Fatherliness, had failed like a splitten sail and left him beating blindly in the void. "My God, my God, why hast thou forsaken me?"

He came strangely up to life in the anguish of that cry. Suddenly he put up his hand and touched the cold stones of his sepulcher. He was dead then, and was alive. Lying very still for pure weakness, his spirit returned half unwittingly by the old track and traveled toward God fumblingly. As a drowsy child at the breast, he sucked comfort, the ineffable, divine support. It flowed. Slowly the slacked spirit filled. Power

Scenes of Jesus' suffering (left) and Resurrection (right) flank the central Crucifixion on this 14th-century painted fabric.

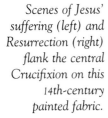

Angels hover over a
shrouded Jesus, laid to rest
in his tomb. The artist,
William Blake (1757–1827),
is as well known today
for his mystical poems as
he is for his engravings of
religious subjects.

Carved out of soft rock, Jewish burial places often had several chambers, such as this one with an entrance marked by a menorah.

Burial Customs in Ancient Palestine

In Jesus' day, the dead of wealthy families were typically laid to rest in family burial places in use for generations, either caves or tombs cut into soft rock. Although criminals were usually interred in the trench graves where the poor were laid to rest, Jesus did not receive a criminal's burial. Since his own family would not have owned a burial spot near Jerusalem, a follower named Joseph of Arimathea arranged to bury Jesus in his own unused tomb in a garden near Golgotha. Such tombs usually had one or more irregular chambers with ledges where the bodies were placed and were accessible only by a short, low-ceilinged, ramplike shaft. No coffin was used. As suggested in the Gospels, a rough boulder or a specially cut closing stone blocked the entrance, basically to protect the

corpse from jackals. The dead were usually buried promptly, as Jesus was, because the Jews did not embalm their deceased and bodies decomposing rapidly in the Middle Eastern heat created a health hazard. Normally, the corpse was immediately washed and anointed with spices, including aloes and myrrh, then wrapped in linen, with special care taken to bind the chin to keep it from lowering. In funeral processions, which were arranged by the nearest of kin, the bereaved cried aloud or sang ritual lamentations and beat their breasts, sometimes donning sackcloth or rolling in the dust, while hired musicians and professional mourners added to the public demonstration of grief.

A sarcophagus found in the tomb shown above, at Beth Shearim, Israel

came upon him. God was not dead nor forsaking. He hung upon that and waited for a word.

Outside in the dawn dusk a bird, awakened by the swaying of his bough in the first waft of the morning, bubbled over with the joyous urge of the spring. The sound of it filtered through the rock crevices in a thin, clear trickle of song. He laid off the grave cloth and began to feel for the round stone which he knew should close the mouth of the grave. Calling on those reserves of power for which he had always been remarkable, he applied his shoulder to the stone. It yielded to the pressure and slid along the groove.

He made out the soft bulk of the olive trees, all awake and astir to catch the first streak of the morning, and the *tink, tink* of water falling from a pipe into a stone basin. Following it he came to the fountain from which the garden was watered, and drank and bathed his wounds. He was startled for a moment by the swaying of a garment against him, and then he perceived it to be the gardener's cloak left hanging in the tree, a long, brown hooded garment. He drew its folds around him as a protection against the warning chill of dawn. Knowing the ways of working folk, he groped in the split hollow of an ancient olive tree and found a lump of figs tied in a cloth and a flask with a few swallows of wine in it. When he had eaten and drunk, he bound up his feet with the cloth and sat down on the stone bench of the fountain to think what had befallen him.

He was dead—else why had they buried him?—and he was alive again. The currents of the Eternal Being circulated through him with peace and healing.

The dusk of the dawn cleared to ineffable blueness, in which the domes and towers of Jerusalem swam, islanded in light. Round about, single high peaks, which still retained the winter whiteness, glowed like outposts of the heavenly host. The gates of the city clattered to let in the hordes of market gardeners with their donkeys, camped since the night before outside the walls, and presently in the cool dimness he saw the women climbing the hill path toward the place of sepulchers. They came peering through the dawn, for they were not certain of any mark by which they should know it, except that it was a new tomb wherein never man was laid. Their voices came up to him clearly through the morning stillness, and he knew at once what their errand was when he heard them troubling lest they had come so early there would be no one about to take away the stone from the door.

*Following his death on the cross, according to a
Christian tradition, Jesus descended into
hell to liberate souls in suffering there. In this
16th-century painting, an aged Adam and an Eve
still clutching her apple are among the rescued.*

MARY MAGDALENE AND
THE OTHER MARY

Our Master lies asleep and is at rest:
   His heart has ceased to bleed, his eye to weep:
The sun ashamed has dropped down in the west;
   Our Master lies asleep.

Now we are they who weep, and trembling keep
   Vigil, with wrung heart in a sighing breast,
While slow time creeps, and slow the shadows
   creep.

Renew thy youth, as eagle from the nest;
   O Master, who hast sown, arise to reap;—
No cock-crow yet, no flush on eastern crest:
   Our Master lies asleep.

CHRISTINA ROSSETTI, 1830–1894

*The so-called harrowing of hell—Jesus' freeing of the souls condemned
to the netherworld—is shown in a 14th-century Greek painting. At bottom,
the women at the empty tomb learn of the Resurrection from an angel.*

As the holy women approach the tomb in the left rear, the Roman guards fall in terror before the risen Jesus. The tapestry is based on a design by Raphael, a painter to the popes in Rome early in the 16th century.

EASTER

Most glorious Lord of lyfe, that on this day
Didst make thy triumph over death and sin,
And having harrowd hell, didst bring away
Captivity thence captive, us to win:
This joyous day deare Lord, with joy begin,
And grant that we, for whom thou diddest dye,
Being with thy deare blood clene washt from sin,

May live for ever in felicity:
And that thy love we weighing worthily,
May likewise love thee for the same againe;
And for thy sake, that all lyke deare didst buy,
With love may one another entertayne.
So let us love, deare love, lyke as we ought:
Love is the lesson which the Lord us taught.

EDMUND SPENSER, c. 1552–1599

And behold, there was a great earthquake; for an angel of the Lord descended from heaven and came and rolled back the stone, and sat upon it. His appearance was like lightning, and his raiment white as snow. And for fear of him the guards trembled and became like dead men.

MATTHEW 28:2–4

WHEN THE HEAVENS WERE SEEN TO OPEN

Although attesting to the Resurrection, none of the four Evangelists actually describes Jesus rising from his tomb. The fragmentary GOSPEL OF PETER, a noncanonical source that may date as early as Matthew, Mark, Luke, and John, contains this striking scene.

PILATE GAVE THEM PETRONIUS the centurion with soldiers to watch the sepulchre. And with them there came elders and scribes to the sepulchre. And all who were there, together with the centurion and the soldiers, rolled thither a great stone and laid it against the entrance to the sepulchre and put on it seven seals, pitched a tent and kept watch. Early in the morning, when the Sabbath dawned, there came a crowd from Jerusalem and the country round about to see the sepulchre that had been sealed.

Now in the night in which the Lord's day dawned, when the soldiers, two by two in every watch, were keeping guard, there rang out a loud voice in heaven, and they saw the heavens opened and two men come down from there in a great brightness and draw nigh to the sepulchre. That stone which had been laid against the entrance to the sepulchre started of itself to roll and gave way to the side, and the sepulchre was opened, and both the young men entered in.

When now those soldiers saw this, they awakened the centurion and the elders. And whilst they were relating what they had seen, they saw again three men come out from the sepulchre, and two of them sustaining the other, and a cross following them, and the heads of the two reaching to heaven, but that of him who was led of them by the hand overpassing the heavens. And they heard a voice out of the heavens crying, "Thou hast preached to them that sleep," and from the cross there was heard the answer, "Yea."

Those men therefore took counsel with one another to go and report this to Pilate. And whilst they were deliberating, the heavens were again seen to open, and a man descended into the sepulchre. When those who were of the centurion's company saw this, they hastened by night to Pilate, abandoning the sepulchre which they were guarding, and reported everything that they had seen, saying, "In truth he was the Son of God."

Pilate said, "I am clean from the blood of the Son of God, upon such a thing have you decided." Then all came to him, beseeching him and urgently calling upon him to command the centurion and the soldiers to tell no one what they had seen. "For it is better for us," they said, "to make ourselves guilty of the greatest sin before God than to fall into the hands of the people of the Jews and be stoned."

Emerging from his tomb, Jesus treads upon a stunned guard. The alabaster relief dates to the late 14th century.

EASTER MORNING

Tomb, thou shalt not hold Him longer:
Death is strong, but life is stronger;
Stronger than dark, the light;
Stronger than the wrong, the right;
Faith and hope triumphant say,
"Christ will rise on Easter Day!"

While the patient earth lies waking
Till the morning shall be breaking,
Shuddering 'neath the burden dread
Of her Master, cold and dead,
Hark! she hears the angels say,
"Christ will rise on Easter Day!"

And when sunrise smites the mountains,
Pouring light from heavenly fountains,
Then the earth blooms out to greet
Once again the blessed feet;
And her countless voices say,
"Christ has risen on Easter Day!"

PHILLIPS BROOKS, 1835–1893

A GUARD OF THE SEPULCHER

I was a Roman soldier in my prime;
Now age is on me and the yoke of time.
I saw your Risen Christ, for I am he
Who reached the hyssop to Him on the tree;
And I am one of two who watched beside
The Sepulcher of Him we crucified.
All that last night I watched with sleepless eyes;
Great stars arose and crept across the skies.
The world was all too still for mortal rest,
For pitiless thoughts were busy in the breast.
The night was long, so long, it seemed at last
I had grown old and a long life had passed.
Far off, the hills of Moab, touched with light,
Were swimming in the hollow of the night.
I saw Jerusalem all wrapped in cloud,
Stretched like a dead thing folded in a shroud.
Once in the pauses of our whispered talk
I heard a something on the garden walk.
Perhaps it was a crisp leaf lightly stirred—
Perhaps the dream-note of a waking bird.
Then suddenly an angel burning white
Came down with earthquake in the breaking light,
And rolled the great stone from the Sepulcher,
Mixing the morning with a scent of myrrh.
And lo, the Dead had risen with the day:
The Man of Mystery had gone his way!

Years have I wandered, carrying my shame;
Now let the tooth of time eat out my name.
For we, who all the wonder might have told,
Kept silence, for our mouths were stopt with gold.

EDWIN MARKHAM, 1852–1940

*The marks of his cruel torment clearly visible, Jesus
extends a blessing as he stands beside his tomb. The guards
in Hans Pleydenwurff's 15th-century painting look more
drowsy than terror-stricken.*

The ornate interior of Jerusalem's Church of the Holy Sepulcher

Where Was Jesus Buried?

Hallowed by ancient tradition, the possible site of Jesus' burial is today venerated within the walls of the Church of the Holy Sepulcher in Jerusalem's Old City. The structure also marks the place where he was executed, reflecting the remark in John's Gospel that the tomb was near Golgotha.

The area that encompassed the execution and burial sites, which had been an old stone quarry just outside Jerusalem, was enclosed within the city walls by King Agrippa I in A.D. 41. After the Roman emperor Hadrian destroyed the city in 135, the quarry was filled in and a new temple to the goddess Aphrodite was built on the spot. The city was renamed Aelia Capitolina after Hadrian's family. When the emperor Constantine began to support Christianity two centuries later, he ordered the bishop of Jerusalem to uncover the site of Jesus' Resurrection. The discovery of the true cross — and by inference the site of the Crucifixion and burial of Jesus — is attributed to Constantine's mother, Helena. Constantine funded the construction of the

The modest garden tomb is also proposed as the site of Jesus' burial.

first Church of the Holy Sepulcher; unfortunately, his engineers cut away the rock and demolished the orginal entrance to the tomb, including its large anteroom. His grandiose edifice, inaugurated in 335, endured until marauding Persians burned it to the ground in the seventh century. For more than a thousand years, churches were periodically built to commemorate the tomb, only to be destroyed or severely damaged by warfare, fire, earthquakes, or the deterioration of age. Today's church dates, for the most part, from the 19th century.

Tourists in Jerusalem are often directed to the so-called garden tomb beside the road to Nablus as the site of Jesus' burial. Because of the peaceful, verdant setting that recalls John 19:41 ("Now in the place where he was crucified there was a garden . . ."), this spot has taken hold in the popular imagination. But historians as well as the archeologists who have probed the ground beneath the Church of the Holy Sepulcher agree that it is the more likely historical site of the burial and Resurrection.

A late-15th-century Italian artist carefully positioned the figures in his Resurrection scene to fit the semicircular space available.

A FEAR THAT MADE THEM DEAD MEN

The bribing of the Roman guard, related only by Matthew, appears also in THE ACTS OF PILATE, one of several documents regarding the alleged activities of the procurator that circulated among early Christians. The following excerpt begins with Joseph of Arimathea defending himself before the Jewish elders who protested his burial of Jesus.

JOSEPH CAME FORTH and said to them: "Why are you angry with me, because I asked for the body of Jesus? See, I have placed it in my new tomb, having wrapped it in clean linen, and I rolled a stone before the door of the cave. And you have not done well with the righteous one, for you did not repent of having crucified him, but also pierced him with a spear."

Then the Jews seized Joseph and commanded him to be secured until the first day of the week. They said to him: "Know that the hour forbids us to do anything against you, because the Sabbath dawns. But know also that we do not count you worthy of burial but shall give your flesh to the birds of heaven."

Joseph answered: "This word is like that of the boastful Goliath, who insulted the living God and the holy David. For God said by the prophet: 'Vengeance is mine, I will repay, says the Lord.' And now he who is uncircumcised in the flesh, but circumcised in heart, took water and washed his hands before the sun, saying: 'I am innocent of the blood of this righteous man. You see to it.' And you answered Pilate: 'His blood be on us and on our children.' And now I fear lest the wrath of God come upon you and your children, as you said."

When the Jews heard these words, they were embittered in their hearts, and laid hold on Joseph and seized him and shut him in a building without a window, and guards remained at the door. And they sealed the door of the place where Joseph was shut up.

And on the Sabbath the rulers of the synagogue and the priests and the Levites ordered that all should present themselves in the synagogue on the first day of the week. And the whole multitude rose up early and took counsel in the synagogue by what death they should kill him. And when the council was in session they commanded him to be brought with great dishonor. But when they opened the door they did not find him and were astonished and filled with consternation because they found the seals undamaged.

And while they still sat in the synagogue and marvelled because of Joseph, there came some of the guard which the Jews had asked from Pilate to guard the tomb of Jesus, lest his disciples should come and steal him. And they told the rulers of the synagogue and the priests and the Levites what had happened: how there was a great earthquake. "And we saw an angel descend from heaven, and he rolled away the stone from the mouth of the cave, and sat upon it, and he shone like snow and like lightning. And we were in great fear, and lay like dead men. Then we heard the voice of the angel speaking to the women who waited at the tomb: 'Do not be afraid. I know that you seek Jesus who was crucified. He is not here. He has risen, as he said. Come and see the place where the Lord lay. And go quickly and tell his disciples that he has risen from the dead and has gone forth into Galilee.'"

The Jews asked: "To what women did he speak?" The members of the guard answered: "We do not know who they were." The Jews said: "At what hour was it?" The guard answered: "At midnight." The Jews said: "And why did you not seize the women?" The guard said: "We were like dead men through fear, and gave up hope of seeing the light of day; how could we then have seized them?"

The Jews said: "As the Lord lives, we do not believe you." The members of the guard said to the Jews: "So many signs you saw in that man and you did not believe; and how can you believe us? You rightly swore: As the Lord lives. For he does live."

Again the members of the guard said: "We have heard that you shut up him who asked for the body of Jesus, and sealed the door, and that when you opened it you did not find him. Therefore give us Joseph and we will give you Jesus." The Jews said: "Joseph has gone to his own city." And the members of the guard said to the Jews: "And Jesus has risen, as we heard from the angel, and is in Galilee."

And when the Jews heard these words, they feared greatly and said: "Take heed lest this report be heard and all incline to Jesus." And the Jews took counsel, and offered much money and gave it to the soldiers of the guard, saying: "Say that when you were sleeping his disciples came by night and stole him. And if this is heard by the governor, we will persuade him that it is true and keep you out of trouble."

Jesus rises from his tomb in this painting by Hendrick van den Broeck (c. 1523–1601), a masterpiece adorning the Vatican's Sistine Chapel. The red cross on a white banner is the traditional artistic symbol of the Resurrection.

Time has pitted the surface but not dulled the vivid colors of this 11th-century enamel book cover depicting the angel greeting Mary Magdalene at the tomb.

And when the sabbath was past, Mary Magdalene, and Mary the mother of James, and Salome, bought spices, so that they might go and anoint him. And very early on the first day of the week they went to the tomb when the sun had risen.

MARK 16:1–2

AN ASTONISHING DISCOVERY

Matthew, Mark, and Luke all place Mary Magdalene among the women who came to the tomb on the day after the Jewish Sabbath to anoint the body of Jesus. In her 1935 novel KING OF THE JEWS, Mary Borden follows the account of John, who says she went there alone and was thus the first to discover that Jesus had risen.

IT WAS EARLY IN THE MORNING when the women started for the tomb. The sun had not yet risen; the deep streets were filled with shadow; the great battlemented walls were ghostly in the twilight. But dim figures with bundles on their backs were already abroad; shadowy caravans of pilgrims were passing out into the country through the city gates, for people who had come to the feast from distant villages were already taking the road home.

There were a number of women in the group that was going to the sepulcher. But Mary Magdalene was not with them; she had gone on ahead while it was still dark.

"We will find her waiting outside the sepulcher," one woman said. "She cannot bear to be far away from her master and will want to stay where he is."

"She watched outside the tomb all the first night," another woman added. "The boy John found her there in the morning and persuaded her to come back to his house. But last night, when she had been with us preparing the things needful for the anointing, we could see that she was straining like a dog on a leash to be back at her place by the sepulcher. She went a little while ago, though it was still very dark."

It was growing lighter as the women made their way toward the city gate. When they reached it, they saw

through the arch that the sky was beginning to glow in the East, and they stood a moment all together, looking across the awful gulf of the Jordan valley.

They huddled together on the far side of the road, away from the gully where the crosses were, then turned and hurried up the path that led to the garden where he was laid. As they pressed forward eagerly, clutching their precious baskets tight, one whispered to another breathlessly, for the path began to climb among steep rocks, "Who will roll the stone away for us from the door of the sepulcher? We can never roll away the stone by ourselves; it is too great."

And now they had reached the garden and there was a little gate leading into it between shrubberies, and the gate stood open. It was still dark among the trees. They could see nothing but shadowy masses of

An outsized angel stays the three women come to the tomb as the Roman guards doze on their spears. Only fragments of the ninth-century ivory carving's original frame remain.

leaves and the path like a tunnel under them. But suddenly the figure of a woman appeared on the path, running toward them.

It was Mary Magdalene and she cried out when she saw them, "The stone is rolled away! The tomb is empty! They have taken away the Lord and I know not where they have laid him! I have looked everywhere." And indeed, all her clothing was stained with earth and there were bits of twigs and leaves in her hair as if she had been through the undergrowth on her hands and knees. But she would not stop to tell them more. She only looked at them wildly when they took hold of her and cried, "I must tell Peter." Flinging them off, she ran away down the path toward the city gate.

The pilgrims by now were pouring out of the city gate. By families and tribes and village communities, some with wagons piled high with luggage and women and children sitting perched on the luggage; some with laden donkeys, some with camels; they crowded through the gateway and their village rabbis walked with them like shepherds, each one leading home a flock of sheep; and all these travelers stared at the distraught woman who came running down to the gate, her red hair flying out behind her like a banner, and ducked between the wagons and donkeys and camels like an animal pursued, and ran on against the stream of people into the city.

Peter was coming down the stairs from the upper room with his bundle on his back and his stick in his hand, when she ran into the courtyard like one demented, her hair streaming over her shoulders and covered all over with dust. She cried out from below, "They have taken away the Lord out of the sepulcher and we know not where they have laid him."

He stared at her stupidly, and she stared up at him, panting for breath. But when he still hesitated, she cried out furiously, "The tomb is empty. Do you not understand? The body of the Lord is gone," and she made as if to drag him down the stairs. But now he ran. He leapt past her and ran out of the courtyard into the street and she ran after him. And the streets were filled with people, but Peter pounded his way through them with Mary Magdalene at his heels. And they passed the door of the house where the Lord's mother lay and the boy John was just coming out of it, and Mary called to him as they ran, "The tomb is empty. They have taken away the body of the Lord." And when John heard it, he came with them in a

flash, and they ran all three back through the streets the way Mary had come. But John outran Peter, for he was swift on his feet as a young deer.

It was much lighter now. The sky was glorious over the gulf of the wasteland to the East. But a sound of lamentation rose from the garden as they ran up the path to the little gate. A great sighing wail, like the crying of a flock of birds, rose from the trees, and when they came in sight of the tomb, there were all the women gathered before it, bowed to the ground weeping, and the great stone that had closed the door of the tomb was rolled away, just as Mary had said.

The lad John was the first to reach the sepulcher. He ran past the women to the gaping door in the rock, and the women saw him stoop down and look. But he did not go in. He fell back from the door, his youthful face white as death. And then Peter came rushing up and pushed past him and plunged into the tomb, and the boy John went in after him. And all the women held their breath when they went in. And Mary Magdalene, who had come after Peter, waited a little apart from the others.

The light was dim in the tomb. But when their eyes were accustomed to it, Peter and John saw the linen cloth that had wrapped him lying there and the napkin that had been about his head was not lying with the linen cloth, but folded together in a place by itself. But they found not the body of the Lord Jesus, and they came out of the tomb into the sunlight and the women saw in Peter's face that it was true, the body was gone.

They stared at him with stricken faces. The precious baskets lay forgotten on the ground. Someone had stolen their master. What did it mean? Who had come in the night and taken away the body?

They looked to Peter, waiting for him to speak and tell them who could have done this wicked thing. But

The angel, the three women, and the stunned guards are all worked into the intricate filigree of this late-10th-century English illuminated manuscript.

The three women, each with her jar of ointment, hear the amazing news from the angel: Jesus has risen. The richly detailed painting is the work of the brothers Hubert (c. 1366–1426) and Jan (c. 1370–c. 1440) van Eyck, founders of the Flemish school of painting.

Peter said nothing. He only stood there staring, with his mouth working as if he were muttering to himself or praying, but making no sound. And then they saw that all his great heavy body was shaking, and when they saw that, they began to be very frightened.

And one whispered, "The Romans have done it. The guard must have taken him." But another said, "No, it was the high priest who hated him and placed a guard at the tomb, so that we could not get near him." But still another said, "Perhaps the councillor himself has moved the body to another place," and they called out to Peter, "We must find the Master!" And at that they began to wail again, beating their breasts, and went on weeping louder and louder, till the little wood round the tomb throbbed with their wailing and a frenzy was like to have seized on them, for some began to knock their heads on the ground and tear their clothing; but Peter spoke suddenly, telling them in a stern voice to stop their crying out and to be silent.

"Go and warn your husbands," he said. "Go and tell all the followers of Jesus what has happened. Go quickly, but go quietly, secretly. Let no man see aught in your faces."

They stared, appalled by the look of him and the sound of his voice. "Why?" they whispered.

"Because it will be said," he answered, "that we, the friends of Jesus, have stolen the body, and there is no knowing what the authorities will do to us."

None of them had thought of this. They didn't take in the meaning of it now. But they got to their feet quickly, for they were accustomed to obeying him. And they drew their shawls over their heads with trembling hands and began to creep away. Peter and John followed them down the path.

But Mary Magdalene did not move from her place. She was alone in the garden after the others had departed, and it was very still. There were only the little sounds of birds twittering in the trees, and the sun was just rising through the branches.

Joy Crowding Her Heart

In this extract from BEHOLD THE MAN, *a work published in 1941, Toyohiko Kagawa blends the narratives of the three synoptic Gospels with that of John. Thus, his Mary Magdalene is with the others at the discovery of the empty tomb but lingers behind when they leave and encounters Jesus in the garden.*

MARY MAGDALENE WAS FIRST at the sepulcher. Joanna followed her, stooping down to look into the cavern. She heard Mary's quick intake of breath, and then she herself felt the quickening of her startled heart. The body of Jesus was not there!

The jar of sweet ointment fell from Joanna's hands with a crash. Mary looked down blindly at the shattered pieces on the cave's floor. As the fragrance drifted up to her slowly, her throat grew painfully tight. Was it not enough that they had crucified her beloved master? Could they not let the dead rest in peace?

Beside her, she heard Salome breathe: "Behold!"

She lifted her head and through eyes blurred with tears saw, in the dimness of the tomb, two white figures, one at the head and one at the foot, where the body of Jesus had lain. For the shaking of her lips, Joanna could utter no sound. Nor could she look longer upon the figures, for the strange glistening of their raiment.

There came a voice from the sepulcher, and it was like no voice which Joanna had ever heard. "Fear not: for I know you seek Jesus who was crucified. He is not here, for he is risen, as he said. Go quickly and tell his disciples that he goes before you into Galilee. There shall you see him. Lo, I have told you."

When Joanna came to herself she was with Salome and Mary, the mother of James, hastening along the road back to Jerusa-lem. How or when she had left the sepulcher, she knew not. Only one thing she knew. They must find Peter and John and the others. They must tell them of the astounding events.

Salome said suddenly: "But—but where is Mary Magdalene?"

"Is she not with us?" asked Joanna. She turned her head, half expecting to see a figure hurrying to overtake them. But there was nought upon that road but the pale hue of dawn.

Mary Magdalene could not leave. She stood outside the sepulcher and the tears she could not shed before, fell now. She was frightened, bewildered and, above everything, desolate. In her agony, she walked blindly in the garden, not able to see her way because of tears. Dimly, she was aware of a man approaching.

"Woman," said the stranger, "why do you weep?"

She did not answer. Why did she weep? There was reason in plenty. None, she moaned inwardly, had ever known such cause for grief.

"Whom do you seek?"

The man's voice seemed to her far away, and she wished that he would go away and leave her with her sorrow. Yet, he might know something of what had occurred here. Perhaps he was the gardener.

"Sir," she said pleadingly, "if you have borne him hence, tell me where you have laid him, and I will take him away."

"Mary!"

That voice of infinite compassion! She turned, shaking from head to foot, and blinked the tears from her eyes.

"Rabboni!"

It was he! It was the Master! It was Jesus of Nazareth. Joy crowded into her heart. There was room for nought else. She flung herself forward to touch him, to hold him.

Jesus said to her: "Touch me not, for I am not yet ascended to my Father: but go to my brethren, and say to them that I ascend to my Father and God and to your Father and God."

Jesus soars above his tomb, a scene worked in miniature within the initial letter of this Italian music manuscript.

And they found the stone rolled away from the tomb, but when they went in they did not find the body. While they were perplexed about this, behold, two men stood by them in dazzling apparel; and as they were frightened and bowed their faces to the ground, the men said to them, "Why do you seek the living among the dead?"

LUKE 24:2–5

Angels frolic among a profusion of flowers, fruit, and vegetables framing Mary Magdalene and Jesus at the tomb. The artist, Jan Brueghel the Younger (1601–1678), was known for his floral landscapes, as was his father and namesake.

And he said to them, "Do not be amazed;
you seek Jesus of Nazareth, who was
crucified. He has risen, he is not here . . . .
But go, tell his disciples and Peter
that he is going before you to Galilee; there
you will see him, as he told you."

MARK 16:6–7

A DREAM TO ALTER
THE FACE OF THE WORLD

The angel's injunction to Mary Magdalene and the other
women at the tomb appears in the first three
Gospels; in John, it is Jesus himself who gives the
command. One who heard the tidings directly from Mary
is the narrator of BY AN UNKNOWN DISCIPLE,
an anonymous work of fiction published in 1919.

N THE EVENING BEFORE I was to set out for Galilee, I went to the garden of Gethsemane by way of the path outside the south wall along which the temple officials had led Jesus to Caiaphas. I climbed between the olive trees to where Jesus had stood looking at the sunset and stopped close to the dry stone wall where I could see all Judea spread out before me. The day had been hot, and a haze hung over the mountains of Moab and hid their color. The sun had scorched the land and there was no glory in it now. It seemed to me that the beauty had vanished from the earth.

After a time I turned aside. Why should I stay there? Life was ugly and barren. There was no joy left in it. I crossed the open space where Jesus had gone apart to pray, and passed, as he had done, between the twisted boughs of the olives. A narrow track led higher up the mountain and I followed it until I came to where the olives ceased, giving place to tall cypresses and a few forest trees. Was it here that Jesus had prayed in his agony? What did it matter? He had been killed in spite of his prayers. What was the good of loving when death came to end all?

I sat down and leaned my head against one of the trees. Somehow the touch of the wild tree comforted me. The garden had been planted by man, the olive trees and the stone wall were man's work, and man was cruel and stupid. There was no hope in a world ruled by men. But God had made the forest trees.

I stayed there for a long time, quieted, marvelling at the strong twist in the trunk of a cypress and the wonder of the grey shadow on its green boughs. The sun was declining and the heat haze still hid the distant mountains when I heard a gay voice singing and a woman in the blue clothing of a peasant turned the corner of the path and came towards me. It was Mary Magdalene. I looked at her in amazement. Were all women heartless as all men were cruel? Jesus was dead and the world was black to me, but the sunshine was still golden to her. And she had seemed to love him.

Mary came nearer and at the sight of my face her song stopped.

"How can you sing, Mary, when Jesus is dead?" I said, and turned to go.

But she caught me by the sleeve. "Jesus is not dead," she cried, and I stopped short, a wild impossible hope springing upon me.

"What do you mean, Mary? I saw him die."

"And so did I. But I have seen him since," she said.

"Seen him? Are you mad?" I said.

She shook her head. "You have not heard? Sit down and I will tell you."

So we sat down at the foot of the tree.

"You cannot think that I could be so callous," she said. "I who loved him more than any. Had I not more to love him for?"

Her eyes filled with tears, and she put her hand on my arm. I sat silent, ashamed of my suspicion of her.

"I was broken for days after his death. But look at me now. Am I the same woman who stood weeping beneath the cross, hopeless and in misery?"

"What has happened to you, Mary?" I asked.

"I have seen Jesus," she said. "At first I thought it was the gardener. But then I saw that it was Jesus."

"You were dreaming, Mary. You have deceived yourself," I said, but she shook her head and smiled.

"You think I am a wild woman who cannot tell truth from dreams. And I tell you, no, I am not mad. Look at me and see if it is not true. Could I be happy if Jesus was really dead, if he was only a dreamer and his vision of the kingdom impossible? Others have seen

The risen Jesus cautions Mary Magdalene not to touch him, a scene popular with artists through the centuries, who usually called such works "Noli me tangere" (Latin for "Touch me not"). This Italian painted wood panel dates to the 14th century.

*Mary Magdalene sinks to a kneeling position and reaches to touch
her master in this painting by Martin Schongauer (c. 1445–1491), a German artist
also considered the finest engraver of his time (see page 77).*

him too. Men everywhere are asking, 'How have these barbarous and contemptible people suddenly become wise? Who has given them this? How have they been instructed?' Our minds are fervent like a fire that burns out of control."

"It is only a dream, Mary," I said dully.

"Would Peter spread the good news with such fire for a dream?" she cried. "They say of him that he was feeble of understanding, but that now he is inspired, and men hear from him things that enrich them and make life great and noble. Can this be without the finger of God?"

I threw myself face downwards on the ground. I could not listen to her talk, for there was no hope within me, and it broke my heart. Mary touched me gently on the shoulder and said, "It does not matter whether you believe that I saw Jesus or dreamed. What matters is that we must spread the news of his kingdom. A dream can alter the face of the world."

And she went away and left me there under the trees of God.

It was in Galilee, on the mountain where I had first heard Jesus teach, that hope came back to me. I had wandered away from the village, and climbed the mountain and sat looking down on the great plain with its vineyards and olive gardens, and the thin grey smoke that rose in the air as the women made ready the evening meal. The voices of the children driving the cattle home came from the plain, and far in the distance a cow lowed to her calf and the sheep baaed to their lambs. Darkness was falling, but I could not go. The light faded and blackness covered the land. I bowed my head on my arms and sat on, too tired for sleep, too hopeless for pain, too sad for tears. All night I sat there, and in the morning came the dawn.

First there came the stillness. No bird cheeped, no wild beast cried aloud. A faint glimmer of light showed the dark masses of the forests on the hills, and the dim silver line of the sea. The golden light spread and touched the land and color awoke again in earth and sky. The sun came up behind the mountains and the shadows lay from east to west along the plain. It was then that the vision came to me. I saw nothing, but as the dawn spread slowly over the land, waking the earth to beauty, something awoke in my heart.

I do not know what it was. I have no words to tell of it. The earth lay before me bathed in a clear radiance that transfigured each familiar place and gave the world the beauty of a dream. And yet it was still the earth. The forests and moors, the mountains and valleys, were the same, but another light lay upon them. So it was with my soul. An intense, still joy awoke in my heart, a joy in which there was no shadow of restlessness, and the old gay sense of something added to life came back to me. It seemed as though Jesus had watched by me all night and I had not known it. The place was full of his presence.

The glory of the vision blinded me, and I hid my eyes. There was no death. Each night the beauty of the earth died into darkness, each dawn in wonder the light rose again on it. It was so with the spirit of man. In tribulation and in agony happiness died, but in beauty and glory joy lived again. I rolled over on my face on the coarse mountain grass and lay there thinking. The greatest miracle in the world had happened to me. A remembrance of beauty and love and immortal passion, the romance of the earth and of life had taken hold of me. The smallest, meanest things had gained a power of signifying the greatest, noblest things. Nothing was impossible to love.

The children had begun to drive the cattle out. Their shrill cries rose in the air before I stirred. When I sat up and looked at the earth again it was broad, garish day. The beauty of the world no longer caught my breath away. In the bustle of life my vision must fade, but I did not mind. I had seen the eternal beauty that lies hidden in the commonplace. There was work to do, and like Peter and the disciples I must do it, no matter what the cost. So I rose to my feet to go back to my village and take up my work again.

MARY MAGDALENE

At dawn she sought the Savior slain,
To kiss the spot where He had lain
And weep warm tears, like springtime rain;

When lo, there stood, unstained of death,
A man that spoke with low sweet breath;
And "Master!" Mary answereth.

From out the far and fragrant years
How sweeter than the songs of seers
That tender offering of tears!

RICHARD BURTON, 1861–1940

At first mistaking Jesus for the gardener, Mary Magdalene recognizes him only when he speaks her name. His subsequent injunction that he is not to be touched because he has yet to ascend to his Father is depicted by the Italian master Antonio Correggio (1494–1534) at left and by the Russian painter Aleksandr Ivanov (1806–1858) below.

EASTER CHORUS

Christ is arisen.
  Joy to thee, mortal!
Out of His prison,
  Forth from its portal!
Christ is not sleeping,
  Seek Him no longer;
Strong was His keeping,
  Jesus was stronger.

Christ is arisen.
  Seek Him not here;
Lonely His prison,
  Empty His bier;
Vain His entombing,
  Spices and lawn,
Vain the perfuming,
  Jesus is gone.

Christ is arisen.
  Joy to thee, mortal!
Empty His prison,
  Broken its portal!
Rising, He giveth
  His shroud to the sod;
Risen, He liveth,
  And liveth to God.

JOHANN WOLFGANG
VON GOETHE, 1749–1832

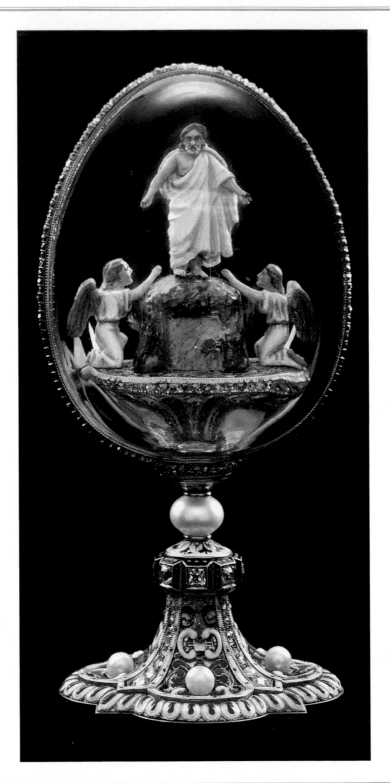

*Flanked by two
angels, Jesus rises
from his tomb within
a rock crystal egg,
a gift of Russian czar
Alexander III to his
wife in 1887.*

EASTER HYMN

Death and darkness get you packing,
Nothing now to man is lacking;
All your triumphs now are ended,
And what Adam marred is mended;
Graves are beds now for the weary,
Death a nap, to wake more merry;
Youth now, full of pious duty,
Seeks in thee for perfect beauty;
The weak and aged, tir'd with length
Of days, from thee look for new strength;
And infants with thy pangs contest
As pleasant, as if with the breast.
  Then, unto Him, who thus hath thrown
Even to contempt thy kingdom down,
And by His blood did us advance
Unto His own inheritance,
To Him be glory, power, praise,
From this, unto the last of days!

HENRY VAUGHAN, 1622–1695

EASTER HYMN

Christ the Lord is risen to-day,
Sons of men and angels say:
Raise your joys and triumphs high,
Sing, ye heavens, and earth reply.

Love's redeeming work is done,
Fought the fight, the battle won;
Lo! our Sun's eclipse is o'er,
Lo! He sets in blood no more.

Vain the stone, the watch, the seal;
Christ hath burst the gates of hell!
Death in vain forbids His rise;
Christ hath opened Paradise!

Lives again our glorious King:
Where, O Death, is now thy sting?
Once He died, our souls to save:
Where thy victory, O Grave?

CHARLES WESLEY, 1707–1788

Real pearls set on gold stems make up this fantasy bouquet of lilies of the valley, created by the house of Fabergé for the Russian imperial family.

CHORUS FOR EASTER

Awareness is on us, now, of the several heavens
Unto which we ascended,
Unfailingly, after the long Golgothas
And the vinegar-drinking ended.

None made it known, none made it understood,
Clearly, what dying is,
Nor how the hurting, heaped-up hill of bone
Was climbing unto this.

We have forgotten, now, or nearly forgotten
Each Gethsemane,
As Christ forgot . . . as this new springing bough,
It well may be,
Forgets the leafless winter, to avow
The green leaf that we see.

DAVID MORTON, 1886–1957

A SONG AT EASTER

If this bright lily
  Can live once more,
And its white promise
  Be as before,
Why can not the great stone
  Be moved from His door?

If the green grass
  Ascend and shake
Year after year,
  And blossoms break
Again and again
  For April's sake,

Why can not He,
  From the dark and mold,
Show us again
  His manifold
And gleaming glory,
  A stream of gold?

Faint heart, be sure
  These things must be.
See the new bud
  On the old tree! . . .
If flowers can wake,
  Oh, why not He?

CHARLES HANSON TOWNE,
1877–1949

Another gift of Czar Alexander to his wife, a basket of wood anemones set with diamonds is concealed within a rich translucent strawberry Easter egg.

That very day two of them were going to a village named Emmaus, about seven miles from Jerusalem . . . . While they were talking and discussing together, Jesus himself drew near and went with them. But their eyes were kept from recognizing him.

LUKE 24:13, 15–16

JOINED BY A STRANGER ON THE ROAD TO EMMAUS

First Mary Magdalene at the tomb, then the two men walking to Emmaus, later the disciples fishing on the Sea of Galilee—those to whom the risen Jesus revealed himself often failed at first to recognize him. Robert Payne, in this selection from THE LORD JESUS, *identifies one of the wayfarers as Nathanael, although Luke names only Cleopas, a person nowhere else mentioned in the Gospels.*

IT WAS ONE OF THOSE EVENINGS when every tree seems to have been dipped in crystal, and the scarlet anemones on the hills glowed like molten rubies. In the cool greenish light of evening the furrowed earth looked softly pale, as though dissolving, and the white fruit trees resembled coral branches, and no birds sang. It was the ghostliness which comes with an oncoming storm.

Nathanael and Cleopas had set out from Jerusalem in the forenoon; now their shadows were lengthening. During the journey they exchanged few words between them, until they came close to Emmaus. Then, when it was growing darker, and their spirits were oppressed by the memories that crowded on them with the coming of night, they spoke more often, with long silences between.

"Is he alive or dead—that's the question!" Cleopas said sharply, planting his staff firmly on the ground. "If he is alive, where is he? And if he is dead, what have the tomb-robbers done to him? Well, I saw the empty tomb! How do you explain it, Nathanael?"

"Did not the woman say she saw him?" Nathanael said after a pause.

"Yes, she did. She said there was a gardener standing in the garden, and wearing a hat to shade his face, and she knew he was Jesus. But when I asked her to describe him—whether there were wounds on his hands and feet, and whether there was blood on his forehead from the crown of thorns, and what clothes he was wearing, why, she answered nothing at all. Well, I believe the rats ate up his flesh, or the tomb broke open in the thunderstorm, or the grave-robbers found him! As for the story of the angel sitting on the tomb—why, that's an old wives' tale. It was a fool's journey, and we were fools to follow him! I shall have no sleep at night, thinking of the trick he has played upon us! You have your faith, but as for me I won't believe he is alive until I see him with my own eyes."

"Then what will you do?"

"I will do what all men do when they see a friend who has returned. I shall run into his arms with such joy that the sound of my cry will be heard for a hundred miles! I loved him with all my heart, but loving a dead man is something else altogether. Didn't he say: 'Let the dead bury the dead'? Well, let the dead Christ bury the dead Christ!"

With these words Cleopas shook his head, fell into a long silence, and said nothing more until the walls of Emmaus came in sight.

The small white-walled village lay in a hollow among vineyards and fruit trees. It was set a little way from the Roman road, and was reached through the grove of walnuts. The two men were halfway through the walnut grove when they heard footsteps behind them. Nathanael looked over his shoulder, but there was no one in sight. Probably the man, whoever he was, was hidden by the walnut trees, or it might be someone walking within the town. It had been a strange afternoon, with a lowering sky and the threat of a storm; they were glad to be close to the village, for the strangeness and emptiness of the evening frightened them. The wind was rising, and a thick white dust came through the trees.

The sound of footsteps grew louder, and soon they became aware that someone else was walking near them. There were three long bluish shadows on the dusty road between the walnut trees. They turned and saw a man of middle height, who wore the costume of a Passover pilgrim, and to judge by the blue tassels on the edge of his cloak, he was a rabbi or a scribe. His gown was covered with dust, and to keep the dust from his mouth and nostrils he wore a scarf over the lower part of his face, and he concealed his hands within the folds of his cloak. They saw only the deep smoldering eyes, and they could barely guess at the shape of his face.

The man must have heard the muttering of Cleopas, for he said: "Why are you so sad, brother?"

"We are all sad these days," Cleopas answered. "Who can be happy now that Jesus is dead?"

"Look upon me," said the stranger quietly. "Surely you know me?" he insisted.

"I see you are a rabbi and a learned man, but you have a rag across your mouth—"

"Surely you know my voice?"

"There are many who speak like you. Forgive me, I do not remember everyone I have seen."

"Look upon me," the stranger repeated, and his hand tore away the scarf covering his mouth.

He looked at the stranger, but it was too dark for him to see

The moment of recognition—Jesus blessing the disciples' bread—is depicted by Caravaggio with his customary elegance and restraint.

the man's features clearly. The hand was wet with blood, but it meant nothing to him, for the stranger might have scratched it on a thorn tree.

"Surely you know me!" the stranger said. "Have we journeyed together all these years in vain? I plucked you, Cleopas, from the fields one day when you were sick unto death, and you, Nathanael, I plucked you from under a fig tree. Do you not know me?"

"Yes, we know you," Cleopas answered, but he spoke like a man who did not know.

In silence they walked into Emmaus. Night had settled on the walled village and the heavens were streaming with stars. They walked through the shadowy streets like sleepwalkers, and when they came to an inn Nathanael said: "Abide with us, for it is late and the day is far spent, and let us feast as we feasted in days gone by."

And still Nathanael did not believe that Jesus was at his side. He would glance at the stranger, who was very pale and curiously withdrawn, speaking in an unrecognizable voice, his eyes glowing like coals which have been blown upon. It was perhaps some messenger of Jesus, or a brother, or even a distant relative. Nathanael felt no alarm at the stranger's presence. Often during his journeys some stranger would accost him, talk for a while and then vanish on his own errands. What puzzled him more than anything else was the unnatural stillness which had descended upon the village. At this hour of the evening you expected to hear a great number of distinct sounds—caravans unloading for the night, women singing at the fountain, the cracking of whips, drunken voices. But even the birds which usually sang in the evening sky were silent.

The disciples en route to Emmaus do not initially recognize Jesus; the stone relief for a monastery was carved about the year 1100.

SLOW TO PERCEIVE THAT HE WAS ALIVE

*Not until he blessed bread, broke it, and gave
it to them at the evening meal did the two disciples
recognize Jesus. Elizabeth Stuart Phelps, in
an excerpt from THE STORY OF JESUS CHRIST, reveals
the two slowly awakening to his magnetism.*

IT WAS LATE AFTERNOON of the first Easter, when two of the eleven, restless with sorrow, went for a country walk to a little place called Emmaus. Life and light throbbed in the soft wind, in the gentle scenery. Thousands of birds were in the air. The soul of spring swayed by dreamily. But the hearts of the twain were as heavy as the clods of the grave. Their Lord was dead.

In the bewilderment of fresh bereavement, they talked drearily—of him, of his great life, of his piteous death, of all that was precious and of all that was confusing to them in his history; of the failure of his purposes, of the ruin of their hopes and of his.

A stranger joined them as they were walking and entered into their conversation. They thought him a very ignorant man, though he had not that appearance, for he questioned them minutely about the life and death of their rabbi. Was there a foreigner in Jerusalem who had not heard what had happened? They answered him with a sort of surprised condescension, but they readily began to talk about their Lord; indeed, they could not speak of anything else.

But as they strolled and talked, their feeling about the stranger underwent one of the swift transformations which simple minds experience in the presence of a superior. This was no ordinary tourist. This was a master of knowledge. He spoke of the Hebrew Messiah; of the meaning of ancient prophetic poetry; of the possibilities hidden in the scriptures. He spoke of the recent events that had shaken Palestine—of the national hopes and of the national shame.

The two disciples felt deeply drawn to the stranger; their thoughts took a high turn; courage and faith swept back upon their despairing hearts like fire from heaven upon an abandoned altar. They clung so to the stranger that, when he would have left them and passed on up the country road, they begged him to accept their hospitality. So he indulged them, smiling, and went to supper with them in their simple house of entertainment. There it seemed the only right thing for him to do was to take the head of the table and serve; his hosts did not even wonder why. And it seemed to be wholly expected that he should ask the blessing of God upon the bread. Then it seemed not strange, in any way, when the two began slowly and quietly to understand who he was. And they who loved and mourned a dead Christ, lifted their eyes and perceived that he was alive.

THE WALK TO EMMAUS

It happened, on a solemn eventide,
Soon after he that was our surety died,
Two bosom friends, each pensively inclined,
The scene of all those sorrows left behind,
Sought their own village, busied, as they went,
In musings worthy of the great event:
They spake of him they loved, of him whose life,
Though blameless, had incurred perpetual strife,
Whose deeds had left, in spite of hostile arts,
A deep memorial graven on their hearts.
The recollection, like a vein of ore,
The farther traced, enriched them still the more;
They thought him, and they justly thought him, one
Sent to do more than He appeared t'have done;
To exalt a people, and to place them high
Above all else, and wondered he should die.
Ere yet they brought their journey to an end,
A Stranger joined them, courteous as a friend,
And asked them, with a kind engaging air,
What their affliction was, and begged a share.
Informed, he gathered up the broken thread,
And, truth and wisdom gracing all he said,
Explained, illustrated, and searched so well
The tender theme, on which they chose to dwell,
That reaching home, "The night," they said, "is near,
We must not now be parted, sojourn here."
The new acquaintance soon became a guest,
And, made so welcome at their simple feast,
He blessed the bread, but vanished at the word,
And left them both exclaiming, " 'Twas the Lord!
Did not our hearts feel all he deigned to say,
Did they not burn within us by the way?"

WILLIAM COWPER, 1731–1800

*As Jesus blesses the bread—the wound of the nail clearly visible on his right hand—
the disciples turn to each other in confirmation of their dawning recognition that Jesus is with
them. The painting is by the Spanish master Velázquez (1599–1660).*

Still bearing the banner symbolizing his Resurrection, Jesus stands amid the gathered disciples. The 15th-century German altarpiece is in Munich's Alte Pinakothek.

As they were saying this, Jesus himself stood among them. But they were startled and frightened, and supposed that they saw a spirit. And he said to them, "Why are you troubled, and why do questionings rise in your hearts? See my hands and my feet, that it is I myself."

LUKE 24:36–39

LOVE AND JOY STRUGGLING WITH FEAR AND INCREDULITY

Hastening back to Jerusalem from their unsettling encounter at Emmaus, Cleopas and his companion found the 11 disciples gathered with others and learned that Jesus had appeared to Simon Peter—a meeting otherwise mentioned only by the apostle Paul. In THEY SAW THE LORD, *a work published in 1947, Bonnell Spencer likens the gathering in the upper room to a typical Sunday congregation.*

WHEN THE TWO DISCIPLES returned from Emmaus, they found the door of the upper room locked. The same fear which had precipitated their flight caused the assembled disciples to guard themselves against intruders. Perhaps they were unduly alarmed. The authorities probably were content to leave them unmolested as long as they remained in hiding and refrained from contradicting the official report that they had stolen our Lord's body from the tomb.

Cleopas and his companion knocked at the door and were identified. Bursting into the room, they cried, "We have seen the Lord."

They were greeted with the words, "The Lord is risen indeed, and hath appeared to Simon."

Discussion there doubtless was. Many must have found the truth hard to believe. Cleopas and his companion elaborated their confirming testimony. Some were convinced. Others plied them with questions. Still others expressed doubt and incredulity.

There, on Easter night, were gathered all the types which one finds in the average congregation on any

Sunday. Some—Peter, Mary Magdalene, Cleopas and his companion—have already had a vivid experience of the risen Lord. There are usually a few in any Christian gathering whose faith rests on a deep experience of its truth which has been vouchsafed to them. They can bear witness with assurance, for they have seen the Lord.

Others, like John and Mary the mother of Jesus, are men and women of great faith. Without having seen, they have believed. Their full-hearted response has given them an insight into the truth. They understand, because they know God. They need neither a vivid personal experience nor the testimony of others to convince them. They are the mystics who find the truth by the hidden path of love.

Others, still, believe on the basis of the testimony of those who have seen. It is enough for them to know that our Lord's accredited witnesses so testify. They constitute the majority of the faithful.

Finally, there are those who find it hard to believe. Doubts and questions assail their minds. They are not hostile, nor are they indifferent. They want to learn. They long to believe. But they cannot convince themselves of the truth. These are the earnest seekers after God, who do not yet realize that they have already been found by him.

In spite of their fear, in spite of their varying degrees of faith, the disciples gathered in the upper room on the first Easter night. And those who gathered saw the Lord. For suddenly the discussion terminated in a breathless hush. Jesus stood in their midst and said, "Peace be unto you."

This may be called our Lord's first official appearance. Three times before, the risen Christ had shown himself to one or another of his disciples in what were private appearances. Each had a specific purpose, meeting the particular need of the person concerned. Mary Magdalene was lifted from bewildered frustration to a level of intimacy with the risen Lord. Peter was relieved of the burden of repented sin that he might be restored to his place in the apostolic circle. Cleopas and his companion were rescued from their misguided flight and brought back to the fellowship. In each instance, the private appearance was a necessary step in preparing the recipient to participate in the experience of the upper room.

The appearance in the upper room had no purpose except to manifest the reality of our Lord's Resurrection. Only a public appearance could do that. Our Lord does not ask us to believe on the basis of any individual's revelation. The authority to which he appeals and through which he manifests himself is the corporate witness of the faithful.

They all saw and heard him. As each glanced hastily about the room, he realized that the others were participating in exactly the same experience. All were shrinking back from the terrible majesty of that Figure, flattening themselves against the wall. Love and joy struggled with fear and incredulity. They were overwhelmed by the impossible wonder of it.

In two complementary images from a medieval German manuscript, the risen Jesus proclaims his message of salvation to the expectant disciples.

A dubious Thomas strains to reach the wound in Jesus' side; the ivory plaque dates to the late 9th or early 10th century.

Now Thomas, one of the twelve, called the Twin, was not with them when Jesus came. So the other disciples told him, "We have seen the Lord." But he said to them, "Unless I see in his hands the print of the nails, and place my finger in the mark of the nails, and place my hand in his side, I will not believe."

JOHN 20:24–25

THE MAN WHO COULD NOT BELIEVE

Mentioned only in passing by the other Evangelists where they name the 12 disciples, Thomas comes alive in John's Gospel. In this excerpt from his 1959 work THE MASTER'S MEN, *William Barclay fills in the details of Thomas's appearances in the fourth Gospel and draws a lesson from his story.*

THOMAS FIRST APPEARS in the Lazarus story as the man of courage. News had come that Lazarus was ill, and for two days Jesus made no move at all. Then he prepared to go to Bethany, a village close to Jerusalem, one of those in which pilgrims to the Passover normally lodged.

By this time the Jewish authorities in Jerusalem were determined that Jesus should die; to go to Jerusalem seemed a suicidal act of recklessness. What made it worse was that news had come that Lazarus was dead, and to go to Jerusalem now seemed not only reckless, but also useless. When Jesus intimated his intention to go to Jerusalem, the disciples came very near to abandoning him. And then there came the voice of the normally silent Thomas: "Let us also go that we may die with him."

It is easy for an optimist to be loyal in a difficult situation, for an optimist always expects the best. It is much harder for a pessimist to be loyal, for a pessimist always expects the worst. Thomas, constitutionally a pessimist, could see nothing but disaster ahead; but for him that was no reason for turning back. For Thomas there might be death, but there could never be disloyalty. And it may well be that it was Thomas

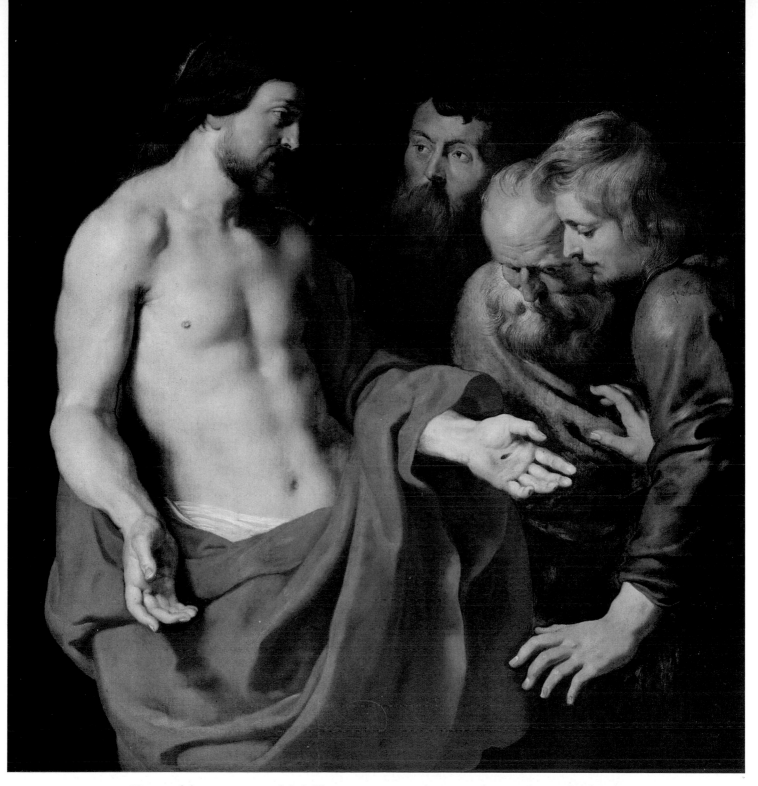

His incredulity giving way to belief, Thomas gazes in wonderment at the wounds Jesus has bared.
The scene, which includes two other disciples, is the central panel of a triptych by the celebrated Flemish painter
Peter Paul Rubens (1577 1610) that hangs in the Royal Museum of Fine Arts in Antwerp, Belgium.

Jeremiah and Isaiah hover over an early Renaissance scene of Jesus revealing his wound to Thomas. Their presence shows that Jesus fulfills Old Testament prophecies that the wounded Messiah would heal the wounds of others.

who rallied the faltering loyalty of the other eleven, on that day when Jesus announced his intention of going to Jerusalem.

Thomas was also the man who was bewildered in those days towards the end. In the upper room Jesus was seeking to persuade the dull minds of the disciples to see the Cross, and to see what lay beyond the Cross. "Whither I go you know," he said, "and the way you know." Thomas broke in: "Lord, we know not whither thou goest; and how can we know the way?" And Thomas received the great answer from Jesus: "I am the way, the truth and the life."

Jesus was saying to him: "Thomas, I know that you do not understand what is happening. No one understands. But whatever happens, *you have got me.*" In this world, in the last analysis, what we need is not an argument but a presence.

Thomas is best remembered as the man who could not believe. When Jesus had died upon the Cross, and when it seemed that the end had finally come, Thomas's only desire was to be alone. So it happened that when Jesus came back to the disciples, Thomas was not there and he utterly refused to believe the good news. He said that he would not believe unless he actually saw and touched and handled the nail-prints in Jesus' hands and the gash of the spear in his side. Thomas had to see before he would believe.

Ultimately, Thomas became the man of devotion and of faith. Jesus came back. He invited Thomas to put his finger in the nail-prints and his hand in his side. And confronted with the risen Lord, Thomas breathed out the greatest confession of faith in the New Testament: "My Lord, and My God."

Two outstanding facts emerge from the story of Thomas. The first truth is that *Jesus blames no man for wanting to be sure.* Jesus did not blame Thomas for his doubts; Jesus knew that once Thomas had fought his way through the wilderness of his doubts he would be the surest man in Christendom. Jesus never says to a man: "You must have no doubts." Rather he says: "You must never profess a faith of which you are not absolutely sure, and you must fight your battle until you reach your certainty." But it must be noted that certainty came to Thomas, not through intellectual conviction of the truth of a creed, but through first-hand experience of the power and the presence of Jesus Christ. Thomas became sure, not of things about Jesus Christ, but of Jesus Christ himself.

The second truth is that *certainty is most likely to*

come to a man in the fellowship of believers. When Thomas was alone, he was doubly alone. By cutting himself off from the fellowship of men Thomas had also cut himself off from Jesus Christ; and it was when he came back into that fellowship that he met Christ again. That is not to say that a man cannot find Jesus Christ in the solitude and the silence; but it is to say that nowhere is a man more likely to find Christ than in the company of those who love Christ.

The Fourth Gospel gives us one more glimpse of Thomas, for Thomas was there when Jesus came back to meet his men beside the Sea of Galilee. Thomas had learned his lesson; from now on he was one with the fellowship of believers.

UNBELIEVING THOMAS

There was a seal upon the stone,
    A guard around the tomb:
The spurned and trembling band alone
    Bewail their Master's doom.
They deemed the barriers of the grave
Had closed o'er Him who came to save;
    And thoughts of grief and gloom
Were darkening, while depressed, dismayed,
Silent they wept, or weeping prayed.

He died;—for justice claimed her due,
    Ere guilt could be forgiven:
But soon the gates asunder flew,
    The iron bands were riven;
Broken the seal; the guards dispersed,
Upon their sight in glory burst
    The risen Lord of Heaven!
Yet one, the heaviest in despair,
In grief the wildest was not there.

Returning, on each altered brow
    With mute surprise he gazed,
For each was lit with transport now,
    Each eye to heaven upraised.
Burst forth from each th' ecstatic word—
"Hail, brother, we have seen the Lord!"
    Bewildered and amazed
He stood; then bitter words and brief
Betrayed the heart of unbelief.

Days passed, and still the frequent groan
    Convulsed his laboring breast;
When round him light celestial shone,
    And Jesus stood confessed.
"Reach, doubter! reach thy hand," he said;
"Explore the wound the spear hath made,
    The front by nails impressed:
No longer for the living grieve,
And be not faithless, but believe."

Oh! if the iris of the skies
    Transcends the painter's art,
How could he trace to human eyes
    The rainbow of the heart;
When love, joy, fear, repentance, shame,
Hope, faith, in swift succession came,
    Each claiming there a part;
Each mingling in the tears that flowed,
The words that breathed—"My Lord! My God!"

THOMAS DALE, 1797–1870

As he vowed he would do before accepting the Resurrection, Thomas places his hand in Jesus' wounded side. The painting is by Giovanni Francesco Barbieri (1591–1666), known as Guercino, and is in the Vatican collection.

AT DAYBREAK,
FISH AND BREAD WITH JESUS

*John concludes his Gospel with Jesus' appearance
to those disciples who had returned to Galilee to resume
their lives as fishermen—an appearance the angel
had foretold to the women come to the tomb. As he had
done when he recruited them as disciples, Jesus
demonstrated his mastery over nature by
bringing fish to their empty nets. Robert Payne's
version is from his novel* THE LORD JESUS.

ON ONE OF THOSE CLEAR NIGHTS when the fishing in the region of the Seven Springs could be expected to produce a satisfactory haul, the fishermen found nothing in their nets. This was not unusual. They were accustomed to failure, as they were accustomed to success. It was a calm night, very warm, and they were content to glide slowly in search of fresh fishing grounds, moving along the eastern shores of the lake until the moon went down and it was time to light their lamps. If there were any fish, they would usually rise to the lamps. There were no fish. They blew out their lamps and drifted across the lake, the seines sweeping between the boats on the off-chance that a few catfish might fall into their nets.

With the dawn they returned to Capernaum. There was no one on the beach except a solitary man standing by a tamarisk tree, wearing a gown of some grey material. He stood there, looking out across the lake, like a man lost in dreams. They were a hundred yards from the shore when they thought they heard him calling to them.

"Who is it?" Jona shouted to Petros to be heard above the loud chorus of bird-song. "Can you hear him?"

"No doubt it is someone who wants to be ferried across the lake, or some ne'er-do-well who has nothing better to do than look for sand crabs."

"Then look again," Jona shouted, and this time there was a quivering excitement in his voice. "Surely it is Jesus, or someone like Jesus!"

In the watery light the man standing by the tamarisk tree assumed the aspect of shadows.

As the boats drew nearer to the shore, the fishermen all gazed at the tamarisk tree. Then they saw the familiar gesture, the arms raised in blessing, and they heard the voice coming across the water, saying: "Children, did you catch any fish?"

"No," they shouted back in the half-light.

"Then cast your net to starboard, and you will find them," the voice said, and they immediately threw their nets overboard.

The fish were there, blue and green and white, filling the shallows, weighing down the nets, and gliding in great schools just below the surface of the water. Andreas pulled on the ropes and was afraid the nets would be torn, so many fish were rushing into them. He called out for help to Jona, who was on the other boat, but Jona was gazing towards shore and shielding his eyes with his hands. Nor was there any help to be obtained from Petros, who had jumped overboard and was now swimming ashore; but since he had to swim through shoals of fish he reached the shore only a little before the others.

The sky was clearing. The leaden greyness of the lake was turning to silver. Beside the tamarisk tree a charcoal fire was burning. There were fish lying on it, and some bread; and the smell of the coals and the cooked fish and the warm bread drifted enticingly over the lake.

In sequential scenes illustrating John 21:1–14, Peter struggles toward Jesus on the shore of the Sea of Tiberias and the disciples gather for breakfast with their risen master. The Austrian altarpiece is dated 1525–1530.

Synagogue and Church

In the very beginning, believers in Jesus did not separate themselves from their fellow Jews. Like Pharisees, Sadducees, Essenes, and lesser-known groups, they seemed to form a new sect of Judaism — sometimes called "the Way"; and the first Christians preached in synagogues whose members shared many of the same beliefs and were already familiar with the Scriptures. Later, as missionaries carried the Gospel out into the Greco-Roman world, services that included gentiles were initially held in synagogues; but soon there were churches specifically for gentile converts. The new faith's confrontation with Hellenism, or Greek culture, produced significant changes in emphasis. For example, gentile Christians did not share the fervent conviction of Jewish believers that the end of the world and the redemptive return of Jesus were imminent. On the other hand, they willingly accepted such Judaic concepts as monotheism along with the Old Testament precepts of morality.

Soon, the gentile Christianity that grew out of the early churches began to predominate over the Jewish Christianity that was centered in synagogues. In fact, as the faith spread in the West, it failed in Palestine, partly because it did not give encouragement to the Zealots, who wanted to rise up against Rome, and partly because its essential ideas and beliefs struck many traditional Jews as too revolutionary. Perhaps as early as A.D. 50, Jews and Christianized Jews split, even rioting against each other in Rome, and soon the gulf between synagogue and church had widened beyond the point of reconciliation.

Medieval artists represented the synagogue as blindfolded against Christianity.

A crowned figure standing for the church completes the pair at Strasbourg Cathedral.

The rays of the rising sun gleamed on the wet skin of Petros as he knelt in the sand. Jesus fanned the flames with the hem of his gown. Soon they were all gathered around the charcoal fire, warming themselves, for the wind was cold in the early dawn. The larks were still singing, and Jesus still fanned the flames with the hem of his gown.

Andreas came up with more fish, and laid them beside the charcoal fire. Seeing the mountains of fish on and around the charcoal fire, he burst out laughing: "Shall we feast all day, Lord? Shall we feast through a week of Sundays? Surely there is more than we need!"

Jesus blessed the fish. There was color in his cheeks, and the wounds in his hands and feet were healing, leaving only brown scars. He gave them bread and fish, and blessed them, and then took some bread and fish for himself. The wind rippled through his beard, and his eyes gleamed in the silver light spreading over the lake.

"It is good," he said, and smiled at them all, reserving for Jona a smile of special sweetness.

"Shalt thou stay with us?" Jona asked.

"I shall stay for a little while."

"And then?"

"I shall go on a journey."

"Shall I go with thee?"

"No, thou shalt stay on earth, and remain here until I come."

"Will it be long, Lord?"

"Not very long."

There was silence, then, until Petros rose abruptly and placed his two heavy hands on the shoulders of Jesus and gazed into the face of the Lord.

"Thou art he," he said in a trembling voice, and Jesus smiled sadly.

"Did you doubt that I would ever leave you?" Jesus said, and there was a hint of weariness in his voice. "Did you doubt it? Surely you love me beyond any doubt! Surely it is so!"

"I have always loved thee."

"Then feed my lambs."

The smoke rose from the cooking fire.

"Do you love me?" Jesus said again, and Petros answered: "I have loved thee always."

The seven disciples mentioned by John crowd the boat in this 12th-century Bavarian manuscript illumination of Jesus' appearance to them after a night of fishing in vain on the Sea of Tiberias.

ning from Bethsaida and Capernaum to see the fishermen's catch, and join in the feast.

"Where is Jesus?" Jona asked.

"He will return in a little while," Petros said, and soon they went to their own homes.

LOVEST THOU ME?

A group had gathered on the shore that bounds
The restless waters of Tiberias.
The weary fishermen, who, all night long,
Had cast their nets in vain, now saw amazed
The wondrous product of their later toil,
And, half in terror, cried—"It is the Lord!"
And He—mysterious Man!—whom late they saw
Expire in agony upon the Cross,
Stood calmly in their midst and hushed their fear.

Impetuous Peter, bolder than the rest,
Had met his Master first, and sought to prove
His zealous confidence and greater love.
Him loving, yet reproving for his warmth,
The Lord addressed:—"Thou son of Jonas, hear!
And answer truly if thou lovest me?"
Thrice fell this question on his anxious ear,
While wonder first, and then dismay and grief,
Oppressed him as his answer thus he made:—
"Yea, Lord, Thou knowest that I love thee well."

"Then *feed my lambs*," the Holy Shepherd said:
"If me thou lovest more than all beside,
Then, *feed my lambs!* If thou wilt prove thy zeal,
And thus insure thy Master's welcome praise,
Go *feed my lambs!* I ask no arduous toil—
No deed of high emprise thy powers shall task,
I only bid thee *feed my lambs!*" He said,
And soon for heav'n departed, there to watch
His under-shepherds while they guard his flock.

Oh ye, whose holy privilege it is
To serve him thus, see that ye *feed His lambs!*
So shall ye gain the evidence ye seek,
That your commission bears His sacred seal:
So shall ye prove your love—and so acquire
The rich reward on which your hopes are fixed.

JULIAN CRAMER

In a softer voice Jesus said: "Be good to my lambs. Be at peace. The Kingdom of Heaven is at hand!"

Then he warmed his hands on the charcoal fire and said slowly: "Behold, I am the lamb of sacrifice, in whom you are anointed! I am the feast! I am the fish and the wine and the bread! Let there be feasting in my name until the end of the world!"

"Shall it be a wedding feast?" Jona asked.

"Yes, a wedding feast," Jesus said, and then he kissed them one by one and went down to the lake.

From being white and grey, the lake became blue and gold, shattering in its brilliance. The night mist melted away, the birds sang, the sun spread in hot waves over the lake. Smoke curled from the roofs of the houses, and the people came out of their houses in the freshness of the new dawn. Children came run-

In the final verses of Matthew's Gospel, Jesus appears to the 11 disciples gathered on a mountain in Galilee—as Jesus, speaking through the women who came to the tomb, had directed them to do. Duccio's version is dated about 1311.

*Then he led them out as far as Bethany,
and lifting up his hands he blessed
them. While he blessed them, he parted
from them, and was carried up into
heaven. And they returned to Jerusalem
with great joy.*

LUKE 24:50–52

GOING HOME TO HIS FATHER

*According to the book of Acts, 40 days passed between the
Resurrection and the Ascension of Jesus. During that
period, suggests G. M. Anderson in this selection from
MARY, HIS MOTHER, his disciples' despair gradually gave
way to wonderment and joy. The narrative is in the form
of diarylike writings attributed to the mother of Jesus.*

*God extends a hand to
draw Jesus into heaven.
His mother, Mary, is
among those who
witness the Ascension
in this ninth-century
manuscript illumination.*

H, SUCH A DARK NIGHT as we have had! But such
a glorious daybreak this! Apocalypses of glory await us. To triumph over death, surely
that is the miracle of all miracles.

He appeared again to
some of our company
and explained all the
prophecies concerning
himself, showing that
all the things that had
happened to him had
been plainly foretold
and that we should have
understood them if it
were not for our mis-
conceptions about the
nature of his Kingdom.

It seems so plain now
that it is all over. Why
did we not understand
those Scriptures?

Did he not tell us over
and over again that he
was to die? But none of
us understood. And that
he would rise again. But
we could not compre-

*A sixth-century Syrian artist depicted
Jesus ascending to heaven in a chariot of fire—as did
the Old Testament prophet Elijah. Below Jesus
are symbols of the four Evangelists (see page 69).*

hend. Surely there was cause for his gentle reproof that
we were slow of heart to understand the Scriptures.

But it is plain now, even to the sword that was to
pierce my own soul.

We do not know yet the nature of the Kingdom.
He comes, he goes—now he is visible, now invisible;
doors cannot bar him out or hold him in. Every time
he appears we ask what and when? He answers,
"Wait. Power is coming. And you will witness to the
whole world, beginning in Jerusalem. I cannot say
much to you now; you would misunderstand as you
did before. I am going to my Father and we will send
reinforcements; then it will be clear as noonday, and
you will know what to do. But they will not know—
they who crucified me. They will come and bow at
your feet and ask you the way; and you will know the
way and the nature of the Kingdom."

He has invited us out to Mount Olivet tomorrow
and will talk with us further there about the Kingdom.
Peter thinks he might call for the 75,000 angels that
he said he could have called, but did not, when he
was arrested in Gethsemane. He says that if Jesus
could not withstand the ferocity and wickedness of

men, how can we unless it is the intention of Jesus to use armies of angels. . . .

As we stood around him at Mount Olivet today, he began to rise from the ground.

"I am going home," he said, "home to my Father, who has given to me all authority in heaven and on earth. Return to Jerusalem and wait. Power will come. Wait till it comes. Mine is the Kingdom and the power and the glory. The offices you sought are yours. I am trusting the administration to you. I will be with you and stand by you. For whatever help you need, call on me, and you shall receive; the resources of heaven may be commandeered. Trust and go forward, fearing nothing. Establish the Kingdom throughout the whole world; it is to swallow up all other kingdoms and will never end."

Then a cloud enveloped him and carried him up and up till he disappeared from our sight.

We stood riveted to the spot in speechless awe. As we gazed into the heavens two angels descended, saying, "He will come back again, as he told you."

Then they vanished.

Overjoyed, we returned to Jerusalem, and waited and prayed for the return of Jesus and the coming of the Kingdom. . . .

This is the ninth day and he has not come yet. We are waiting and praying. He will come. Where is he when we see him not? Marshalling the invisible hosts? Did he not tell Pilate's court that they would see him coming in the clouds of heaven? . . .

Tenth day—Pentecost, and strange things are happening. A roaring, as of wind; fiery tongues playing on the apostles; multitudes of people rushing together; the apostles speaking out the story of Jesus in languages they had never learned—the languages of the nationalities that were before them.

Peter tells them they murdered the Messiah, but that God raised him up; that he now is over all things in heaven and on earth, and he it is who sends forth the signs they see and hear.

His slayers are panic-stricken and cry for mercy. They are afraid of vengeance; for what king ever triumphed without then wreaking vengeance? But the apostles offer them mercy, because that is the kind of kingdom Christ's Kingdom is.

Three thousand joined today—the first day. Signs and wonders are everywhere. They thought his cause was dead, but it has broken out again with overwhelming power. It sweeps on like a resistless tide.

AWAY

I can not say, and I will not say,
That he is dead—he is just away.
With a cheery smile and a wave of the hand,
He has wandered into an unknown land,
And left us dreaming, how very fair
It needs must be, since he lingers there.
And you—O you, who so wildly yearn
For the old-time step and the glad return,
Think of him faring on, as dear
In the love of There as the love of Here.
Think of him as the same, I say;
He is not dead—he is just away.

JAMES WHITCOMB RILEY, 1849–1916

The Ascension is at center in this embroidered religious vestment, named for the ninth-century emperor Charlemagne but probably dating to a much later period. The reverse side, which features the Transfiguration, can be seen on page 223.

As they were looking on, he was lifted up, and a cloud took him out of their sight. And while they were gazing into heaven as he went, behold, two men stood by them in white robes, and said, "Men of Galilee, why do you stand looking into heaven? This Jesus, who was taken up from you into heaven, will come in the same way as you saw him go into heaven."

ACTS OF THE APOSTLES 1:9–11

The vision of Jesus ascending to heaven caused the disciples to return to Jerusalem with great joy, and thereafter to bless God continually in the temple. Rembrandt's version, dated 1636, is in Munich's Alte Pinakothek.

AFTER FORTY DAYS, CARRIED UP INTO HEAVEN

The Ascension of Jesus, mentioned in Mark as well as Luke but omitted from Matthew and John, is confirmed in the first chapter of Acts of the Apostles, a continuation of the Gospel of Luke. Bonnell Spencer, in this excerpt from THEY SAW THE LORD, attempts to reconcile the two versions.

IN LUKE'S FIRST ACCOUNT, the Ascension might seem to follow immediately after the appearance of Christ on Easter night. This, of course, is impossible. It would not leave time for the other recorded appearances and Luke precludes this false impression by saying in Acts that our Lord was "seen of them forty days." But the fact that his Gospel runs the two events together makes it probable that the latter started where the former had occurred, in the upper room.

It was most appropriate that our Lord's final appearance should take place in the Holy City. There he had entered into his kingdom on Palm Sunday. There he had won his kingdom on Good Friday. Now he was about to establish that kingdom among men. It was not a new kingdom, but was the continuation and the sublimation of the old. It fulfilled the purpose for which the Jews were the chosen people. Many of them, especially the official leaders, refused to follow Christ from the old Israel into the new. Our Lord had had to train and authorize new leaders to take their places. But the continuity was emphasized by having the new dispensation emanate from the capital of the old. Therefore, he assembled his disciples in Jerusalem to terminate his Resurrection appearances and to prepare them to become, in the full sense of the word, his body the Church.

The disciples were about to pass through another period of transition which would result in a new and permanent relationship with Christ. The first transition had taken place during the three days when our Lord's body lay in the tomb. At first, the apostles had followed Christ as a man among men. That relationship came to an end in his death. During Eastertide, he appeared to them from time to time in his risen body, showing "himself alive after his passion by many infallible proofs." This form of his self-manifestation was now to give way to the third. His followers were not to be dependent on intermittent Resurrection appearances for their knowledge of him. He willed to make himself more readily accessible than that, abiding with us in word and sacraments until the end of time.

In order to make them understand that they were no longer to expect him to appear on earth in his risen body, he led them out to the Mount of Olives near Bethany and, after he had blessed them, "He was taken up; and a cloud received him out of their sight."

He wanted his disciples to realize that his risen body was leaving the earth to take its place at the right hand of God. How else could he have given that note of finality?

It would not have been enough simply to disappear. All the other Resurrection appearances had terminated in that way. That would have left the disciples expecting him to return as he had before. It would not have done for him to walk away from them over the brow of the hill. That would have given the impression that he was still roaming the earth. He could not die a second time, for one of the essential characteristics of his risen body is that it is beyond death. How could he express the teaching he had to give except by taking his body either up into the air or down into the earth? Today, in spite of all our modern astronomy, we continue to think of heaven as up and hell as down. Thus the appropriate gesture by which to show that he was finally parted from us, as far as the visibility of his Resurrection body is concerned, is still to be "carried up into heaven."

The Ascension reveals the destiny which God has prepared for men. Jesus remains incarnate. He did not take our human nature merely to lay it aside again either at death or after he had demonstrated the Resurrection. He united it to himself permanently. He has raised it to the right hand of God, which is a figurative way of saying that man in Christ has been given the place of highest honor, has been taken up into the Godhead itself.

The disciples sensed the significance of the Ascension at the moment when Christ was taken up into heaven. For this reason, they felt none of the grief of Calvary at his parting from them. They realized that he had but gone before to prepare a place for them, remembering his promise, "I, if I be lifted up from the earth, will draw all men unto me." And so they "returned to Jerusalem with great joy: and were continually in the temple, praising and blessing God."

The right panel of a triptych by Hans Memling (c. 1430–1495) shows the disciples and Mary as prayerful observers of Jesus disappearing into the clouds above.

Harvesting wheat has changed little in the centuries since Jesus' time; this field is outside a Judean village.

Pentecost: The Feast of Weeks

As the Greek term Pentecost suggests, the annual Feast of Weeks, or Shavuot, took place 50 days after Passover began. Considered the second most important of all of the ancient Jewish celebrations, and one of the three occasions on which all males were required to appear before the Lord at the temple, this joyful festival marked the end of the grain harvest. It was also a reaffirmation of Yahweh's covenant with his people, for the successful harvest proved that he had taken care to sustain them through the previous year. Following the Old Testament injunction for a "cereal offering of new grain," two loaves of leavened, salted bread were offered at the Shavuot ceremony. The use of yeast, unique to this ritual in Hebraic practice, suggests an origin as a Canaanite agricultural festival adopted by the Israelites when they gave up their wanderings and settled down to become farmers in Palestine.

After the founding of the Christian church at Pentecost, and especially after the temple was destroyed in A.D. 70, the interpretation of Shavuot gradually changed. Since it was believed that Moses brought the Ten Commandments down from Sinai 50 days after the original Passover in Egypt, the feast became a commemoration of the giving of the Torah and the Covenant of Sinai. For Christians, Pentecost

celebrates the miracle of the birth of the church, a dramatic affirmation that God's plan of redemption applies to all of the world's people, not the Jews alone. The gift of the Holy Spirit that day was considered to be the dawn of a new age in which believers then and now were enjoined to become missionaries until the Gospel message is heard "to the end of the earth" (Acts 1:8).

Young members of a kibbutz in Israel's Negev region celebrate Shavuot with a ritual harvest dance.

BLASPHEMY THAT MUST BE STOPPED

The visitation of the Holy Spirit that left the assembled disciples with the gift of speaking in other languages led to a mass baptism in Jerusalem that day—an event that can be called the birth of Christianity. James Martin retold the story in THE EMPTY TOMB, a work of fiction in the form of letters from Caiaphas to his father-in-law and predecessor as high priest, Annas.

T HE JESUS AFFAIR has flared up again and is much worse than before. Today is Pentecost, of course, and the Nazarene crowd have caused a fearful commotion. They have begun, after all, to proclaim publicly their blasphemous and nonsensical doctrine of the resurrection of Jesus and have succeeded in setting the whole city by the ears.

All their sympathizers—a little more than a hundred, it is estimated—were gathered together this morning when their mad obsession concerning the crucified carpenter seemed to overwhelm their minds and they began to make such a tumult that a large crowd was attracted, thinking no doubt that it was a drunken brawl and that they might see some fun. When the crowd had gathered, that big fisherman who is one of them, Simon by name, started to proclaim that Jesus was risen from the dead and from all accounts a great deal of excitement was engendered.

That, you may think, is bad enough, but, if it had been all, there would have been little reason for concern. Unfortunately and well-nigh unbelievably, large numbers of the listeners appear to have embraced the false teaching and made a public declaration of their intention to take their stand on the side of the Nazarenes. This makes the situation a great deal worse.

Not only is it infuriating, it is perplexing! This affair has had mysterious and puzzling features all along and this latest development is no exception. Why, it is seven weeks since Jesus was crucified and it was only two days later that the tomb was found empty and the Nazarenes were started on this ridiculous delusion that Jesus had risen from the dead. Why did they wait until now before coming out into the open?

I would have thought that if they were going to take this line, the best time to take it, from their point of view, was right away. I cannot see what they have gained by waiting. It is true that, most surprisingly, they seem to have made a spectacular start today and won a large crowd over to their persuasion. But that can be no more than a flash in the pan.

No doubt when we get the details we shall find that their "converts" are some riff-raff of the city lacking enough intelligence or religious background to know what they are doing. Nobody with any sense could have anything to do with the preposterous doctrine they are preaching. . . .

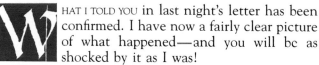

HAT I TOLD YOU in last night's letter has been confirmed. I have now a fairly clear picture of what happened—and you will be as shocked by it as I was!

The Nazarenes, about a hundred and twenty of them, were met together in a house, a hullabaloo broke out, a crowd gathered, Simon the fisherman began to preach the resurrection of Jesus and many were apparently convinced and converted. Whether the preaching was planned or spontaneously embarked upon I do not know and it makes little difference anyhow. But I have more to tell you about the content of Peter's preaching. He had rather a lot to say, and it will not make any more pleasant hearing for you than it did for me. Not only did he allege that Jesus was risen from the grave, he said a great many other things as well. Two were particularly offensive.

First, he had the audacity to make a public accusation of us—yes, you and me and the rest. He asserted that we were murderers, that we had plotted against

Their number restored to 12 with the election of Matthias to take Judas's place, the apostles were gathered in Jerusalem—traditionally the upper room used for the Last Supper— when the Holy Spirit descended as tongues of fire. The 10th-century manuscript at left has the correct number; only 10 are in the one at right, dating to the early 11th century.

an innocent man who was none other than Messiah and foully contrived his death. What an impudent nerve the man must possess to behave in such an outrageous fashion! We were doing our obvious duty and my conscience for one is clear. All the same, we cannot tolerate this sort of thing. It is bad for discipline and good order. This illiterate fisherman and his henchmen will require to be taught a sharp lesson, and the sooner the better.

But I have still to tell you the best of the story, or the worst of it, whichever you care to term it. The Nazarenes must be completely mad! Their delusion that Jesus is risen might well be taken as sufficient proof of madness even if there was nothing else. The fact that after a lapse of seven weeks they suddenly start shouting their nonsensical belief from the housetops, with the apparent expectation of getting others to accept it, is a further token of minds that are unhinged. So is their irrational and irreligious contention that the Jesus who was found guilty of blasphemy, who was condemned as a felon and crucified to death, is, after all, Messiah. And surely no sane person would stand up in public in this city under our very noses and call us murderers!

But what I have to tell you now caps everything else and is far and away the maddest thing of all. They are suggesting, Annas—and, mark you, this is sober fact—that Jesus is both Messiah and *Lord*. They are calling him Lord and trying to persuade their hearers to accept him as such. This is the worst blasphemy that has ever been heard of *and it must be stopped*.

As for the additional fact that the Nazarenes have somehow managed to persuade others to side with them in their blasphemy, that, I must confess, floors me completely. I told you already that they made a number of converts as a result of their preaching yesterday. I presume that means these converts accept the claims the Nazarenes are making and are prepared to agree with them, not only that Jesus is Messiah, not only that he is risen from the dead, but also that he is divine. I cannot for the life of me conceive how anyone, no matter how ignorant or how irreligious, could ever come to be persuaded of that.

Created in the mid-12th century, this enamel and copper gilt French plaque has the hand of God directing the tongues of fire to the disciples' heads.

THE GIFT OF TONGUES

Not hopeless did they grieve; for o'er the soul
His last bequest has shed a gleam of joy;
"A comforter to come" restrained their tears,
A steadfast faith suppressed the rising sigh,
And expectation raised their downcast eyes.
Nor vain their hope; for now with sudden burst
A rushing noise through all that sacred band
Silence profound and fixed attention claimed,
A chilling terror crept through every heart,
Mute was each tongue, and pale was ev'ry face:
The rough roar ceased; when, borne on fiery wings,
The dazzling emanation from above
In brightest vision round each sacred head
Diffused its vivid beams; mysterious light!
That rushed impetuous through th' awaking mind,
Whilst new ideas filled the passive soul,
Fast crowding in with sweetest violence.
'Twas then amazed they caught the glorious flame,
Spontaneous flowed their all-persuasive words,
Warm from the heart, and to the heart addressed,
Deep sunk their force in ev'ry captived ear.

O see the crowd, pressing with eager steps
To catch the flowing periods as they fall;
See how, with wond'ring rapture, they devour
The pleasing accents of their native tongue;
See how, with eyes uplifted, they advance,
With outstretched hands and smiles of social love,
To greet the partners of their native soil.
O catch the varying transports in their looks,
In awful wonder see each passion lost,
When ev'ry nation urged an equal claim.
Fond men, forbear; and know the voice of truth,
By weak restraints of language unconfined,
Flows, independent, from that radiant shrine
From whence the dayspring draws her glitt'ring store
To shine on all with undistinguished ray,
And scatter dazzling light on ev'ry clime.

CHARLES JENNER

The work of Titian (c. 1490–1576), this painting of Pentecost acquires a three-dimensional effect by its setting between pillars topped by an arch in the church of Santa Maria della Salute in Venice.

Now when they
heard these things
they were enraged,
and they ground
their teeth against
him [Stephen].
. . . and stopped
their ears and
rushed together
upon him. Then
they cast him out
of the city and
stoned him; and
the witnesses
laid down their
garments at the
feet of a young
man named Saul.

ACTS OF THE APOSTLES
7:54, 57–58

In garb befitting his
office as a deacon of
the Jerusalem church,
Stephen sinks beneath
the stones cast by the
enraged mob. The artist,
Adam Elsheimer
(1578–1610), worked
principally in Rome,
where he was called
"Il Tedesco" (Italian
for "the German")
because of his
foreign birthplace.

CHRISTIANITY'S FIRST MARTYR

One of the first seven deacons of the Jerusalem church,
Stephen challenged the Jewish religious hierarchy as
"stiff-necked people, uncircumcised in heart and ears"
and accused them of responsibility for Jesus'
betrayal and murder. A consenting bystander at
Stephen's punishment—death by stoning—was a young
man named Saul, the future apostle Paul. Sholem
Asch dramatized the event in his novel THE APOSTLE.

THE FIELD OF STONING lay outside the city. It was not really a field; it was a pit on the summit of a hill. Around the sides of the pit lay heaps of stones—the soil of Jerusalem and of the countryside nearby was sown with rocks. The bottom of the pit was not visible because of the stones which covered it, stones which had been thrown into it in the course of executions, stones on which there were, here and there, flecks of dried blood.

The clothes were ripped off the accused; a multitude of hands flung him down into the stony pit, and a voice cried: "Witnesses, come forward and do your duty. Fulfill the commandment: 'And the hand of the witnesses shall be the first against him!'"

The two witnesses threw off their mantles of burlap. Tattered and wretched these mantles were, but the garment of the poor is precious to them. "Who will guard the garments of the witnesses?"

Saul cried out that he would guard the mantles of the witnesses, sat down on the bundle of garments by the edge of the pit, and saw the first stones fly down on the condemned man.

White body covered suddenly with blood . . . another stone . . . then a rain of stones . . . white, bloody body kneeling . . . falling . . . rising . . . a half body dipped in stones, and a half body rising naked out of the sea of stones. The last rays of the sun falling on the white body, making patches of silver amid patches of blood. . . . Then two naked hands, like silver wings, uplifted toward the sun, a white face lifted to the sky, a high voice, the ringing, metallic voice of the preacher: "Lord, Jesus, receive my soul!"

Saul dropped his eyes. He would look no more. But he could not shut out the voice, ringing still, but dying away: "Father, forgive them. . . ."

The very night of the execution Saul was driven to visit once more the field of stoning. It did not for an instant occur to him that the sentence carried out against the blasphemer and misleader had been an unjust one or that it had served any but the divine purpose; what filled him with restlessness was the utter self-certainty of the proponent of the wrong. He saw again the ecstatic face of Stephen, he heard the cry with which he relinquished his soul to the highest authority: "Father, forgive them!" According to report these were the very words which their rabbi had uttered when he was dying under the tortures of the heathens. Could a blasphemer and misleader die thus?

And if he could, if all of them could, whence the source of their strength? What were the springs which fed them? To give up life for the cause of God was the highest achievement of which man was capable, the highest condition to which he could attain; it was the fulfillment of the great commandment: "And thou shalt love the Lord with all thy soul." But how could he, Saul, admit that these men drew their strength from the fount of true holiness? That could not be.

When he reached the summit, and looked down into the hollow, he started back. The intimates of the dead preacher had already lifted the body out of the pit, acting not in shame and fear, but as men act at the burial of a great saint who has given up his life for the sanctification of the Name.

Saul drew his mantle up over his face, in order that he might not be recognized, and mingled with the funeral procession. He listened to the murmuring voices, and he heard praises of the dead man being uttered not only by his companions in the faith, but also by important scribes and Pharisees, who were joining freely in exalting the death of the blasphemer and misleader as the death of a saint, a pure and holy death, and condemning the execution as nothing less than an act of murder.

But it was not in the nature of Saul to be intimidated by the words and thoughts of others. What happened this night was that he understood for the first time the vastness of the danger represented by the new sect; for if sages and teachers and prominent rabbis could permit themselves to participate in the funeral of a blasphemer, and join in the eulogies which were uttered for him, then it was indeed ill with Israel. The zeal of the Lord was strengthened that night in Saul; he was convinced, more than ever, of the justice of his cause. Heaven and earth would have to be moved, but the fire which had been lit by the men of Galilee would have to be extinguished.

Thrown from his mount and blinded by a light from heaven, Saul sprawls on the ground in Caravaggio's depiction of the future apostle's dramatic conversion.

Saul, still breathing threats and murder against the disciples of the Lord, went to the high priest and asked him for letters to the synagogues at Damascus, so that if he found any belonging to the Way, men or women, he might bring them bound to Jerusalem.

ACTS OF THE APOSTLES 9:1–2

YIELDING TO THE BOUNDLESS POWER OF TRUTH

A consenting witness to the martyrdom of Stephen, Saul became the scourge of the early Christian church, in time asking permission to extend his vendetta from Jerusalem to Damascus. En route there, he had a vision that changed his life—and the history of the world. Rex Miller recreated the moment in his 1949 novel I, PAUL.

F YOU APPROACH DAMASCUS by the Jerusalem road you will reach a point, not far outside the city wall, where desert suddenly gives way to garden. Along this road I passed, one bright midday in early spring, just thirty years ago.

The members of our little caravan, sensing the approaching end of the tedious six-day journey from Jerusalem, were in high spirits. The sun beat hotly upon our shoulders, and from the padding hoofs of the camels clouds of fine dust arose and all but smothered us. We could see ahead the fresh greenness of the well-watered plain, and the gleaming whiteness of the city's houses among their groves and gardens.

I was elated at the prospect of activity within the famous, ancient, beautiful city that lay ahead. These Nazarenes should learn that, even in the distant seclusion of a pagan city, no Jew could elude the watchfulness of the temple authorities at Jerusalem! My next appearance before the Sanhedrin would be in the nature of a triumph. Here, they would say, is the gallant young soldier of the faith, returned from a brief campaign with a train of dangerous captives.

As at this instant our caravan was passing from days of desert drought and solitude into the smiling, rose-decked suburbs of Damascus, even so it seemed to me that I was passing from years of discipline and struggle into the realization of my fondest hopes: into a position of leadership and authority in the religion of my fathers, with wealth and power and domestic bliss its natural accompaniments.

These were my dreams when suddenly there came a blinding flash of light, brighter than ever the noonday sun had shone upon the desert. I stumbled from my mount and fell prostrate in the dust, trembling with shock and fear.

"Saul, Saul," came a voice from I could not tell where, "why do you persecute me?"

"Who are you, my Lord?" I asked in my confusion, my question revealing that I knew the dread answer.

"I am Jesus," came the reply, fulfilling all my fears. "I am Jesus whom you persecute. Why do you fight against that which you know to be the right?"

It was true. All this plotting, this constant hatred, these murders and imprisonments; I had known that they were wrong. But like one under the spell of a magician I had gone on and on, persecuting, binding, killing. These words, so simple, so straightforward, had broken a spell that held me bound more tightly than any of my prisoners. In an instant I saw Truth, and yielded to its boundless power.

"Lord," I asked, still trembling and astonished, "what would you have me do?"

"Arise," came the answer. "Go into the city, and it will be told you what to do." That was all. So little said. So much achieved.

My companions, thrown into confusion, had crowded around me. Some had seen the blinding flash, they said; others had heard the voice; but only I had grasped the meaning of it all.

I stood up. I could see nothing, although my eyes were open. The light, that shining, glorious light, was still around me. I heard the voice of Jesus say: "Saul, I have appeared to you to make you my minister, and my witness both as to these things which you have seen, and those things in which I will appear to you. I now send you to the Gentiles, to open their eyes, and to turn them from darkness to light, and from the power of Satan to God, that they may receive forgiveness for their sins, and an inheritance among those who are made holy through faith in me."

These words came to me as my companions in the caravan, disturbed by my continued blindness, were offering their hands to guide me to Damascus.

Recalling the event, it is not lost upon me that here, in my extremity, I found the first evidence of loving-kindness that had been vouchsafed me for many months. There had been no place for deeds of kindness in my life. It had been a life of scheming, of political intrigue, of bigotry and persecution. There had been no time for simple friendship; all was striving for a selfish goal, disguised as zeal for my religion.

These comrades of the Jerusalem road lifted me and led me into the city, to the house of one Judas in the street called Straight, a kindly man. They did not know it—I did not know it then—but now it is clear to me that their loving care was but the response to something I had newly gained: a brotherly affection for my fellow men. My brief vision of the Master, and the words I heard, had given this quality to me.

Three days I stayed in Judas's house. They were three days such as Jesus must have spent in the sepulcher, and I came out from that house, even as Jesus came out from the tomb, resurrected.

As a curiously white-bearded Jesus speaks to him from heaven, Saul sinks with his stumbling horse. The Damascus he approaches is more reminiscent of a French walled town at the time this manuscript illumination was executed, about 1410, than the first-century Syrian city.

The midday sun with fiercest glare,
Broods o'er the hazy, twinkling air;
   Along the level sand
The palm tree's shade unwavering lies,
Just as thy towers, Damascus, rise,
   To greet yon wearied band.

The leader of that martial crew
Seems bent some mighty deed to do,
   So steadily he speeds,
With lips firm closed and fixed eye,
Like warrior when the fight is nigh,
   Nor talk nor landscape heeds.

What sudden blaze is round him poured,
As though all heaven's refulgent hoard
   In one rich glory shone?
One moment—and to earth he falls;
What voice his inmost heart appals?
   Voice heard by him alone.

For to the rest both words and form
Seem lost in lightning and in storm,
   While Saul, in wakeful trance,
Sees deep within that dazzling field
His persecuted Lord revealed,
   With keen yet pitying glance.

And hears the meek upbraiding call
And gently on his spirit fall,
   As if th' Almighty Son
Were prisoner yet in this dark earth,
Nor had proclaimed his royal birth,
   Nor his great power begun.

"Ah! wherefore persecut'st thou me?"
He heard and saw, and sought to free
   His strained eye from the sight;
But heaven's high magic bound it there,
Still gazing, though untaught to bear
   Th' insufferable light.

"Who art thou, Lord?" he falters forth:—
So shall sin ask of heaven and earth
   At the last awful day.
"When did we see thee suffering nigh,
And passed thee with unheeding eye?
   Great God of judgment, say?"

Ah! little dream our listless eyes
What glorious presence they despise,
   While in our noon of life,
To power or fame we rudely press,
Christ is at hand to scorn or bless,—
   Christ suffers in our strife.

JOHN KEBLE, 1792–1866

Paul narrowly escaped martyrdom in the ancient theater at Ephesus.

Apostle to the Gentiles

Paul was not the first early Christian to envision an evangelical mission to gentiles, but he became the most zealous and pivotal figure in the crusade. In his preaching and writing, he helped resolve the crucial questions raised by Judaic tradition: Must gentile converts, like most Jewish Christians, circumcise their male infants, refuse to eat pork, and avoid associating with pagans? Paul recognized that the issue was whether salvation comes from following the Old Testament commandments, or from the forgiveness that Jesus gives freely to his believers. He chose the latter: Baptism meant that the convert was free from the demands of the law of Moses. He endured much controversy before convincing the leaders of the Jerusalem congregation, then the center of Christianity, to grant full membership to the legion of gentile converts he made throughout the Roman world.

He was raised
on the third day in
accordance with the
scriptures, and . . .
he appeared to
Cephas, then to the
twelve. Then he
appeared to more
than five hundred
brethren at one
time, most of whom
are still alive,
though some have
fallen asleep. Then
he appeared to
James, then to all
the apostles. Last
of all, as to one
untimely born, he
appeared also to me.

1 CORINTHIANS 15:4–8

Scenes relating to the
conversion of Saul
appear on this page
from a ninth-century
illuminated manuscript:
the vision on the road
to Damascus (top); the
instruction to the disciple
Ananias to restore Saul's
sight (center); and the
inflammatory preaching
that forced him to flee
Damascus by night.

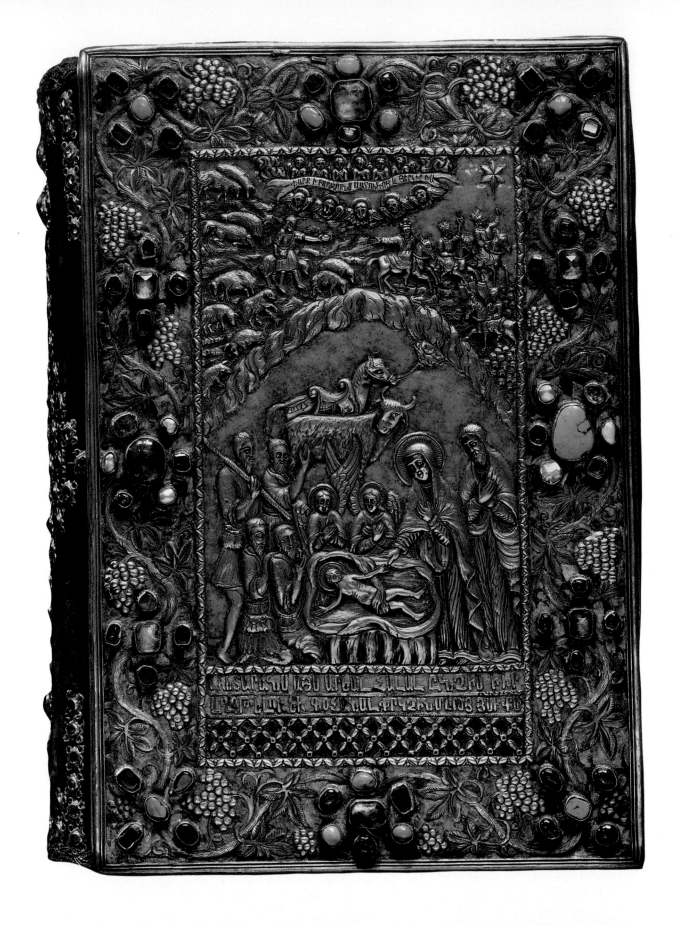

The story of Jesus is encapsulated on the covers of a 14th-century Armenian Bible, a treasure of the Metropolitan Museum in New York. On the front (opposite) is the Nativity; on the back (at left) is the Resurrection. Carved and hammered silver, gilt, enamel, and semiprecious stones decorate the incised vellum covers, which have somewhat unequal shades of color because of the manner in which the volume was long stored.

Jesus Among Us

For 2,000 years succeeding generations have pondered
and cherished Jesus. In the early centuries of the Christian era,
devout writers tried to fill in the gaps in the Gospel narratives with
imaginative embellishments. The Middle Ages brought pious
meditations on his life by a clergy hoping to reach the illiterate masses.
So-called rationalist scholars in the 19th century searched for the
historical Jesus, presenting him as a laborer, a storyteller, a
medical practitioner, even a humorist.

Despite such wide-ranging attempts to recreate or even
invent a Jesus apart from the Scriptures, common
people the world over have never lost sight of the man and
his message. To them he is changeless yet adaptable
to each new era, the village carpenter of Nazareth who spans
the globe, the one who brings love, solace, and hope in
times of sorrow, satisfaction and gratitude in times
of triumph. On the following pages are works of art and
writing through which the modern world continues
to celebrate the life of Jesus.

*In this work by the
German expressionistic
painter and illustrator
Emil Nolde (1867–1956),
Jesus turns his back
to the disciples who
seek to prevent parents
from bringing their
children for a blessing.
The canvas is at the
Museum of Modern
Art in New York.*

And in that region there were shepherds out in the field, keeping watch over their flock by night. And an angel of the Lord appeared to them, and the glory of the Lord shone around them, and they were filled with fear.

LUKE 2:8–9

This tender Nativity scene by the American artist N. C. Wyeth (1882–1945) was used to illustrate a Christmas tale in the December 1912 issue of the then popular Scribner's *magazine.*

TO JESUS ON HIS BIRTHDAY

For this your mother sweated in the cold,
For this you bled upon the bitter tree:
A yard of tinsel ribbon bought and sold;
A paper wreath; a day at home for me.
The merry bells ring out, the people kneel;
Up goes the man of God before the crowd;
With voice of honey and with eyes of steel
He drones your humble gospel to the proud.
Nobody listens. Less than the wind that blows
Are all your words to us you died to save.
O Prince of Peace! O Sharon's dewy Rose!
How mute you lie within your vaulted grave.
　　The stone the angel rolled away with tears
　　Is back upon your mouth these thousand years.

EDNA ST. VINCENT MILLAY, 1892–1950

THE FIRST CHRISTMAS TREE

The angel who brought tidings of Jesus' birth to the shepherds, the poet and journalist Eugene Field wrote, selected one of the trees in the forest for a special mission. His story appeared in A LITTLE BOOK OF PROFITABLE TALES, *published in 1889–1890.*

WHEN THE MORNING CAME the angels left the forest,—all but one, who remained behind and lingered near a tiny tree, so small it scarcely ever was noticed. Then a cedar asked: "Why do you tarry with us, angel?" And the angel answered: "I stay to guard this sacred tree, that no harm shall come to it."

The little tree felt quite relieved by this assurance, and it held up its head more confidently than ever before. And how it thrived and grew, and waxed in strength and beauty! The cedars said they never had seen the like. The sun seemed to lavish its choicest rays upon the little tree, heaven dropped its sweetest dew upon it, and the winds never came to the forest that they did not forget their rude manners and linger to kiss the little tree and sing it their prettiest songs. No danger ever menaced it, no harm threatened; for the angel never slept,—through the day and through the night the angel watched the little tree and protected it from all evil.

So the years passed, the angel watching his blooming charge. Sometimes the beasts strayed toward the little tree and threatened to devour its tender foliage; sometimes the woodman came with his axe, intent upon hewing down the straight and comely thing; sometimes the hot, consuming breath of drought swept from the south, and sought to blight the forest and all its verdure: the angel kept them from the tree. Serene and beautiful it grew, until it was no longer a little tree, but the pride and glory of the forest.

One night the tree heard someone coming through the forest. Hitherto the angel had hastened to its side when men approached; but now the angel strode away and stood under the cedars yonder.

"Dear angel," cried the tree, "can you not hear the footsteps of someone approaching? Don't leave me!"

"Have no fear," said the angel; "for he who comes is the Master."

The Master came to the tree and beheld it. He placed his hands upon its trunk and branches, and the tree was

The 20th-century French artist Jean Charles used brilliant colors for a Nativity scene executed in a primitive cubist style.

THE FLIGHT INTO EGYPT

Through every precinct of the wintry city
Squadroned iron resounds upon the streets;
Herod's police
Make shudder the dark steps of the tenements
At the business about to be done.

Neither look back upon Thy starry country,
Nor hear what rumors crowd across the dark
Where blood runs down those holy walls,
Nor frame a childish blessing with Thy hand
Towards that fiery spiral of exulting souls!

Go, Child of God, upon the singing desert,
Where, with eyes of flame,
The roaming lion keeps thy road from harm.

THOMAS MERTON, 1915–1968

This flight into Egypt, painted by the Yugoslavian artist Ivo Dulcic in 1916, hangs in the Vatican Museum of Contemporary Christian Art.

thrilled with a strange and glorious delight. Then he stooped and kissed the tree, and fell upon his knees and prayed. The tree heard him; and all the forest was still, as if it were standing in the presence of death. And when the morning came, lo! the angel had gone.

Then there was a great confusion in the forest and a sound of rude voices and a clashing of swords and staves. Strange men appeared, uttering loud oaths and cruel threats, and the tree was filled with terror. It called aloud for the angel, but the angel came not.

The forest was sorely agitated, but it was in vain. The strange men plied their axes with cruel vigor, and the tree was hewn to the ground, its beautiful branches cut away and cast aside and its soft, thick foliage strewn to the mercies of the winds.

"They are killing me!" cried the tree. "Why is not the angel here to protect me?" But no one heard the piteous cry, none but the other trees of the forest; and they wept.

Then the cruel men dragged the despoiled and hewn tree from the forest, and the forest saw that beauteous thing no more. But the wind that swept down from the city the following night tarried in the forest awhile to say that it had seen the tree upraised that very day on Calvary,—the cross on which was stretched the body of the dying Master.

French painter Georges Rouault (1871–1958) achieved renown for his expressionistic religious paintings. The colors in this view of Nazareth reflect his apprenticeship in a workshop that produced stained glass.

WHEN THE MIRACLE WORKER SMILED

Among the many writers who have woven stories around the theme of Jesus' love of children is novelist Frank Norris, from whose posthumously published work of 1906, THE JOYOUS MIRACLE, the following selection is taken. The legend of Jesus making clay birds fly can be traced back to the so-called INFANCY GOSPEL OF THOMAS, a noncanonical work dating to the second century.

IT WAS A LONG TIME AGO," said Mervius. "I was a lad. For the children of our village—that is to say, my little cousin Joanna, my brother Simon, the potter's son Septimus, a lad named Joseph, whose father was the olive presser, and myself—the village green was the playground.

"It was there one day that Septimus showed us how to model clay into pots and drinking vessels, and afterward even into the form of animals: dogs, fishes, and the lame cow that belonged to the widow at the end of the village. Simon made a wonderful beast that he assured us was a lion, with twigs for legs, while Septimus and I patted and pinched our lump of clay to look like a great pig.

"Joanna—she was younger than all the rest of us—was fashioning little birds, clumsy, dauby little lumps of wet clay without much form. She was very proud of them, and set them in a row upon a stick, and called for us to look at them. As boys will, we made fun of her and her little clumsy clay birds, because she was a girl, and Simon, my brother, said: 'Ho, those aren't like birds at all. More like bullfrogs.'

"She was too brave to let us see her cry, but she got up and was just about to go home across the green when Simon said to me and to the others: 'Look, quick, Mervius, here comes that man that father spoke about, the carpenter's son.' And he pointed across the brook, down the road that runs from the city over toward the lake. Joanna stopped and looked where he pointed; so did we all.

"He came up slowly along the road near the brook where we children were sitting. When he noticed us all standing there and looking at him quietly, he crossed the brook, sat on the bank, took Joanna on his knee, and asked us what we had been doing. We showed him our array of clay birds and animals.

"We were all about him, on his shoulders, on his knees, in his arms, and Joanna in his lap. 'See, see my birds,' she said. She had her arms around his neck. 'They said they were not pretty. They are pretty, aren't they, quite as pretty as their birds?'

" 'Prettier, prettier,' he said. 'Look now.' He set Joanna's shapeless little lumps before him in a row, looked at them, and at last touched one with his fingertip, then—Did you ever see, when corn is popping, how the grain swells, swells, swells, then bursts forth into whiteness? So it was then. No sooner had that little bird of Joanna's, that clod of dust, that poor bit of common clay felt the touch of his finger than it awakened into life and became a live bird—and white, white as the sunshine, a beautiful little white bird that flew upward on the instant, with a tiny, glad note of song pouring from its throat.

"We children shouted aloud, and Joanna danced and clapped her hands. And then it was that the carpenter's son smiled. He looked at her as she looked up at that soaring white bird, and smiled, smiled, just once, and then fell calm again.

"He rose to go, but we hung about him and clamoured for him to stay.

" 'No,' he said, as he kissed us all, 'I must go.' He crossed the brook and looked back at us.

" 'Can't we go with you?' we cried to him. He shook his head.

" 'Where I am going you cannot go. But,' he added, 'I am going to make a place for just such as you.' "

Vivid colors enhance the primitive simplicity of this version of Jesus accepting the gift of the lad with loaves and fish; it is the work of 20th-century American artist Jean Heiberg.

ALL ARE HIS BRETHREN

At the age of 30, the distinguished French Protestant clergyman, philosopher, and music scholar Albert Schweitzer took up the study of medicine and eight years later, in 1913, embarked for French Equatorial Africa, where he founded the Lambaréné Hospital. Rewarded for his efforts on behalf of the underprivileged with the 1952 Nobel Peace Prize, Schweitzer explained his feelings about his patients in ON THE EDGE OF THE PRIMEVAL FOREST.

AS TO OPERATIONS, ONE UNDERTAKES in the forest, naturally, only such as are urgent and which promise a successful result. The one I have had to perform most often is that for hernia, a thing which afflicts the Negroes of Central Africa much more often than it does white people, though why this should be so we do not know. They also suffer much more often than white people from strangulated hernia in which the intestine becomes constricted and blocked, so that it can no longer empty itself. It then becomes enormously inflated by the gases which form and this causes terrible pain. Then, after several days of torture, death takes place, unless the intestine can be got back through the rupture into the abdomen.

Our ancestors were well acquainted with this terrible method of dying, but we no longer see it in Europe because every case is operated on as soon as ever it is recognized. "Let not the sun go down upon your strangulated hernia" is the maxim continually impressed upon medical students. But in Africa this terrible death is quite common. There are few Negroes who have not as boys seen some man rolling in the sand of his hut and howling with agony till death came to release him. So now, the moment a man feels that his rupture is a strangulated one—ruptures are far rarer among women—he begs his friends to put him in a canoe and bring him to me.

How can I describe my feelings when a poor fellow is brought to me in this condition? I am the only person within hundreds of miles who can help him. Because I am here and am supplied by my friends with the necessary means, he can be saved like those who came before him in the same condition and those who will come after him, while otherwise he would merely have fallen a victim to the torture. This does not mean merely that I can save his life. We must all die. But that I can save him from days of torture is what I feel as my great, ever-new privilege. Pain is a more terrible lord of mankind than even death itself.

So when the poor moaning creature comes, I lay my hand on his forehead and say to him: "Don't be afraid! In an hour's time you shall be put to sleep and when you wake you won't feel any more pain!"

Very soon the sufferer is given an injection of omnipon; the doctor's wife is called to the hospital and, with the help of a native named Joseph, she makes everything ready for the operation. When that is to begin she administers the anesthetic and Joseph, in a pair of rubber gloves, acts as assistant.

The operation is finished and in the hardly lighted dormitory I watch for the sick man's awakening. Scarcely has he recovered consciousness when he stares about him and ejaculates again and again: "I have no more pain! I have no more pain!" His hand feels for mine and will not let go its clasp of gratitude.

Then I begin to tell him that it is the Lord Jesus who has told the doctor and his wife to come to the Ogowe River and that white people in Europe give them the money to live here and cure the sick Negroes of the region.

The African sun is shining through the coffee-bushes into the dark shed, but we, black and white, sit side by side, and feel that we know by experience the meaning of the words "And all ye are brethren!" Would that my generous friends in Europe could come out here and live through one such hour!

*The face of Jesus
in plaster by 20th-century American
artist Norman LaLiberté*

JESUS, HER PATIENT

Widely admired for her work among the poor of Calcutta and winner of the Nobel Peace Prize in 1979, Mother Teresa by her life exemplifies charity to others as the truest form of serving Jesus. Following is her daily prayer.

DEAREST LORD, may I see you today and every day in the person of your sick, and whilst nursing them minister to you. Though you hide yourself behind the unattractive disguise of the irritable, the exacting, the unreasonable, may I still recognize you and say, "Jesus, my patient, how sweet it is to serve you."

Lord, give me this seeing faith, then my work will never be monotonous. I will ever find joy in humoring the fancies and gratifying the wishes of all sufferers.

O beloved sick, how doubly dear you are to me, when you personify Christ; and what a privilege is mine to be allowed to tend you.

Sweetest Lord, make me appreciative of the dignity of my vocation and its responsibilities. Never permit me to disgrace it by giving way to unkindness or impatience. And, while you are Jesus my patient, deign also to be to me a patient Jesus, bearing with my faults, looking only to my intention, which is to love and serve you in the person of each of your sick.

Lord, increase my faith, bless my effort and work, now and for evermore.

The Last Supper painted in 1955 by the Spanish surrealist Salvador Dali (1904–1989) is among the most admired works in the collection of the National Gallery of Art in Washington, D.C.— formal in composition yet emotionally powerful.

*The face of Jesus in mosaic, a work by the Italian futurist
Gino Severini (1883–1966)*

*And going a little farther he fell on his
face and prayed, "My Father, if it be possible,
let this cup pass from me; nevertheless,
not as I will, but as thou wilt."*

MATTHEW 26:39

BEHIND EVERY SAYING IN THE GOSPELS:
ONE MAN'S EXPERIENCE

*On September 18, 1961, United Nations Secretary-
General Dag Hammarskjöld died in an airplane crash
while on a peacekeeping mission to Africa. A
manuscript he had written in secret was subsequently
published as MARKINGS, a remarkable book of
meditations that revealed what he called
"my negotiations with myself—and with God."
The following entry was written a few
months before his death.*

I DON'T KNOW WHO—or what—put the question,
I don't know when it was put. I don't even
remember answering. But at some moment I
did answer *Yes* to Someone—or Something—
and from that hour I was certain that existence is
meaningful and that, therefore, my life, in self-surren-
der, had a goal. From that moment I have known
what it means "not to look back," and "to take no
thought for the morrow."

Led by the Ariadne's thread of my answer through
the labyrinth of Life, I came to a time and place where
I realized that the Way leads to a triumph which is a
catastrophe, and to a catastrophe which is a triumph,
that the price for committing one's life would be reproach, and that the only elevation possible to man
lies in the depths of humiliation. After that, the word
"courage" lost its meaning, since nothing could be
taken from me.

As I continued along the Way, I learned, step by
step, word by word, that behind every saying in the
Gospels stands *one* man and *one* man's experience.
Also behind the prayer that the cup might pass from
him and his promise to drink it. Also behind each of
the words from the cross.

In the Silence of Prayer, the Presence of Christ

Born into a wealthy Jewish family in Paris, Simone Weil was a staunch opponent of fascism and, when France fell to the Nazis, she joined the Free French government in England. Refusing to eat any more than her countrymen were allotted, she died in 1943, partly from undernourishment. Though drawn to Catholicism by an early mystical experience of Jesus, Weil was never baptized but, as the following letter to a priest reveals, made prayer a part of her daily life.

I MAY SAY THAT NEVER at any moment in my life have I "sought for God." For this reason, which is probably too subjective, I do not like this expression and it strikes me as false. As soon as I reached adolescence, I saw the problem of God as a problem the data of which could not be obtained here below, and I decided that the only way of being sure not to reach a wrong solution, which seemed to me the greatest possible evil, was to leave it alone. So I left it alone. I neither affirmed nor denied.

I knew quite well that my conception of life was Christian. That is why it never occurred to me that I could enter the Christian community. I had the idea that I was born inside. But to add dogma to this conception of life, without being forced to do so by indisputable evidence, would have seemed to me like a lack of honesty. For it seemed to me certain, and I still think so today, that one can never wrestle enough with God if one does so out of pure regard for the truth. Christ likes us to prefer truth to him because, before being Christ, he is truth. If one turns aside from him to go toward the truth, one will not go far before falling into his arms.

Last summer, studying Greek with a friend, I went through the Our Father word for word in Greek. We promised each other to learn it by heart. I do not think he ever did so, but some weeks later, as I was turning over the pages of the Gospel, I said to myself that since I had promised to do this thing and it was good, I ought to do it. I did it. The infinite sweetness of this text so took hold of me that for days I could not stop myself from saying it over all the time.

Since that time I have made a practice of saying it through once each morning with absolute attention. The effect of this practice is extraordinary and sur-prises me every time, for, although I experience it each day, it exceeds my expectation at each subsequent repetition.

At times the very first words tear my thoughts from my body and transport it to a place outside space where there is neither perspective nor point of view. At the same time, filling every part of this infinity of infinity, there is silence, a silence which is not an absence of sound but which is the object of a positive sensation, more positive than that of sound. Sometimes, also, during this recitation or at other moments, Christ is present with me in person, but his presence is infinitely more real, more moving, more clear than on that first occasion when he took possession of my heart and soul.

I have told you that you are like a father to me. But these words only express an apology. Perhaps at bottom they only correspond to a feeling of affection, of gratitude and admiration. For as to the spiritual direction of my soul, I think that God himself has taken it in hand from the start and still looks after it.

> *"When you pray, go into your room and shut the door and pray to your Father, who is in secret; and your Father who sees in secret will reward you."*
> MATTHEW 6:6

The French painter André Derain (1880–1954) was influenced by primitive artists—as can be seen in this Last Supper.

> *When the centurion and those who were*
> *with him, keeping watch over Jesus,*
> *saw the earthquake and what took place,*
> *they were filled with awe, and said,*
> *"Truly this was the Son of God!"*
>
> MATTHEW 27:54

THEY KNEW NOT WHAT THEY DID

Leader of the nonviolent movement for civil rights in the
United States, Martin Luther King, Jr., won the
Nobel Peace Prize four years before his assassination
in 1968. In STRENGTH TO LOVE, *a work published in 1963,*
King revealed what the cross symbolized for him.

VERY TIME I LOOK AT THE CROSS I am reminded of the greatness of God and the redemptive power of Jesus Christ. I am reminded of the beauty of sacrificial love and the majesty of unswerving devotion to truth. It causes me to say with the poet John Bowring:

In the cross of Christ I glory,
Towering o'er the wrecks of time;
All the light of sacred story
Gathers round its head sublime.

But I can never turn my eyes from that cross without also realizing that it symbolizes a strange mixture of greatness and smallness, of good and evil. As I behold that uplifted cross I am reminded not only of the unlimited power of God, but also of the sordid weakness of man. I think not only of the radiance of the divine, but also of the tang of the human. I am reminded not only of Christ at his best, but of man at his worst.

We must see the cross as the magnificent symbol of love conquering hate and of light overcoming darkness. But in the midst of this glowing affirmation, let us never forget that our Lord and Master was nailed to that cross because of human blindness. Those who crucified him knew not what they did.

Faustio Pirandello's painting of Jesus and the two thieves
hangs in the Vatican Museum of Contemporary Christian Art.

CITIZEN OF THE WORLD

No longer of Him be it said,
"He hath no place to lay His head."

In every land a constant lamp
Flames by His small and mighty camp.

There is no strange and distant place
That is not gladdened by His face.

And every nation kneels to hail
The Splendor shining through its veil.

Cloistered beside the shouting street,
Silent, He calls me to His feet.

Imprisoned for His love of me
He makes my spirit greatly free.

And through my lips that uttered sin
The King of Glory enters in.

JOYCE KILMER, 1886–1918

Although painted in oil,
this Crucifixion by Abraham
Rattner (1895–1978) has
the quality of a stained-glass
window. The striking
cubist image belongs to the
Santa Barbara Museum
of Art in California.

*As Jesus passed on from there, he
saw a man called Matthew sitting at the tax
office; and he said to him, "Follow me."*

MATTHEW 9:9

OBEYING A TAP ON THE SHOULDER

*Lacking the education he needed to become a
foreign missionary, Peter Marshall left his native Scotland
for the United States in 1927 and worked at several
jobs before being accepted as a candidate for the ministry.
As a preacher at Washington's historic New York Avenue
Presbyterian Church and as chaplain of the United States
Senate, Marshall gained renown for his sermons, some of
which appeared in 1949 in* MR. JONES, MEET THE MASTER.
In one sermon he spoke of his own calling.

*Two women in a field
of gold cradle the body
of Jesus in this work
by Japanese artist
Tsugouharu Foujita
(1886–1968).*

NOW, IF YOU WERE WALKING down the street, and someone came up behind you and tapped you on the shoulder . . . what would you do? Naturally, you would turn around. Well, that is exactly what happens in the spiritual world.

A man walks on through life—with the external call ringing in his ears but with no response stirring in his heart, and then suddenly, without any warning, the Spirit taps him on the shoulder.

What happens? He turns round. The word "repentance" means "turning round." He repents and believes and is saved.

The "tap on the shoulder" is the almighty power of God acting without help or hindrance upon an elect fallen sinner so as to produce a new creature and lead him into the particular work which God has for him.

God calls men to preach.

How did preaching arise in the first place? By what right does a man stand before his fellows, Bible in hand, and claim their attention?

Not because he is better than they are . . .

Not because he has attended a theological seminary and studied Hebrew . . . Greek . . . and theology.

But primarily because he is obeying a "tap on the shoulder." Because God has whispered to him in the ear and conscripted him for the glorious company of those voices crying in the wilderness of life.

The preacher is conscious of being *called,* as we say, and that means that he is responding to an inward urge that could not be resisted . . . an urge that grew out of a providential arrangement of his life and his circumstances to the great end that he should become an ambassador of the Chief—an urge that grew into a conviction that only by obeying could he ever find that joy and satisfaction of a life lived according to the plan of God.

God brought Moses from minding the sheep . . .

He took Amos from the herds of Tekoa . . .

He beckoned Peter, James, and John from the fishing boats and their nets . . .

From the mills, the factory, and the farm they come . . . From the ranks of mediocrity, or the gutters of sin He calls them . . . changes them . . . and makes them His messengers.

The true minister is in his pulpit not because he has chosen that profession as an easy means of livelihood, but because he could not help it, because he has obeyed a summons that will not be denied.

Such was my tap on the shoulder.

How to Hide Jesus

There are people after Jesus.
They have seen the signs.
Quick, let's hide him.
Let's think;
   carpenter,
   fishermen's friend,
   disturber of religious comfort.
Let's award him a degree in theology,
a purple cassock
and a position of respect.
They'll never think of looking here.
Let's think;
His dialect may betray him,
His tongue is of the masses.
Let's teach him Latin
and seventeenth-century English,
they'll never think of listening in.
Let's think;
   humble,
   Man of Sorrows,
   nowhere to lay his head.
We'll build a house for him,
somewhere away from the poor.
We'll fill it with brass and silence.
It's sure to throw them off.

There are people after Jesus.
Quick, let's hide him.

STEVE TURNER, 1949–

*This pietà—Jesus taken
down from the cross
and placed in his mother's
arms—is characteristic
of the poetic, exuberant
style of the Russian-
born French painter Marc
Chagall (1887–1985).*

> *Thomas said to him, "Lord, we do not know where you are going; how can we know the way?" Jesus said to him, "I am the way, and the truth, and the life; no one comes to the Father, but by me."*
>
> JOHN 14:5–6

JESUS: THE MAN WHO BELONGS TO THE WHOLE WORLD

In the wake of the Second World War, Mohandas K. Gandhi—called Mahatma ("great-souled") by the Hindu people he was to lead to independence—was asked what Jesus meant to him. His answer was published in the popular weekly magazine Liberty.

ALTHOUGH A GREAT PART OF MY LIFE has been devoted to the study of religion and to discussion with religious leaders of all faiths, I know that I cannot avoid seeming presumptuous in writing about the figure of Jesus and trying to explain what significance and meaning he has had for me. I do so solely because I have been told more than once by certain Christian friends that, since I am not a Christian and do not (to quote their exact words) "accept him in my innermost heart as the only-begotten Son of God," I can never realize the full meaning of his teachings, and therefore can never draw upon the greatest source of spiritual strength known to man.

Whether or not this is true in my case, it seems to me to be a mistaken point of view. I believe that it is incompatible with the message that Jesus brought to the world. For he, surely, was the greatest example of one who wished to give to all, to withhold from none, whatever their creed.

I believe that Jesus himself, if he lived among men today, would bless the lives of many who perhaps had never heard his name, if they lived in accordance with the virtues that his life so imperishably illustrated, the virtues of unselfishness and loving kindness toward one's fellow men.

It is this, I think, that above all was important to him, just as it is written in the great book of Chris-tianity—"Not he that crieth Lord, Lord, but he that doeth his will."

What, then, has Jesus meant to me? To me he is a great world teacher. To his followers, he was and is the only-begotten Son of God. Whether or not I accept this, does he affect my life the less? Is all the grandeur of his teaching thus automatically barred from me? I cannot believe so.

The adjective "begotten" has a meaning for me that I like to think is deeper and possibly grander than its literal one. To my mind it implies spiritual birth. My interpretation, in other words, is that in his own life Jesus stood nearest to God. And it is in this sense that I look upon him as the Son of God.

But I believe that there is something of this spirit, which in Jesus was expressed in the fullest measure, in all mankind. I must believe that; if I did not, I would be a cynic, and to be a cynic is to be lifeless, empty; it means that one condemns the whole race of man.

There is every apparent reason for cynicism, certainly, when one beholds the bloody carnage that Europe's aggressors wrought in the Second World War, when one thinks of the misery and suffering spread over the surface of the globe, the pestilence and plague and hunger that inevitably and terribly follow in the wake of warfare. In the face of that, how can one speak seriously of the spirit of the divine in man? Because these acts of terror and bloodshed appall man's conscience; because he knows that they are evil; because, in his innermost heart and mind, he deplores them. And because, when he is not misled, deceived, and corrupted by false leaders and false arguments, man has in his breast an impulse of kindness and compassion, which is the spark of the divine, and which one day, I believe, will be brought forth to the full flowering that is inherent in it.

It is an example of such a flowering that is seen in the figure and life of Jesus. I refuse to believe that there were any who did not profit by his example and by his atoning for their sins, whether or not they consciously realized it.

The lives of all were to some degree, great or small, changed and benefited by his presence, his actions, and the words of his voice.

It is impossible, I think, to weigh the merits of the world's several religions, and unnecessary and pointless even to attempt to do so. But in each one, I believe, there was an original common impulse—the desire to help and to improve the life of all men. I interpret the miracles of Jesus not in a literal sense, which seems to me unimportant, but as the dramatic and unforgettable expression of this impulse, as the most vivid lesson possible to impart—not to pass by the sick and suffering, not to judge those who, in the world's eyes, have sinned, but to forgive them and thus help them to enter a new and better life.

These lessons stand for us today as they stood for the men and women of Jesus' own time.

Jesus gave mankind, in these lessons and in his life, the great goal toward which to aspire. It is because there is such a goal, and because there was such a figure as that of Jesus, that I cannot be pessimistic, but instead am hopeful and confident of the future. And it is because his life has this significance and meaning for me that I do not regard him as belonging to Christianity alone, but rather to the whole world, to all its peoples, no matter under what name they worship.

Paul Gauguin (1848–1903), a modern master of French art, was moved by the spirituality of peasants in Brittany to paint such works as this Crucifixion, in which women in traditional dress kneel at a roadside shrine.

Further Reading

Andersen, Jean Jones. *Encounters at Bethlehem*. New York/ Mahwah, N.J.: Paulist Press, 1985.

Anderson, G. M. *His Mother, A Story of Our Lord*. St. Louis: The Bethany Press, 1930

Anonymous. *By an Unknown Disciple*. New York: George H. Doran Company, 1919.

Asch, Sholem. *The Apostle*. New York: G. P. Putnam's Sons, 1943.

Asch, Sholem. *Mary*. New York: G. P. Putnam's Sons, 1949.

Asch, Sholem. *The Nazarene*. New York: G. P. Putnam's Sons, 1939.

Austin, Mary. *The Green Bough*. New York: Doubleday & Co., 1913

Barclay, William. *The Master's Men*. London: SCM Press Ltd., 1959.

Bishop, Jim. *The Day Christ Died*. New York: Harper & Brothers, 1957.

Bishop, Jim. *The Day Christ Was Born*. New York: Harper & Brothers, 1959/1960.

Bonser, Edna Madison. *The Little Boy of Nazareth*. New York: Harper & Brothers, 1930.

Borden, Mary. *King of the Jews*. Boston: Little, Brown, and Company, 1935

Brownrigg, Ronald. *The Twelve Apostles*. London: Weidenfeld and Nicolson, 1974.

Buck, Pearl S. *The Story Bible*. Edinburgh: Bartholomew House Ltd., 1971.

Buckmaster, Henrietta. *Paul: A Man Who Changed History*. New York: McGraw-Hill Book Company, 1965.

Buechner, Frederick. *Peculiar Treasures*. New York: Harper & Row, Publishers, 1979.

Caldwell, Taylor, and Jess Stearn. *I, Judas*. New York: Atheneum, 1977.

Clark, Thomas Curtis, ed. *The Master of Men, Quotable Poems About Jesus*. New York: Richard R. Smith, Inc., 1930.

Cross, Colin. *Who Was Jesus?* New York: Atheneum, 1970.

Darton, Alice W. *His Mother*. New York: The Macmillan Company, 1927.

Douglas, Lloyd C. *The Big Fisherman*. Boston: Houghton Mifflin Company, 1948.

Douglas, Lloyd C. *The Robe*. Boston: Houghton Mifflin Company, 1942.

Daniel-Rops. *Jesus and His Times*. New York: E. P. Dutton & Co., Inc., 1954.

Davie, Donald, ed. *The New Oxford Book of Christian Verse*. Oxford/New York: Oxford University Press, 1981.

Dickens, Charles. *The Life of Our Lord*. London: Associated Newspapers Ltd., 1934.

Edwards, R. A. *The Upper Room*. London: Methuen & Co. Ltd., 1941.

Farrar, Frederic W. *Life of Christ*. Grand Rapids, Mich.: Zondervan Publishing House, 1949.

Fleg, Edmond. *Jesus*. New York: E. P. Dutton & Co., 1935.

Gibran, Kahlil. *Jesus, The Son of Man*. New York: Alfred A. Knopf, 1928

Goodspeed, Edgar J. *A Life of Jesus*. New York: Harper & Brothers, Publishers, 1950.

Goudge, Elizabeth. *God So Loved the World*. New York: Coward-McCann, Inc., 1951.

Goudge, Elizabeth. *The Well of the Star*. New York: Coward-McCann, Inc. 1941.

Holland, J. G., ed. *Christ and the Twelve*. Springfield, Mass.: Bill, Nichols & Company, 1871.

Holmes, Marjorie. *The Messiah*. New York: Harper & Row, Publishers, 1987.

Holmes, Marjorie. *Three from Galilee*. New York: Harper & Row, Publishers, 1985.

Holmes, Marjorie. *Two from Galilee*. Old Tappan, N.J.: Fleming H. Revell Company, 1972

Jacobs, Joseph. *Jesus as Others Saw Him*. New York: Bernard G. Richards Co., Inc., 1925.

Kagawa, Toyohiko. *Behold the Man*. New York and London: Harper & Brothers, 1941.

Kennedy, Charles W., trans. *Early English Christian Poetry*. London: Hollis & Carter, 1952.

Kirkland, Winifred. *Discovering the Boy of Nazareth*. New York: The Macmillan Co., 1944

Komroff, Manuel. *In the Years of Our Lord*. New York: Harper & Brothers, 1942.

Leonard, William Ellery. *The Poet of Galilee*. New York: B. W. Huebsch, 1909.

Lawson, James Gilchrist, ed. *The Best Loved Religious Poems*. New York: Fleming H. Revell Company, 1933.

Luther, Martin. *Luther's Meditations on the Gospels* (Translated and arranged by Roland H. Bainton) Philadelphia: The Westminster Press, 1962.

Marshall, Peter. *Mr. Jones, Meet the Master*. New York: Fleming H. Revell Company, 1949/1950.

Marshall, Peter. *The First Easter*. New York: McGraw-Hill Book Company, Inc., 1959.

Martin, James. *The Empty Tomb*. New York: Harper & Brothers, Publishers, 1960.

Mauriac, François. *Life of Jesus*. New York/Toronto: Longmans, Green and Co., 1937.

Mauriac, François. *The Son of Man*. London: Burns & Oates, 1960.

Maus, Cynthia Pearl. *Christ and the Fine Arts*. New York and London: Harper & Brothers, 1938.

Miller, Rex. *I, Paul: An Autobiography of the Apostle to the Gentiles*. New York: Duell, Sloan and Pearce, 1940.

Mills, James R. *The Gospel According to Pontius Pilate*. San Francisco: San Francisco Book Company, 1977.

Morrison, James Dalton, ed. *Masterpieces of Religious Verse*. New York: Harper & Brothers, 1948.

Nazhivin, Ivan. *According to Thomas*. New York and London: Harper & Brothers, 1930.

O'Shea, Denis. *The First Christmas*. Milwaukee: The Bruce Publishing Company, 1952.

Oursler, Fulton. *The Greatest Story Ever Told*. New York: Doubleday, 1949.

Payne, Robert. *The Lord Jesus*. London/New York/Toronto: Abelard-Schuman, 1964.

Paul, Leslie. *Son of Man, The Life of Christ*. New York: E. P. Dutton & Co., Inc., 1961.

Phelps, Elizabeth Stuart. *The Story of Jesus Christ*. Boston and New York: Houghton, Mifflin and Company, 1897.

Poteat, Edwin McNeill. *These Shared His Passion, Cross and Power*. New York: Harper & Brothers, 1948.

Sayers, Dorothy L. *The Man Born to Be King*. New York: Harper & Brothers, 1943.

Sheen, Fulton J. *Life of Christ*. New York/Toronto/London: McGraw-Hill Book Company, Inc., 1958.

Slack, Elvira, ed. *Christ in the Poetry of Today*. New York: The Womans Press, 1928.

Spencer, Bonnell. *They Saw the Lord*. New York: Morehouse-Gorham Co., 1947.

Steinmann, Jean. *The Life of Jesus*. Boston/Toronto: Little, Brown and Company, 1963

Wagenknecht, Edward. *The Story of Jesus in the World's Literature*. New York: Creative Age Press, Inc., 1946.

Wallace, Lew. *Ben-Hur: A Tale of the Christ*. New York: Harper & Brothers, 1880

Wallis, Charles L., ed. *A Treasury of Poems for Worship and Devotion*. New York: Harper & Brothers, 1959.

Walsh, Thomas, ed. *The World's Great Catholic Poetry*. New York: The Macmillan Company, 1940.

Madonna and child by Raphael

Illustration Credits

Picture research by Carousel Research, Inc.

2, Paolo Veronese, Last Supper, 16th century, Pinacoteca di Brera, Milan, Art Resource/Scala; 4, Initial Q with angel appearing to Zechariah and birth of Jesus, c. 1000, Pierpont Morgan Library, New York, Ms. 333, fol. 51r; 6, left, Hanging triptych showing the Nativity (center cameo, Italian 13th century), gold and enamel, French 15th century, Cleveland Museum of Art; 6, right, Duccio di Buoninsegna, The Nativity, c. 1308-1311, National Gallery of Art, Washington, DC, Andrew W. Mellon Collection; 7, left, Adoration of the Magi, 16th century, Museo Lazaro Galdiano, Madrid, Art Resource/Giraudon; 7, right, Cope fastening with Annunciation, Cathedral Treasury, Aachen, Art Resource/Scala; 8, left, Vicenzo Campi, Christ Disputing Among the Doctors, 16th century, S. Bartolomeo, Busseto, Art Resource/Scala; 8, right, Paolo Veronese, Baptism of Christ, 16th century, Galleria Palatina, Florence, Art Resource/Alinari; 9, left, Duccio di Buoninsegna, Calling of the Apostles Peter and Andrew, c. 1308-1311, National Gallery of Art, Washington, DC, Samuel H. Kress Collection; 9, right, Jean Fouquet, Mary Magdalene at the Feast of Simon, Hours of Etienne Chevalier, 15th century, Musée Condé, Chantilly, Art Resource/Giraudon; 10, left, Lorenzo Lippi, Christ and the Samaritan Woman at the Well, 1644, Kunsthistorisches Museum, Vienna, Artothek; 10, right, Workshop of Giorgio Andreoli, Prodigal Son amid the Swine, 16th century, The Metropolitan Museum of Art, Robert Lehman Collection, 1975; 11, left, Ford Madox Brown, Christ Washing the Apostle's Feet, 19th century, Tate Gallery, London, Art Resource/Tate Gallery, London; 11, right, Limoges enamel plaque showing Christ at the Praetorium, 16th century, Bargello, Florence, Art Resource/Giraudon; 12, left, El Greco, Christ Carrying the Cross, 16th century, Museo di Arte Catalana, Barcelona, Art Resource/Scala; 12, center, Agnolo Bronzino, Deposition from the Cross, 16th century, Musée des Beaux-Arts, Besançon, Art Resource/Giraudon; 12, right, Taddeo Gaddi, The Resurrection, 14th century, Accademia, Florence, Art Resource/Scala; 13, left, Enamel plaque with Jesus blessing, 13th century, Musée Dobrée, Nantes, Art Resource/Giraudon; 13, center, Mathieu Le Nain, Supper at Emmaus, 17th century, Louvre, Paris, Art Resource/Scala; 13, right, The Pentecost from the Hours of François de Guise, 1350-1400, Musée Condé, Chantilly, Art Resource/Giraudon; 14, Georges Rouault, Christ on the Cross, 20th Century, Private Collection, Bridgeman Art Library; 15, Reliquary Shrine of the Virgin and Child, 1325-1350, The Metropolitan Museum of Art, The Cloisters Collection, 1962. Photograph by Malcolm Varon.

THE MESSIAH

16, Tree of Jesse, 15th century, church of St. Lazare, Autun, Art Resource/Scala; 18, German enamel reliquary with cupola, 1180-1190, Victoria and Albert Museum, London; 19, Mosaic showing Isaiah, sixth century, San Vitale, Ravenna, Art Resource/Scala; 20, Annunciation, Visitation and Nativity, Ingeburg Psalter, 13th century, Musée Condé, Chantilly, Ms. 9/1965, Art Resource/Giraudon; 21, Matthias Grünewald, Isenheim altarpiece showing the Annunciation with Isaiah, c.1515, Musée d'Unterlinden, Colmar, Art Resource/Scala; 22, left, Hannah at prayer from the St. Albans Psalter, 12th century, Dombibliothek, Hildesheim, HS G 1; 22, right, Fra Bartolommeo (Baccio della Porta), Adoration, late 15th-early 16th century, Villa Borghese, Rome, Art Resource/Scala; 23, Giotto di Bondone, Flight into Egypt, early 14th century, S. Francesco, Assisi, Art Resource/Scala; 24, Masaccio (Tommaso Guidi), St. Peter baptizing the neophytes, 15th century, Chiesa del Carmine, Florence, Art Resource/Scala; 25, Gathering manna and the Last Supper, Mirror of Human Salvation Manuscript, 15th century, Musée Condé, Chantilly, Ms. 139 (1363), fol. 17v., Art Resource/Giraudon; 26, Fra Angelico, Vision of Ezekiel, 15th century, Museo San Marco, Florence, Art Resource/Scala; 27, Portraits of the four Evangelists from the Gospels of the Abbey of Cisoing, Mid-12th century, Bibliothèque Municipale, Lille, Ms. 479, Art Resource/Giraudon; 28, Arrest of Jesus, S. Francesco, Assisi, Art Resource/Scala; 29, left, Crucifixion from a Psalter (Psalm 22), British Library, London, Ms. Harley 2895, fol. 17r; 29, right, Giotto di Bondone, Crucifix, early 14th century, S. Maria Novella, Florence, Art Resource/Scala; 30, Psalter initial showing the Resurrection of Jesus and Jonah emerging from the big fish (Psalm 69), British Library, London, Ms. Add. 54179, fol. 59v; 31, Tree of Jesse from the Ingeburg Psalter, 13th century, Musée Condé, Chantilly, Ms. 9/1965, Art Resource/Giraudon.

THE NATIVITY

32, Sandro Botticelli, The Mystic Nativity, 1500, National Gallery, London; 34, Andrea Pisano, The South Gate, 1330, Baptistery, Florence, Art Resource/Scala; 35, Domenico Ghirlandaio, Angel Appearing to Zechariah, late 15th century, S. Maria Novella, Florence, Art Resource/Scala; 36, left, Inscription from Second Temple, By courtesy of the Israel Department of Antiquities and Museums; 36, right, Model of Second Temple, Zev Radovan, Jerusalem; 37, Gospel Book of St. Bernward, early 11th century, Hildesheim Cathedral Treasury; 38, Angel, 17th century, Lee Boltin; 39, Antoine Dufour, manuscript page, Lives of Celebrated Women, 1505, Musée Dobrée, ms. 17, fol. 2, Art Resource/Giraudon; 40, top, Manuscript page of missal, Museo Horne, Florence, Art Resource/Scala; 40, bottom, Limousin angel plaque, 12-13th century, Palazzo Venezia, Rome, Art Resource/Scala; 41, Andrea della Robbia, The Annunciation, 15th century, La Verna Sanctuary, Art Resource/Scala; 42, Melozzo da Forli, The Annunciation, 15th century, Pantheon, Rome, Art Resource/Nimatallah; 43, top, Ivory plaque from casket, 11th century, Bargello Museum, Florence, Art Resource/SEF; 43, bottom, Dante Gabriel Rossetti, Ecce Ancilla Domini (Annunciation), 1849, Tate Gallery, London, Art Resource/Tate Gallery; 44, Raphael, The Betrothal, 1504, Brera Gallery, Milan, Art Resource/Scala; 45, Jewish marriage contract, 18th century, Zev Radovan, Jerusalem; 46, Joseph's Dream, 12th century, Bayerische Staatsbibliothek, Munich, CLM 15903, fol. 5v; 47, Fra Angelico, Marriage of the Virgin, 15th century, Prado Museum, Madrid, Art Resource/Scala; 48, Master of the Life of Mary, Marriage of the Virgin, 15th century, Alte Pinakothek, Munich, Art Resource/Scala, 50, The Visitation, c. 1310, The Metropolitan Museum of Art, Gift of J. Pierpont Morgan, 1917; 51, Tapestry, Life of the Virgin, 16th century, Cathedral St. Sauveur, Aix-en-Provence, Art Resource/Lauros-Giraudon; 52, Coptic Textile, Nativity and Visitation, sixth century, Bridgeman Art Library; 53, Andrea della Robbia, The Visitation, S. Giovanni Fourcivitas, Pistoia, Art Resource/Scala; 54, Francesco Granacci, scenes from the Life of Saint John the Baptist, late 15th-early 16th century, The Metropolitan Museum of Art, Gwynne Andrews, Harris Brisbane Dick, Dodge, Fletcher, and Rogers Funds, funds from various donors, Ella Morris Depeyster Gift, Mrs. Donald Oenslager Gift, and gifts in memory of Robert Lehman, 1970. (1970.134.1); 55, Fra Angelico, Inscribing the Name of John the Baptist, 15th century, Museo S. Marco, Florence, Art Resource/Scala; 56, left, St. John the Baptist in the Desert, Bibliothèque Nationale, Paris, lat. 18014, fol. 208; 56, right, Fra Filippo Lippi, detail from The Story of John the Baptist, 15th century, Duomo, Prato, Art Resource/Scala; 57, top, One of the "Bar Cohba" Letters, Zev Radovan, Jerusalem; 57, bottom, View of Qumran, Zev Radovan, Jerusalem; 58, Census Taking, Bayerische Staatsbibliothek, Munich, CLM 15713, fol. 3r; 59, Pieter Brueghel the elder, Census of Bethlehem, 16th century, Royal Museum, Brussels, Art Resource/Scala; 60, left, Tree of Jesse, mid-12th century, Douai, Bibliothèque Municipale, Art Resource/Giraudon; **60, center,** Tree of Jesse, Bayerische Staatsbibliothek, Munich, CLM 15711, fol. 31v; **61,** Mary and Joseph Taxed, Corpus Christi College Library, Oxford, MS. C.C.C. 410, fol 13r; **62-63,** Codex Aureus of Echternach, 11th century, Germanisches Nationalmuseum Nürnberg, fol. 18v, fol. 19r; **64,** Virgin and Child, late 13th century, Freiburg im Breisgau, Art Resource/Giraudon; **65, center,** Enamel and gold cross showing the Nativity, sixth to eighth century, Biblioteca, Vatican, Art Resource/Scala; **65, right,** Byzantine ivory statuette of the Virgin and Child, 11th century, The Metropolitan Museum of Art, Lee Boltin; **66, top,** Russian icon of the Virgin and Child, private collection, Laurie Platt Winfrey, Inc.; **66, bottom left,** African wooden statuette of the Madonna and Child, 20th century, Collection Maurice Lavanoux, Lee Boltin; **66, bottom right,** Chinese ivory statuette of the Madonna and Child, 19th century, Church of Notre-Dame, Huy, Lee Boltin; **67,** Korean painting of Madonna and Child, 19th century, Maryknoll Sisters' Museum, Lee Boltin; **68,** The Nativity, 12th century, Museo Arte Catalana, Barcelona, Art Resource/Scala; **69, center,** Limoges enamel plaque, 13th century, Musée Départemental, Rouen, Art Resource/Giraudon; **69, corners,** Symbols of Evangelists, Golden Altar, c. 1020, Cathedral, Aachen, Art Resource/D.Y.; **70,** Jean Fouquet, Adoration of the Shepherds, Hours of Etienne Chevalier, 15th century, Musée Condé, Chantilly, Art Resource/Giraudon; **71, top,** Pol de Limbourg, Nativity, Trés Riches Heures du Duc de Berry, 15th century, Musée Condé, Chantilly, fol. 44v, Art Resource/Giraudon; **71, bottom,** Annunciation to the Shepherds, Ingeburg Psalter, 13th century, Musée Condé, Chantilly, Ms. 9/1965, fol. 16v, Art Resource/Giraudon; **72,** Annunciation to the Shepherds, The Playfair Book of Hours, Victoria and Albert Museum, London, Ms. L 475-1918, fol. 64r, Art Resource/Victoria and Albert Museum; **73,** Georges de La Tour, The Adoration of the Shepherds, 17th century, Louvre, Paris, Art Resource/Scala; **74,** Charles Le Brun, Adoration of the Shepherds, 17th century, Louvre, Paris, Art Resource/Scala; **75,** Sano di Pietro, Annunciation to the Shepherds, 15th century, Pinacoteca, Siena, Art Resource/Scala; **76,** Rembrandt van Rijn, Adoration of the Shepherds with the Lamp, c. 1654, Art Resource/Marburg; **77,** Martin Schongauer, Birth of Christ, 15th century, Art Resource/Marburg; **78, left,** Silvestro dei Gherarducci and his workshop, gradual manuscript showing the Nativity in an initial P, late 14th century, Pierpont Morgan Library, M. 653.1; **78, right,** and **79, top and bottom,** Details of musicians from a choral manuscript, Biblioteca Nazionale, Naples, Ms. VA 14F, fol. 47r, Art Resource/Scala; **80,** Federico Barocci, The Circumcision, 1590, Louvre, Paris, Art Resource/Scala; **81,** Fra Angelico, The Presentation in the Temple, 15th century, Prado, Madrid, Art Resource/Scala; **82,** Epigraph of Adoration, Galleria Lapidaria, Vatican, Art Resource/Scala; **83,** Stained glass of Journey of the Magi, c.1200, Canterbury, Cathedral, Art Resource/Manu Sassoonian; **84,** Albrecht Altdorfer, The Adoration of the Magi, late 15th–early 16th century, Städelsches Kunstinstitut und Städtische Galerie, Frankfurt, Artothek; **85, top,** Domenico Ghirlandaio, Adoration of the Magi, late 15th century, Uffizi, Florence, Art Resource/Alinari-AGC; **85, bottom,** Adoration of the Magi, Duomo, Cividale del Friuli, Art Resource/Scala; **86,** Sandro Botticelli, Adoration of the Magi, 15th century, Uffizi, Florence, Art Resource/Scala; **87,** Girolamo da Cremona, Adoration of the Magi, Duomo libreria Piccolomini, Siena, Art Resource/Scala; **88,** Three Kings, Mexican folk art, Lee Boltin; **89, top left,** Astrological map, New York Public Library; **89, top right,** Sadao Watanabe, Nativity, 1970, Vatican Museum of Contemporary Christian Art, Lee Boltin; **89, bottom,** Annunciation to the Magi, 14th century, Sant'Abbondio, Como, Art Resource/Scala; **90, left,** Ivory plaque, dream of Joseph, ninth century, Musée Départemental, Rouen, Art Resource/Giraudon; **90, right,** Book of Hours, 14th century, Victoria and Albert Museum, London, Art Resource/Bridgeman; **91,** Massacre of the Innocents, 1491, Bayerische Staatsbibliothek, Munich, Art Resource/Marburg; **92, left,** Massacre of the Innocents, early 13th century, Bibliothèque Municipale, Rouen, Art Resource/Giraudon; **92, right,** Giovanni Pisano, Massacre of the Innocents, early 14th century, Duomo, Pisa, Art Resource/Scala; **93,** Ceramic plate, Massacre of the Innocents, 1566, Bargello Museum, Florence, Art Resource/Nimatallah.

THE HIDDEN YEARS

94, Simone Martini, Christ Discovered in the Temple, 14th century, Walker Art Gallery, Liverpool, Bridgeman Art Library; **96,** Bartoleme Esteban Murillo, The Flight into Egypt, 17th century, Detroit Institute of Arts, Bridgeman Art Library; **97, left,** Vittore Carpaccio, The Flight into Egypt, c. 1500, National Gallery of Art, Washington, DC; **97, right,** The Flight into Egypt, 13th century, Museo Bargello, Florence, Art Resource/SEF; **98, top left,** José Rafael Aragón, The Flight into Egypt, 19th century, Museum of International Folk Art, Santa Fe, bequest of Charles D. Carroll.; **98, top right,** The Sacred Family, Graphische Sammlung Albertina, Vienna, Art Resource/Nimatallah; **98, bottom,** Rembrandt van Rijn, The Flight into Egypt: Crossing a Rill, 1654, Pallant House, Chichester, Bridgeman Art Library; **99,** Miracle of the Palm Tree, 15th-16th century, The Metropolitan Museum of Art, Rogers Fund (38.184); **100,** Nicolas Poussin, The Rest on the Flight into Egypt, 17th century, Hermitage, Leningrad, Bridgeman Art Library; **101,** Guido Reni, The Flight into Egypt, late 16th-early 17th century, Bradford City Art Gallery & Museums, Bridgeman Art Library; **102,** Map of the world, Bibliothèque Nationale, Paris, Art Resource/Giraudon; **103,** Joseph's dream from the Codex Egberti, 10th century, Stadtbibliothek, Trier, fol. 12 v; **104,** Sir John Everett Millais, Christ in the House of His Parents, 19th century, Tate Gallery, London, Bridgeman Art Library; **105,** Georges de La Tour, Joseph the Carpenter, 17th century, Louvre, Paris, Art Resource/Scala; **106,** The Fallen Idols, Bibliothèque Nationale, Paris, ms. lat. 2688, fol. 17; **107,** John Rogers Herbert, Youth of our Lord, 19th century, Guildhall Art Gallery, London, Bridgeman Art Library; **108,** Christ Among the Doctors, c. 1500-1510, The Metropolitan Museum of Art, Gift of J. Pierpont Morgan, (16.32.218); **109,** Christ among the doctors, Historisches Museum, Basel; **110,** Raphael, Story of Moses, Parting of the Red Sea, early 16th century, Vatican, Art Resource/Scala; **111,** William Holman Hunt, The Finding of the Saviour in the Temple, 19th century, Birmingham City Art Gallery, Bridgeman Art Library; **112,** Christ in the Temple, Naumburg Cathedral, Art Resource/Scala; **113, top,** Christ with the Doctors, 12th century, San Marco, Venice, Art Resource/SEF; **113, bottom,** Giovanni di Paolo, The Child Jesus Disputing in the Temple, 15th century, Isabella Stewart Gardner Museum, Boston, Art Resource/ISG; **114,** William C. T. Dobson, Jesus Returning to Nazareth with His Parents, 19th century, Tate Gallery, London, Art Resource/Tate Gallery; **115,** Rembrandt van Rijn, Christ Between His Parents, Returning from the Temple, 1654, The Metropolitan Museum of Art, Bequest of Mrs. H.O. Havemeyer (29.107.7); **116,** Carolingian ivory bookcover plaque, ninth century, Victoria and Albert Museum, Art Resource/Victoria and Albert Museum.

HIS MINISTRY ON EARTH

118, Carl Vogel von Vogelstein, Suffer the Little Children Come Unto Me, Gallerie d'Arte Moderne, Florence, Art Resource/AGC; **120,** Domenico Veneziano, Saint John in the Desert, c. 1445, National Gallery of Art, Washington, DC, Samuel C. Kress Collection; **121,** Donatello, St. John the Baptist, Chiesa dei Frari, Venice, Art Resource/Scala; **122,** Fra Filippo Lippi, detail from The Story of St. John the Baptist, 15th century, Duomo, Prato, Art Resource/Scala; **123,** Andrea Pisano, The South Gate, 1330, Baptistery, Florence, Art Resource/Scala; **124, top,** St. John the Baptist, 17th century, Kremlin, Moscow, Art Resource/Beniaminson; **124, bottom,** Mosan enamel plaque showing the Baptism of Christ, 12th century, The Metropolitan Museum of Art, Gift of J. Pierpont Morgan, (17.190.430); **125,** Baptism of Christ shown in the cupola mosaics, Baptistery, Ravenna, Art Resource/Scala; **126,** Giotto di Bondone, The Baptism of Christ, early 14th century, Scrovegni Chapel, Padua, Art Resource/Scala; **127, left,** Baptismal font, 12th century, Hildesheim Cathedral, Diözesanmuseum Hildesheim; **127, right,** Ivory pastoral staff showing the Baptism of Christ, Museo dell'Opera Metropolitana, Siena, Art Resource/Scala; **128, top,** Piero Della Francesca, The Baptism of Christ, 15th century, National Gallery, London, Bridgeman Art Library; **128, bottom,** Coptic manuscript showing the Baptism of Christ, Bibliothèque Nationale, Paris; **129,** Pupil of Veit Stoss, wood sculpture of the Baptism of Christ, 15th century, The Metropolitan Museum of Art, Rogers Fund (12.130.1); **130,** Ottavio Vannini, The Baptism of Christ, 17th century, Musée des Beaux-Arts, Nantes, Bridgeman Art Library; **131**, Ann Johnson, Baptisam of Our Savour, c. 1840, Abby Aldrich Rockefeller Folk Art Center, Williamsburg; **132**, Manuscript depicting the temptation of Jesus and Daniel before the god Bel, 15th century, Musée Condé, Chantilly Ms. 139, fol. 14v., Art Resource/Giraudon; **133**, Paolo Veronese, The Baptism and Temptation of Christ, 16th century, Brera Gallery, Milan, Art Resource/Scala; **134**, Desert near Sinai, Zev Radovan, Jerusalem; **135**, Temptation of Christ, 1491, Staatsbibliothek, Munich, Art Resource/Marburg; **136**, Codex Aureus of Echternach, 11th century, Germanisches Nationalmuseum Nürnberg, fol. 20r; **137**, James Joseph Jacques Tissot, Christ Borne up Unto a Pinnacle of the Temple, 19th century, Superstock; **138**, Hans Suess von Kulmbach, The Calling of Peter, late 15th-early 16th century, Uffizi, Florence, Art Resource/AGC; **139**, Domenico Ghirlandaio, The Calling of Peter and Andrew, 1481-82, Sistine Chapel, Rome, Art Resource/Scala; **140**, Historiated initial showing the Baptism and Temptation of Jesus and the calling of the Apostles, Bibliothèque Nationale, Paris, Ms. lat. 16746, fol. 28v; **141, top**, Sadao Watanabe, The Calling of Peter and Paul, 1970, Lee Boltin; **141, bottom**, Mosaic showing the calling of Peter and Andrew, S. Apollinare Nuovo, Ravenna, Art Resource/Scala; **142, left**, Silver and gilt chalice showing Apostles, 1230-1250, The Metropolitan Museum of Art, The Cloisters Collection (47.101.26); **142, right**, Ivory showing Christ with the twelve Apostles, sixth century, Musée des Beaux-Arts, Dijon, Art Resource/Giraudon; **143**, Michelangelo Mersis da Caravaggio, The Calling of St. Matthew, 1599-1602, S. Luigi dei Francesi, Rome, Art Resource/Scala; **144**, Juan de Flandes, The Marriage Feast at Cana, 16th century, The Metropolitan Museum of Art, The Jack and Belle Linsky Collection (1982.60.20); **145**, Wedding at Cana, 1491, Staatsbibliothek, Munich, Art Resource/Marburg; **146**, Duccio di Buoninsegna, the wedding at Cana, predella panel, c. 1311, Duomo, Siena, Art Resource/Scala; **147**, Ivory plaque depicting the wedding at Cana, 11th century, Schlossmuseum Treasury, Berlin, Art Resource/Marburg; **148**, Master of the Catholic Kings, The Marriage of Cana, c. 1495/97, National Gallery of Art, Washington, DC, Samuel H. Kress Collection; **149, top**, Ivory plaque showing the wedding at Cana from the throne of Archbishop Maximian, 545-56, Museo Arcivescovile, Ravenna, Art Resource/Scala; **149, bottom**, Tapestry with the wedding at Cana, 16th century, Musée des Tissus, Lyon, Art Resource/SEF; **150, top**, Synagogue at Capernaum, 4th century, Israel, Art Resource/SEF; **150, bottom**, Silver and gilt megillah, 18th century (South Russia), Judaica Collection of Max Berger, Vienna, Erich Lessing/Magnum; **151**, Durs Rudy, Jesus and the Disciples, c. 1810, Rare Book Department, Free Library of Philadelphia; **152**, Holkham Picture Bible, British Museum Library, London add. ms. 47682, fol 22v.; **153, top**, Byzantine manuscript, Biblioteca Vaticano, Rome, gr. 1613, p. 1, Menologium of Basil II; **153, bottom**, Codex Aureus of Echternach, 11th century, Germanisches Nationalmuseum Nürnberg, fol. 19v; **159**, Rembrandt van Rijn, Christ Healing the Sick, 17th century, Victoria and Albert Museum, London, Art Resource/Victoria and Albert Museum; **160**, Raphael, The Healing of the Paralytic, 16th century, Ducale Palace, Mantua, Art Resource/Scala; **161, left**, The Healing of the Paralytic at Capernaum, c. 1520-1525, The Metropolitan Museum of Art, Gift of Mrs. Henry Goldman, 1944; **161, right**, Healing of the Paralytic, sixth century, S. Apollinare Nuovo, Ravenna, Art Resource/Scala; **162**, J. Bridges, Christ Healing the Mother of Simon Peter, 19th century, Agnew & Sons, London, Bridgeman Art Library; **164**, Medical instruments, Museo Nazionale Atestino, Este, Art Resource/Scala; **165**, Ivory diptych showing the miracles of Jesus, c. 450-460, Victoria and Albert Museum, London; **166, top**, Healing of the leper, ninth century, Universitätsbibliothek, Düsseldorf, Ms. Cod. B 113, fol. 5r, Alexander Glaser; **166, bottom**, Codex Egberti, 10th century, Stadtbibliothek, Trier, fol. 21v; **167**, Nicolas Poussin, Christ Healing the Blind of Jericho, 17th century, Louvre, Paris, Art Resource/Giraudon/EPA; **168**, Master of the Darmstädter Passion, Christ Raises the Widow's Son at Nain, 15th century, Bayerische Staatsgemäldesammlungen, Munich, Artothek; **169**, Golden Gospel Book of Henry III, 11th century, Escorial, Madrid, cod. Vitr. 17, fol. 30r., Archiv für Kunst und Geschichte, Berlin; **170, left**, Limbourg Brothers, Trés Riches Heures du Duc de Berry, 15th century, Musée Condé, Chantilly, fol. 164r, Art Resource/Giraudon; **170, right**, Healing the woman with the issue of blood, sixth century, S. Apollinare Nuovo, Ravenna, Art

Resource/Scala; **172, top**, Gospels of Otto III, late 10th century, Bayerische Staatsbibliothek, Munich, CLM 4453, fol. 44r; **172, bottom**, Giovanni Domenico Tiepolo, Jesus in the House of Jairus, c. 1790-1804, The Art Institute of Chicago, restricted gift of Mrs. Tiffany Blake; **173**, George Percy Jacomb-Hood, The Raising of Jairus' Daughter, late 19th-early 20th century, Guildhall Art Gallery, London, Bridgeman Art Library; **174**, Mary Magdalene in Prayer, 17th century, The Metropolitan Museum of Art, Gift of Irwin Untermyer, 1964; **175**, Maestro Giorgio Andreoli, Mary Magdalene Anointing the Feet of Christ in the House of Simon the Pharisee, 1528, The Metropolitan Museum of Art, Robert Lehman Collection, 1975; **176**, Giovanni da Milano, Jesus in the Pharisee's House, mid 14th century, Rinuccini Chapel of S. Croce, Florence, Art Resource/Scala; **177**, Imitator of Dirk Bouts, Christ in the House of Simon, early 16th century, City of York Art Gallery, Bridgeman Art Library; **178**, Holkham Picture Bible, British Museum Library, London add. ms. 47682, fol 20v.; **179**, Virgil Solis, 16th century; **180**, Sainte Chapelle Lectionary, c. 1280, British Library, London, Additional Ms. 17341, fol 41a, Art Resource/Marburg; **181, left**, J. Schnorr von Carolsfeld, Jesus and the Samaritan Woman, 19th century, Art Resource/Marburg; **181, right**, Rembrandt van Rijn, Christ with the Samaritan Woman, 17th century, Art Resource/Marburg; **182, left**, The Samaritan Pentateuch, 16th century, Zev Radovan, Jerusalem; **182, right**, Gerizim, ruins of Samaritan temple, Zev Radovan, Jerusalem; **183**, Giovanni Domenico Tiepolo, Christ and the Samaritan Woman, private collection, Bridgeman Art Library; **184**, Gustave Moreau, Salome, 19th century, private collection, Bridgeman Art Library; **185**, Andrea Pisano, Beheading of St. John, The South Gate, 1330, Baptistery, Florence, Art Resource/Scala; **186, left**, Michelangelo Merisi da Caravaggio, The Beheading of St. John the Baptist, 1608, Valletta Cathedral, Malta, Art Resource/Scala; **186, right**, Donatello, Herod's Feast, late 14th-early 15th century, church of S. Giovanni, Siena, Bridgeman Art Library; **187, top**, Sea of Tiberias, Marvin Newman; **187, bottom**, Coins from time of Herod Antipas, Zev Radovan, Jerusalem; **188**, Lorenzo Monaco, Herod's Banquet, late 14th-early 15th century, Louvre, Paris, Bridgeman Art Library; **189**, Titian, Salome with the Head of John the Baptist, 16th century, private collection, Bridgeman Art Library; **190**, Gerino da Pistoia, Multiplication of the Loaves, S. Lucchese, Poggibonsi, Art Resource/Scala; **191, top**, Liberale da Verona or Giralomo da Cremona, Multiplication of the loaves and fish from a choral book, Piccolomini Library, Duomo, Siena, Art Resource/Scala; **191, bottom**, Limbourg Brothers, Trés Riches Heures du Duc de Berry, 15th century, Musée Condé, Chantilly, fol. 158v, Art Resource/Giraudon; **192**, Multiplication of the loaves and fish, Victoria and Albert Museum, Art Resource/Victoria and Albert Museum; **193**, Christ walking on the sea, c. 1260, Hofbibliothek Aschaffenburg, cod. 13, fol. 29, Hofbibliothek Aschaffenburg/Foto Fuchs; **194**, Jacopo Tintoretto, Christ at the Sea of Galilee, 16th century, Superstock; **195, left**, J. Schnorr von Carolsfeld, The Sinking Peter, 19th century, Art Resource/Marburg; **195, right**, Sea of Galilee, Richard T. Nowitz; **196**, Rembrandt van Rijn, The Storm on the Sea of Galilee, 17th century, Isabella Stewart Gardner Museum, Boston, Art Resource/ISG; **197, top**, Storm at sea, 1491, Bayerische Staatsbibliothek, Munich, Art Resource/Marburg; **197, bottom**, Gospels of Abbess Hitda von Meschede, Hessisches Landesmuseum Darmstadt, Ms. 1640, fol. 117; **199**, Raphael, The Miraculous Draught of Fishes, 16th century, Pinacoteca, Vatican, Art Resource/Scala; **200**, Jan Brueghel the elder, Christ Preaching on the Sea of Galilee, late 16th-early 17th century, private collection, Bridgeman Art Library; **201**, The Good Shepherd, late third century, Museo Pio Cristiano, Vatican, Art Resource/Scala; **202-203**, Frederick Krebs, The Prodigal Son Manuscript, c. 1800, The State Museum of Pennsylvania/Pennsylvania Historical and Museum Commission; **204**, The Good Samaritan from the Rossano Gospels, sixth century, Cathedral Library, Rossano, Art Resource/Scala; **205, left**, Carl Julius Milde, The Merciful Samaritan, 19th century, Superstock; **205, right**, Sarcophagus showing the Good Shepherd, Louvre, Paris, Art Resource/Giraudon; **206**, Historiated initial showing Jesus casting out the demons from the Winchester Bible, 12th century, Winchester Cathedral Library, Bible, vol. III, fol. 215r, Courtesy of The Dean and Chapter of Winchester; **207, top**, James Joseph Jacques Tissot, The Swine Driven into the Sea, 19th century, Superstock; **207, bottom**, Codex Egberti, 10th century, Stadtbibliothek, Trier, fol. 26v; **208, left**, Limbourg Brothers, Trés Riches Heures du Duc de Berry, 15th century, Musée Condé, Chantilly, fol. 166r, Art Resource/Giraudon; **208, right,** Devil, c. 1960, Museum of International Folk Art, Santa Fe; **209**, Briton Riviere, The Miracle of the Gadarene Swine, 1883, Tate Gallery, London, Art Resource/Tate Gallery; **210**, Fra Angelico, Sermon on the Mount, 15th century, Museo San Marco, Florence, Art Resource/Scala; **211**, Sermon on the Mount, c. 1110-1120, Staatliche Graphische Sammlung, Munich, inv. no. 39789; **213**, Christ Instructing on The Lord's Prayer, 2nd half of the 13th century, British Library, London, Yates Thompson Ms. 11, fol. 52v, Courtesy of the Trustees of the British Library, London; **214**, Virgil Solis, 16th century; **215**, Abel Grimmer, Pharisees Censuring Christ, late 16th-early 17th century, private collection, Bridgeman Art Library; **216**, Jan Vermeer, Christ in the House of Mary and Martha, 17th century, National Gallery of Scotland, Edinburgh, Bridgeman Art Library; **217**, William Blake, Christ in the House of Martha and Mary, late 18th-early 19th century, Victoria and Albert Museum, London, Bridgeman Art Library; **218, top,** Raising of Lazarus on an ivory pyxis from Syria, fifth century, Hessisches Landesmuseum, Darmstadt; **218, bottom,** Resurrection of Lazarus, 15th century, Louvre, Paris, Bridgeman Art Library/Giraudon; **219**, Fra Angelico, The Raising of Lazarus, 15th century, Museo San Marco, Florence, Art Resource/Scala; **220**, Carel Fabritius, The Raising of Lazarus, 17th century, Museum Narodowe, Warsaw, Bridgeman Art Library; **221**, J. B. Corneille, The Resurrection of Lazarus, Musée des Beaux-Arts, Rouen, Art Resource/Giraudon; **222**, Raphael, The Transfiguration, early 16th century, Pinacoteca, Vatican, Art Resource/Scala; **223**, Dalmatic of Charlemagne, early 15th century?, St. Peter's, Museo del Tesoro, Vatican, Art Resource/Scala; **224, top,** View of Mount Hermon, Israel, Richard T. Nowitz; **224, bottom,** Mount Tabor, Church of the Transfiguration, Zev Radovan, Jerusalem; **225**, Giovanni Bellini, The Transfiguration, 15th-early 16th century, Museo Correr, Venice, Art Resource/Scala.

THE FINAL DAYS

226, The Last Supper, Flemish tapestry, 16th century, The Metropolitan Museum of Art, Robert Lehman Collection, 1975 (1975.1.1915); **228**, Nicolas Froment, Feast in the House of Simon, right wing of a triptych depicting the raising of Lazarus, 15th century, Uffizi, Florence, Art Resource/Scala; **229**, Feast in the House of Simon with Mary Magdalene and Flagellation of Christ, 13th century, Musée Municipal, Semur-en-Auxois; **230**, Duccio di Buoninsegna, The Entry into Jerusalem, c. 1311, Duomo Museum, Siena, Art Resource/Scala; **231, bottom left,** Palm Sunday procession, David Harris; **231, bottom right,** Capital showing palm tree, David Harris; **232, top,** Limbourg Brothers, Trés Riches Heures du Duc de Berry, 15th century, Musée Condé, Chantilly, fol. 173v, Art Resource/Giraudon; **232, bottom,** Entry into Jerusalem from the Rossano Gospels, sixth century, Cathedral Library, Rossano, Art Resource/Scala; **233**, Pietro Lorenzetti, Entry into Jerusalem, 14th century, Church of S. Francesco, Assisi, Art Resource/Scala; **234**, Tilman Riemenschneider, Entry into Jerusalem, left wing of altarpiece, 16th century, Church of St. Jakob, Rothenburg, Erich Lessing/Magnum; **235, top,** Entry into Jerusalem on the Pala d'Oro antependium, c.1100, cathedral of San Marco, Venice, Erich Lessing/Magnum; **235, bottom,** Jesus riding on a donkey, 16th century, Victoria and Albert Museum, London, Art Resource/Victoria and Albert Museum; **236**, El Greco, Christ Driving the Traders from the Temple, 16th century, National Gallery, London; **237**, Rembrandt van Rijn, Christ Driving the Money Changers from the Temple, 17th century, private collection, Art Resource; **238, top,** Joseph Mallord William Turner, Christ Driving the Traders from the Temple, 19th century, Tate Gallery, London, Art Resource/Tate Gallery; **238, bottom,** Giotto di Bondone, Driving the Merchants from the Temple, early 14th century, Scrovegni Chapel, Padua, Art Resource/Scala; **239, left,** Driving the Money Lenders from the Temple, 15th century, Staatsbibliothek, Munich, Art Resource/Marburg; **239, right,** School of Quentin Metsys, Jesus Chasing the Money Lenders from the Temple, 16th century, Musée Royal des Beaux-Arts, Antwerp, Art Resource/Giraudon; **240**, The Last Supper, early 16th century, The Metropolitan Museum of Art, Bequest of Michael Friedsam, 1931. (32.100.143); **241**, The Last Supper, 15th century, Ronald Sheridan/Ancient Art & Architecture; **242, top,** Pietro Lorenzetti, The Last Supper, 14th century, church of S. Francesco, Assisi, Art Resource/

Scala; **242, bottom,** Duccio di Buoninsegna, The Last Supper, c. 1311, Duomo Museum, Siena, Art Resource/Scala; **243**, Philippe de Champaigne, The Last Supper, 17th century, Louvre, Paris, Art Resource/Giraudon; **244, top,** The Last Supper, c. 1750-1775, Victoria and Albert Museum, London, Art Resource/Victoria and Albert Museum; **244, bottom,** Ivory plaque showing the Last Supper, c. 1100, Walters Art Gallery, Baltimore; **245, top,** German embroidered panel showing the Last Supper, 1300-1310, The Art Institute of Chicago; **245, bottom,** Ivory liturgical comb with scenes of Jesus' final days, Victoria and Albert Museum, London, Art Resource/Victoria and Albert Museum; **246, top,** Albrecht Durer, Christ Washing the Feet of the Disciples, late 15th-early 16th century, The Metropolitan Museum of Art, Gift of Junius S. Morgan, 1919 (19.73.179); **246, bottom,** School of Arezzo, Christ Washing the Disciples' Feet, c. 1390, private collection, Bridgeman Art Library; **247, top,** Kiddush cup for Passover, 1698, Jewish Museum, New York, Art Resource/Jewish Museum, photo: Malcolm Varon; **247, bottom,** Illuminated page from a "Yehuda" Haggadah manuscript, 15th century, Zev Radovan, Jerusalem; **248**, Fra Angelico, Christ and the Communion to the Apostles, 15th century, Museo San Marco, Florence, Art Resource/Scala; **249**, Leonardo da Vinci, The Last Supper, c. 1495, S. Maria delle Grazie, Art Resource/Scala; **250, left,** Ivory holy water bucket showing Judas receiving the silver, c. 980, Victoria and Albert Museum, London; **250, right,** Manuscript page showing Judas receiving the silver, c. 1190, Bayerische Staatsbibliothek, Munich, CLM 935, fol. 51v; **251**, English Psalter page showing Judas receiving the silver; Christ in the garden of Gethsemane, early 13th century, Bayerische Staatsbibliothek, Munich, CLM 835, fol. 25r; **252**, Andrea Mantegna, Christ in the Garden, 15th century, Musée des Beaux-Arts, Tours, Art Resource/Giraudon; **253, top right,** Christ in the Garden at Gethsemane, 14th century, Bibliothèque Nationale, Paris; **253, bottom,** Agony in the Garden, 16th century, The Metropolitan Museum of Art, Gift of J. Pierpont Morgan, 1918; **254**, Fra Angelico, Agony in the Garden, 15th century, Pinacoteca Civica, Forli, Art Resource/Scala; **255**, Francisco de Goya y Lucientes, The Agony in the Garden, 18th-19th century, private collection, Bridgeman Art Library; **256**, Giovanni Bellini, Agony in the Garden, c. 1460, National Gallery, London, Bridgeman Art Library; **257**, Sandro Botticelli, Agony in the Garden, 15th century, Royal Chapel, Grenada, Bridgeman Art Library; **258, top,** Jean Fouquet, The Arrest of Jesus, Hours of Etienne Chevalier, 15th century, Musée Condé, Chantilly, Art Resource/Giraudon; **258, bottom,** Manuscript page showing the arrest of Jesus, Isabella Stewart Gardner Museum, Boston, Art Resource/ISG; **259**, Sassetta (Stefano di Giovanni), The Betrayal of Christ, 15th century, Courtesy of the Founders Society, Detroit Institute of Arts; **260**, Pietro Lorenzetti, The Arrest of Jesus, 14th century, church of S. Francesco, Assisi, Art Resource/Scala; **261**, Holy water bucket showing scenes of Jesus' final days, c. 980, Victoria and Albert Museum, Art Resource/Victoria and Albert Museum; **262**, Martin Didier, Limoges enamel plaque showing Jesus before Caiaphas, 16th century, Musée des Beaux-Arts, Niort, Art Resource/Giraudon; **263**, Giotto di Bondone, Christ before Caiaphas, early 14th century, Scrovegni Chapel, Padua, Art Resource/Scala; **264**, Duccio di Buoninsegna, Christ before Annas and the Betrayal of Peter, c. 1311, Duomo Museum, Siena, Art Resource/Scala; **265**, Painted glass panel showing the suicide of Judas, c. 1520, The Art Institute of Chicago; **266**, Manuscript illumination showing the suicide of Judas, Pierpont Morgan Library, MS. 147, fol. 21; **267**, Mattia Preti, Pilate Washing His Hands, 17th century, The Metropolitan Museum of Art, Purchase, Gift of J. Pierpont Morgan and Bequest of Helena W. Charlton, by exchange, Gwynne Andrews, Marquand, and Rogers Funds, Victor Wilbour Memorial Dund, The Alfred N. Punnett Endowment Fund, and funds from various donors, 1978; **268**, Antonio Ciseri, Ecce Homo, Galleria d'Arte Moderna, Florence, Art Resource/Scala; **269**, Rembrandt van Rijn, Christ before Pilate, c. 1635-36, The Metropolitan Museum of Art, Gift of Henry Walter, 1917; **270, top,** Stained glass panel showing the flagellation of Jesus, 13th century, Victoria and Albert Museum, London, Art Resource/Victoria and Albert Museum; **270, bottom,** Stone inscription with Pilate's name, Erich Lessing/Magnum; **271**, Bernardo Martorelli, The Flagellation of St. George, 15th century, Louvre, Paris, Art Resource/Scala; **272, top left,** Albrecht Dürer, The Mocking of Christ, c. 1498, Staatsbibliothek, Munich, Art Resource/Marburg; **272, top right,** Limoges enamel plaque showing the flagellation of Jesus, before 1520, Victoria and Albert Museum, London, Bridgeman Art Library; **272, bottom**, Jaime Huguet, The Flagellation of Christ, c. 1450-60, Louvre, Paris, Art Resource/Scala; **273**, Ivory statuette, late 13th century, Museum Mayer van den Bergh, Antwerp, Erich Lessing/Magnum; **274**, Ecce Homo, 17th century, The Metropolitan Museum of Art, The Metropolitan Museum of Art, Ann and George Blumenthal Fund, 1973 (1973.286); **275**, Michelangelo Merisi da Caravaggio, Ecce Homo, late 16th-early 17th century, Galleria di Palazzo Rosso, Genoa, Art Resource/Scala; **276**, Albrecht Dürer, The Road to Calvary, 1527, private collection, Bridgeman Art Library; **277, top right**, Giovan Battista Naldini, Christ Carrying the Cross, 16th century, Badia, Florence, Art Resource/Scala; **277, bottom**, Christ Carrying the Cross, left wing of an ivory diptych, 14th century, Musées des Antiquités, Rouen, Art Resource/Giraudon; **278, top**, Easter Sunday procession, Jerusalem, Marvin Newman; **278, bottom**, Francisco Zurbarán, The Holy Face (Veronica's Veil), 17th century, Nationalmuseum, Stockholm, AR; **279, left**, Hieronymus Bosch, Ecce Homo, late 15th-early 16th century, Museum voor Schone Kunsten, Ghent, Art Resource/Scala; **279, right**, Raphael, Christ Falls on the Way to Calvary, 16th century, Prado, Madrid, Bridgeman Art Library; **280**, Van Valkenborough, The Crucifixion, private collection, Bridgeman Art Library; **281, left**, Choir screen relief showing the nailing of Jesus to the cross, Dom St. Marien, Havelberg, Art Resource/Marburg; **281, right**, Ivory bishop's staff showing the Crucifixion, 14th century, Bargello, Florence, Art Resource/Giraudon; **282**, Lorenzo Monaco, The Crucifixion, late 14th-early 15th century, Louvre, Paris, Bridgeman Art Library/Giraudon; **283, top**, Fra Angelico, The Crucifixion, 15th century, Museo San Marco, Florence, Art Resource/Scala; **283, bottom**, Russian icon showing Roman soldiers at Jesus' tomb, 17th century, private collection, Laurie Platt Winfrey, Inc.; **284, top left**, Donatello, Crucifixion, 15th century, Bargello, Florence, Art Resource/Scala; **284, top right**, Matthias Grünewald, Isenheim Altar showing scene of the Crucifixion, closed position of wings, c.1515, Musée d'Unterlinden, Colmar, Art Resource/Giraudon; **284, bottom right**, Giovanni Cimabue, The Crucifixion, late 13th century, church of S. Domenico, Arezzo, Art Resource/Scala; **284, bottom left**, Crucifixion from the Rabbula Gospels, 586, Biblioteca Laurenziana, Florence, cod. Plut. I, 56, fol. 13r, Art Resource/Scala; **285, top left**, Ivory plaque showing the Crucifixion, 9th-10th century, Bargello, Florence, Art Resource; **285, top right**, Donatello, Crucifix, 15th century, Basilica del Santo, Padua, Art Resource/Scala; **285, bottom**, Barnaba di Modena, Processional banner showing scene of Jesus crucified, 14th century, Victoria and Albert Museum, London, Bridgeman Art Library; **287**, Andrea Mantegna, The Crucifixion, 15th century, Louvre, Paris, Artz Resource/Scala; **288**, Peter Paul Rubens, The Descent from the Cross, 17th century, Musée des Beaux-Arts, Lille, Bridgeman Art Library; **289, top**, Pendant with scene of Pieta, 16th century, The Metropolitan Museum of Art, The Friedsam Collection, Bequest of Michael Friedsam, 1931; **289, bottom left**, Guilio Clovio, The Deposition and Shroud of Turin, 16th century, Galleria Sabauda, Turin, Art Resource/Scala; **289, bottom right**, Shroud of Turin, Turin, Photo Researchers: Gianni Tortoli/Science Source; **290**, Fra Angelico, The Deposition, 15th century, Museo San Marco, Florence, Art Resource/Scala; **291**, Michelangelo Buonarroti, Pieta, 1553-1555, Cathedral, Florence, Art Resource/Scala; **292, top**, Reliquary casket of the True Cross, 817-24, Museo Sacro, Biblioteca Apostolica, Vatican; **292, bottom**, Entombment of Christ, Victoria and Albert Museum, London, Bridgeman Art Library; **293**, Pieter Lastman, Entombment of Christ, early 17th century, Musée des Beaux-Arts, Lille, Bridgeman Art Library.

SAVIOR AND REDEEMER

294, Andrea Mantegna, The Resurrection, 15th century, Museo Communale, Tours, Art Resource/Scala; **296, top left**, Jean Fouquet, Hours of Etienne Chevalier, 15th century, Musée Condé, Chantilly, Art Resource/Giraudon; **296, bottom**, Scenes of Christ's Passion, 14th century, Louvre, Paris, Art Resource/Scala; **297**, William Blake, Angels Hovering above Jesus, late 18th-early 19th century, Victoria and Albert Museum, London, Bridgeman Art Library; **298, top**, Burial catacomb, Beth Shearim, Israel, Zev Radovan, Jerusalem; **298, bottom**, Decorated sarcophagus, Beth Shearim, Israel, Zev Radovan, Jerusalem; **299, left**, Descent into Limbo, 16th century, Bargello, Flor-

ence, Art Resource/Scala; **299, right**, Anastasis, Harrowing of Hell, 14th century, Byzantium-Constantinople?, Walters Art Gallery, Baltimore; **300**, Raphael, The Resurrection, 16th century, Gallery Arazzi, Vatican, Art Resource/Scala; **301**, The Resurrection, late 14th century, Beauvais, Art Resource/Marburg; **302**, Hans Pleydenwurff, The Resurrection, 15th century, Alte Pinakothek, Munich, Art Resource/Scala; **303, top**, Church of the Holy Sepulcher (interior), Jerusalem, Richard T. Nowitz; **303, bottom**, Garden Tomb, Jerusalem, Richard T. Nowitz; **304**, Nicola di Maestro Antonio, The Risen Christ, second half of the 15th century, City of York Art Gallery, York, Bridgeman Art Library; **305**, H. van der Broeck, The Resurrection of Christ, Sistine Chapel, Vatican, Art Resource/Scala; **306, left**, Angel greeting Mary Magdalene at the sepulcher, 11th century, Duomo, Milan, Art Resource/Scala; **306, right**, Three Marys at the tomb, ninth century, Bargello, Florence, Art Resource/Giraudon; **307**, Three Marys at the tomb from the Winchester Pontifical, late 10th century, Bibliothèque Municipale, Rouen, Art Resource/ Giraudon; **308**, Van Eyck Brothers, Three Marys at Christ's Grave, late 14th-early 15th century, Museum Boymans-van Beuningen, Rotterdam, Bridgeman Art Library; **309**, Girolamo da Cremona, The Resurrection, Duomo Libreria Piccolomini, Siena, cod. 23.8, c.2, Art Resource/Scala; **310**, Jan Brueghel the younger, Christ and Mary Magdalene, late 16th-early 17th century, Rafael Valls Gallery, London, Bridgeman Art Library; **311**, Master of the Codex of St. George, Noli me Tangere, 14th century, Bargello, Florence, Art Resource/Scala; **312**, Martin Schongauer, Noli me Tangere, 15th century, Musée d'Unterlinden, Colmar, Bridgeman Art Library; **313, top**, Antonio Correggio, Noli me Tangere, c. 1534, Prado, Madrid, Bridgeman Art Library; **313, bottom**, Ivanov Aleksandr, Christ Appearing to Mary Magdalene, 19th century, State Museum, St. Petersburg, Art Resource/Scala; **314–315**, The Forbes Magazine Collection, New York; **316**, Ivory plaque with scenes of Jesus appearing on the road to Emmaus, ninth century, The Metropolitan Museum of Art, The Cloisters Collection, 1970. (1970.324.1); **317, left**, Michelangelo Merisi da Caravaggio, The Supper at Emmaus, late 16th-early 17th century, National Gallery, London, Art Resource/Nimatallah; **317, right**, Jesus on the road to Emmaus, c.1100, Cloister of Santo Domingo, Silos, Art Resource/Marburg; **319**, Diego Rodriguez de Silva y Velazquez, The Supper at Emmaus, 17th century, The Metropolitan Museum of Art, Bequest of Benjamin Altman, 1913. (14.40.631); **320**, Master of the Heisterbach Altar, Christ Appearing to the Apostles, c. 1450, Staatsgalerie, Bamberg, Artothek; **321**, Manuscript showing Jesus appearing to the Apostles, Kupferstichkabinett, Staatliche Museen zu Berlin, Preussischer Kulturbesitz, cod. 78A3, fols. 1v, 2r; **322**, Ivory plaque showing Doubting Thomas, late 9th-early 10th century, Staatliche Museen, Berlin, Art Resource/Marburg; **323**, Peter Paul Rubens, Central panel from the Rockox Triptych showing the incredulity of Thomas, 17th century, Royal Museum of Fine Arts, Antwerp, Art Resource/Scala; **324**, G. Toscani, The Incredulity of Thomas, Accademia, Florence, Art Resource/AGC; **325**, Il Guercino (Giovanni Francesco Barbieri), The Incredulity of Thomas, 17th century, Pinacoteca, Vatican, Art Resource/Scala; **326**, Jesus appearing to the Apostles on the Sea of Tiberias from the Mömpelgarter Altar, 1525-1530, Kunsthistorisches Museum, Vienna; **327, left**, Statue of Synagogue; **327, right**, Statue of Ecclesia, 13th century, both: Strasburg Cathedral, Art Resource/Marburg; **328**, Jesus appearing to the Apostles, 12th century, Bayerische Staatsbibliothek, Munich, CLM 15903, fol. 44 r; **329**, Duccio di Buoninsegna, Christ Appearing at Galilee, c. 1311, Duomo Museum, Siena, Art Resource/Scala; **330, left**, The Ascension from the Sacramentary of Archbishop Drogo of Metz, mid-ninth century, Bibliothèque Nationale, Paris, Ms. lat. 9428, fol. 71v.; **330, right**, The Ascension from the Rabbula Gospels, 586, Biblioteca Laurenziana, Florence, Art Resource/Scala; **331**, Dalmatic of Charlemagne, early 15th century?, St. Peter's, Museo del Tesoro, Vatican, Art Resource/Scala; **332**, Rembrandt van Rijn, The Ascension of Christ, 1636, Alte Pinakothek, Munich, Artothek; **333**, Hans Memling, The Ascension of Christ from the right panel of the Triptych of the Louvre, 15th century, Louvre, Paris, Art Resource/Scala; **334, top**, Reaping wheat in a village in Judea, Zev Radovan, Jerusalem; **334, bottom**, Celebrating Shavuot in Kibbutz Beeri in Central Negev, Zev Radovan, Jerusalem; **335, left**, Pentecost from the Evangeliary of Henry II, 1002-14, Bayerische Staatsbibliothek, Munich, CLM 4452, fol. 135v; **335, right**, Pentecost from the Winchester Pontifical, late 10th century,

Bibliothèque Municipale, Rouen, Art Resource/Giraudon; **336**, Enamel plaque of Pentecost from the workshop of Godefroid de Clare, 1150-1175, The Metropolitan Museum of Art, The Cloisters Collection, 1965. (65.105); **337**, Titian, Pentecost, 16th century, S. Maria della Salute, Venice, Art Resource/ Scala; **338**, Adam Elsheimer, The Stoning of St. Stephen, late 16th-early 17th century, National Gallery of Scotland, Edinburgh, Bridgeman Art Library; **340**, Michelangelo Merisi da Caravaggio, Conversion of St. Paul, late 16th-early 17th century, S. Maria del Popolo, Rome, Art Resource/Scala; **341**, The Conversion of St. Paul, 1410, Bibliothèque Nationale, Paris, Ms. Fr. 2810, fol. 131; **342**, Amphitheater at Ephesus, Art Resource/Vanni; **343**, Scenes from the life of St. Paul, ninth century, Bibliothèque Nationale, Paris, Ms. Lat. 1, fol. 386v; **344, 345,** The Nativity and the Resurrection from the metalwork front and back bookcovers of an Armenian Bible, 13th century, The Metropolitan Museum of Art, Gift of Mrs. Edward S. Harkness, 1916.

Jesus Among Us

346, Emil Nolde, Christ Among the Children, 1910, The Museum of Modern Art, New York, Gift of Dr. W.R. Valentiner; **348**, N. C. Wyeth, The Nativity, 1912, Collection of Mr. and Mrs. Douglas Allen, photograph courtesy of the Brandywine River Museum; **349, left,** Jean Charles, The Nativity, 20th century, Collection of Maurice Lavanoux, Lee Boltin; **349, right,** Ivo Dulcic, Flight into Egypt, 1916, Vatican Museum of Contemporary Christian Art, Lee Boltin; **350**, George Rouault, Nazareth, 20th century, Vatican Museum of Contemporary Christian Art, Art Resource/Scala; **351**, Jean Heiberg, Miracle of the Loaves and Fishes, 20th century, Collection Cronin, Lee Boltin; **352**, Norman LaLiberté, The Face of Jesus, 20th century, Collection Cronin, Lee Boltin; **353**, Salvador Dali, The Sacrament of the Last Supper, 1955, National Gallery of Art, Washington, DC, Chester Dale Collection; **354**, Gino Severini, Volto di Cristo, 20th century, Vatican Museum of Contemporary Christian Art, Lee Boltin; **355**, André Derain, The Last Supper, 1911, The Art Institute of Chicago, Gift of Mrs. Frank L. Lillie; **356**, Faustio Pirandello, Crucifixion, 20th century, Vatican Museum of Contemporary Christian Art, Art Resource/Scala; **357**, Abraham Rattner, Crucifixion in Blue (Composition II), 1953, Santa Barbara Museum of Art, Gift of Mrs. Sterling Morton from the Preston Morton Collection; **358**, Tsugouharu Foujita, Pieta, 20th century, private collection, Bridgeman Art Library; **359**, Marc Chagall, Red Pieta, 20th century, Vatican Museum of Contemporary Christian Art, Art Resource/Scala; **361,** Paul Gauguin, Yellow Christ, 1889, Albright-Knox Art Gallery, Buffalo. **364** Raphael, Madonna and Child, 16th century, Alte Pinakothek, Munich, Art Resource/ Scala; **370**, Pietro Perugino, Baptism of Christ, c. 1498, Kunsthistorisches Museum, Vienna, Art Resource/Erich Lessing; **384**, Mosaic, Museo di S. Sofia, Istanbul, Art Resource/Scala.

The baptism of Jesus by Pietro Perugino

Acknowledgments

Grateful acknowledgment is made to the following for permission to use copyrighted material:

Abelard-Schuman for "Are Your Shoulders Strong Enough?"; "A Prophet Without Honor in His Own Country"; "At Daybreak, Fish and Bread with Jesus"; "Like the Coming of a Storm on a Cloudless Day"; "A Man Who Bled Like Everyone Else"; and "Joined by a Stranger on the Road To Emmaus" from *The Lord Jesus* by Robert Payne. Copyright © 1964 by Robert Payne. Reprinted by permission of JCA Literary Agency, Inc.

Abingdon Press for "A New And Faithful Son" from *The Old Testament Roots of Our Faith* by Paul and Elizabeth Achtemeier. Copyright © 1962 by Abingdon Press. Reprinted by permission of Paul and Elizabeth Achtemeier.

Abingdon/Nashville for "The Lord's Prayer" from *The Sermon on the Mount* by Roger L. Shinn. Copyright © 1954, 1962 by United Church Press. Reprinted by permission of The Pilgrim Press/United Church Press.

Atheneum Publishers for "A Sinner Only In His Own Innocence" from *I, Judas* by Taylor Caldwell and Jess Stearn. Copyright © 1977 by Taylor Caldwell and Jess Stearn. Reprinted by permission of Writers House Inc.

Bartholomew House Ltd. for "The Answered Prayer" from *The Story Bible* by Pearl S. Buck and Lyle Kenyon Engel. Copyright © 1971 by Pearl S. Buck and Lyle Kenyon Engel. Reprinted by permission of Harold Ober Associates, Inc.

Bethany Press for "Going Home To His Father" from *His Mother* by George M. Anderson. Copyright © 1930 by G.M. Anderson. Reprinted by permission of Christian Board of Publication.

The Bruce Publishing Co. for "In Obedience to the Imperial Edict" from *The First Christmas* by Denis O'Shea. Copyright © 1952 by The Bruce Publishing Company. Reprinted by permission of Macmillan Publishing Company.

The Christian Century for "The Annunciation" by Theodosia Garrison.

Coward-McCann, Inc. for "The Heavens Opened, The Light Shown Down" and "An Eager Young Mind Thirsting For Knowledge" from *God So Loved the World* by Elizabeth Goudge. Copyright © 1951 by Elizabeth Goudge; "Finding Their Way" from *The Well of the Star* by Elizabeth Goudge. Copyright © 1941 by Elizabeth Goudge. Reprinted by permission of David Higham Associates.

Crossroad Publishing Co. for "Understanding Prophecies in Light of Their Fulfillment" from *The Gospel According to St. Matthew* Vol. 1 by Wolfgang Trilling. English translation copyright © 1969 by Herder & Herder, Inc; "A Joy That Filled Her Soul and Spirit" and "Describing His Mission in Words Taken from Isaiah" from *The Gospel According to St. Luke* Vol. 1 by Alois Stöger. English translation copyright © 1969 by Burns & Oates, Limited, London. Reprinted by permission of The Crossroad Publishing Company.

Doubleday Inc. for "When a Young Girl Danced"; "Too Much to Expect of Any Man"; "Blessed Among Women"; and "Standing On The Heights With Evil Itself" from *The Greatest Story Ever Told* by Fulton Oursler. Copyright © 1949 by Fulton Oursler. Reprinted by permission of Doubleday, a division of Bantam Doubleday Dell Publishing Group, Inc.

E.P. Dutton Company, Inc. for "Cataclysms of Nature Announce His Death"; "A Seed for the Fostering Earth"; and "Bound for Bethlehem" from *Jesus and His Times* by Henri Daniel-Rops, translated by Ruth Millar, translation copyright © 1954, 1956 by E.P. Dutton; "The Power That Flowed From Him" from *Jesus* by Edmond Fleg, translated by Phyllis Megroz, translation copyright © 1935, copyright © renewed 1963 by E.P. Dutton; "The Last Supper" from *Singing Drums* by Helen Welshimer. Copyright © 1937 by E.P. Dutton, copyright © renewed 1965 by Ralph Welshimer. Used by permission of E.P. Dutton,

an imprint of New American Library, a division of Penguin Books USA Inc.

Wm. B. Eerdmans Publishing Co. for "A Name From Heaven" and "Struck Dumb for Disbelief" from *The Mystery of Bethlehem* by Herman Hoeksema. Copyright © 1944 by William B. Eerdmans Publishing Co. Copyright © 1986 by Reformed Free Publishing Association; "Jesus: He Was Indeed the Coming One" from *The Time Is Fulfilled* by F.F. Bruce. Copyright © by The Paternoster Press Ltd.

Epworth Press for "Not Knowing He Was Lost Until Jesus Found Him" by W. Russell Maltby from *Obiter Scripta,* edited by F.B. James, Epworth, 1952. Reprinted by permission of Reverend Graham Slater.

Mahatma Gandhi for "One Who Belongs to All Mankind" from "What Jesus Means to Me." Reprinted by permission of Navajivan Trust.

Harper & Brothers for "Simon The Cyrenian, Speaks" from *The Black Christ and Other Poems* by Countee Cullen. Copyright © 1929 by Harper & Brothers. Copyright © renewed 1957 by Ida M. Cullen. Reprinted by permission of GRM Associates, Inc. Agents for the Estate of Ida M. Cullen; "Lessons From A Boat" from *Christ and the Fine Arts* by Cynthia Pearl Maus. Copyright © 1938, © 1959 by Cynthia Pearl Maus. Reprinted by permission of the estate of Cynthia Pearl Maus; "The Faith that Made Him Well" from *In the Years of Our Lord* by Manuel Komroff. Copyright © 1942 by Manuel Komroff, reprinted by permission of the estate of Manuel Komroff; "Don't Be Afraid. It Is I" and "The Resurrection and the Life" from *The Man Born To Be King* by Dorothy L. Sayers. Copyright © 1943 by Dorothy L. Sayers. Reprinted by permission of the Watkins/Loomis Agency, Inc.; "Coming Home to His Father's House" from *The Little Boy of Nazareth* by Edna Madison Bonser. Copyright © 1930 by Richard R. Smith, Inc. Copyright © renewed 1958 by Virginia Bonser Brooks; "On the Eve of the First Miracle" and "The Presentiment of an Appalling Fate" from *According to Thomas* by Ivan Nazhivin, translated by Emile Burns. Copyright © 1930 by Harper & Brothers. Copyright © renewed 1958 by Harper & Brothers; "Blasphemy that Must Be Stopped" from *The Empty Tomb* by James Martin. Copyright © 1960 by James Martin; "If the Prophet Elisha Could Come Again" and "A Farewell to Carpentry" from *These Shared His Cross* by Edwin McNeill Poteat. Copyright © 1940, 1941, 1948 by Harper & Brothers Publishers; "By Order of Pontius Pilate: Thirty-Nine Strokes" and "For Someone Without Fear, One Place Is as Safe as Another" from *These Shared His Passion, Cross and Power* by Edwin McNeill Poteat. Copyright © 1940, 1941, 1948 by Harper & Brothers; "In Token of Repentance: Baptism" and "None Greater than the Baptist" from *A Life of Jesus* by Edgar J. Goodspeed. Copyright © 1950 by Harper & Brothers; "When the Time Grew Short" and "The Wrath of Herod" from *The Day Christ Was Born* by Jim Bishop. Copyright © 1959, 1960 by Jim Bishop; "An Underlying Tension at the Passover Feast" and "Deep in the Realm of Agony" from *The Day Christ Died* by Jim Bishop. Copyright © 1957 by Jim Bishop; "Joy Crowding Her Heart" and "Ministering to Those in the Upper Room" from *Behold the Man* by Toyohiko Kagawa. Copyright © 1941 by Harper & Brothers. Copyright © renewed 1968; "Thirty Pieces of Silver for Jesus" from *Earthbound and Other Poems* by Helene Mullins. Copyright © 1929 by Harper & Brothers. Copyright © renewed 1956 by Helene Mullins. All reprinted by permission of HarperCollins Publishers.

Harper & Row for "They Knew Not What They Did" from *Strength to Love* by Martin Luther King, Jr. Copyright © 1963 by Martin Luther King, Jr. Reprinted by permission of Joan Daves Agency; "The Infinite Sweetness of Prayer" from *Waiting For God* by Simone Weil. Copyright © 1951; Copyright © renewed 1979 by G.P. Putnam's Sons. Reprinted by permission of The Putnam Publishing Group and Librairie A. Fayard. "A Very Special Son" from *Three From Galilee* by Marjorie Holmes. Copyright © 1985 by Marjorie Holmes; "De-

Index

Pages numbers in **bold** type refer to illustrations.

Jesus in mosaic, from Istanbul's Hagia Sophia